CAMBRIDGE
UNIVERSITY PRESS

CAMBRIDGE
Primary English

Teacher's Resource 1

Gill Budgell

CAMBRIDGE
UNIVERSITY PRESS

University Printing House, Cambridge CB2 8BS, United Kingdom

One Liberty Plaza, 20th Floor, New York, NY 10006, USA

477 Williamstown Road, Port Melbourne, VIC 3207, Australia

314–321, 3rd Floor, Plot 3, Splendor Forum, Jasola District Centre, New Delhi – 110025, India

103 Penang Road, #05–06/07, Visioncrest Commercial, Singapore 238467

Cambridge University Press is part of the University of Cambridge.

It furthers the University's mission by disseminating knowledge in the pursuit of education, learning and research at the highest international levels of excellence.

www.cambridge.org
Information on this title: www.cambridge.org/9781108783514

First published 2015
Second edition 2021

20 19 18 17 16 15 14 13 12 11 10 9 8 7 6 5 4 3 2 1

Printed in Great Britain by CPI Group (UK) Ltd, Croydon CR0 4YY

A catalogue record for this publication is available from the British Library

ISBN 978-1-108-78351-4 Paperback with digital access

Additional resources for this publication at www.cambridge.org/go

....

NOTICE TO TEACHERS IN THE UK

....

〉Contents

Digital resources

The following items are available on Cambridge GO. For more information on how to access and use your digital resource, please see inside front cover.

Active learning

Assessment for Learning

Developing learner language skills

Differentiation

Improving learning through questioning

Language awareness

Metacognition

Skills for Life

Letter for parents – Introducing the Cambridge Primary and
    Lower Secondary resources

Lesson plan template

Curriculum framework correlation

Scheme of work

Audio files

Diagnostic check and answers

Answers to Learner's Book activities

Answers to Workbook activities

Glossary

You can download the following resources for each unit:

Differentiated worksheets and answers

Language worksheets and answers

〉Acknowledgements

The authors and publishers acknowledge the following sources of copyright material and are grateful for the permissions granted. While every effort has been made, it has not always been possible to identify the sources of all the material used, or to trace all copyright holders. If any omissions are brought to our notice, we will be happy to include the appropriate acknowledgements on reprinting.

Excerpts from the *Approaches to learning and teaching* series, courtesy of Cambridge University Press and Cambridge Assessment International Education: cambridge.org/approachestolearning

Unit 1: Illustrations and story adapted from *It's much too early!* by Ian Whybrow (Cambridge Reading Adventures). Published by Cambridge University Press 2016. Story used by permission of Ian Whybrow; Excerpts from *Don't Spill the Milk* by Stephen Davies, illustrated by Christopher Corr reproduced by the permission of Andersen Press; Extracts and illustrations from *Hide and Seek* by Lynne Rickards, (Cambridge Reading Adventures). Published by Cambridge University Press 2016; Excerpt from *THE PARK IN THE DARK* by Martin Waddell, Text © 1989 Martin Waddell, Reproduced by permission of Walker Books Ltd, London SE11 5HJ www.walker.co.uk **Unit 2:** Extracts and illustrations from *My First Train Trip* by Lynne Rickards, (Cambridge Reading Adventures). Published by Cambridge University Press 2016; Excerpt from *A Week in the Holidays* by Gill Budgell published by Cambridge University Press; Excerpts and illustrations from *Cloud Nine* written by Gill Budgell reproduced by permission of Franklin Watts, an imprint of Hachette Children's Books; **Unit 3:** *One, Two, Buckle my Shoe* by Gill Budgell and Kate Ruttle, reproduced by permission of Cambridge University Press; Excerpts from *I got the Rhythm* by Schofield Morrison copyright 2014, reproduced by permission of Bloomsbury Publishing Inc; Adapted extract and illustrations from *Red is a Dragon* copyright 2001 by Roseanne Thong, Used with permission of Chronicle Books LLC, San Francisco; **Unit 4:** Excerpts from *The Runaway Chapati; A Chapati; Run, Run; Stop, Come Back!* by Gill Budgell and Kate Ruttle reproduced by permission of Cambridge University Press with Illustrations by Stephen Waterhouse; Adapted extract from *The Big Pancake* by Susan Gates & Alan Rogers, Cambridge Reading Adventures, Cambridge University Press; Adapted extract from *One Day in the Eucalyptus, Eucalyptus Tree* by Daniel Bernstrom Illustrated By Brendan Wenzel. Text Copyright 2016 by Daniel Bernstrom Illustrations Copyright 2016 by Brendan Wenzel. Reproduced by permission of HarperCollins Publishers; **Unit 5:** Excerpt from *Make Colours* by Gill Budgell, by of Cambridge University Press, photographs Graham Portlock; Excerpt from *More-Igami* by Dori Kleber and illustrated by G. Brian Karas Reproduced by permission of Walker Books Ltd, London SE11 5HJ www.walker.co.uk, Text© 2016 Dori Kleber, Illustrations © G. Brian Karas; **Unit 6:** Excerpt from 'Sand in your fingernails' by John Foster, published in *Poems for the Very Young* (Kingfisher Books), used by kind permission of the author; 'Sand' and 'Sick' © 1988 Shirley Hughes from *OUT AND ABOUT* by Shirley Hughes Reproduced by permission of Walker Books Ltd; Excerpt from 'Laughing Time' from *Laughing Time: Collected Nonsense* by William Jay Smith, illustrated by Fernando Krahn. Copyright 1990 by William Jay Smith. Reprinted by permission of Farrar, Straus and Giroux Books for Young Readers and the Estate of William Jay Smith; Excerpt from *Bad Day, Good Day* by Roderick Hunt, illustrated by Jan Lewis , published by Oxford University Press; **Unit 7:** 'The Grass House' © 1988 Shirley Hughes From OUT AND ABOUT by Shirley Hughes Reproduced by permission of Walker Books Ltd; Excerpts and illustrations from *How to Catch a Star* by Oliver Jeffers, Reproduced by permission of HarperCollins Publishers Ltd © 2004, Oliver Jeffers; Excerpt from *We're Going on a Bear Hunt* by Michael Rosen and Helen Oxenbury. Written by Michael Rosen & illustrated by Helen Oxenbury Reproduced by permission of Walker Books Ltd and Simon & Schuster; Exterpts from *Bedtime for Monsters* by Ed Vere 2011, published by Puffin, © Ed Vere, Reproduced by permission of Penguin Books Limited; Extract from Crabs by Andy Belcher (Cambridge Reading Adventures), published by Cambridge University Press; Page spread from *My First Dictionary*, Published by Dorling Kindersley; **Unit 9:** Excerpt from 'Rainbow' by Gill Rujaro Magwenzi, from *Out and About* (Cambridge Reading). Published by Cambridge University Press; 'Thunder' by Romesh Gunesekera (Copyright Romesh Gunesekera) Reprinted by permission of A M Heath & Co. Ltd. Authors' Agents; 'One Wet Day' by Richard Edwards (abridged), reproduced by kind permission of the author.

Thanks to the following for permission to reproduce images:

Cover image by Omar Aranda (Beehive Illustration); *downloadable worksheet 8* DeltaImages/Getty Images; *Diagnostic Test* JGI/Jamie Grill/Getty Images, George Zoumas/EyeEm/Getty Images

> Introduction

Welcome to the new edition of our Cambridge Primary English series.

Since its launch, the series has been used by teachers and learners in over 100 countries for teaching the Cambridge Primary English curriculum framework.

This exciting new edition has been designed by talking to Primary English teachers all over the world. We have worked hard to understand your needs and challenges, and then carefully designed and tested the best ways of meeting them.

As a result of this research, we've made some important changes to the series. This Teacher's Resource has been carefully redesigned to make it easier for you to plan and teach the course.

The series now includes digital editions of the Learner's Books and Workbooks. This Teacher's Resource also offers additional materials available to download from Cambridge GO. (For more information on how to access and use your digital resource, please see inside front cover.)

The series uses the most successful teaching approaches like active learning and metacognition and this Teacher's Resource gives you full guidance on how to integrate them into your classroom.

Formative assessment opportunities help you to get to know your learners better, with clear learning intentions and success criteria as well as an array of assessment techniques, including advice on self and peer assessment.

Clear, consistent differentiation ensures that all learners are able to progress in the course with tiered activities, differentiated worksheets and advice about supporting learners' different needs.

All our resources include extra language support to enable teaching and learning in English. They help learners build core English skills with vocabulary and grammar support, as well as additional language worksheets.

We hope you enjoy using this course.

Eddie Rippeth

Head of Primary and Lower Secondary Publishing, Cambridge University Press

› About the author

Gill Budgell

Gill is the director of Frattempo Ltd, which is a consultancy business specialising in educational and publishing services. She has over 30 years' experience of education as a teacher, publisher, researcher and writer of early years and primary English language resources.

Before establishing Frattempo, Gill was an in-house educational primary publisher for 14 years, and prior to that followed the usual route of class teacher to senior adviser. She is qualified in supporting the needs of bilingual pupils and specialises in English language and literacy resources. She has developed, written and published many outstanding and award-winning print and digital primary resources with industry partners.

Gill is an industry judge for both BETT and ERA educational awards in the UK, and has worked extensively in international markets as both teacher and trainer.

> How to use this series

All of the components in the series are designed to work together.

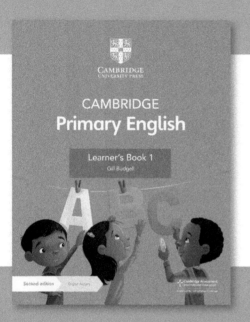

The Learner's Book is designed for learners to use in class with guidance from the teacher. It offers complete coverage of the curriculum framework. A variety of investigations, activities, questions and images motivate learners and help them to develop the necessary skills. Each unit contains opportunities for formative assessment, differentiation and reflection so you can support your learners' needs and help them progress.

A digital version of the Learner's Book is included with the print version and is available separately. It includes simple tools for learners to use in class or for self-study.

The skills-focused write-in Workbook provides further practice of all the topics in the Learner's Book and is ideal for use in class or as homework. A three-tier, scaffolded approach to skills development promotes visible progress and enables independent learning, ensuring that every learner is supported. Teachers can assign learners questions from one or more tiers for each exercise, or learners can progress through each of the tiers in the exercise.

A digital version of the Workbook is included with the print version.

The Teacher's Resource is the foundation of this series and you'll find everything you need to deliver the course in here, including suggestions for differentiation, formative assessment and language support, teaching ideas, answers, diagnostic check and extra worksheets. Each Teacher's Resource includes:

- a **print book** with detailed teaching notes for each topic
- **Digital Access** with all the material from the book in digital form plus editable planning documents, extra guidance, worksheets and more.

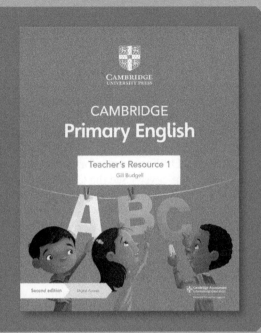

The Phonics Workbooks A and B are designed for learners to use in class in Kindergarten and Stage 1 or at home. These are write-in workbooks which work alongside Cambridge Primary English to support the early stages of reading (grapheme-phoneme correspondences, decoding), writing (letter formation and word/phrase/sentence writing) and spelling (encoding). This Teacher's Resource references any specific links to the Phonics Workbooks. There is additional information for teachers at the back of each Phonics Workbook.

A letter to parents, explaining the course, is available to download from Cambridge GO (as part of this Teacher's Resource).

> How to use this Teacher's Resource

This Teacher's Resource contains both general guidance and teaching notes that help you to deliver the content in our Cambridge Primary English resources. Some of the material is provided as downloadable files, available on **Cambridge GO**. (For more information about how to access and use your digital resource, please see inside front cover.) See the Contents page for details of all the material available to you, both in this book and through Cambridge GO.

Teaching notes

This book provides **teaching notes** for each unit of the Learner's Book and Workbook. Each set of teaching notes contains the following features to help you deliver the unit.

The **Unit plan** summarises the topics covered in the unit, including the number of learning hours recommended for the topic, an outline of the learning content and the Cambridge resources that can be used to deliver the topic.

Session	Approximate number of learning hours	Outline of learning content	Resources
1.1 At home	1	Explore the idea of known places. Read and talk about a family story set at home and answer questions about it.	Learner's Book Session 1.1 Workbook Session 1.1

The **Background knowledge** feature outlines specific skills, resources, grammar and subject knowledge that you can familiarise yourself with in order to help you teach the unit content effectively.

Learners' prior knowledge can be informally assessed through the **Getting started** feature in the Learner's Book.

The **Teaching skills focus** feature covers a teaching skill and suggests how to implement it in the unit.

BACKGROUND KNOWLEDGE

Before you begin to teach this unit, you may find it helpful to:

*   prepare ways to talk with learners about the concept of the past and the past tense

TEACHING SKILLS FOCUS

Skills for Life

The activities throughout this book aim to develop key skills for the 21st century. These include:

Reflecting the Learner's Book, each unit consists of multiple sections. A section covers a learning topic.

At the start of each session, the **Learning plan** table includes the learning objectives, learning intentions and success criteria that are covered in the session. The learning objectives that are the main focus of the lesson are in bold, followed by those that are partially covered.

It can be helpful to share learning intentions and success criteria with your learners at the start of a session so that they can begin to take responsibility for their own learning.

LEARNING PLAN

Learning objectives		Learning intentions	Success criteria
Main focus	**Also covered**	• Talk about places they know.	• Learners can talk about places they know.
1Rv.02, 1Rs.01, 1Ra.04	1Rv.01, 1Ri.01, 1Ri.05, 1Ri.09		

There are often **common misconceptions** associated with particular learning topics. These are listed, along with suggestions for identifying evidence of the misconceptions in your class and suggestions for how to overcome them.

Common misconception

Misconception	How to identify	How to overcome
We can read the pictures instead of the words.	Ask learners to talk about a picture. Then together read the words on the page.

Are they the same thing? | Discuss the fact that although pictures can support our understanding and add extra information, we also have to read (decode and understand) the words on the page. |

For each topic, there is a selection of **starter ideas**, **main teaching ideas** and **plenary ideas**. You can pick out individual ideas and mix and match them depending on the needs of your class. The activities include suggestions for how they can be differentiated or used for assessment. **Homework ideas** are also provided.

Starter idea

Book cover (10–15 minutes)

Resources: Learner's Book, Session 1.2: Getting started and/or book cover of *It's Much Too Early!* by Ian Whybrow

Description: Ask learners what they know about the cover of a storybook. Ask: *What do you know it will include?* Share ideas.

Ask learners to work in pairs to look at the book

Main teaching ideas

1 Listen for language patterns (20–30 minutes)

Learning intention: to read and identify repeated phrases and sentences in a text

Resources: Learner's Book, Session 1.2, Activity 1

Description: Split the class into four groups. Give each group a phrase or sentence from the story in Activity 1.

The **Language support** feature highlights specific vocabulary and uses of English throughout the unit that learners might not have encountered before, or may struggle with. It contains suggestions on how to approach these with your class and examples to help them better understand.

LANGUAGE SUPPORT

Learners will become more familiar with the repeated phrases and sentences in *It's Much Too Early!* by recalling and then retelling the story from Session 1.1.

The **Cross-curricular links** feature provides suggestions for linking to other subject areas.

CROSS-CURRICULAR LINKS

Science: Gather a selection of toys, including a scooter, if possible. Encourage learners to think about the materials each toy is made from (wood, plastic, metal, glass, rock, paper or fabric).

Digital resources to download

This Teacher's Resource includes a range of digital materials that you can download from Cambridge GO. (For more information about how to access and use your digital resource, please see inside front cover.) This icon ⬇ indicates material that is available from Cambridge GO.

Helpful documents for planning include:

- **Letter for parents – Introducing the Cambridge Primary and Lower Secondary resources:** a template letter for parents, introducing the Cambridge Primary English resources.
- **Lesson plan template:** a Word document that you can use for planning your lessons.
- **Curriculum framework correlation:** a table showing how the Cambridge Primary English resources map to the Cambridge Primary English curriculum framework.
- **Scheme of work:** a suggested scheme of work that you can use to plan teaching throughout the year.

Each unit includes:

- **Differentiated worksheets:** these worksheets are provided in variations that cater for different abilities. Worksheets labelled 'A' are intended to support less confident learners, while worksheets labelled 'C' are designed to challenge more confident learners. Answer sheets are provided.
- **Language worksheets:** these worksheets provide language support. Answer sheets are provided.

Additionally, the Teacher's Resource includes:

- **Diagnostic check and answers:** a test to use at the beginning of the year to discover the level that learners are working at. The results of this test can inform your planning.
- **Answers to Learner's Book activities**
- **Answers to Workbook activities**
- **Glossary**

In addition, you can find more detailed information about teaching approaches.

🎧 **Audio** is available for download from Cambridge GO (as part of this Teacher's Resource and as part of the digital resources for the Learner's Book and Workbook).

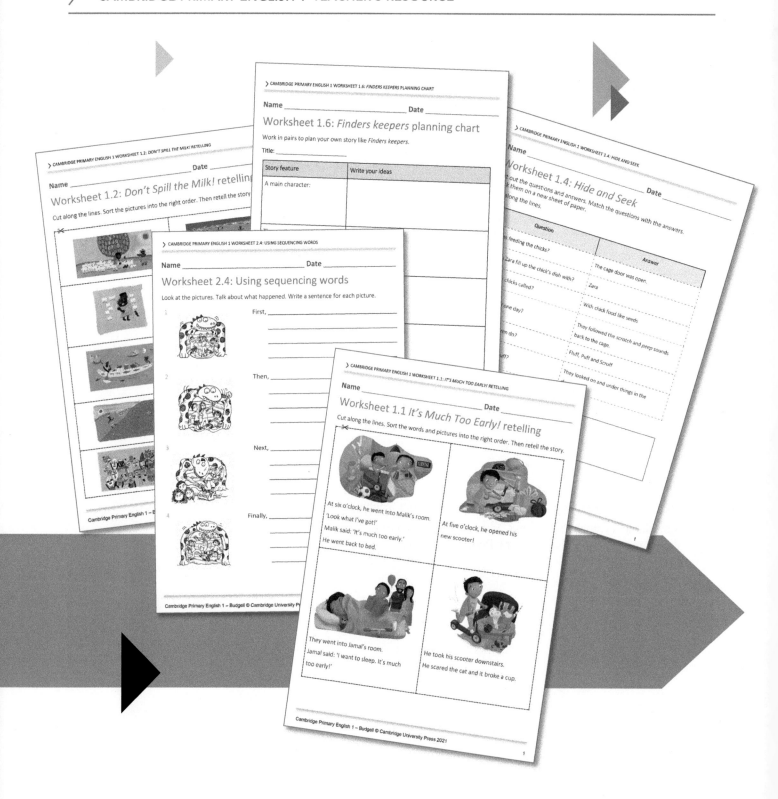

> CAMBRIDGE PRIMARY ENGLISH 1 WORKSHEET 1.6: FINDERS KEEPERS PLANNING CHART

Name _____ Date _____

Worksheet 1.6: *Finders keepers* planning chart

Work in pairs to plan your own story like *Finders keepers*.

Title: _____

Story feature	Write your ideas
A main character:	

> CAMBRIDGE PRIMARY ENGLISH 1 WORKSHEET 1.2: DON'T SPILL THE MILK! RETELLING

Name _____ Date _____

Worksheet 1.2: *Don't Spill the Milk!* retelling

Cut along the lines. Sort the pictures into the right order. Then retell the story

Cambridge Primary English 1 – B

> CAMBRIDGE PRIMARY ENGLISH 1 WORKSHEET 1.4: HIDE AND SEEK

Name _____ Date _____

Worksheet 1.4: *Hide and Seek*

...out the questions and answers. Match the questions with the answers.
...k them on a new sheet of paper.
...along the lines.

Question	Answer
...s feeding the chicks?	The cage door was open.
...Zara fill up the chick's dish with?	Zara
...chicks called?	With chick food like seeds
...one day?	They followed the scratch and peep sounds back to the cage.
...en do?	Fluff, Puff and Scruff
...uff?	They looked on and under things in the

1

> CAMBRIDGE PRIMARY ENGLISH 1 WORKSHEET 2.4: USING SEQUENCING WORDS

Name _____ Date _____

Worksheet 2.4: Using sequencing words

Look at the pictures. Talk about what happened. Write a sentence for each picture.

1   First, _____

2   Then, _____

3   Next, _____

4   Finally, _____

Cambridge Primary English 1

> CAMBRIDGE PRIMARY ENGLISH 1 WORKSHEET 1.1: IT'S MUCH TOO EARLY! RETELLING

Name _____ Date _____

Worksheet 1.1 *It's Much Too Early!* retelling

Cut along the lines. Sort the words and pictures into the right order. Then retell the story.

At six o'clock, he went into Malik's room.
'Look what I've got!'
Malik said: 'It's much too early.'
He went back to bed.

At five o'clock, he opened his new scooter!

They went into Jamal's room.
Jamal said: 'I want to sleep. It's much too early!'

He took his scooter downstairs.
He scared the cat and it broke a cup.

Cambridge Primary English 1 – Budgell © Cambridge University Press 2021

1

> About the curriculum framework

The information in this section is based on the Cambridge Primary English curriculum framework (0058) from 2020. You should always refer to the appropriate curriculum framework document for the year of your learners' assessment to confirm the details and for more information. Visit www.cambridgeinternational.orglprimary to find out more.

The Cambridge Primary English curriculum has been designed to help learners to become confident communicators. They will learn to apply reading, writing, speaking and listening skills in everyday situations, as well as develop a broad vocabulary and an understanding of grammar and language. Through this curriculum, learners will develop evaluation skills, learn to appreciate texts from different cultures and learn to write for different audiences and purposes.

The Cambridge Primary English curriculum framework is split into three strands: reading, writing and speaking and listening. For more information, visit the Cambridge Assessment International Education website.

A curriculum framework correlation document (mapping the Cambridge Primary English resources to the learning objectives) and scheme of work are available to download from Cambridge GO (as part of this Teacher's Resource).

> About the assessment

Information about the assessment of the Cambridge Primary English curriculum framework is available on the Cambridge Assessment International Education website: **https://www.cambridgeinternational.org/primary**

> Approaches to learning and teaching

The following are the teaching approaches underpinning our course content and how we understand and define them.

Active learning

Active learning is a teaching approach that places learners' learning at its centre. It focuses on how learners learn, not just on what they learn. We, as teachers, need to encourage learners to 'think hard', rather than passively receive information. Active learning encourages learners to take responsibility for their learning and supports them in becoming independent and confident learners in school and beyond.

Assessment for Learning

Assessment for Learning (AfL) is a teaching approach that generates feedback which can be used to improve learners' performance. Learners become more involved in the learning process and, from this, gain confidence in what they are expected to learn and to what standard. We, as teachers, gain insights into a learner's level of understanding of a particular concept or topic, which helps to inform how we support their progression.

Differentiation

Differentiation is usually presented as a teaching approach where teachers think of learners as individuals and learning as a personalised process. Whilst precise definitions can vary, typically the core aim of differentiation is viewed as ensuring that all learners, no matter their ability, interest or context, make progress towards their learning intentions. It is about using different approaches and appreciating the differences in learners to help them make progress. Teachers therefore need to be responsive, and willing and able to adapt their teaching to meet the needs of their learners.

Language awareness

For all learners, regardless of whether they are learning through their first language or an additional language, language is a vehicle for learning. It is through language that learners access the learning intentions of the lesson and communicate their ideas. It is our responsibility, as teachers, to ensure that language doesn't present a barrier to learning.

Metacognition

Metacognition describes the processes involved when learners plan, monitor, evaluate and make changes to their own learning behaviours. These processes help learners to think about their own learning more explicitly and ensure that they are able to meet a learning goal that they have identified themselves or that we, as teachers, have set.

Skills for Life

How do we prepare learners to succeed in a fast-changing world? To collaborate with people from around the globe? To create innovation as technology increasingly takes over routine work? To use advanced thinking skills in the face of more complex challenges? To show resilience in the face of constant change? At Cambridge, we are responding to educators who have asked for a way to understand how all these different approaches to life skills and competencies relate to their teaching. We have grouped these skills into six main Areas of Competency that can be incorporated into teaching, and have examined the different stages of the learning journey and how these competencies vary across each stage.

These six key areas are:

* Creativity – finding new ways of doing things, and solutions to problems
* Collaboration – the ability to work well with others
* Communication – speaking and presenting confidently and participating effectively in meetings
* Critical thinking – evaluating what is heard or read, and linking ideas constructively
* Learning to learn – developing the skills to learn more effectively
* Social responsibilities – contributing to social groups, and being able to talk to and work with people from other cultures.

Cambridge learner and teacher attributes

This course helps develop the following Cambridge learner and teacher attributes.

Cambridge learners	Cambridge teachers
Confident in working with information and ideas – their own and those of others.	**Confident** in teaching their subject and engaging each learner in learning.
Responsible for themselves, responsive to and respectful of others.	**Responsible** for themselves, responsive to and respectful of others.
Reflective as learners, developing their ability to learn.	**Reflective** as learners themselves, developing their practice.
Innovative and equipped for new and future challenges.	**Innovative** and equipped for new and future challenges.
Engaged intellectually and socially, ready to make a difference.	**Engaged** intellectually, professionally and socially, ready to make a difference.

Reproduced from Developing the Cambridge learner attributes *with permission from Cambridge Assessment International Education.*

More information about these approaches to teaching and learning is available to download from Cambridge GO (as part of this Teacher's Resource).

Approaches to learning and teaching English

In this new edition of Cambridge Primary English we offer an integrated approach to language skills (speaking, listening, reading and writing). This means that in each English lesson you can expect a focus on learning objectives from each strand of the curriculum framework. Each Learner's Book contains nine units: two long units and one shorter unit per 10-week term. Each long unit of 12 sessions has been designed to be delivered over four weeks, with three lessons per week, plus a revision session. If your timing is different we hope the materials are flexible enough for you to be able to fit them to your requirements. The shorter units of six sessions are intended to be delivered over two weeks, plus a revision unit. The units per term may be taught in any order with progression being built in per term, rather than unit-by-unit, to add further flexibility for the use of the programme and to allow for more cross-curricular matching.

Listening and speaking are a focus for effective communication, but also underpin reading and writing skills too. We consolidate and develop the sub-strands including: making yourself understood; showing understanding; group work and discussion; performance; and reflection and evaluation. We have included additional listening activities in this edition and there is enhanced support for developing listening and speaking skills in authentic and exciting contexts. Audio tracks actively promote good pronunciation of English and you will find recordings of all the texts from the Learner's Book in this Teacher's Resource.

Across each stage for reading and writing we introduce a wide range of fiction and non-fiction texts including fiction genres, poetry and non-fiction text-types for different purposes. There is a broad selection of authentic texts from around the world, which have been included to promote reading for pleasure as well as an understanding of meaning and the conventions and features of different types of writing.

For reading and writing we orchestrate rich coverage of each sub-strand and are still mindful to integrate listening, speaking, reading and writing skills as follows:

Word structure (phonics and spelling): We assume schools have followed a systematic phonics programme with decodable reading books and that increasingly learners are encouraged to enjoy and explore texts with less restricted word choice. We believe that phonics knowledge is a strong basis for reading and spelling, and that learners need to be both taught and have time to explore spelling patterns, rules and exceptions. By actively focusing the learners' attention on activities and useful rules in the context of the lesson, this course aims to improve the average spelling age in your classroom. Phonic workbooks are provided for Stage 1 and may be of some use for learners who need further or repeated practice in basic phonics at Stage 2.

The downloadable spelling lists in this Teacher's Resource are a supplement to the spelling activities at the back of the Learner's Book. Embedded throughout the notes are **Spelling links**; these are intended to suggest opportunities at which the indicated spelling areas can be looked at in greater detail.

There are three spelling spreads included at the back of each Learner's Book. Each spread contains specific spelling activities to address some of the spelling objectives in a systematic way to ensure complete coverage of all the objectives. They can be used at the teacher's discretion as part of a wider session or as part of a dedicated spelling session. The answers to the spelling activities are included at the end of this Teacher's Resource.

A suggested spelling session format

- **SAY the word and SEE the word.** Introduce words both orally and visually so the children see each word and hear the sound simultaneously to develop auditory perception. Use flash cards, words appearing on a screen or written on the board.

- **PLAY with the word.** They write it in the air or on their desk with a finger, mime it to a partner, write it on a slate or paper and hold it up, do visual memory activities with a partner: look at a word, close eyes and spell it. These activities provide immediate feedback and develop visual memory. Clap the sounds to demonstrate how the word is broken into syllables. Let the children find their own associations to help them remember words e.g. *ear* in h*ear* or *ache* in head*ache*.

- **ANALYSE the word.** Spelling rules can be helpful here to explain how words are built up, why letters move, how sounds change from one word to another and how patterns fit into words.

- **USE the word – make up a sentence.** Activities are provided in the Learner's Book but you can add to these by playing spelling games. Younger children enjoy spelling 'snap' or 'bingo'; older children might enjoy a spelling challenge/ladder or a competition that involves winners.

- **LEARN the word.** They commit the word to memory while writing it out in a wordbook or personal spelling notebook. Tests or assessments need not be repetitive weekly activities but learners do need incentive to internalise the spelling of words and to see they are making progress.

Vocabulary and language: We provide multiple experiences and strategies for securing vocabulary, including saying a word and then writing it, exploring context, grammatical features and a word's relationship to other words (word families, prefixes, suffixes etc.). We also explore texts with learners to reflect on writers' choices of vocabulary and language. In the final sessions of each unit we then innovate on the text vocabulary or language to apply learning and try out new found skills and knowledge.

Practical ideas for the classroom

Words and spellings need to be highlighted and enriched at every opportunity in the classroom.

1 Encourage personal word books or cards: include words covered in spelling sessions and ones they look up in the dictionary. At the back, suggest learners develop a bank of words they would like to use (especially powerful, descriptive or unusual words). Word meanings can also be included. Some children may benefit by using colours or underlining/highlighting to identify tricky bits or root words.

2 Have a classroom display of aspirational words or themed words around a topic (any learning area).

3 Have plenty of large spelling resources – online and print dictionaries, thesauruses, etc.

4 Set up spelling buddies as a first line of check if a dictionary or thesaurus does not help.

5 Play word games such as word dominoes or phonic pairs on a set of cards as a memory game.

6   Highlight and discuss word origins and have a merit system for anyone with interesting words or word information to share.

7   Display lists of words with similar sounds or letter patterns (either at the start, middle or end) – write the words large in the handwriting taught at the school joined up if appropriate to stimulate visual and kinaesthetic knowledge.

8   Have an interactive word list of interesting words, or words that match a spelling rule or word pattern being focused on. Add to it whenever anyone comes across a relevant word.

9   Consider an alphabet of vowel sounds and consonant sounds as a display or frieze around the walls.

10 If handwriting lessons are timetabled, add word patterns and sounds into those sessions.

11 Research free web resources to create your own crosswords and word searches linked to vocabulary in themes and spelling rules you are working on.

Grammar and punctuation: Whilst being mindful of reading for pleasure and text coherence, we focus on the grammar and punctuation arising from a text so that learners experience new learning in context. We have respected both teacher and learners' capacity for understanding and using correct metalanguage in the classroom and especially in writing activities.

Structure of texts: An exciting range of authentic texts is provided for discussion, performance, reflection and as models for learners' own writing. This is especially true in the final sessions of each unit when learners aim to write within the support of frameworks or scaffolds.

Interpretation of and creation of texts: Whilst the units provide a rich and broad selection of texts, it is also expected that learners are enjoying texts outside of the course, but aligned in some way to the topic or theme. Differentiation within each activity ensures that all learners can explore authentic texts and experiment with creative ideas and writing.

Appreciation and reflection of reading: We support the ethos of reading for pleasure and encourage learners to reflect and evaluate their wider reading from an early age. Links to Cambridge Reading Adventures (CRA) series are provided and offer a perfect bridge for learners between the texts in the Learner's Books, Book Band graded reading books in CRA and the wider world of authentic texts. We adopt 'assessment for learning' strategies to encourage learners to work independently and in pairs or groups to discuss their reading (and wider learning), to share experiences and to respond to others' ideas and experiences.

Presentation and reflection of writing: We encourage learners to adopt a write, reflect/evaluate and improve cycle of working from an early age. We encourage them to present their own work and listen for feedback as well as to talk about their own ideas and others'. Handwriting is an important part of writing and this series encourages best practice in handwriting but does not teach it explicitly. We recommend using the *Cambridge Penpals for Handwriting* series alongside *Cambridge Primary English* for teaching handwriting.

> Setting up for success

Our aim is to support better learning in the classroom with resources that allow for increased learner autonomy while supporting teachers to facilitate learner learning. Through an active learning approach of enquiry-led tasks, open-ended questions and opportunities to externalise thinking in a variety of ways, learners will develop analysis, evaluation and problem-solving skills.

Some ideas to consider to encourage an active learning environment are as follows:

- Set up seating to make group work easy.
- Create classroom routines to help learners to transition between different types of activity efficiently, e.g. move from pair work to listening to the teacher to independent work.
- Source mini-whiteboards, which allow you to get feedback from all learners rapidly.
- Start a portfolio for each learner, keeping key pieces of work to show progress at parent–teacher days.
- Have a display area with learner work and vocab flashcards.

Planning for active learning

We recommend the following approach to planning. A blank Lesson Plan Template is available to download to help with this approach.

1 **Planning learning intentions and success criteria:** these are the most important feature of the lesson. Teachers and learners need to know where they are going in order to plan a route to get there.

2 **Plan language support:** think about strategies to help learners overcome the language demands of the lesson so that language doesn't present a barrier to learning.

3 **Plan starter activities:** include a 'hook' or starter to engage learners using imaginative strategies. This should be an activity where all learners are active from the start of the lesson.

4 **Plan main activities:** during the lesson, try to: give clear instructions, with modelling and written support; coordinate logical and orderly transitions between activities; make sure that learning is active and all learners are engaged; create opportunities for discussion around key concepts.

5 **Plan assessment for learning and differentiation:** use a wide range of Assessment for Learning techniques and adapt activities to a wide range of abilities. Address misconceptions at appropriate points and give meaningful oral and written feedback which learners can act on.

6 **Plan reflection and plenary:** at the end of each activity and at the end of each lesson, try to: ask learners to reflect on what they have learnt compared to the beginning of the lesson; build on and extend this learning.

7 **Plan homework:** if setting homework, it can be used to consolidate learning from the previous lesson or to prepare for the next lesson.

To help planning using this approach, a blank Lesson plan template is available to download from Cambridge GO (as part of this Teacher's Resource).

For more guidance on setting up for success and planning, please explore the Professional Development pages of our website **www.cambridge.org/education/PD**

>1 Places we know

Unit plan

Session	Approximate number of learning hours	Outline of learning content	Resources
1.1 At home	1	Explore the idea of known places. Read and talk about a family story set at home and answer questions about it. Explore using pictures in texts to support understanding.	Learner's Book Session 1.1 Workbook Session 1.1
1.2 Retelling	1.5	Re-read a text to notice repetition of words and phrases. Create sentences to retell the story.	Learner's Book Session 1.2 Workbook Session 1.2 ⬇ Worksheet 1.1 ⬇ Language worksheet 1A
1.3 Helping at home	1	Listen to and read the first part of a story. Predict what happens next.	Learner's Book Session 1.3 Workbook Session 1.3
1.4 Joining in	1.5	Listen to and read the second part of a story. Answer questions about the story. Read words with adjacent consonants.	Learner's Book Session 1.4 Workbook Session 1.4 ⬇ Worksheet 1.2 Phonics Workbook A
1.5 Story maps and retelling	2	Talk about and make a story map to retell a story. Act the story in a group.	Learner's Book Session 1.5 Workbook Session 1.5 ⬇ Worksheet 1.3

Session	Approximate number of learning hours	Outline of learning content	Resources
1.6 At school	1.5	Talk about schools and classrooms. Read a classroom story. Match questions about the story to answers.	Learner's Book Session 1.6 Workbook Session 1.6 ⬇ Worksheet 1.4
1.7 Changing and retelling	1.5	Talk about real and pretend pets. Retell a story using pictures. Write sentences to match pictures. Change a story and retell it orally.	Learner's Book Session 1.7 Workbook Session 1.7 ⬇ Differentiated worksheets 1A–C
1.8 When things we know look different	1.5	Listen to and discuss a rhyming text. Form questions and act parts of the text to show non-verbal responses.	Learner's Book Session 1.8 Workbook Session 1.8
1.9 Out and about	1.5	Listen to and follow a text using pictures. Explore, find and use words in a story. Pretend to be a character, and to ask questions.	Learner's Book Session 1.9 Workbook Session 1.9
1.10 Story endings	1.5	Describe things in detail. Talk about story endings and read one. Act the story in a group.	Learner's Book Session 1.10 Workbook Session 1.10 ⬇ Worksheet 1.5
1.11 Planning and writing	2	Explore the features of a story we know. Talk about choices we make when writing a story. Plan and write a similar story.	Learner's Book Session 1.11 Workbook Session 1.11 ⬇ Worksheet 1.6 ⬇ Worksheet 1.7 Phonics Workbooks A and B

Session	Approximate number of learning hours	Outline of learning content	Resources
1.12 Look back	1	Check writing. Talk about the stories in the unit. Think about learning.	Learner's Book Session 1.12 Workbook Session 1.12 ⬇ Language worksheet 1B
Cross-unit resources			
Diagnostic check			
Learner's Book Check your progress			
Learner's Book Projects			

BACKGROUND KNOWLEDGE

Before you begin to teach this unit, it might be helpful to familiarise yourself with:

- ways to talk with your learners about:
  - places that are familiar to them at home, at school, or out and about
  - personal information and feelings
  - understanding humour (you could share some examples from the texts in this unit)
- phonics, including: letter-to-sound correspondence; words with adjacent consonants; blending and segmenting words and understanding syllables, e.g. *Penda, downstairs*. Use pictures where needed to support understanding and help with unfamiliar words
- using repetition to support fluency
- using rhyme to support spelling
- sequencing of pictures, words, stories
- number words and *o' clock* time.

TEACHING SKILLS FOCUS

Skills for life

The activities throughout this book aim to develop key skills for the 21st century. These include:

- critical thinking: learners analyse, evaluate and understand
- collaboration: learners work together
- creativity: learners generate new ideas as well as improve and innovate on existing ideas
- communication: learners share ideas effectively

- independence: learners work with little or no guidance
- problem-solving: learners explore and apply strategies
- information-handling: learners begin to research using books and it.

At the end of this unit, consider how well you were able to challenge learners to develop 21st-century skills. What would need to change for you to become more reflective, innovative, confident, engaged or responsible as a teacher?

Cambridge Reading Adventures

Learners may enjoy these other fiction titles from Cambridge Reading Adventures that follow the unit theme:

- *Late for School* by Claire Llewellyn (Yellow Band: easier than the unit texts)
- *Take Zayan with You!* by Peter Millett (Green Band: same level as *Hide and Seek*)
- *Omar in Trouble* by Gabby Pritchard (Orange Band: harder than the unit texts)

1.1 At home

LEARNING PLAN

Learning objectives		Learning intentions	Success criteria
Main focus	**Also covered**	• To talk about places they know.	• Learners can talk about places they know.
1Rv.02, 1Rs.01, 1Ra.04	1Rv.01, 1Ri.01, 1Ri.05, 1Ri.09, 1Ri.11, 1Ri.12, 1Ri.13, 1Ra.02, 1Wv.01, 1Wg.01, 1SLm.01, 1SLm.02, 1SLm.03, 1SLg.04, 1SLp.01, 1SLp.05, 1SLp.02	• To listen to a story set at home, finding information in the pictures. • To talk about the story sequence.	• Learners can listen to and read a story set at home, finding information in the pictures. • Learners can talk about the story sequence.

LANGUAGE SUPPORT

Learners will benefit from reading the Cambridge Reading Adventures book *It's Much Too Early* by Ian Whybrow and re-reading the text in the original print format. They may like to act the story to reinforce the language patterns. They may also achieve this by using simple character puppets for story retelling.

Common misconception

Misconception	How to identify	How to overcome
We can read the pictures instead of the words.	Ask learners to talk about a picture. Then together read the words on the page. *Are they the same thing?*	Discuss the fact that although pictures can support our understanding and add extra information, we also have to read (decode and understand) the words on the page.

Starter idea

Places we know (10–15 minutes)

Resources: Learner's Book, Session 1.1: Getting started; pictures or photos of familiar places

Description: Ask learners to talk about places they know, to elicit key vocabulary such as *home, school, park* and *beach.*

Explain that this unit is all about places we know and ask learners to share their initial ideas and experiences.

Ask learners to explore and talk about the pictures in Getting started together in pairs. Then ask them to give feedback on what they noticed and were able to name.

Are there some places that are not familiar to them? Are there other places they would add?

Main teaching ideas

1 Words and pictures (15–30 minutes)

Learning intention: to use pictures in texts to support understanding

Resources: Learner's Book, Session 1.1, Activity 1; a variety of clocks

Description: Tell learners they are going to read the first sentence of a story.

Write the opening sentence on the board: *At five o'clock, Jamal got out of bed and looked at the presents.* Read it together, pointing to each word as you do so.

Ask learners to read the sentence again in this way, working in pairs.

Ask pairs of learners to explore the picture. Ask: *What else does the picture tell them about this story?*

Read the questions in the Learner's Book together and ask for verbal responses.

Share ideas and talk about the importance of looking at pictures carefully for extra detail and information. Ask learners to show in the picture where they found the information.

If possible, show a variety of clocks, to consolidate number recognition and to talk about time.

> **Differentiation ideas:** Support learners by providing the opening sentence as a sentence strip so they may more easily point and follow when reading it.

Challenge learners by asking them to comment on a very small detail in the picture, e.g. *How are the presents wrapped?*

Answers:
Jamal is in his bedroom / at home in his bedroom; It's four o'clock / It's very early; He's awake because it's his birthday / He's excited / He can't sleep / He wants to open his presents.

2 *It's Much Too Early!* (20–30 minutes)

Learning intention: to listen to a story set at home; to listen for a repeated phrase and point to pictures

To talk about the story sequence.

Resources: *It's Much Too Early!* (Learner's Book, Session 1.1, Activity 2); Track 01; Workbook, Session 1.1

Description: Tell learners they will now listen to the rest of this story about Jamal's birthday.

Initially, ask them to just listen and look at the pictures.

On a second listening, ask learners to count the number of times they hear the story title: *It's Much Too Early!* (four excluding the title)

Talk about their first impressions of the story.

Draw their attention to the mascot question. Explore how they guessed or did not guess the present was a scooter.

Ask learners to read the story in their pairs.

Learners can complete the Workbook Session 1.1 activities for Session 1.1 in class now.

> **Differentiation ideas:** Support learners by sitting them in a pair with a more confident reader and/ or working with a group to read the story again together.

Challenge learners to point to the words as they listen and to the phrase *It's much too early* when they hear it.

3 Time (12–20 minutes)

Learning intention: to talk about a story sequence

Resources: Learner's Book, Session 1.1, Activity 3

Description: Ask learners to look back at the pictures of the story to focus on each time Jamal gets up and key events.

If possible, rehearse numbers and number formation as learners notice the clock in each picture.

Ask learners to rehearse the sentences for five, six and seven o'clock. *At five o'clock Jamal got out of bed,* etc.

Encourage learners to think about what they do in the morning and share ideas.

> **Differentiation ideas:** Support learners to share, draw and sequence their ideas about what they do in the mornings, e.g. get out of bed, wash, eat breakfast.

Challenge learners to draw and write a sentence for their morning sequence of activities.

Answers:
a   May include: At 5:00 Jamal got out of bed / went into Mum and Dad's room; At 6:00 Jamal went into Malik's room; At 7:00 Jamal took his scooter downstairs / Mum went downstairs.
b   Learners' own responses

Plenary idea

Play Which Picture? (5 minutes)

Resources: *It's Much too Early!* (Learner's Book, Session 1.1); Track 01

Description: Ask learners to play a game of Which Picture?

Split learners into pairs. The first learners should choose a picture from the story in Learner's Book Session 1.1 and describe it. The second learner should point to the picture they think is being described.

Learners should then swap roles and repeat the activity.

CROSS-CURRICULAR LINKS

Maths: Use the pictures from the story to explore the correct formation of numbers and o'clock time-telling using analogue clocks.

Homework ideas

Learners complete the Workbook Session 1.1 activities if not completed in class.

They talk to their family about a time when they have got up 'much too early' and share this story on return to school.

Answers for Workbook

Answers might include:

1 I can see a clock / a globe / a bed / presents / a scooter.

2 What time is it?; Go back to bed, Jamal!; It's much too early!; What are you doing?

3 I can't sleep; I love my new scooter; I want to ride my new scooter; I love red.

1.2 Retelling

LEARNING PLAN

Learning objectives		Learning intentions	Success criteria
Main focus	**Also covered**	• To notice repeated words and phrases.	• Learners can notice repeated words and phrases.
1Rv.05, 1Rg.03, 1Ri.06, 1Wv.02	1Rw.04, 1Rv.02, 1Rg.02, 1Rs.01, 1Rs.03, 1Ri.01, 1Ri.14, 1Ra.02, 1Wg.01, 1Ws.01, 1Wc.02, 1Wc.03, 1SLm.05, 1SLg.01, 1SLp.01	• To retell the story using pictures. • To write sentences with the same language pattern as a story.	• Learners can retell the story using pictures. • Learners can write sentences with the same language pattern as a story.

LANGUAGE SUPPORT

Learners will become more familiar with the repeated phrases and sentences in *It's Much Too Early!* by recalling and then retelling the story from Learner's Book Session 1.1.

Print and distribute the repeated phrases from the story to groups of learners, read them aloud and ask learners to stand up when they hear their phrase to help them to listen actively. Similarly, sequencing pictures of the story held will support comprehension.

Explain the meaning of the contraction *it's*.

Common misconception

Misconception	How to identify	How to overcome
You must stop for a while at each full stop.	Ask learners to listen to you reading a short passage from any class book. Read the sentences first with long pauses at each full stop and then fluently. Ask learners which sounds best.	Ask learners to read aloud to practise fluency in recognising full stops but not letting them interrupt the flow of the meaning.

Starter idea

Book cover (10–15 minutes)

Resources: Learner's Book, Session 1.2: Getting started; and/or book cover of *It's Much Too Early!* by Ian Whybrow

Description: Ask learners what they know about the cover of a storybook. *What do you know it will include?* Share ideas.

Ask learners to work in pairs to look at the book cover of *It's Much Too Early!* in Getting started or online/in print. Ask: *What can you see?* Try to elicit the key features: front cover, title, cover illustration/picture, author name and illustrator name.

Work through the questions in the Learner's Book to help them to notice specific punctuation.

If you have access to a print copy of the book, challenge learners to consider the back cover, too.

Main teaching ideas

1 Listen for language patterns (20–30 minutes)

Learning intention: to read and identify repeated phrases and sentences in a text

Resources: Learner's Book, Session 1.2, Activity 1; Workbook, Session 1.2, Activity 1; Language worksheet 1A

Description: Split the class into four groups. Give each group a phrase or sentence from the story in Activity 1.

Ask learners to listen as you read the story again. Explain that learners should jump up when they hear their phrase or sentence.

Now draw learners' attention to the speech bubbles in the Learner's Book.

Explain that you want them to work in small groups or pairs to re-read the text and work out where the phrases and sentences are repeated, who says them and how many times.

You can use Workbook Session 1.2 Activity 1 in class now for further practice of identifying who says what.

> **Differentiation ideas:** Support learners by asking them to find just one or two of the phrases or sentences.

Challenge learners further using Language Worksheet 1A to identify verbs ending –ed.

Answers:

Words and sentences	a How many times?	b Who says them?
Go back to bed, Jamal!	*Two*	*Dad and Malik*
It's much too early!	*Four*	*Dad, Malik, Mum and Jamal*
At ___ o'clock …	*Four*	*The storyteller*

2 Picture sorting and retelling (30–45 minutes)

Learning intention: to sequence and retell a story by pictures

Resources: Learner's Book, Session 1.2, Activity 2; Worksheet 1.1

Description: Remind learners how important pictures can be to help them to understand a story.

Ask learners to work in pairs to sort the pictures of the story into the right order. Then, together as a class, agree on the correct sequence.

Ask learners to work together in pairs again to use the pictures to retell the story in their own words.

Encourage learners to use the repeated phrases and sentences in Learner's Book Session 1.2 Activity 1 to help them.

Remind them to use their voice to make their story interesting (refer to the punctuation points in Getting started).

You can provide Worksheet 1.1 *It's Much Too Early!* retelling now for learners who need some support to sequence text to match the pictures.

Assessment focus: Allow time for some learners to present their story retellings and encourage listeners to give feedback. Provide some sentence starters: *I liked the way …, I liked it when …, I think the … could be a bit better, Perhaps next time they could …*

> **Differentiation ideas:** Support learners by providing Worksheet 1.1 *It's Much Too Early!* retelling, which has both text and pictures to sort.

Challenge learners to present or record their retellings.

Answers:
Story similar to this:

f   It was Jamal's birthday.
    He tried to go to sleep, but he wanted to open
    his presents.

b   At 5 o'clock he opened his new scooter!

h   He went into Mum and Dad's room and said,
    'Look what I've got!'
    They said: 'It's much too early.'
    He went back to bed.

a   At 6 o'clock he went into Malik's room and
    said 'Look what I've got!'
    Malik said: 'It's much too early!'
    He went back to bed.

d   He took his scooter downstairs. He scared the
    cat and the cat broke a cup.

g   At 7 o'clock Mum came downstairs. She said:
    'It's much too early!' They went back to bed.

e   At eight o'clock it was time to get up. But where
    was Jamal?

c   They went into Jamal's room.
    Jamal said: 'I want to sleep. It's much too early!'

3   **Use a language pattern to write similar
    sentences (20–30 minutes)**

Learning intention: to use a language pattern to
write similar sentences

Resources: Learner's Book, Session 1.2, Activity 3;
large pieces of paper; a scooter, if possible

Description: Remind learners that one of the
repeated sentences in the story is the title of the
book: *It's Much Too Early!*

Show learners the pictures of the scooter in the
Learner's Book, or other pictures of scooters or a
real scooter!

Talk about what you could say about the scooter
using the language pattern: *Put that scooter down.
It's much too ….* Show them the example in the
Learner's Book Session 1.2 Activity 3: *Put that
scooter down! It's much too red and shiny!*

Ask learners to work in groups of three or four
on large pieces of paper, or individually in their
notebooks.

Learners draw or paint a red scooter and then
write sentences about it around the outside, using
some of the adjectives provided the Learner's
Book Session 1.2 Activity 3. Make sure learners

understand they need to repeat the language pattern
each time.

> **Differentiation ideas:** Support learners to create
only one or two sentences and to write them on
their poster/in their notebooks.

Challenge learners to write more sentences using
their own ideas and adjectives.

Answers:

b   Learners' own sentences, but may include: Put
    that scooter down! It's much too heavy!; It's much
    too big!; It's much too noisy!; It's much too new!

Plenary idea

Circle time (5–10 minutes)

Resources: a list of simple questions

Description: Ask learners to sit in a circle.

Stand in the middle with a lightweight inflatable ball.

Explain to learners that if they catch the ball, you will
ask them a question, and they have to answer using the
pattern: *No, it's much too …*

Throw the ball to a learner and ask them a question.
For example:

- Question: *Can we go home yet?* Answer: *No, it's
  much too early!*

- Question: *Can we eat breakfast now?* Answer: *No,
  it's much too late!*

Continue asking questions that need these replies. Vary
as learner confidence grows. For example:

- Question: *Can you lift an elephant?* Answer: *No, it's
  much too heavy!*

- Question: *Can you hear the snow falling?* Answer:
  No, it's much too quiet!

CROSS-CURRICULAR LINKS
Science: Gather a selection of toys, including a scooter, if possible. Encourage learners to think about the materials each toy is made from (wood, plastic, metal, glass, rock, paper or fabric).

Homework ideas

Learners complete the Workbook Session 1.2 activities
if not completed in class.

They look again at the picture of Jamal's presents in Learner's Book Session 1.2 Activity 2 and draw what they think might be in the unopened presents.

Answers for Workbook

1   Hooray: Jamal; It's only 7 o'clock: Mum; Where is Jamal?: Malik

2   Look out: Jamal; Happy Birthday, Jamal!: Mum, Dad and Malik; I want to sleep!: Jamal; Where is Jamal?: Malik

3   May include: Mum: But it's much too early.; Dad: Go back to bed, Jamal!, Jamal: Here I come!

1.3 Helping at home

LEARNING PLAN

Learning objectives		Learning intentions	Success criteria
Main focus	**Also covered**	• To listen to and read a story about helping at home.	• Learners can listen to and read a story about helping at home.
1Rs.01, 1Ri.07, 1Ri.10, 1Ra.02	1Rw.01, 1Rv.01, 1Rv.02, 1Rg.03, 1Ri.01, 1Ri.05, 1Ri.12, 1Ri.13, 1Ra.01, 1Ra.04, 1Ra.06, 1Ww.01, 1Wv.02, 1Wg.04, 1Wp.01, 1SLm.03, 1SLp.01, 1SLg.04	• To join in with what a character says in a story. • To say what they think happens next.	• Learners can join in with what a character says in a story. • Learners can say what they think happens next.

LANGUAGE SUPPORT

Learners may benefit from being able to play in a 'home' corner or role-play area to act some of the ways they may help at home. Visiting a class of younger children to do this may benefit some learners so that they can rehearse appropriate language orally.

Providing the printed book *Don't Spill the Milk!* would allow learners to revisit the text and look at the brightly coloured and detailed illustrations to further support understanding of the story.

Some pre-teaching of vocabulary may be useful: *grasslands, masked dancers, dunes.*

Common misconception

Misconception	How to identify	How to overcome
Long words are difficult to spell.	Ask learners to spell *grasslands*. Some learners may struggle, but some may be able to explain what they did to spell the word. This may include clapping the syllables and/or splitting it into two words: *grass* and *lands*, to help them.	Look at compound words and two-syllable words in the story to allow learners to recognise and practise them, e.g. *droplet* (of milk) and *mountain*.

Starter idea

Helping at home (5–10 minutes)

Resources: Learner's Book, Session 1.3: Getting started

Description: Ask learners to share what jobs they do at home to help their family members. If you have taught learners to work with partners, ask them to share ideas together and then report back.

Talk about the pictures in Getting started to stimulate further discussion about who does what at home and what learners are allowed to do with help, or alone. Ask: *What do you most and least like to help with?*

You may wish to start creating a 'Helping at home' class display with sentences and pictures to share learners' experiences. This can be added to throughout the session.

Main teaching ideas

1 *Don't Spill the Milk!* Part 1 (20–30 minutes)

Learning intention: to listen to and follow a story using pictures, repeating specific parts of the text

Resources: *Don't Spill the Milk!*, Part 1 (Learner's Book, Session 1.3, Activity 1); Track 02

Description: Tell learners that this story is about a girl who wants to help her mummy. Her daddy is working away from home, and so she offers to take him some milk.

Ask learners to listen as you read aloud the text extract from *Don't Spill the Milk!* by Stephen Davies and Christopher Corr in the Learner's Book or play the audio. Encourage them to point to each picture as they listen, to show they are following the story.

Ask learners to describe what they have heard. Ask: *What did you understand about the story?*

Ask them to listen again, but this time to repeat what Penda says to encourage herself on her journey (the italicised text in the story). Pause your reading or the audio to allow learners time to repeat these parts.

Ask learners what they think of Penda's advice to herself, and to reflect on whether they sometimes do the same. What do they say to themselves or think?

Ask learners if they noticed any rhyming words in section 4 (*shiver, quiver, river*). Can they extend the rhyme? (*giver, sliver* or nonsense words such as *bivver*) You may also wish to pick up on the non-standard use of *don't* in: *milk don't float.*

> **Differentiation ideas:** Ask some learners to listen for the name of the girl in the story and where she is heading.

Challenge some learners to listen out for each instruction Penda gives herself: *Don't slip, Walk tall, Don't shiver, Don't look, never give up.*

Answers:
Learners point to pictures as they listen and join in with the words spoken by Penda.

2 Check understanding (10–15 minutes)

Learning intention: to read sentences about the story to check understanding

Resources: Learner's Book, Session 1.3, Activity 2; Workbook, Session 1.3, Activities 1 and 2

Description: Read each sentence with learners.

Some learners may be less familiar with the terms *true* and *false*. Ask learners to decide whether they will say *yes* or *no* / *true* or *false* for each answer.

Discuss their answers as a class.

You can use Workbook Activities 1 and 2 here to focus on pencil grip and control in copying patterns linked to the illustrations in the story.

> **Differentiation ideas:** Support groups of learners by reading the sentences aloud and then working with them to say their responses orally.

Challenge learners by asking them to write their own sentences for a similar activity in their notebooks.

Answers:
a true; b true; c false

3 Predict (10–15 minutes)

Learning intention: to make predictions

Resources: Learner's Book, Session 1.3, Activity 3

Description: Ask learners how this first part of the story ends and elicit: *At last Penda arrived at the grasslands!*

What do learners think she sees/hears/smells/feels/touches when she gets to the grasslands?

Remind them how we can use our senses to really imagine being in the story, like Penda.

Ask them to share their ideas about what might happen next. Encourage fanciful ideas and challenge learners to give explanations, too.

Agree on three possible outcomes. Keep these safe so you can return to them in the next session when the story is completed.

> **Differentiation ideas:** Support learners by providing some possible endings for them to consider and discuss.

Challenge learners to say why they have predicted something: *I think that because …*

Answers:
Learners' own responses. They know why Penda is going so responses may include: she finds her daddy and goes home; she gets lost and can't find her daddy; etc.

Plenary idea

Left and right (5–10 minutes)

Description: Ask learners to listen again to one of the things Penda says to herself: *Left foot, right foot, never give up, girl. Left hand, right hand, all the way up now.*

Show learners how to create an *L* shape between the thumb and the forefinger of the left hand to help them remember which is their left hand (and left foot on the same side).

Repeat Penda's words with your back slightly to the class so you can show them left and right.

Ask them to perform the sentences for you with words and actions.

CROSS-CURRICULAR LINKS

Geography: Find out more about different terrains including: grasslands, dunes, mountains and plains (where the giraffes were). Ask learners what sort of animals might live in the different terrains.

Art: Ask learners to create vibrant painted copies of some of the patterns in the storybook illustrations.

Homework ideas

Learners complete the Workbook Session 1.3 activities if not completed in class.

They help someone at home and report back on what they did.

Answers for Workbook

1   Learners copy the patterns on the pots: horizontal lines; vertical lines; and zig-zags.

2   Learners copy the patterns on the baskets: circles; criss-crosses; and lines.

3   Learners copy the patterns on the sheets: wavy; dotty; circles and dots; concentric circles; and ovals.

1.4 Joining in

LEARNING PLAN

Learning objectives		Learning intentions	Success criteria
Main focus	**Also covered**	• To listen and join in with some repeated parts of a story.	• Learners can listen and join in with some repeated parts of a story.
1Rw.03, 1Ri.12, 1Ri.13, 1Ra.02, 1Ww.02	1Rv.02, 1Rv.05, 1Rg.03, 1Rs.01, 1Ri.05, 1Ri.07, 1Ri.09, 1Ra.01, 1SLr.02	• To answer questions about a story.	• Learners can answer questions about a story.
		• To find and read words with two consonants next to each other.	• Learners can find and read words with two consonants next to each other.

LANGUAGE SUPPORT

Learners will benefit from revisiting the pictures of Part 1 of the story in Learner's Book Session 1.3 and hearing the reading of Part 2 with accurate expression, e.g. 'I don't believe it!' **wailed** Penda; 'It's not all gone,' **whispered** dad; 'Huh?' said Penda.

Picture cards of the dunes, masked dancers, the river, white giraffes and the mountains will help as prompts for learners to say the words as they join in with the story. Consider cutting up the pictures from Worksheet 1.2 *Don't Spill the Milk!* retelling for this purpose.

Starter idea

Story recall, Part 1 (5–10 minutes)

Resources: Learner's Book, Session 1.4: Getting started

Description: Ask learners to work in small groups to talk about and quickly draw what they remember about Part 1 of the story.

Ask for their ideas, encouraging accurate recall and use of language patterns where possible.

Encourage them to reflect on what they had remembered (words, places, character names, general points or details) and how they remembered this information. Tell them that they are now going to listen to and follow the second part of the story.

Main teaching ideas

1 *Don't Spill the Milk!*, Part 2 (20–30 minutes)

Learning intention: to listen to and follow a story using pictures, repeating specific parts of the text

Resources: *Don't Spill the Milk!*, Part 2 (Learner's Book, Session 1.4, Activity 1); Track 03; Worksheet 1.2

Description: Ask learners to listen as you read the text aloud or play the audio. Learners should follow the text by looking at the pictures, as they did in the previous session.

On a second listen, ask learners to join in and say the words that are repeated and shown in pictures: *dunes, masked dancers, the river, white giraffes, the mountains.* Pause and use the pictures from Worksheet 1.2 *Don't Spill the Milk!* retelling (see Language support earlier) if helpful to prompt learners to say the words.

> **Differentiation ideas:** Ask some learners to sit with more confident readers or for a more confident reader to point to the pictures if displayed on a shared board so that the sequence is clear.

Challenge some learners to say what they think happens at the end of the story, e.g. Penda walks home back through the different settings. This can be picked up again in Session 1.5 with puppet retellings.

Answers:
Learners point to pictures and join in with words represented by pictures in the text.

2 Comprehension (15–30 minutes)

Learning intention: to answer questions orally or in writing to demonstrate comprehension

Resources: Learner's Book, Session 1.4, Activity 2

Description: Read each question with learners and discuss the answers as a class.

Ask learners to write or draw their answers in their notebooks.

As learners work, move around the classroom and check their pencil grips, letter formation and correct use of punctuation.

If you only want learners to respond orally, check they are responding with clear spoken language and correct sentence structures and tenses.

> **Differentiation ideas:** Support learners by working with them in a group to answer their questions and/or by providing answers for them to match to the questions.

Challenge learners by asking them to write some questions about this part of the story for a partner to answer.

Answers:
a   She saw her daddy, a mango tree and some sheep.
b   He was sitting under a mango tree.
c   A big fat mango landed in the bowl.

3 Words with adjacent consonants (10–15 minutes)

Learning intention: to read words with adjacent consonants

Resources: Learner's Book, Session 1.4, Activity 3; letter cards to spell the words *milk, just, spilt, stop* and *drop*

Description: Write the story title on the board: *Don't Spill the Milk!* Ask learners to look at the word *spill.*

Ask them to say the sounds in the word. Model how to add a sound button under each phoneme: /s/ /p/ /i/ /ll/. Remind them that *ll* is two letters, but one sound.

Hand out letter cards for each word in the activity (*milk, just, spilt, stop* and *drop*) to different learners. Ask them to sort themselves into the correct order to spell the word you tell them. Others say if they are correct by blending the sounds to read the word.

Repeat for the other words.

You may like to use Workbook Session 1.4 and/or Phonics Workbook A, (pages 34–36), for further practice of reading and spelling words with adjacent consonants.

> **Differentiation ideas:** Support learners by providing a copy of the text so they can mark it up and/or ask each pair to search for just one of the words.

Challenge learners to use each word in a sentence and write it and/or to write other words ending –*lk*, –*st* and –*lt*, and beginning *sp*–, *st*– and *dr*–.

Answers:
Learners read the words and find them in the text. Some appear more than once.

Plenary idea

What else? (5–10 minutes)

Description: Ask learners to think about the word *splosh*, which is used to describe the mango falling from the tree into the milk bowl.

Ask: *What else goes splosh?*

Do learners know other similar words that begin with *spl*, e.g. *splash*?

Can they say 'Splish, splash, splosh!'?

CROSS-CURRICULAR LINKS

Maths: Develop understanding of fractions by cutting a mango or other fruit (real or pretend) into different shares, e.g. into two (for two people) or into three as in the story. Practise sharing.

Art: Ask learners to paint or make a model bowl from dough or clay. Ask: *What will you put in your bowl to show your love for someone in your family?* Make a class display of the love bowls.

Homework ideas

Learners complete the Workbook Session 1.4 activities if not completed in class.

They work with an adult to find out more about other festivals that involve masks.

Answers for Workbook

1   **a** milk; **b** slip; **c** stop; **d** Left; **e** drop

2   h/a/n/d: band, stand

m/a/s/k: task (but note *ar* pronunciation of *a* in this word), tusk

s/p/i/ll: spin, spit

s/t/o/p: still, stand

j/u/s/t: dust, must

3   **a** spill; **b** stop; **c** drop; **d** sand; **e** milk;
    f mask

1.5 Story maps and retelling

LEARNING PLAN

Learning objectives		Learning intentions	Success criteria
Main focus	**Also covered**	• To make a story map.	• Learners can make a story map.
1Rs.01, 1SLm.03, 1SLp.04	1Rv.01, 1Rs.02, 1SLm.01, 1SLm.04, 1SLm.0	• To retell a story using a story map.	• Learners can retell a story using a story map.
		• To retell a story using puppets.	• Learners can retell a story using puppets.

LANGUAGE SUPPORT

Re-use the picture word cards from Session 1.4 (the things Penda saw and where she went) if helpful to reinforce vocabulary as well as sequence the story again. With learners, use the images again to show how Penda returns seeing and doing the same things all the way back home to her mum.

Acting the story using puppets will help learners to revisit the story structure and language patterns.

If using the print book, the illustrations on the first and last spreads are very good for reinforcing the story sequence.

Common misconception

Misconception	How to identify	How to overcome
Story titles tell you what happens in a story.	Show learners a range of storybooks and discuss the titles. You may include *Don't Spill the Milk!* Ask how many learners think titles are: • for telling you what happens in a story • for giving you an idea of what a story is about. • Nothing to do with the story.	Create a class display of story titles the class have read and enjoyed. When learners are writing their own stories, remind them that a title should not tell us what happens and spoil the story.

Starter idea

Story maps (10–15 minutes)

Resources: Learner's Book, Session 1.5: Getting started; Workbook, Session 1.5; samples of story maps (posters or online)

Description: Talk to learners about how they used pictures in Session 1.4 to help them to retell the story.

Look at the story map in Getting started.

What can the learners tell you about the story by looking at the story map?

You can use Workbook Session 1.5 Activities 1–3 in class now to reinforce the story sequence before learners create their own story maps.

Main teaching ideas

1 Make a story map (30–50 minutes)

Learning intention: to make a story map

Resources: Learner's Book, Session 1.5, Getting started and Activity 1; large pieces of paper; felt-tip pens

Description: Tell learners they will now create their own story maps of *Don't Spill the Milk!*

Remind them that Penda goes all the way to see her daddy in the grasslands … and back again. How can they show that return journey?

Split the class into pairs. Give each pair two large pieces of paper – one for planning and one for making their final story map.

As they work, support learners to put the story events in the correct order (they have practised this in previous sessions).

Encourage learners to annotate their story maps like the example provided in Getting started.

> **Differentiation ideas:** Support learners by pairing good artists with those good at sequencing and spelling.

Challenge learners by asking them to annotate the map including the important parts of the text as practised in Sessions 1.3 and 1.4. Ask them to include other detail from the story in their pictures.

Answers:
Correct order: G, B, I, D, F, H, A, J, E, C
Learners' own drawings and writing

2 Story map retellings (30–50 minutes)

Learning intention: to use a story map to retell a story in their own words

Resources: Learner's Book, Session 1.5, Activity 2; learners' story maps; audio or video recording equipment if possible

Description: Once the story maps are completed, invite pairs to use them to retell their stories. Encourage them to use language from the original story where possible.

Fix the story maps onto an easel so learners can point to them as they talk.

If possible, consider recording some of the retellings so you can enjoy revisiting them at later stages or share them with other classes.

Talk about tips for retelling the story:

• Say the story title and check that everyone is sitting ready to listen before you begin.

- Speak clearly.
- Try to make the retelling interesting for listeners, e.g. by varying your voice and using non-verbal cues (you might pretend to cry when the mango falls in the bowl and spills the milk).

Talk about what we might do to listen well and how we can show that to the person speaking.

Take the opportunity to invite peer feedback at the end of each retelling, if there is time. Ask: *What went well? What could be better?*

> **Differentiation ideas:** Support learners to retell the story by asking questions to elicit responses. If you have paired different-skilled learners as suggested in Activity 1, ensure both learners participate in the retelling.

Challenge learners to incorporate the language patterns of the story and to include some of their own.

Answers:
Learners' own pictures and sentences

3 Puppets (30–40 minutes)

Learning intention: to make puppets to retell a story in character

Resources: Learner's Book, Session 1.5, Activity 3; Worksheet 1.3; puppets; small sticks (if stick puppets); scissors (to be used carefully); recording equipment; construction bricks, dough, junk modelling (for constructing the terrain of Penda's journey if desired)

Description: Ask learners to make puppets to retell the story.

They may make these themselves (finger puppets, sock puppets, small dough puppets or even construction brick puppets) or use Worksheet 1.3 *Don't Spill the Milk!* puppets for guidance.

Some learners may wish to use their puppets in conjunction with their story maps to retell the story. Others may wish to build a 3D story map with junk materials so that they can show their puppet walking the journey over the *uppy downy dunes,* etc.

Allow time for performances and again consider recording some of these and encouraging peer feedback.

> **Differentiation ideas:** Support learners by providing narration for the story and prompting them to say the correct part at the correct time.

Challenge learners to elaborate on the words the puppets say.

Answers:
Learners' own puppets and performances

Plenary idea

Puppets (5–10 minutes)

Resources: pictures of puppets or the learners' models

Description: Ask: *How many different kinds of puppets can you name?* They might suggest: Sock, finger, stick, shadow, hand, string, pop-up, ventriloquist's, life-size fancy dress costumes …

Explore puppet vocabulary and begin a class display or working wall of it.

CROSS-CURRICULAR LINKS
Science: Explore how sound becomes quieter as it travels from a source. Enable learners to notice the difference in voice volume when they stand really close to a presenter compared to standing on the other side of the classroom.

Homework ideas

Learners complete the Workbook Session 1.5 activities if not completed in class.

They draw a story map for another story they know.

Answers for Workbook

1 Penda, mum, Daddy correctly labelled
2 Pictures and words correctly matched
3 Correct pictures drawn for each label from the story.

1.6 At school

LEARNING PLAN

Learning objectives		Learning intentions	Success criteria
Main focus	Also covered	• To talk about schools and classrooms using *and*.	• Learners can talk about schools and classrooms using *and*.
1Rw.05, 1Rg.04, 1Ri.13, 1Wg.05	1Rw.03, 1Rv.01, 1Rv.05, 1Ri.09, 1Ri.11, 1Ra.03, 1Ra.06, 1Ww.03, 1SLm.02, 1SLg.03, 1SLp.01, 1SLp.03	• To use phonics to read a story set in a classroom. • To match questions and answers.	• Learners can use phonics to read a story set in a classroom. • Learners can match questions and answers.

LANGUAGE SUPPORT

Learners will benefit from handling the print book of the story to support understanding, if possible. Check learners are familiar with the game Hide and Seek.

Common misconception

Misconception	How to identify	How to overcome
We just keep adding *and* each time we add something in a list.	Ask learners which answer is more usual when answering the question: *What are the chick's names?* *Fluff **and** Puff **and** Scruff* or *Fluff, Puff **and** Scruff.* Tell them that if we are adding two things together, we use *and* between them. In a list of several things, we tend to just use *and* at the end before the last thing.	When learners are speaking or writing, remind them about how to use *and*. Using *Fluff, Puff and Scruff* as a mnemonic may help.

Starter idea

Different schools and classrooms (10–20 minutes)

Resources: Learner's Book, Session 1.6: Getting started

Description: Talk about schools and classrooms – draw learners' attention to the photos and captions in Getting started and read the captions together.

Talk about other kinds of schools including those relevant to the learners' experiences:

• School of the Air, where learners' classrooms are at home and they learn online.

• Mobile Schools with bus classrooms.

Give learners time to talk about their school and classroom in pairs.

Tell the learners that this session is about a story in a school setting. Ask: *What sort of classroom do you think it will be?*

Main teaching ideas

1 *Hide and Seek* (20–30 minutes)

Learning intention: to read a simple text with some independence using phonic skills

Resources: *Hide and Seek* (Learner's Book, Session 1.6, Activity 1); Track 04

Description: Tell learners that the surprise about this classroom is that they are allowed to have pet chicks in it!

Note: The idea of pets in a classroom may need exploring further in your school if this is not a usual occurrence. Explore notions of real and pretend so learners appreciate the humour of pets in school.

Read the story to the learners first and ask them to listen out for what happens.

Elicit that one chick seems to go missing or to be playing Hide and Seek. Ask: *Do you know the game?* Explain the game if necessary.

If appropriate, ask learners to try to read the story in pairs independently, or you may prefer to work in guided-reading groups.

Ask learners what they thought of the end of the story. Ask: *What had happened?*

> **Differentiation ideas:** Support learners with reading by working with a group or reading the story aloud with them and modelling how to run a finger under each word. Stop to use phonics on some decodable words e.g. *p–e–ck*.

Challenge learners to read the story alone and to make a list of words they are not sure about, and where they were able or unable to use phonics. Discuss those words with those learners to model how to tackle them. At the end of the session, invite learners to read aloud the different sections in pairs.

2 Questions and answers (15–20 minutes)

Learning intention: to match questions with correct answers

Resources: Learner's Book, Session 1.6, Activity 2; Worksheet 1.4; scissors (to be used carefully); glue

Description: Ask learners to look at the questions and answers in the Learner's Book.

Together, read the questions. Explain to learners that they have to find the matching answer.

You can provide Worksheet 1.4 Hide and Seek now, which enables learners to cut and stick the matching pairs.

Check answers with learners as a class, asking different learners or groups to contribute.

> **Differentiation ideas:** Support learners by asking them to work in pairs with one question at a time. Then work as a group to stick the questions and answers from Worksheet 1.4 Hide and Seek together.

Challenge learners to copy the questions or the question numbers in their notebooks and to copy the correct answer to match.

Answers:
a 2; **b** 3; **c** 5; **d** 1; **e** 6; **f** 4

3 Use *and* (20–30 minutes)

Learning intention: to join two words and sentences together using *and*

Resources: Learner's Book, Session 1.6, Activity 3; Workbook, Session 1.6

Description: Read the story again and ask learners to stand up each time they hear the word *and*.

Draw their attention to the Language focus Box in the Learner's Book Session 1.6 Activity 3.

If time, prepare the two parts of the table of phrases and sentences in the Learner's Book on cards or signs and a star sign with *and* written on it.

Ask one learner to stand with the first part of the phrase or sentence, and then another learner to stand with the second part of the phrase or sentence. Ask the class where the learner holding *and* should stand (between them). Repeat with different learners for the five phrases and sentences in the Learner's Book.

Ask learners to write the complete phrase or sentence in their notebooks and to draw a picture for each.

> **Differentiation ideas:** Support learners by playing the game using *and* (see Description) in smaller groups or as table-top game.

Challenge learners to write their own game like this with further examples linked to the story.

Answers:

a   Miss Garcia looked in the cage and she found Scruff.

b   Fluff, Puff and Scruff

c   Beno looked on the floor and Kofi looked under a desk.

d   She liked to fill up their dish and watch them peck.

e   Hide and seek.

Plenary idea

Leaving in pairs (5–10 minutes)

Description: Ask two learners to volunteer to be teachers.

The 'teachers' must ask learners to leave the class in pairs, saying, e.g. *Anna **and** Dan may leave now.*

Keep going until only the 'teachers' are left, and then you can say: *Everyone else has left **and** now you two may leave.*

> ### CROSS-CURRICULAR LINKS
>
> Science: As a class, find out what chicks need to survive.

Homework ideas

Learners complete the Workbook Session 1.6 activities if not completed in class.

They read to a pet at home (or to a toy pet if there are no pets at home). There is some evidence that reading to a pet can enhance reading for pleasure (and gives a good excuse to read aloud to a patient listener!).

Answers for Workbook

1   Hide **and** Seek

Zara liked to fill up the chick's dish **and** watch them peck.

The chicks were called Fluff, Puff **and** Scruff.

One day the cage door was open **and** Zara looked inside.

She looked **and** looked, but Scruff was gone.

2   a   Some classrooms are inside and some (classrooms) are outside.

b   Some classrooms have pets and the children look after them.

c   Learners' own sentences

3   Fluff, Puff and Scruff

Scritch, Scatch and Snatch (or similar, repeating the –*tch* letters and sound)

Peep, Tweet and Sweet (or similar, repeating the ee letters and sound)

Learners' own names for chicks

1.7 Changing and retelling

LEARNING PLAN

Learning objectives		Learning intentions	Success criteria
Main focus	**Also covered**	• To retell a story using pictures.	• Learners can retell a story using pictures.
1RS.01, 1Ri.06, 1Ws.01, 1Wc.03, 1SLm.03	1Rv.03, 1Ri.01, 1Ri.02, 1Ra.04, 1Ra.06, 1Wv.01, 1Wv.03, 1Wg.05, 1Wc.02, 1SLs.02, 1SLg.01, 1SLp.04	• To write sentences to match pictures. • To change the story and retell it.	• Learners can rewrite sentences to match pictures. • Learners can change a story and retell it.

LANGUAGE SUPPORT

Provide books and pictures about pets to support vocabulary and comprehension of the topic.

Common misconception

Misconception	How to identify	How to overcome
The letter *a* at the end of word always sounds like /a/ for apple.	Ask learners to tell you the name of the girl and teacher in the story *Hide and Seek*. Listen to their pronunciations of Zara and Miss Garcia. Can they hear that the final *a* should be unstressed, as in *schwa*? This sound is more like an *ugh* sound!	Remind learners when they are reading aloud or spelling that sometimes they might need to try to use this *ugh* sound for letter *a* to help them to work out the word or its spelling, especially if the word ends in *a*.

Starter idea

Classroom pets (10–15 minutes)

Resources: Learner's Book, Session 1.7: Getting started; pictures of/stories about a range of real and fantasy pets

Description: Learners may not have experience of pets so be sensitive to different cultural backgrounds here.

Remind learners that in the *Hide and Seek* story the learners were allowed to have classroom pets: chicks.

Ask them what sort of classroom pets they would choose if they could. Allow time for their ideas and explanations.

Use any pictures or other stories about classroom pets you have gathered to share with learners.

Share ideas and use the pictures in Getting started as further stimulus.

Tell learners they will be writing about their chosen class pet in this session, so they should try to remember their thoughts here.

Main teaching ideas

1 Retell a story using pictures (20–30 minutes)

Learning intention: to retell a story using pictures

Resources: Learner's Book, Session 1.7, Activity 1

Description: Tell learners they will first retell the story *Hide and Seek* using the pictures in the Learner's Book.

Ask learners to work in pairs to try to recall the events of the story, using appropriate or repeated words and phrases.

Listen in to retellings as you circulate and intervene to support or challenge learners.

Select a few pairs to perform their retellings and invite others to give feedback.

> **Differentiation ideas:** Support learners by rehearsing vocabulary and language structures together: *Zara liked …*; *One day …*; *They looked …*; *Let's listen*; *Scratch*; *Peep*.

Challenge learners to use direct speech in their retellings and voices for the different characters.

Answers:
Learners' own retellings

2 Write captions (20–30 minutes)

Learning intention: to write sentences to match pictures for a written retelling

Resources: Learner's Book, Session 1.7, Activity 2; Workbook, Session 1.7; Differentiated worksheets 1A–C

Description: Tell learners that now they are going to write sentences for each picture from their retellings. You can provide Differentiated worksheets 1A–C here.

If working without worksheets, carry on with the Learner's Book prompts – word banks relating to character names, setting, places in the classroom and noises. Show learners how you want them to set out their work in their book, e.g. they could draw each picture and then write the caption underneath.

As you circulate, encourage learners to use their phonics knowledge to check spellings and remind them to use correct punctuation.

> **Differentiation ideas:** Use Differentiated worksheets 1A–C.

Answers:
Learners' own sentences

3 Change the story (20–30 minutes)

Learning intention: to change a story and retell it orally

Resources: Learner's Book, Session 1.7, Activity 3; Workbook, Session 1.7

Description: Remind learners of their class pet choices in Learner's Book Session 1.7 Getting started.

Ask questions to help them remember, e.g. *Who chose a real animal/pretend animal?*

Tell learners they will now work with their partners to change the story so it is about their chosen class pet.

Show them the questions in the Learner's Book to help them with their plans.

Give learners time to make their choices and tell the story to a different pair of learners.

You can use the Workbook Session 1.7 activities in class now for further support with ideas.

Invite some learners to share their new story with the class.

> **Differentiation ideas:** Support learners using the Differentiated worksheet activities

Challenge learners to write or record audio of their new story.

Answers:
Learners' own stories

Plenary idea

Where would you look? (5–10 minutes)

Description: Ask learners where they would look in the classroom if they had a missing classroom pet.

Rehearse prepositions: *I would look in / under / on / behind / next to …*

Ask individual learners to respond to the question.

If there is time, repeat the activity with the question: *If you were a classroom pet, where would you hide in this classroom?*

> **CROSS-CURRICULAR LINKS**
>
> **Maths:** Make a simple block graph or pictogram to show the most popular classroom pet choices in the class.

Homework ideas

Learners complete the Workbook Session 1.7 activities if not completed in class.

They find a favourite story at home and talk about how they could change the ending.

Answers for Workbook

1 Learners' own drawings and sentences

2–4 Learners' own sentences

1.8 When things we know look different

LEARNING PLAN

Learning objectives		Learning intentions	Success criteria
Main focus	**Also covered**	• To listen to a rhyming story.	• Learners can listen to a rhyming story.
1Rv.05, 1Ri.09, 1Ra.04, 1Ra.06, 1Wg.04	1Rg.02, 1Rs.01, 1Rs.03, 1Ra.01, 1Wp.02, 1Wp.06, 1SLs.01, 1SLs.02, 1SLg.03, 1SLg.04, 1SLr.02	• To ask questions about the story to work out its meaning.	• Learners can ask questions to work out the meaning of a story.
		• To draw and write about other things they know that can look different.	• Learners can draw and write about other things they know that can look different.

LANGUAGE SUPPORT

Pre-teach any vocabulary (e.g. *creaks*, *haunty hall*, *shivery*, *flee*) or language structures (e.g. *It looks like …*) that you think learners may not know.

For listening, you may need to provide some visual support for some learners – even just the characters. Use the book *The Park in the Dark* (available in print or online) for pre-teaching to ensure the listening activity is beneficial.

Common misconception

Misconception	How to identify	How to overcome
Listening well is only about using our ears.	Ask learners to listen to the opening of the rhyming story. Ask what they hear. (words, a voice) Ask them what the words and voice are telling them. (names, an adventure, that it's nighttime, where they are going …)	Talk about good listening strategies. Ask: *What helps us to hear more than just words and a voice or music?* *Should we close our eyes? Listen several times? Talk with a partner to share ideas?* Create a poster of 'Good Listening Skills' for the classroom.

Starter idea

The ways things can look (10–20 minutes)

Resources: Learner's Book, Session 1.8: Getting started; realia to reinforce the teaching point, e.g. a stone or twig that might look like something else; a camera

Description: Using any resources available, provide examples of things that look different to what they actually are. Ask learners what they see. For example, do they see a stone, or a bird's eye? Find out how imaginative learners can be in expressing their ideas.

Together, look at the pictures in Getting started and discuss them. Ask: *What are they? What do they look like?* Learners' answers may include: an insect can look like a leaf; a car covered in snow can look like a snowy monster; a log can look like a snake.

It possible, take learners outside to search for things that might look different and record what they find with photos or drawings.

Main teaching ideas

1 *The Park in the Dark* listening activity (20–30 minutes)

> **Learning intention:** to demonstrate listening skills and to respond in a way that demonstrates comprehension and/or imagination
>
> **Resources:** *The Park in the Dark* (Learner's Book, Session 1.8, Activity 1); Track 05; Workbook, Session 1.8, Activities 1 and 2
>
> **Description:** Tell learners to listen to a rhyming story. If any learners already know the story, ask them not to share the surprise so that others can work it out for themselves!
>
> Tell learners that the story is about three friends who go out at night to somewhere they know and love. But something happens. Ask them to listen out for what happens.
>
> Play the audio and ask learners to draw what they think 'the THING' is.
>
> Give learners time to share ideas in pairs and then in the class.
>
> Establish that 'the THING' is a train … and it scares the characters so they run back home.
>
> Ask learners if anyone knows the title of the story (*The Park in the Dark*). Write the title on the board and focus on the use of capital letters.

You can use Workbook 1.8 Activities 1 and 2 in class now for further practice of letter formation.

> **Differentiation ideas:** Support learners by pausing the audio, discussing and asking questions as prompts, e.g. *What would make this sort of noise at night?* If necessary, use picture prompts to further stimulate discussion, e.g. pictures of a train, plane, giant …

Challenge learners to retell a summary of the story.

Audioscript: *The Park in the Dark*

When the sun goes down and the moon comes up and the old swing creaks in the dark, that's when we go to the park, me and Loopy and Little Gee, all three.

Softly down the staircase, through the haunty hall, trying to look small, me and Loopy and Little Gee, we three.

It's shivery out in the dark on our way to the park, down dustbin alley, past the ruined mill, so still, just me and Loopy and Little Gee, just three.

In the park in the dark by the lake and the bridge, that's when we see where we want to be, me and Loopy and Little Gee. WHOOPEE!

And we swing and we slide and we dance and we jump and we chase all over the place, me and Loopy and Little Gee, the Big Three!

And then the THING comes! YAAAAA AAAIII OOOOOEEEEEEE!

RUN RUN RUN shouts Little Gee to Loopy and me and we flee, me and Loopy and Little Gee, scared three.

Back where we've come through the park in the dark and the THING is roaring and following, see? After me and Loopy and Little Gee, we three.

Up to the house, to the stair, to the bed where we ought to be, me and Loopy and Little Gee, safe as can be, all three.

Martin Waddell

Answers:
1 a The THING is a train, but this may not be obvious without the pictures in the book; accept all reasonable answers.
   b Learners' own drawings

2 Ask questions (20–30 minutes)

Learning intention: to ask and write questions about a text

Resources: Learner's Book, Session 1.8, Activity 2; *The Park in the Dark* (Learner's Book, Session 1.8); Track 05; speech bubble shapes

Description: Play the audio again and ask listeners to work in pairs to write questions they would like to ask the characters in the rhyming story. Learners should write in the third person.

Draw their attention to the Writing tip about remembering to use a question mark at the end of a sentence that is a question.

You may wish to ask learners to write their best two questions in a speech bubble shape and share these with the class.

Create a class display of the speech bubbles to show the variety of learners' questions.

Consider role playing the narrator in the story (the toy monkey 'me') and answering learners' questions. You can swap with a learner if anyone feels confident enough to try to do the same.

> **Differentiation ideas:** Support learners by providing some question options from which they can choose, or work with a group to write two group questions.

Challenge learners to work independently to write a question about the characters, the setting and the events in different categories.

Answers:
Learners' own questions, but may include:
Are you people? (no, they are toys and you may wish to flag that they are friends as it would be unwise for young learners in real life to go out alone to the park in the dark) *How do you feel at the park at first? What happens? Why are you scared? What do you do?*

3 Non-verbal communication (10–20 minutes)

Learning intention: to show how non-verbal communication can reflect word meanings

Resources: Learner's Book, Session 1.8, Activity 3; Track 05

Description: Read one sentence from the story that can be acted out easily.

Ask volunteers how they would act the sentence to show its meaning, e.g. *And we swing and we slide and we dance and we jump and we chase all over the place, me and Loopy and Little Gee, the Big Three!*

Ask all learners to join in with the agreed actions or facial expressions.

Then ask learners, in groups of three, to do the same with each of the phrases from the story in the Learner's Book, or give different groups one phrase each.

Give groups time to practise before asking them to share performances.

> **Differentiation ideas:** Support learners by giving them just one phrase to work on and explaining the word meanings first.

Challenge learners to create more than one performance and to work out some of the meanings for themselves. Ask how they did that.

Answers:
Learners' own performances

4 Compare things (20–30 minutes)

Learning intention: to draw and write comparative sentences

Resources: Learner's Book, Session 1.8, Activity 4; sheets of A4 paper (one for each learner)

Description: Remind learners of the Learner's Book Session 1.8 Getting started activity, look back at the photos and revisit any artefacts you shared.

Talk about how things can look different at night or in poor light because we cannot see so well. This may well stimulate discussion about night fears so proceed with sensitivity and caution.

Hand out sheets of A4 paper. Ask learners to draw something on one side and then to turn it over and draw what it might look like in different circumstances (including in the dark) on the other side.

Show the example in the Learner's Book and model the writing of the sentence.

Give learners time to write their own sentences.

> **Differentiation ideas:** Support learners by providing some 'mix and match' ideas, e.g. coat stand / bear; tree / old hand; tree trunk / monster's foot; a sock on the floor / a mouse.

Challenge learners to fold their paper into three rows so they can draw and write more than one thing.

Answers:
Learners' own drawings and sentences

Plenary idea

Listening (5 minutes)

Description: Ask learners to close their eyes and listen.

Perform an action, e.g. opening and closing the door. Ask them to say what you were doing.

Ask: *What did you hear? How did you guess?*

> **CROSS-CURRICULAR LINKS**
>
> **Science:** Ask learners to listen for all the sounds they can hear around them for two minutes. Create a class soundscape.

Homework ideas

Learners complete the Workbook Session 1.8 activities if not completed in class.

They try to find and share a similar storybook online called *Shark in the Park!* by Nick Sharratt.

Answers for Workbook

1 Capitals copied correctly
2 A different sequence of capitals, correctly formed
3 WHOOPEE!; whoopee!
4 Learners' own words, but similar to: Hooray! Yipee!
5 Title copied with correct use of capital letters and lower case; Learners' own titles, e.g. The THING in the park; Little Gee, Loopy and Me; Learners' own cover drawings.

1.9 Out and about

LEARNING PLAN

Learning objectives		Learning intentions	Success criteria
Main focus	**Also covered**	• To listen to and follow a text using pictures.	• Learners can listen to and follow a text using pictures.
1Rw.07, 1Rv.01, 1Ri.10, 1SLs.02, 1SLp.04	1Rv.02, 1Rv.05, 1Ri.01, 1Ri.09, 1Ri.12, 1Ra.01, 1Ra.03, 1Ra.06, 1Wg.04, 1SLm.03, 1SLm.04, 1SLs.02, 1SLg.01	• To explore, find and use words in a story. • To pretend be a character, and to ask questions.	• Learners can explore, find and use words in a story. • Learners can pretend be a character, and to ask questions.

LANGUAGE SUPPORT

Learners need support with 'same' and 'different', but the visual nature of the Getting Started activity will support this.

The very structured language patterns in this text will support bilingual learners and provide opportunities to practise common English sayings.

Common misconception

Misconception	How to identify	How to overcome
We can use the word *thing* to talk about people.	Ask learners: Can we say: *Bear asked everything?* (No, because we use *thing* to talk about 'things' and *body* or *one* to talk about people or animals. So here, we would say: *Bear asked everybody*.)	Make a class poster or display to show these useful words and their relationship to each other. *Anything/something/everything Anybody/somebody/everybody*

Starter idea

Spot the difference (10–15 minutes)

Resources: Learner's Book, Session 1.9: Getting Started

Description: Ask learners if they can remember the story *Hide and Seek*. What happened? Did Zara look carefully in the cage or was Scruff always there but she did not see him?

Talk about the similarities with *The Park in The Dark*: the toys couldn't see the train properly in the dark, and the sound scared them.

Use these examples to emphasise that we need to see and look carefully to really understand things.

Check understanding of the concept of 'Spot the difference'. Have any learners played spot the difference before?

Ask learners to close their eyes for a moment. Draw a simple picture on the board of Bear. Then a copy of the bear, but add one clear difference. Ask learners to open their eyes and to say what is different about the bears.

Ask learners to look at the pictures in Getting started.

Give them a set time to find all six differences. Who finishes the fastest?

Ask the winners to explain what they found and show others.

Reflect on what helps them to look very carefully.

Main teaching ideas

1 *Finders keepers* (10–15 minutes)

Learning intention: to listen to and follow a text using pictures

Resources: *Finders keepers*, Part 1 (Learner's Book, Session 1.9, Activity 1); Track 06

Description: Explain to learners that they are going to listen to part of a story about a boy who is trying to find his scarf.

Ask learners to listen to the audio of the story, or read it aloud to them. Encourage them to point to the words and pictures as they listen, to help them follow the text.

> **Differentiation ideas:** Support learners by pairing weaker readers with stronger readers or by working with a group to show them how to use a finger to track words as they listen.

Challenge learners to read different character parts in a class reading: Ashraf, Rat, Cat, Fox.

2 Answering questions (10–15 minutes)

Learning intention: to listen and follow a text using pictures

Resources: Learner's Book, Session 1.9, Activity 2; *Finders keepers*, Part 1 (Learner's Book, Session 1.9)

Description: Tell learners they are now going to read the story and answer some questions about it.

Before they start, explain that Ashraf is trying so hard to find his scarf that he has forgotten to look *carefully*. Ask learners to look carefully at the pictures as they read, to see if they can spot the thing that Ashraf hasn't noticed. You may remind them that they had to look carefully in the Getting Started activity.

At the end of the story, ask: *What did Ashraf not see?* [Fox had taken Ashraf's scarf and was wearing it]

Ask learners why Fox says he hasn't seen Ashraf's scarf. You could use this as a starting point for discussions about telling the truth if appropriate.

Remind learners that this unit is about 'places we know'. Ask: *Where is this story taking place? Do we know or do we have to guess?* (we have to guess as there is little background in the pictures.)

> **Differentiation ideas:** Support learners to read this part of the story in pairs, or ask them to read around the class – one sentence per learner.

Answers:

a   In the woods

b   That fox is wearing Ashraf's scarf.

3   Exploring words (20–30 minutes)

Learning intention: to explore, find and use words in a story

Resources: Learner's Book, Session 1.9, Activity 3; *Finders keepers*, Part 1 (Learner's Book, Session 1.9); Track 06; Workbook, Session 1.9

Description: Show learners the Language focus box in the Learner's book and how the words *no*, *some* and *any* often go with the words *where*, *body*, *way* and *thing* to make new words.

Split the class into three groups. Give each group a word to listen out for: *anywhere, something, nobody*.

Read the story aloud and ask groups to stand up or clap when they hear their word.

Set them to work alone or in pairs to make a note to show how many times they find each of the words. They should then copy three sentences containing one of the three words.

You can use the Workbook Session 1.9 activities now for further consolidation of who says what in the story.

> **Differentiation ideas:** Support learners by repeating the listening game in a smaller group and/or by providing the words on separate cards.

Challenge learners to explore the word 'every' in combinations with *where*, *body*, *way* and *thing* (see Common misconception earlier). What can they work out?

Answers:

a   anywhere: 3; something: 2; nobody: 1.

4   Hot seat (10–20 minutes)

Learning intention: to pretend be a character, and to ask questions

Resources: Learner's Book, Session 1.9, Activity 4

Description: Remind learners that Fox did not tell the truth. Do they think Fox is feeling guilty? Can we always have things we want? Is it ever okay to not tell the truth? How do they feel about Fox?

Tell them that one person is going to pretend to be Fox – the stealer of the scarf.

Select a learner to play Fox. They should be able to respond articulately to the questions posed. If you have not played this kind of game before, you may need to play the role of Fox first to model how it's done.

Ask Fox to sit at the front of the class or in the middle of a circle.

Rehearse asking questions by posing some of the questions in the Learner's Book, and then begin the game. Try to ensure as many learners as possible have the opportunity to pretend to be Fox.

If time, make a class display of Fox and your class questions.

> **Differentiation ideas:** Support learners by pairing them in a productive way, e.g. pairing an articulate learner with a shy learner.

Challenge learners to think of their own questions to ask. Challenge learners to see the humour in Fox's denials as well as to draw comparisons with young children who may also say such things whilst they are learning about the importance of telling the truth!

Answers:
Your, or learners' own, exploring notions of truth

Plenary idea

Ask Ashraf questions (10–20 minutes)

Description: As done in Activity 3, now ask someone willing to be Ashraf to sit in the chair.

Ask: *What questions would we like to ask Ashraf?*

If time, swap to include other characters. Ask: *What does Cat think?*

CROSS-CURRICULAR LINKS
Science: Use the vocabulary of 'same' and 'different' in science teaching, e.g. when looking at how humans are the same and different, and sorting materials. Science: Explore binoculars or a telescope that allow us to see stars in the night sky in more detail.

Homework ideas

Learners complete the Workbook Session 1.9 activities if not completed in class.

They make a Spot the Difference game for a friend to play.

Answers for Workbook

1   **a** nothing; **b** something; **c** nobody; **d** somebody
2   **a** everything; **b** anything; **c** everybody; **d** anybody
3   Learners' own sentences
4   **a** anywhere; **b** anything; **c** Nobody

1.10 Story endings

LEARNING PLAN			
Learning objectives		**Learning intentions**	**Success criteria**
Main focus	**Also covered**	• To describe things in detail. • To talk about story endings and read one. • To act the story in a group.	• Learners can describe things in detail. • Learners can talk about story endings and read one. • Learners can act the story in a group.
1Rs.01, 1Ri.07, 1SLp.04	1Rv.01, 1Ri.09, 1Ri.13, 1Ra.01, 1Ra.03, 1Ra.06, 1SLm.04, 1SLg.01		

LANGUAGE SUPPORT
Rehearse polite language with learners, reminding them of words such as *please* and *thank you* as well as asking for help (Please can you help me?) and answering questions negatively, but politely, as in the story (No, I'm sorry).

Common misconception

Misconception	How to identify	How to overcome
We only need a few words to describe things in detail.	Ask the class to listen to you describing something simple in the class. Ask them if you had to use a few or a lot of words to make your description.	Show learners how using more words make it easier to understand what is being described. Begin with few words. e.g. it's blue. Gradually build your description by adding words to show how more words makes the description clearer. Remind learners of this in their own speech and writing.

Starter idea

1 Play a game: Back to back
(10–30 minutes)

Resources: Learner's Book, Session 1.10: Getting started; some pictures for learners to describe

Description: Ask learners to give you instructions to draw Bear's hat (it's a triangle with a curved bottom line and it's red). Does it look right if you try to draw it?

Ask if learners already know the game of Back to back. If not, model it first with two volunteers.

Two learners sit back to back. One learner is given a simple picture to describe whilst the other learner must draw it.

Learners should compare the two pictures. If the describer has used careful words, the picture drawn should be very similar to the original.

Learners can then swap and play a few times with different pictures.

Main teaching ideas

 1 Predict and check (20–30 minutes)

Learning intention: to predict the ending of the story and then to read it

Resources: *Finders keepers,* Part 2 (Learner's Book, Session 1.10, Activity 1); Track 07; Workbook, Session 1.10

Description: Ask learners to share ideas about how they think this story might end. Take all ideas and write them in a list. You can return to this list at the end of the session.

Ask learners to then read to the end of the story. Some may do this independently whilst others will need paired or group support.

You can use the Workbook Session 1.10 activities now to further explore the meaning and language of the story.

> **Differentiation ideas:** Support learners by reading the text with them in a group. Much of the vocabulary is decodable and recycled from *Finders keepers*, Part 1, so encourage independence where you can.

Challenge learners to explain the use of capitals in the text. Is Ashraf shouting, angry or something else?

Answers:
Learners' own responses, but may include: Ashraf finds/doesn't find his scarf; Ashraf remembers that Fox was wearing a scarf; Ashraf gets a new scarf; etc.

2 To talk about story characters
(20–30 minutes)

Learning intention: to talk about story characters and give opinions

Resources: Learner's Book, Session 1.10, Activity 2

Description: Ask learners in groups to decide what the characters in the story are like.

Together, read and respond to the statements provided in the Learner's Book to support learners to express their opinions about the different story. For example:

- Ashraf is kind:
    - Is he kind to Rat?
    - Is he kind to Fox?
- Owl is helpful:
    - How does he help Ashraf to find his hat?
    - Does Owl help anyone else?

You may wish to give different groups one question to explore before then sharing ideas.

Ask learners how they would get something that they want (would they ask first?) and what they might do to get something back that belongs to them. This is a good opportunity to talk about managing our own feelings and behaviours.

› **Differentiation ideas:** Support learners by allowing them to work in groups.

Challenge learners to find and use words in the text that might help them to say why they feel the way they do.

Answers:
Learners' own responses

---

3 **Make masks and act the story in groups (30–60 minutes)**

Learning intention: to perform the story in character

Resources: Learner's Book, Session 1.10, Activity 3; Worksheet 1.5

Description: Ask learners to work in small groups to make animal masks for: Ashraf, Rat, Cat, Fox and Owl. Learners can adapt the mask template on Worksheet 1.5 for each character in the story.

If learners prefer, masks can be worn around the neck or stuck to jumpers to avoid covering faces.

Once the masks are made, give groups time to rehearse their performances of the story.

Point out, if they have not noticed, that the author uses colour to show different character's speech.

As you circulate, support all learners with ideas and encouragement as they act the story.

› **Differentiation ideas:** Support learners by placing them in groups comprising some learners who would like to be challenged and some learners who would benefit from additional support.

Challenge learners to include non-verbal communication (using body language) to tell show how the characters are feeling.

Answers:
Learners' own creations and performances

Plenary idea

Watch online (5–10 minutes)

Resources: online access

Description: Do you know the story *I want my hat back* by Jon Klassen? Search online for an official animated version or promotion of this story and share with the class on screen. Learners may compare *Finders keepers* and this story.

Notice that some add music, sound effects and music.

Which do learners prefer? Why?

Homework ideas

Learners complete the Workbook Session 1.10 activities if not completed in class.

They play the 'back to back' game at home with a family member.

Answers for Workbook

1 Learners' own drawings and sentences. For example: I lost my _____. I found it/did not find it.

2 Ashraf: I lost my scarf/I am sad – or similar Rat It sounds like something I would like to nibble – or similar

Cat: It sounds like something I would like to snuggle in _____

Fox: I like scarves/Ashraf's scarf; I am sorry I stole Ashraf's scarf – or similar.

3 Answers may include: No.; Sorry, I haven't.; I haven't seen any scarves around here.; No I haven't seen your scarf.; I haven't seen anything at all.; What does it look like?; What is a scarf?; Where did you last have it?

1.11 Planning and writing

LEARNING PLAN

Learning objectives		Learning intentions	Success criteria
Main focus	**Also covered**	• To explore the features of a story we know.	• Learners can explore the features of a story they know.
1RS.02, 1Ri.02, 1Wv.02, 1Wg.04, 1Wc.01, 1Wc.02	1Rw.07, 1Rv.03, 1Rg.02, 1Wv.01, 1Wg.03, 1SLg.04	• To talk about choices we make when writing a story.	• Learners can talk about choices they make when writing a story.
		• To plan and write a similar story.	• Learners can plan and write a similar story.

LANGUAGE SUPPORT

This shortened story of *Finders keepers* should now be familiar to learners, but they may benefit from using the worksheets to support their writing outcome.

The repeated language structures (including asking and answering questions) of this story should support learners in their writing. If necessary, work with a group of learners to create a group story, providing them with possible options of what could happen for each blank space in the cloze.

Common misconception

Misconception	How to identify	How to overcome
We only use capital letters at the beginning of a sentence and to begin our names.	Ask learners to find examples in the story text (or cloze) of capital letters and to explain why they are used, e.g. at the beginning of sentences/questions; for emphasis or to show emotion: *YOU! …*	Encourage learners to use this technique in their own writing. Practise the formation of capital letters so they feel confident to use these.

Starter idea

1 Story features (10–15 minutes)

Resources: Learner's Book, Session 1.11: Getting started

Description: Ask learners to remember all the things they noticed about the story *Finders keepers*.

Share ideas and tell them these things are the story 'features' and that we can use them in our own writing if we want to.

Show them the story features in Getting started. Talk about the features together. Can they find and talk about all these story features in *Finders keepers*?

Ask: *Who is the main character/the other characters? What is the problem? What does Ashraf do to try to solve his problem? Does he solve the problem? How does the story end?* As you do this, ask learners to point to the features and pictures in the Learner's Book.

Main teaching ideas

1 Feature questions (20–30 minutes)

Learning intention: to use story features to plan a new story

Resources: Learner's Book, Session 1.11, Activity 1; Worksheet 1.6

Description: Tell learners they will now think about what features they want to borrow from *Finders keepers*, to write their own version of the story. What will they keep and/or change?
Ask them to work in pairs to talk about and answer the questions in the Learner's book. As you circulate, support and challenge learners to be creative. Ask a few learners to share their completed charts as good models of completion.

> **Differentiation ideas:** Support learners by providing options to choose from for each question.

Challenge learners to debate and agree the best options shared in their pairs and to include an additional feature of their choice.

Answers:
Learners' own responses

2 Writing sentences (20–30 minutes)

Learning intention: to use planning notes to write a story

Resources: Learner's Book, Session 1.11, Activity 2; Workbook, Session 1.11; Phonics Workbooks A and B; Worksheet 1.7

Description: Tell learners they will now use their planning notes from the last session to write their own story in sentences.

Remind learners about capital letters at the beginning of sentences, for the character names and for emphasis, as well as using end of sentence punctuation. You can use the Workbook Session 1.11 activities now for further practice of high frequency words in this text. You may also like to use the Phonics Workbooks for further practice of high frequency and tricky words:

Workbook A: pages 13, 15, 19, 25, 29, 31, 43, 45, 49, 51 and 53.

Workbook B: pages 11, 13, 17, 19, 21, 25, 27, 29, 31, 35, 37, 45 and 53.

> **Differentiation ideas:** Support learners by working with them as a group to scribe their sentences.

Challenge learners to add sentences from the original story text to their own story if they can remember them. Ask learners to check, and check again, their spelling, punctuation and handwriting.

Answers:
Learners' own sentences and drawings

3 Zig-zag book (30–60 minutes)

Learning intention: to create a book of their own stories

Resources: Learner's Book, Session 1.11, Activity 3; A3 paper for creating a double-sided, 4-page zig-zag book

Description: Show learners how to fold the paper into half horizontally and then into half and half again to create a 4-page (but double-sided) zig-zag book.

Ask them to rewrite and illustrate their story onto the eight pages.

Make a class display of your zig-zag books.

> **Differentiation ideas:** Support learners by folding the paper for them and cutting up completed Worksheet 1.7 so they can match and stick each section to each page of their zig zag book.

Challenge learners to copy their stories into their zig-zag books and to include some speech bubbles in their illustrations.

Answers:
Learners' own stories

Plenary idea

Story features (5–10 minutes)

Resources: another story book for each group

Description: Show learners another story book. Ask them to work in groups to quickly say what features they notice about their book.

Before they leave the classroom they must list the features they have noticed.

Homework ideas

Learners complete the Workbook Session 1.11 activities if not completed in class.

They research or design some other types of book format, e.g. a pop-up book, an exploding book (content that is folded in a special way so that it 'explodes' when opened!).

Answers for Workbook

1   **a** his;   **b** my, it;   **c** the

2   **a** like;   **b** for, be;   **c** nobody

2   Learners' own responses

1.12 Look back

LEARNING PLAN

Learning objectives		Learning intentions	Success criteria
Main focus	**Also covered**	• To check our writing and share our stories.	• Learners can check their writing and share their story.
1Ra.04, 1Wv.01, 1Wp.06, 1SLp.05, 1SLr.01	1Rs.03, 1SLm.01, 1SLg.02, 1SLg.03	• To talk about the stories in this unit.	• Learners can talk about the stories in this unit.
		• To think about our learning from the unit.	• Learners can think about their learning from the unit.

LANGUAGE SUPPORT

Use the Language worksheet 1B to check knowledge and understanding of the unit vocabulary and to practise spelling.

Common misconception

Misconception	How to identify	How to overcome
Mistakes are bad.	Ask learners if they can remember a time when they made a mistake. Ask them how they felt. Did they learn from it? Have a sensitive class discussion about the value of mistakes.	Establish a classroom culture where mistakes are welcomed as opportunities to learn.

Starter idea

1 Settings (5–10 minutes)

Resources: Learner's Book, Session 1.12: Getting started; books that feature different settings

Description: Talk to learners about books with different single or multiple settings, either reflecting on those in the unit and/or by sharing additional books.

Together, describe and sort the books by setting.

Ask learners if they know of other books with unusual or different settings.

Can they think of other titles he might write about next, e.g. *I love my hat, I want a bigger hat, I saw a hat …*

Ask learners how they changed the original story, *I want my hat back*, to make it their own – they changed the hat (the subject) and the characters. Explain that borrowing ideas from a story is a fun way to write your own!

Main teaching ideas

1 Check writing (10–15 minutes)

Learning intention: to check writing for mistakes

Resources: Learner's Book, Session 1.12, Activity 1; learners' stories from Session 1.11; Workbook, Session 1.12

Description: Discuss the value of mistakes (see Common Misconception).If appropriate, choose an example of a sentence that needs correcting. Write it on the board and work on this together first.

Then ask learners to look at the stories they wrote in the previous session. Can they find one spelling mistake and one word that they could write more neatly?

Ask them to enjoy reading their stories and checking their work. Some learners may wish to share their stories by reading aloud.

Encourage peer-to-peer feedback, but try to ensure it is kept positive.

You can use the Workbook Session 1.12 activities here for further self-correcting practice.

> **Differentiation ideas:** Support learners by working with them in a group when checking their stories or selecting a sentence for them to improve.

Challenge learners to spot punctuation errors, too.

2 The unit stories (10–15 minutes)

Learning intention: to reflect on stories and recall their features

Resources: Learner's Book, Session 1.12, Activity 2; text extracts throughout Unit 1 of the Learner's Book; Language worksheet 1B (vocabulary building)

Description: Ask learners if they can remember the stories from the unit using memory as well as class displays that you may have created.

List the story titles together, encouraging learners to look at the images in the Learner's Book if they cannot remember all of them.

Ask learners to talk about the stories. Ask: *Which did they enjoy most?* Take a class vote. Ask learners to recall the characters and settings for each of the stories to revisit the unit focus of places we know / familiar settings.

You can use Language worksheet 1B (vocabulary building) here for learners to revisit vocabulary of places we know.

> **Differentiation ideas:** Support learners by using book covers in print or in Unit 1 of the Learner's Book, or classroom displays as reminders.

Challenge learners to think of other story settings that could have featured in this unit.

Answers:
Learners' own responses

3 Skill review (10–15 minutes)

Learning intention: to think about learning in terms of language skills

Resources: Learner's Book, Session 1.12, Activity 3; the tune of 'Here we go round the Mulberry Bush'

Description: Familiarise yourself with the tune of 'Here we go round the Mulberry bush'.

Talk about the different language skills: reading, writing, spelling, listening and speaking.

Together, make up an action for each skill.

Using the tune, teach learners to sing the song 'This is the way we … in our English classroom!'.

Use the following phrases and chosen actions after the 'This is the way we':

- read a book
- write a story
- spell a word
- listen well
- speak out loud.

> **Differentiation ideas:** Support learners by modelling both words and actions or asking others in class to model them.

Challenge learners to think of other language skills, e.g. reading a word using phonics or writing letters.

Plenary idea

Skill charades (5–10 minutes)

Description: Make an action (as agreed in Activity 3) for one of the language skills (reading, writing, spelling, listening and speaking) and ask: *What am I doing?*

Ask learners to identify the language skill to ensure they are confident using the correct terms.

Then invite learners to take it in turns to act one of the skills and ask the same question.

Continue playing until time runs out.

Homework ideas

Ask learners to:

- complete the Workbook Session 1.12 activities if not completed in class
- choose a book they liked from this unit or which they enjoy at home
- think of a way to change the title to make it similar but not the same – just like Jon Klassen did with his books, e.g. *Don't Spill the Milk!* might become *Don't Drink the Milk!* or *Don't Spill the Water!*

Answers for Workbook

1 Learners' own drawings
2 wea > we; storys > stories; caled > called; darck > dark; learners' own sentences
3 Learners' own choices

CHECK YOUR PROGRESS

1 It is the place where a story happens.
2 *Shiver, quiver* and *river.*
3 A book cover usually tells you the title of the book, the author, the illustrator and something about the book in a picture or photo (or similar).
4 The park, the dark and the train were real, but the toys and 'the THING' were pretend.
5 **a** ride, side (or similar) **b** peek, week (or similar)
6 Learners' own answers

PROJECT GUIDANCE

These projects build on the reading, writing and understanding learners have developed throughout the unit. Since they have just read several stories that explore familiar settings, the project options here extend the focus and provide opportunities for the learners to choose to work in a group, as a pair or alone. It may be that you prefer to allocate a project to the class.

Group project: Learners should make a class A–Z of places. They may draw on the unit's stories and others they know. This can be created as a working wall and developed over time. Learners will need to use collaboration skills and their creativity.

Pair project: Learners design and make a simple map of Penda's journey. They will need large paper and paint or felt tips. Some may prefer to work with construction bricks or small world resources.

Solo project: Learners paint or draw the setting that they imagined for *Hide and Seek,* by Lynne Ryckards. They can make the setting more elaborate using their own ideas.

Setting up the project

- The projects are designed to encourage creativity and critical thinking. Class projects are more easily manged in class, whilst Pair and Solo projects may be suitable for homework if shared around the later sessions of the unit.

- If you allow learners to choose, ensure that over the course of the year, they have a good mix of project experiences in terms of the three working options.

- In any case they will be most useful if learners are given time to both plan and create the project outcome. Allow one week for learners to work on their project in their own time or in pockets of time.

- Resources will depend on which project learners choose and how they want to create the item, but if possible, try to anticipate needs, e.g. small world resources.

Assessing the project

The most valuable assessment of the projects will be as follows.

- Group and Pair projects: Observations of the learners as they work together to plan and create the outcome. Discussions you have with them will be valuable. The final group or pair outcome will be important, too: did they achieve what they set out to achieve?

- Solo project: If the solo project is being completed at home, ensure that the learner is fully engaged and while working with family members is not letting them do all the work.

- In all cases, outcomes should be shared, celebrated, presented or displayed and discussed.

- In all cases, learners should self- and peer assess – both giving and receiving feedback.

- As you assess each learner's contributions, ask if the learner:
  - engaged with the project independently, or did they need support; if so, what kind of support did they need?
  - had sufficient understanding of the topic to tackle their chosen project with knowledge and skills?
  - demonstrated know-how to plan and list resources needed?
  - used appropriate vocabulary?
  - worked co-operatively as part of a group to plan and prepare the project – or worked well alone if working on the solo project?
  - contributed usefully and respectfully to group discussions?
  - created a successful outcome?
  - showed evidence of having learned from the project process?

>2 Let me tell you!

Unit plan

Session	Approximate number of learning hours	Outline of learning content	Resources
2.1 First experiences	1.5	Talk about first experiences. Read a recount. Use the past tense. Find words beginning with adjacent consonants.	Learner's Book Session 2.1 Workbook Session 2.1 ⬐ Language worksheet 2A Phonics Workbooks A and B
2.2 Retelling with pictures	1.5	Name the parts of a book. Re-read a recount and answer questions about it. Use pictures to retell a recount.	Learner's Book Session 2.2 Workbook Session 2.2 ⬐ Worksheet 2.1
2.3 I remember …	1.5	Listen to a short interview. Practise the alphabet. Create an A–Z of first experiences and write about one.	Learner's Book Session 2.3 Workbook Session 2.3 ⬐ Language worksheet 2B
2.4 What's in a week?	1	Practise the days of the week. Read a diary and answer questions about it.	Learner's Book Session 2.4 Workbook Session 2.4 ⬐ Worksheet 2.2 Phonics Workbooks A and B
2.5 Retelling a diary	1.5	Retell a diary. Transfer information into a chart and answer questions about it.	Learner's Book Session 2.5 Workbook Session 2.5 ⬐ Worksheet 2.2 Phonics Workbook B

Session	Approximate number of learning hours	Outline of learning content	Resources
2.6 Writing a diary	1.5	Talk about different kinds of diaries. Use *and* to talk about things in a diary. Write a diary entry.	Learner's Book Session 2.6 Workbook Session 2.6 ⬇ Differentiated worksheets 2A–C
2.7 A big day out	1.5	Talk about days out. Listen to and read a recount. Use own ideas to answer questions about a recount.	Learner's Book Session 2.7 Workbook Session 2.7 Phonics Workbook B
2.8 Checking understanding	1.5	Re-read a recount and answer questions to check understanding. Sort pictures to retell a recount.	Learner's Book Session 2.8 Workbook Session 2.8 ⬇ Worksheet 2.3 Phonics Workbooks A and B
2.9 Exploring words and writing a recount	1	Explore plurals with –s and –es endings. Use simple time adverbials when writing a recount.	Learner's Book Session 2.9 Workbook Session 2.9 ⬇ Worksheet 2.4
2.10 Holiday news!	1.5	Talk about ways to share news. Listen to and read a postcard and answer questions about it. Identify the beginning and end features of a postcard.	Learner's Book Session 2.10 Workbook Session 2.10
2.11 Planning and writing a postcard	1.5	Explore the features of postcards. Plan and write a postcard.	Learner's Book Session 2.11 Workbook Session 2.11 ⬇ Worksheet 2.5

Session	Approximate number of learning hours	Outline of learning content	Resources
2.12 Look back	1	Talk about spacing a handwritten sample. Check the spacing of own writing. Talk about the recounts in the unit and think about learning.	Learner's Book Session 2.12 Workbook Session 2.12

Cross-unit resources
Learner's Book Check your progress
Learner's Book Projects

BACKGROUND KNOWLEDGE

Before you begin to teach this unit, you may find it helpful to:

- prepare ways to talk with learners about the concept of the past and the past tense as well as personal information, feelings and memories
- familiarise yourself with the different formats that a recount can take, e.g. memories, diaries, letters, postcards, etc. You could also prepare some examples to help explain how a recount can be a narrative, but still give information.
- familiarise yourself with the phonics and grammar elements in this unit, including:

- phonics - letter to sound correspondence, words with adjacent consonants, blending and segmenting words
- sequencing words, pictures and events using time adverbials such as *first*, *then* and *next*

- prepare some examples using days of the week and using the alphabet to organise ideas
- prepare some pictures you can share with learners to aid their understanding of unfamiliar words and concepts.

TEACHING SKILLS FOCUS

Assessment for Learning

Assessment for Learning (AfL) is a very powerful tool to support teaching and learning. It gives teachers insight into learners' own perceptions of their learning and allows us to use that information to focus teaching.

The AfL cycle involves three key questions for the teacher:

What can the learner already do?
What do they already know?

How can I help them to move forwards?

What do they need to know?

Assessment for Learning cycle

What can the learners already do?

What do they already know?

How can I help them to move forwards? / What do they need to know?

AfL is generally associated with formative assessment, which is ongoing and looks forward to future learning (rather than summative assessment, which is usually in the form of tests and looks backwards to what has already been achieved).

Most teachers find some aspects of AfL easier to implement than others and most of us need time and practice to improve our skills. One of the hardest things to accept is sharing responsibility for learning with the learners. To help you to self-assess your own skills, ask yourself question such as:

- What is the impact of self- and peer assessment in a lesson?
- Does assessment only occur at the end of a lesson? When is it most powerful?
- What support might learners need to improve their self and peer assessment skills?

Cambridge Reading Adventures

Learners may enjoy other fiction titles from Cambridge Reading Adventures that follow the unit theme:

- *Omar's First Day at School* by Shoua Fakhouri (Pink B Band) (written in the present tense)
- *The Big City* by Lynne Rickards (Yellow Band) (written in the present tense)
- *A Day at the Museum* by Sibel Sagner, Sevi Senocak and Inci Kartal (Blue Band) (written in the past tense)

2.1 First experiences

Learning objectives		Learning intentions	Success criteria
Main focus	**Also covered**	• To explore and name the parts of a book.	• Learners can explore and name parts of a book.
1Rw.03, 1Ra.04, 1Rs.03, 1Ww.02	1Rv.01, 1Rv.02, 1Ri.01, 1Ri.12, 1Ra.01, 1SLm.01, 1SLg.03, 1SLp.05	• To listen to and share the reading of a recount. • To find and blend words with adjacent consonants.	• Learners can listen to and share the reading of a recount. • Learners can find and blend words with adjacent consonants.

LANGUAGE SUPPORT

If available, learners will benefit from reading the Cambridge Reading Adventures book, *My First Train Trip* and re-reading the text in printed form, but note that the print version is written in the present tense.

Check learners can read and say both forms of the ordinal numbers with you: *first, second, third, fourth, fifth* and *1st, 2nd, 3rd, 4th, 5th.*

Common misconception

Misconception	How to identify	How to overcome
When there are two consonants next to each other, we always say two sounds.	Write the words *shop*, *chat ticket* and *train* on the board. Ask learners to sound out each letter sound (phoneme) and blend to read the words, e.g. *ch-a-t; sh-o-p; t-i-ck-e-t; t-r-ai-n.* Listen out for any learners who are saying two separate sounds for two consonants together. Ask: *What is different about the last word?* (We say a letter sound for each of the two consonants at the start of the word, instead of saying one sound for both.)	Find different examples of words with digraphs, e.g. *chick, fish,* and/or adjacent consonants at the beginning and end of words, e.g. *stop, jump.* Use the Workbook Session 2.1 activities and the Phonics Workbooks for further practice of digraphs (Phonics Workbook A, pages 36–39, and Phonics Workbook B, pages 4–5) and adjacent consonants (Phonics Workbook A, pages 34–35).

Starter idea

Talk about the photos (10–15 minutes)

Resources: Learner's Book, Session 2.1: Getting started; additional pictures or photos of first experiences

Description: Explore some of the vocabulary and key content suggested by the pictures in Getting started.

Ask learners to talk about their memories of doing things for the first time. This will be a theme of this unit and returned to in Session 2.3.

Explain that this unit is about telling people about something we have done (an experience). Ask learners to share their initial ideas.

Ask learners to explore and talk about the pictures in the Learner's Book, in pairs. Then ask them to give feedback on what they recognised or can name (clapping hands, walking, feeding yourself, swimming under water/ opening eyes under water, cycling / riding a bike).

Ask: *Are there some experiences that are not familiar to you? Are there other experiences you would add?*

Ask learners to bring in photos from home during the week to begin a class display of learners doing things as babies or toddlers.

Main teaching ideas

1 Name the parts of a book (15–20 minutes)

Learning intention: to explore and label parts of a book

Resources: Learner's Book, Session 2.1 Activity 1; Language worksheet 2A; a fiction/non-fiction book for each group

Description: Ask learners what they know about the different parts of a book. What do they know it will include? Share ideas.

Hand out a book for each group and give them a few minutes to identify the parts. Ask each group to deliver a mini-presentation to the class. Ensure that they use key vocabulary: *front cover* and *back cover, title, blurb, price, bar code, author, illustration, photo.*

Ask learners to work in pairs to look at the book cover of *My First Train Trip* in the Learner's Book, or online / in print if you have access to it. Ask: *What can you see?*

Work through the questions in the Learner's Book to help them to notice the parts of a book.

You can use Language worksheet 2A here to label the parts of a book.

Answers:
Learners' own correct responses

2 My First Train Trip (20–30 minutes)

Learning intention: to listen to a recount of a first experience

Resources: *My First Train Trip* (Learner's Book, Session 2.1, Activity 2); Track 08

Description: Tell learners they will now listen to a girl telling us about her first experience on a train.

Initially, ask them to just listen and look at the pictures in the Learner's Book as you play the audio or read the text aloud.

Talk about their first impressions of the recount and discuss the artwork (it is a mix of illustrations and photos).

Draw their attention to the question *Did you guess the girl was visiting somebody? How?* Explore how they guessed or did not guess that the purpose of the trip was to visit a family member.

On a second listening, ask learners to follow the text with their fingers.

Ask learners to read the story in pairs.

> **Differentiation ideas:** You can put learners who need support in a pair with a more confident reader and/or work with a group to read the text again together.

Challenge learners to read the text independently.

3 Read sentences in the past tense (15–20 minutes)

Learning intention: to use the past tense in sentences about a recount

Resources: Learner's Book, Session 2.1, Activity 3

Description: Ask learners how they came to school yesterday. Work around the class and check if this was the first time (or the usual way) they came to school like that.

Ask learners if the girl *is* on the train trip (present tense) or *was* on the train trip (past tense). Confirm that she *was* on the train trip (in the past). Ask: *How do you know this?* (The first sentence begins: *Yesterday, I went …*)

Draw learners' attention to the Speaking tip and stress the terms *past tense* and *recount*, if suitable for your learners.

Tell learners they are going to read a few sentences and change them from the present to the past. They are going to 'recount' or 'retell' the experiences.

Read the sentences together. Ask learners to tell you what each sentence would be if the experience was in the past (*yesterday*). Ask for verbal responses.

Ask learners to read the sentences again in this way, working in pairs.

> **Differentiation ideas:** Support learners by playing games that provide further practice of recounting experiences, e.g. providing pictures of different types of transport or places for learners to say *Yesterday, I went on a* [bus]; *Last week I visited the* [zoo].

Challenge learners by asking them to say what sort of words they changed to talk about the past (the verbs).

Answers:
b The station was big. **c** We got a ticket. **d** We found our seat. **e** The train was slow. **f** It was a long train trip. **g** Grandpa was on the platform.

4 **Words beginning with two consonants (15–30 minutes)**

Learning intention: to blend words with adjacent consonants

Resources: Learner's Book, Session 2.1, Activity 4; *My First Train Trip* (Learner's Book, Session 2.1); Track 08; Workbook, Session 2.1; Phonics Workbook A

Description: Write the title of the book in Learner's Book Session 2.1 Activity 2 on the board: *My First Train Trip.*

Ask learners what they notice about the words *Train* and *Trip.* (They both begin with letters *tr.*)

Together, blend the sounds in these words: t-r-ai-n and t-r-i-p. Invite different learners to do this out loud for you, too.

Ask learners to work in pairs and to look back at the text in Activity 2 to find other words that begin with two consonants that make two separate sounds. Ask learners to write the words in a list.

You may want to begin a class display of words beginning with two consonants (two letters and two sounds). If anyone suggests words beginning with letters *th*, remind them that some letters sit together to make one sound, e.g. *sh*, *th*, *ch*.

You can use the Workbook Session 2.1 activities here for further practice of identifying consonants or Phonics Workbook A, pages 34–35.

> **Differentiation ideas:** Support learners by checking that they remember what vowels and consonants are. Ask them to find a word beginning with *st* (*station* or *streets*) and a word beginning with *gr* (*grandpa*).

Challenge learners to cut out their lists and to explore different ways of grouping the words, e.g. words beginning with *st* or those beginning with *s* + another consonant. Ask: *Can you add another word to each group in your list?*

Answers:
Answers may include: station, travelling, platform, free, slow(ing), streets, fields, trees, grandpa

Plenary idea

Find words with adjacent consonants (5 minutes)

Resources: Learner's Book, Session 2.1, or reading books

Description: Ask learners to work in pairs to find a word from the Learner's Book or their reading book that features adjacent consonants.

If their word is correct, they may leave.

CROSS-CURRICULAR LINKS

Maths: Explore ordinal numbers: 1st, 2nd, 3rd, etc.

Link work on past tense sentences to the language of time using weeks, months and years, e.g. *Last week, I went …*, *Last month, I …*, *Last year, I …*

Link work on past tense sentences to analogue time, e.g. *At 7.30 in the morning, I brushed my teeth.*

Homework ideas

Learners complete the Workbook Session 2.1 activities if not completed in class.

They talk to family members about 'first experiences' and bring photos in from home where possible or appropriate.

Answers for Workbook

1   consonants on consonant train and vowels (*a, e, i, o, u*) on the vowel train

2   speed, blue, spoke, stand, blow-up, speed, stepped, close, front, flew, great

3   Learners' own sentences using blends

2.2 Retelling with pictures

LEARNING PLAN

Learning objectives		Learning intentions	Success criteria
Main focus	**Also covered**	• To explore a text about a first experience. • To answer questions about a recount. • To retell a recount using pictures.	• Learners can explore a text about a first experience. • Learners can answer questions about a recount. • Learners can retell a recount using pictures.
1Rs.01, 1Ri.05, 1Ri.06	1Rv.02, 1Wv.01, 1SLm.01, 1SLg.03		

LANGUAGE SUPPORT

Learners will benefit from handling any books available so they can practise naming the different parts.

To help to check comprehension and to encourage active listening, consider printing and handing out words from the recount *My First Train Trip* in

Learner's Book Session 2.1 that are associated with trains (train ride, station, trains, ticket office, tickets, ticket seller, platform, seats, train trip, slowing down). Ask learners to stand up when they hear their word or phrase read aloud.

Common misconception

Misconception	How to identify	How to overcome
Information books only have photos.	Ask learners to look at a collection of non-fiction texts (mainly recounts if possible). Ask them to talk about the different types of illustration and photos.	Discuss the fact that we can illustrate stories and non-fiction books in different ways to give different information. Share a recount text such as *My First Train Trip* to demonstrate an interesting mix of photos and illustrations combined.

Starter idea

Share a memory (15–20 minutes)

Resources: Learner's Book, Session 2.2: Getting started

Description: Ask learners to work in pairs to talk about a memory they have of a favourite experience.

Together, read the question prompts in Getting started before sharing ideas.

Main teaching ideas

1 Listen for words (20–30 minutes)

Learning intention: to read and identify topic words in a text

Resources: Learner's Book, Session 2.2, Activity 1; *My First Train Trip* (Learner's Book, Session 2.1); Track 08

Description: Ask learners to listen and follow the text as you read the recount *My First Train Trip* in Session 2.1 again out loud.

Ask learners to listen out for words to do with a train station and to put up their hand when they hear them.

As learners raise their hands, write a list of the train station vocabulary to model list writing and word bank writing.

Ask: *Can you add more words to the list of topic words?* Suggest: *luggage rack, suitcase, travellers, first class, second class, reserved seats, buffet car*, etc.

> **Differentiation ideas:** Support learners by asking them to listen for just one or two of the words listed.

Challenge learners by asking them to read the recount in pairs and write their own lists of train station vocabulary.

Answers:
train ride, station, trains, ticket office, tickets, ticket seller, platform, seats, train trip, slowing down, train trip

2 Answer questions (20–30 minutes)

Learning intention: to answer questions to check comprehension

Resources: Learner's Book, Session 2.2, Activity 2; Workbook, Session 2.2

Description: Ask learners to sit in a circle. Sit in the middle of the circle.

Tell learners you are pretending to be the little girl on the train trip and you are going to ask them questions about your experience. (Use the questions in the Learner's Book with key question words.)

Ask learners to respond to your questions and check they are using the correct verb forms, e.g. *You were …* (the simple past tense).

Swap places so learners have the chance to role play and answer different questions.

Back at their desks, you may wish learners to work in pairs to write down the answers to the questions in the Learner's Book.

You can use the Workbook Session 2.2 activities now for further practice of checking comprehension.

> **Differentiation ideas:** Support learners by playing the game several times to practise using good language models, particularly in the past tense.

Challenge learners to extend their answers with more detail.

Answers:
Learners' responses, similar to: I was at the station.; The station was big and busy.; We bought a ticket. / We went to the ticket office.; We waited on Platform 5.; I sat at the window because I wanted to look out.; Grandpa was on the platform when I arrived.

3   Sort the pictures to retell a story (20–30 minutes)

Learning intention: to sequence and retell a story by pictures

Resources: Learner's Book, Session 2.2, Activity 3; Worksheet 2.1

Description: Remind learners how important pictures can be to help them to understand a retelling.

Ask learners to work in pairs to sort the pictures of the experience in the Learner's Book into the right order. Then, as a class, agree on the correct sequence.

Ask learners to work in pairs again to use the pictures to retell the experience of the train trip in their own words.

Encourage learners to use the words in Activity 1 to help them.

Remind them to use their voice to make the information clear, e.g. to speak with clear pronunciation and not to rush.

You can provide Worksheet 2.1 *My First Train Trip* retelling now to support learners who may need to cut and stick the pictures to support their retelling.

Allow time for some learners to present their retellings using a loud, clear voice. Ask the presenter to give feedback on the audience. Provide some sentence starters, e.g. *I liked* … (the question from); *I thought* … (everyone listened well); *Some people* … (fidgeted).

> **Differentiation ideas:** Support learners by providing Worksheet 2.1 *My First Train Trip* retelling, which has both text and pictures to sort.

Challenge learners to add more detail to their retelling and to write captions or sentences for each picture.

Answers:
Learners' retellings, similar to the original, but in learners' own words

Plenary idea

Finish the sentence (5–10 minutes)

Resources: sentence starters for recounts

Description: Ask learners to finish sentence starters that you provide, e.g. *Last week I* …; *Yesterday I* …; *When I was three I* ….

Play the game around the class until it is time to leave.

CROSS-CURRICULAR LINKS

Maths: Explore local currency and how it can be used to buy train tickets.

Geography: Research pictures or an online street view or visit the local train station if possible. Support learners to create a model of your nearest station and to label the key features.

Drama: Set up a ticket office in the classroom for learners to role play ticket buying and selling. You may also create a train using rows of chairs.

Homework ideas

Learners complete the Workbook Session 2.2 activities if not completed in class.

They ask learners to find one new fact about travelling by train, e.g. the fastest train can travel at speeds of …; it takes x hours to travel from x to y by train.

Answers for Workbook

1   Learners label the picture correctly.

2   Learners label the picture correctly.

3   Learners draw buildings as the train leaves the city and the countryside.

4   Learners' own ideas, e.g. animals in fields, mountains

2.3 I remember …

LEARNING PLAN

Learning objectives		Learning intentions	Success criteria
Main focus	**Also covered**	• To listen to an interview and talk about first experiences.	• Learners can listen to a short interview and talk about first experiences.
1Rw.01, 1Rv.04, 1Ww.01, 1Wg.04	1Wv.01, 1Wp.01, 1Wp.02, 1SLm.02, 1SLm.03, 1SLg.01, 1SLg.04, 1SLp.05	• To create an alphabet of first-experience memories.	• Learners can create an alphabet of first-experience memories.
		• To write about a first experience.	• Learners can write about a first experience.

LANGUAGE SUPPORT

Learners may benefit from making and displaying an alphabet frieze and from playing alphabet games and singing alphabet songs.

Pictures and photos will support comprehension of first experiences.

Common misconception

Misconception	How to identify	How to overcome
Letter *X* is code for letter *sound* /z/.	Ask learners to say the word *xylophone!* (or any learner's name in your class with a name beginning with *X* and sounded as /z/, e.g. *Xanthe*. Ask what sound *x* makes at the beginning of *xylophone/Xanthe* (/z/). Then, together, blend to read the word *box*, and then the word *exam*. Ask: *What do you notice about the sound we need to say for letter x in those words?* (/k//s/)	Make a class display of *X* words – very few require the letter sound /z/ as in *xylophone*.

Starter idea

I remember … (5–10 minutes)

Resources: *First Day at School* (Learner's Book, Session 2.3, Getting started); Track 09

Audioscript: *First Day at School*

Teacher: I wonder what you can remember about your first day at school?

Boy: I remember that I didn't know what to say or do because I didn't know anybody.

Girl: Yes, I remember that, too. I was hanging on to my mum! I felt shy.

Boy: Did you cry?

Girl: No. I don't think I cried.

Teacher: Well done both of you. Those are good memories. Then how did your first day go after that?

Girl: I remember it felt like a very long time.

Boy: Yes, it felt strange until we started doing things …

Teacher: What sort of things?

Boy: I remember playing outside on a bike …

Girl: Yes! And I remember dressing up with fairy wings!

Boy: And I remember painting a picture and writing my name.

Girl: I remember home time.

Teacher: What do you remember about home time?

Girl: Running to my mum and telling her that school was …

Boy and girl SHOUTING: GREAT!

Description: Ask learners to listen to the short interview about a first day at school.

Play the audio or read the interview aloud.

Before playing the audio or reading a second time, ask learners to listen out for something the boy remembers and something the girl remembers.

Ask learners to share what they heard and then to share their memories of their first day at school.

You may wish to encourage learners to read the interview aloud together from the script, with you reading the teacher's speech, the boys reading the boy's speech and the girls reading the girl's speech.

Main teaching ideas

1 Say the alphabet (15–20 minutes; longer if using Workbook Session 2.3)

Learning intention: to practise the alphabet

Resources: Learner's Book, Session 2.3, Activity 1; Workbook, Session 2.3; alphabet song

Description: Introduce the alphabet using your classroom alphabet frieze or display if you have one. Make sure the alphabet is displayed low in your classroom so that learners can see it and touch it. (You may wish to instruct different learners to run over to touch a specified letter.)

Ask learners if they can say the alphabet or if they know any alphabet songs. Invite performances from learners.

You can use the alphabet song now. As learners listen, encourage them to join in and to point to each letter as they hear it mentioned.

Hand out alphabet letter cards to 26 children. Ask them to sort themselves into a line in the correct order!

You can use the Workbook Session 2.3 activities here, for further alphabet practice.

Ask learners how they remember the alphabet. Encourage them to share their reflections.

> **Differentiation ideas:** Support learners with further alphabet games and songs.

Challenge some learners to say or sing the alphabet alone or in pairs.

2 A–Z of first experiences (15–30 minutes)

Learning intention: to create an A–Z of first experiences

Resources: Learner's Book, Session 2.3, Activity 2; large piece of paper with A–Z chart on it or whiteboard/display board

Description: Tell learners that together you are going to make an A–Z of first experiences.

Look at the chart in the Learner's Book and talk about the examples provided. Ask for learners' own ideas for alphabet experiences. Invite learners to be creative with their ideas and to respond in sentences, making it clear which word matches the letter of the alphabet.

You can use Language worksheet 2B here.

Alternatively, split the class into groups and ask each group to provide ideas for a few letters. Give them time to think and then report back.

> **Differentiation ideas:** Support learners working in groups with examples that they can then match to each letter.

Challenge learners by asking them to write their own sentences for a similar activity in their notebooks.

Answers:
Learners' own responses

3 Write about a first experience (15–30 minutes)

Learning intention: to write a memory

Resources: Learner's Book, Session 2.3, Activity 3

Description: Tell learners they are going to write their own memories using the sentence starters provided in the Learner's Book:

- *I remember the first time I …*
- *I felt …*

Learners may choose experiences from the class A–Z ideas or remember their own.

Learners should write about three experiences and draw pictures to illustrate each of them.

> **Differentiation ideas:** Support learners by asking them to write one memory.

Challenge learners to write more about each memory.

Answers:
Learners' own responses

Plenary idea

What comes next? (5–10 minutes)

Resources: class alphabet frieze

Description: Ask learners to listen to you saying the alphabet and then stopping at different points.

Ask: *What comes next?*

Learners must say the next letter.

If learners become really confident, ask them to take the lead in the game to ask: *What comes next?*

CROSS-CURRICULAR LINKS

Art: Make the class A–Z beautiful with elaborate capital and lower-case letters.

Music: Explore other alphabet poems and rhymes.

Homework ideas

Learners complete the Workbook Session 2.3 activities if not completed in class.

They ask a family member for a memory about taking them to school on their first day. Were they excited or scared about starting school, or both?

Answers for Workbook

1 Learners copy the lower-case letters with correct letter formation and then self-assess.

2 Learners copy the capital letters with correct letter formation and then self-assess.

3 Learners copy the alphabet in lower case and capitals with correct letter formation, thinking about relative size, and then self-assess.

2.4 What's in a week?

LEARNING PLAN

Learning objectives		Learning intentions	Success criteria
Main focus	**Also covered**	• To practise the days of the week.	• Learners can practise the days of the week.
1Rw.07, 1Rs.01, 1Ra.04	1Rv.01, 1Rv.02, 1RS.02, 1Ri.03, 1Ri.04, 1Ra.01, 1SLs.02	• To listen to, talk and read about personal experiences in a diary. To find common words. • To make links with own experiences.	• Learners can listen to, read and talk about a diary, finding common words. • Learners can make links with own experiences.

LANGUAGE SUPPORT

Learners may benefit from making and displaying a days of the week poster, and from singing days of the week songs. Search online for songs with appropriate videos.

Check the transport vocabulary in Session 2.4 and pre-teach if necessary: e.g. *car, bus, roller skates*. Provide as many examples of diary recounts as you can, e.g. *On the Way Home* by Jill Murphy.

Common misconception

Misconception	How to identify	How to overcome
We always say every letter in a word.	Write the word *Wednesday* on the board. Ask learners to say each letter sound, e.g. blend to read the word W-e-d-n-e-s-d-a-y Ask how you can split the word to make it easier. (W-e-d/n-e-s/d-a-y) When learners say *Wed-nes-day*, ask them if that sounds right. Say: *We say: Wens-day.* Establish that in some words there are letters that we do not need to pronounce.	When they meet other silent letters in words during their reading, remind them of the *Wednesday* example.

Starter idea

The days of the week (15–20 minutes)

Learning intention: to practise the days of the week

Resources: Learner's Book, Session 2.4: Getting started; Workbook, Session 2.4

Description: Introduce the days of the week using your classroom poster or display if you have one. Make sure the poster or display is low in your classroom so that learners can see it and touch it. You may wish to instruct different learners to run over to touch a specified day.

Ask learners if they can say the days of the week in order or if they know any days of the week songs. Invite performances from learners.

As other learners listen, encourage them to join in and to point to each weekday word as they hear it.

Ask: *Can you tell me what day of the week it is today? What day was it yesterday?*

Hand out days of the week cards to seven learners. Ask them to sort themselves into a line in the correct order!

You can use the Workbook Session 2.4 activities in class now.

Main teaching ideas

1 A diary (10–15 minutes)

Learning intention: to listen to and read a diary, noticing its features

Resources: *My School Holiday Diary* (Learner's Book, Session 2.4, Activity 1); Track 10

Description: Tell learners they are going to listen to and read a diary about a week in the school holidays.

Ask what they know about diaries and/or tell them that when we write about things we have done on each day, we call it a diary.

Ask learners to listen as you read the text aloud or play the audio.

Before playing the audio or reading aloud for a second time, ask learners to follow the text in the Learner's Book as they listen by looking at the pictures and pointing to each day of the week.

Check learners are confident about the transport vocabulary.

Phonics: model how to blend the letter sounds to read some of the words, e.g. *bus* (consonant, vowel, consonant, CVC) *roller* (unstressed /er/ at the end) and *skates* (split digraph *a-e*); *bike* (split digraph *i-e*); *c-ar* (/ar/ phoneme); *scooter* (unstressed /er/ at the end) and *walking* (tricky *lk* and *ing* endings). Choose the words based on the learners' phonic knowledge and skills.

> **Differentiation ideas:** Support learners by sitting with them in a group or displaying the diary and modelling how to follow the text by pointing to the words as they are said. Repeat so they begin to do it themselves.

Challenge some learners to find words in the diary that have letters in them that we do not pronounce (like *Wednesday* as in Common misconception earlier). They may find *Tuesday*, *library*, *restaurant*, *walked*.

2 Answer questions (15–20 minutes)

Learning intention: to make links to experiences and give opinions

Resources: Learner's Book, Session 2.4, Activity 2

Description: Read each question with learners and discuss the answers as a class.

Then ask learners to write or draw their answers in their notebooks.

As learners work, move around the classroom and check their pencil grips, letter formation and use of punctuation.

If you only want learners to respond orally, check they are responding with clear spoken language and correct sentence structures and tenses.

> **Differentiation ideas:** Support learners by working with them in a group to answer the questions.

Challenge learners by asking them to write some questions about the diary for a partner to answer.

Answers:
Learners' own responses

3 Read some common words (10–15 minutes)

Learning intention: to find common words in a text and read them

Resources: Learner's Book, Session 2.4, Activity 3; *My School Holiday Diary* (Learner's Book, Session 2.4); Track 10; Worksheet 2.2; Phonics Workbooks A and B; word cards of the common words

Description: Ask learners to blend the sounds to read the following common words: *went, to, walked, the, was, my*. Provide the words on cards or write them on the board.

Talk about how phonics can help learners a little, but sometimes words are irregular, so we have to use other strategies to read them, e.g. recognising a word by its letters or shape. You may like to use the Phonics Workbooks for further practice of high-frequency and tricky words:

Phonics Workbook A: pages 13, 15, 19, 25, 29, 31, 43, 45, 49, 51 and 53.

Phonics Workbook B: pages 11, 13, 17, 19, 21, 25, 27, 29, 31, 35, 37, 45 and 53.

Ask learners to work in pairs to find the common words listed in the diary text in Activity 1.

Give them time to read and count the words before sharing answers.

> **Differentiation ideas:** Support learners by providing Worksheet 2.2 Diary retelling so they can mark up the diary text in the top half as they search for the words and count them.

Challenge learners to use each word in a sentence and write it.

Answers:
went: 1, to: 6, walked: 1, the: 4, was: 7, my: 4

Plenary idea

What comes next? (5–10 minutes)

Resources: days of the week poster

Description: Ask learners to say what comes before or after a day of the week that you say, e.g. *What comes before Friday? What comes before Wednesday?*

Work round the class.

If learners become really confident, ask them to take the lead in the game by posing these questions to other learners.

> CROSS-CURRICULAR LINKS

Maths: Explore numbers and time: 7 days in a week, 12 months in a year, 365 days in a year.

Music: Explore other days of the week songs and rhymes. Clap the rhythms of the days of the week.

Homework ideas

Learners complete the Workbook Session 2.4 activities if not completed in class.

They find out how to say the days of the week in a language you do not know very well.

Answers for Workbook

1 days of the week written in order: Tuesday, Wednesday, Thursday, Friday, Saturday, Sunday

2 **b** Thursday; **c** Tuesday; **d** Friday; **e** Sunday; **f** Wednesday; **g** Saturday.

3 **a** day; **b** hay, lay, may, pay, okay, stay, grey, today, etc.

2.5 Retelling a diary

LEARNING PLAN

Learning objectives		Learning intentions	Success criteria
Main focus	**Also covered**	• To retell a diary in the correct order using pictures. • To create a chart to show information. • To answer and write questions about a diary.	• Learners can retell a diary in the correct order using pictures. • Learners can create a chart to show information. • Learners can answer and write questions about a diary.
1Rs.01, 1Ri.06, 1Ri.08, 1Ws.02, 1Wp.04	1Rv.02, 1Rv.03, 1Rv.05, 1Ri.05, 1Ri.12, 1Wv.01, 1Ws.01, 1Wc.03, 1SLm.01, 1SLg.01, 1SLg.03, 1SLp.01		

LANGUAGE SUPPORT

Continue to provide learners with opportunities for practising days of the week by using a days of the week poster, singing days of the week songs and playing games like Clap the Day in Session 2.5 Getting started.

Provide opportunities to orally repeat language structures, e.g. *On _____ I went to the _____.*

Common misconception

Misconception	How to identify	How to overcome
Letters *ow* only make the sound /oa/ as in *low*.	Write the words *cow* and *low* on the board. Ask learners to read them. What do they notice? (In *cow* the *ow* represents the sound /ou/ whereas in *low* the *ow* represents the sound /oa/. Sometimes the same letters have different sounds.	When learners are reading words with *ow* and blending the letters to read a word, remind them that they might need to try different sounds. Have a class phonics chart with different examples of same letters and different sounds on it.

Starter idea

Clap the Day (10–15 minutes)

Resources: Learner's Book, Session 2.5: Getting started; days of the week word cards

Tell learners they are going to play a game and they have to listen carefully.

Explain that:

• learners will get into groups of seven – one for each day of the week

- each learner gets a card with a day of the week on it
- learners memorise their day
- you will say the days of the week in a random order
- when learners hear their day of the week, they should clap loudly.

Play the game.

Continue playing until all learners have clapped.

Main teaching ideas

1 Retell a diary from pictures (30–50 minutes)

Learning intention: to retell a diary using prompt cards

Resources: Learner's Book, Session 2.5, Activity 1 (Holiday diary text from Learner's Book, Session 2.4, Activity 1); seven days of the week cards; three pieces of paper for each group

Description: Tell learners they will work in seven groups and each group will retell what happened on one day from the diary as if they were there, using the pronoun *we*.

Hand out a day of the week card to each group and three pieces of paper for them to draw or write where they went, how they got there and what sort of day it was.

They may use the pictures in the Learner's Book to remind them of the sequence, and the Speaking tip to help them with the language structure.

Move round the classroom to support and challenge groups.

Finally, ask each group to retell their day, starting with Monday and working through to Sunday. Ensure learners notice that, cumulatively, they are retelling the diary of events in the correct order.

> **Differentiation ideas:** Support learners by using mixed-ability groupings.

Challenge learners by asking them to repeat all seven days from the shared group work.

Answers:
Learners' retellings, correctly sequenced

2 Make a chart (30–40 minutes)

Learning intention: to write information into a chart

Resources: Learner's Book, Session 2.5, Activity 2; Phonics Workbook B; Worksheet 2.2; diary prompt cards created in Activity 1; question word cards

Description: Discuss the chart in the Learner's Book.

Talk about the question words: *When? Where? How?* and *What?*

Phonics (Phonics Workbook B, pages 26–27): consider linking this to phonics teaching: words beginning with letters *wh* (two letters, one sound).

Using the prompt cards learners created in Activity 1, create a large wall chart of the diary, with the headings: *When? Where? How?* and *What?* Or, if you prefer, ask learners to create the chart in their notebooks or to use Worksheet 2.2 Diary retelling.

Encourage learners to then retell the diary using their chart, rather than reading the diary sentences from the original text (in Activity 1).

Model how to read the information from the chart to create full sentences and invite learners to join in.

> **Differentiation ideas:** Support learners by providing Worksheet 2.2 Diary retelling.

Challenge learners to record their own version of the chart in their notebooks.

Answers:
Learners' own charts used for retellings in the correct sequence of the diary

3 Use the chart to answer questions (20–30 minutes)

Learning intention: to find information in a chart to answer questions

Resources: Learner's Book, Session 2.5, Activity 3; Workbook, Session 2.5; charts from Activity 2

Description: Ask learners to answer questions using the class chart or the one in their notebooks, or on their worksheet. Together, orally answer the questions before asking learners to write their answers.

As learners write their answers, check for use of capital letters and full stops or question marks.

You can use the Workbook Session 2.5 activities now for further practice of questions.

> **Differentiation ideas:** Support learners by modelling how to find the answers in the chart.

Challenge learners to ask further questions of each other.

Answers:

a   She went to the swimming pool on Saturday.

b   She went to her dad's restaurant on Wednesday.

c   She went to the park on her bike.

d   She went shopping on her roller skates.

Plenary idea

Jump Over It (5–10 minutes)

Resources: a question mark on a card and a full stop on a card

Description: Place two cards on the floor: one with a question mark and one with a full stop.

Ask two learners to:

- stand next to the question mark or full stop card
- listen to a series of statements or questions
- jump over their punctuation mark if they think it goes at the end of each statement or question

Read out a series of statements/questions to play the game.

Ask the learners watching the game to confirm if the learner who has jumped is correct.

Swap learners several times.

Homework ideas

Learners complete the Workbook Session 2.5 activities if not completed in class.

They make up a game using question words.

Answers for Workbook

1 and **2** Learners' spoken and drawn responses

3   Learners' own questions

4   Learners' own questions starting *When, Where, How* and *What*

2.6 Writing a diary

LEARNING PLAN

Learning objectives		Learning intentions	Success criteria
Main focus	**Also covered**	• To talk about personal experiences and express preferences. • To say sentences using information from a diary and using *and*. • To write personal experiences in the form of a diary.	• Learners can talk about personal experiences and express preferences. • Learners can say sentences using information from a diary and using *and*. • Learners can write their personal experiences in the form of a diary.
1Rg.04, 1Wg.04, 1Wg.05, 1Wc.05	1Rs.01, 1Ri.04, 1Wv.01, 1Ws.01, 1Ws.02, 1Wc.02, 1Wp.05, 1Wp.06, 1SLg.04		

LANGUAGE SUPPORT

Learners will benefit from handling a range of diaries or books written in a diary format.

Make a word card featuring the word *and* to use with a small group to demonstrate how to join sentences.

Check learners are familiar with the terminology *full stop* and *question mark*, as well as with the vocabulary required in Activity 1.

Common misconception

Misconception	How to identify	How to overcome
All question words begin with *wh*.	Ask learners to think about what question words begin with and list question words they know. Take ideas and keep going until *how* is mentioned. Talk about how most question words begin with *wh* but that *how* does not.	Make a class list or poster of question words to use when learners need support.

Starter idea

Different diaries (10–20 minutes)

Resources: Learner's Book, Session 2.6: Getting started

Description: Talk about the different diaries – draw learners' attention to the illustrations and captions in Getting started and read the captions together.

Together, match each caption to a diary.

Talk about learners' diary preferences. Ask why they prefer a particular diary.

Tell learners that this session is about writing a diary.

Main teaching ideas

1 Talk about a diary using *and* (20–30 minutes)

   Learning intention: to retell events using the language of recount and the word *and*

   Resources: Learner's Book, Session 2.6, Activity 1; Workbook, Session 2.6

   Description: Tell learners they are going to pretend that they have a diary.

   Direct learners to the pictures in the chart, and add extras if you can, too, to rehearse some of the

vocabulary. Pre-teach some words if necessary, e.g. *desert island, play centre, gym.*

Draw learners' attention to the Language focus box.

Model the sentence structures you wish learners to use, e.g. *On Thursday I went to the cinema and I watched a film. I went by lorry!*

Work through the chart and ensure that lots of learners get the chance to say a sentence using *and.* Repeat this as a plenary activity if you run out of time.

Ask learners to then repeat the activity in pairs. After a while, invite some pairs to share their sentences.

You can use the Workbook Session 2.6 activities now to practise joining sentences with *and.*

> **Differentiation ideas:** Support learners with reading by working with a small group. Say sentences without the day of the week and ask them to say which day it was.

Challenge learners to use different questions, e.g. *On which day did I …?; When did I …?* Can they use *and* in different places in the sentence, e.g. *On Tuesday I went to a café. I ate a sandwich **and** I went by car.*

2 Mix and match (15–20 minutes)

Learning intention: to practise saying a wider range of sentences using *and*

Resources: Learner's Book, Session 2.6, Activity 2; extra pictures of places, transport and activities; three pots

Description: Use the pictures in the Learner's Book (Activity 1) and any additional pictures and ideas to create new combinations and sentences.

This could be played as a Lucky Dip game, e.g. putting images in three pots corresponding to: *Where did you go? What did you do? How did you get there?*.

Learners choose one picture or word from each pot plus a day of the week.

They must put the ideas together to form a recount statement using *and* – as practised in Activity 1.

This could be played as a class initially and then in pairs or small groups.

〉 **Differentiation ideas:** Support learners by asking them to work in mixed-ability pairs or play the game as a group.

Challenge learners to add their own ideas to create fun scenarios and sentences.

Answers:
Learners' own sentences

3 Write a diary (20–30 minutes)

Learning intention: to write a diary

Resources: Learner's Book, Session 2.6, Activity 3; Differentiated worksheets 2A–C

Description: Tell learners that now they will use their ideas from Activity 2 to write their own diary.

You can use Differentiated worksheets 2A–C here to support and challenge learners.

If you prefer, show learners how to fold a piece of paper into four columns so that they have a guide for their writing. Do not expect learners to copy the chart from the Learner's Book.

Allow learners time to complete their diaries and, if appropriate, use them to encourage talk and presentations about what they did. Then ask them to write about what they did on two days (using the example sentence structure from the Learner's Book).

Ask learners to ask each other questions, e.g. *When did you …? Where did you go on …? How did you get to …? What did you do on …?*

〉 **Differentiation ideas:** Use Differentiated worksheets 2A–C.

Answers:
Learners' own responses

Plenary idea

You may leave if … (5–10 minutes)

Description: Ask learners to look at their diary charts from Activity 3.

Make statements starting *You may leave if …:*

• *You may leave if you walked somewhere on a Wednesday.*

• *You may leave if you went to the park on a Monday.* etc.

Keep going until everyone has left the classroom.

Homework ideas

Learners complete the Workbook Session 2.6 activities if not completed in class.

They choose a family member and write a diary about their week. It might be a pet!

Answers for Workbook

1 Correct circling of the word *and*; correct matching of sentences to pictures

2 a They went to the play centre and they met some friends.

  b He got on his bike and he zoomed off up the hill.

3 Learners' own sentences

2.7 A big day out

Learning objectives		Learning intentions	Success criteria
Main focus	**Also covered**	• To talk about days out.	• Learners can talk about days out.
1Rv.01, 1Ri.11, 1Ra.04, 1SLm.03	1Rv.02, 1Rg.03, 1Rg.04, 1Ri.03, 1Ri.04, 1Ri.13, 1Ra.01, 1Ra.03, 1Ra.06, 1Wv.01, 1Wc.02, 1SLm.02, 1SLs.02, 1SLg.02, 1SLg.03, 1SLg.04, 1SLp.05	• To listen to and read a recount of a big day out. • To bring own ideas and experience to understand a story.	• Learners can listen to and read a recount of a big day out. • Learners can bring their own ideas and experience to understand a story.

Pre-teach theme park vocabulary and provide books and pictures about days out to support vocabulary and comprehension of the topic.

Common misconception

Misconception	How to identify	How to overcome
Long words are hard to read.	Write the word *roundabout* on the board. Ask learners to read it. Ask: *Can anyone read this word? How? What did you do?* They may have started blending then guessed, split it into two and blended each smaller word, etc. If no one can read the word, then model the technique of clapping the word and splitting it into two: *round/about; r/ou/n/d round; a/b/ou/t about = roundabout.*	Remind learners, when they are reading aloud or spelling, that sometimes they can try to work out a longer word by splitting it into smaller parts. Provide practice by giving learners longer words to work out.

Starter idea

What is a big day out? (10–15 minutes)

Resources: Learner's Book, Session 2.7: Getting started; pictures/recounts of days out

Description: Learners may not have experience of 'big' or special days out, so be sensitive to this throughout this session.

Remind learners that in *My First Train Trip* in Session 2.1, Activity 2, they read a first-experience recount.

Talk about special days out. Ask if learners have experiences to share of places they like to visit with family and friends. Ask: *Which places do you like to visit?*

Look at the pictures in Getting started to further stimulate the discussion about fun places to go.

Check understanding of the vocabulary.

Ask learners to work in small groups or pairs to choose just one of the places and choose one person to give feedback to the class. Tally the responses and compare. Ask: *Which is the most popular place for a special day out?*

Encourage learners to now write their own responses to the question: *Where do you like to go for a day out?* (This might be different to the experience chosen by their group!)

Tell learners that in this session they will read about a day out at a theme park.

Main teaching ideas

1 A Trip to a Theme Park (30–40 minutes)

Learning intention: to listen to and read a recount of a big day out

Resources: *A Trip to a Theme Park* (Learner's Book, Session 2.7, Activity 1); Track 11; Phonics Workbook B

Description: Tell learners they will first listen to and then read a recount about a girl's special birthday trip to a theme park.

Show the learners the pictures in the Learner's Book. Discuss the fact that the pictures are not photographs so it looks more like a story, but it could be true.

Give learners time to quietly listen to the recount. Play the audio or read the text aloud.

Discuss learners' initial thoughts and then give them time to look through and read the recount.

After a while, stop the class to ask some questions:
- *Who has a birthday?*
- *How old do we think Polly is?*
- *Who goes with Polly?*
- *How many things do they do before the café?*

Re-read the text, pausing at certain places to invite learners to join in with the reading: e.g. *dolphins*; *roundabout*; *Slide and Glide*; *splashed, tired, birthday bag.*

Phonics (Phonics Workbook B, pages 14–15): consider linking to phonics here by using the opportunities in the text to show learners words with split digraph i-e, e.g. *nine, slide, glide.*

> **Differentiation ideas:** Support learners by pairing less confident readers with more confident readers.

Challenge learners to read sections of the recount aloud, noticing full stops.

2 In the birthday bag (10–20 minutes)

Learning intention: to give opinions and listen to others

Resources: Learner's Book, Session 2.7, Activity 2

Description: Ask learners about the birthday bag in the recount. Ask: *What is it and what do you think might be in it? Do the illustrations in the book give any clues?* (no)

Give pairs time to come up with ideas. Invite them to share their ideas.

Give learners time to draw the bag in their notebooks, and then draw and write about the contents of the bag.

As you circulate, encourage learners to use their phonics knowledge to check spellings and remind them to use correct punctuation.

> **Differentiation ideas:** Support learners with spelling words as they label the things in the birthday bag.

Challenge learners to write sentences about the items in their bags and to explain their answers.

Answers:
Learners' own drawings

3 What else happened? (20–30 minutes)

Learning intention: to use own ideas and experiences to talk about a recount

Resources: Learner's Book, Session 2.7, Activity 3; Workbook, Session 2.7; large sheets of paper and pens

Description: Ask learners to think about what else Polly and Sal might have done at the theme park.

Hand out large sheets of paper and pens, so they can record their ideas for sharing.

After a while, invite each group to feed back their ideas.

Invite some learners to share their ideas with the class.

You can use the Workbook Session 2.7 activities in class now to further explore ideas about theme parks

⟩ **Differentiation ideas:** Support learners by prompting/asking questions.

Challenge learners to explain their ideas by retelling the ending of the story, e.g. ask them to embed their ideas into the story. Ask learners to comment on what other learners have said to challenge their listening skills.

Answers:

Learners' own ideas, but may include: They might have gone on a helter skelter / got lost / met dad in the café.

Plenary idea

Long words (5–10 minutes)

Description: Ask learners to work in small groups or pairs to read longer words such as:

- *fantastic*
- *birthday*
- *adventure*
- *lemonade*

Those who work out each word the fastest may explain how they worked it out (see Common misconception earlier).

CROSS-CURRICULAR LINKS

Maths: Draw simple block graphs or pictograms to show the most popular places to go for a big day out.

Science: Use construction toys to build models of theme parks or build a model water slide in a water tray.

Homework ideas

Learners complete the Workbook Session 2.7 activities if not completed in class.

They write a word that rhymes with a list of words from the recount: *cloud, nine, slide, came, show.*

Answers for Workbook

1   Learners' own responses

2   Learners may label: big wheel; helter-skelter; a castle; merry-go-round; dodgems; train; tea-cup ride; rollercoaster; log flume, swinging ship; ice-cream van; ticket booth; pedalos/boats

3   Learners' own responses

2.8 Checking understanding

Learning objectives		Learning intentions	Success criteria
Main focus	**Also covered**	• To explore pronouns.	• Learners can explore pronouns.
1Rv.01, 1Ri.06, 1Ri.13, 1SLm.04	1Rg.05, 1Rs.02, 1Ri.07, 1SLs.02, 1SLg.01, 1SLp.04	• To answer questions about a recount to check understanding.	• Learners can answer questions about a recount to check understanding.
		• To retell a recount from pictures and using actions.	• Learners can retell a recount from pictures and using actions.

LANGUAGE SUPPORT

Revisit pronouns with learners using picture or word cards in matching activities or games. Matching actions to the recount may support some learners with understanding.

Common misconception

Misconception	How to identify	How to overcome
It does not matter if we use *he* or *she* to talk about boys and girls or men and women.	Ask learners to say what is wrong in sentences you are reading aloud. For example: *The boy loved the Slide and Glide. **She** loved to splash.* *Polly and Sal waited in the café because **Dad** was parking the car. **She** said to wait there.* *Polly was happy. **He** was going to have a lovely birthday.* Talk about pronouns for males and females.	Make a class display of pronouns that learners can use when they are unsure. Add pictures to help learners distinguish the differences.

Starter idea

Using pronouns (10–20 minutes)

Resources: Learner's Book, Session 2.8: Getting started; Workbook, Session 2.8; Phonics Workbooks A and B

Description: Ask one learner about another learner: *What is he/she doing?* to prompt the response: *He/She is reading/working/writing,* etc.

Ask a few other learners to ensure the correct use of *he/she*.

Ask the class about something outside, e.g. a bird or a class pet to prompt the response: *It is … flying,* etc.

Then ask a learner about the others in the class: *What are they doing?* to prompt the response: *They are reading/ working/writing,* etc.

Phonics: consider linking to phonics here by flagging the reading and spelling of these common and/or tricky words:

Phonics Workbook A: pages 13, 15, 19, 25, 29, 31, 43, 45, 49, 51 and 53.

Phonics Workbook B: pages 11, 13, 17, 19, 21, 25, 27, 29, 31, 35, 37, 45 and 53.

Choose different learners to ask questions correctly using the third-person singular and plural. Ensure that you give several learners the chance to practise.

Ask learners to match up the pictures and the pronouns in Getting started to consolidate this activity.

You can use the Workbook Session 2.8 activities here for further practice.

Answers:
a: I, she; **b**: we, they; **c**: it; **d**: we, they

Main teaching ideas

1 Read to check understanding (20–30 minutes)

Learning intention: to match questions to answers to check comprehension

Resources: Learner's Book, Session 2.8, Activity 1; *A Trip to a Theme Park* (Learner's Book, Session 2.7); Track 11

Description: Together, re-read *A Trip to a Theme Park* from Learner's Book, Session 2.7, Activity 1.

Then read each question in the Learner's Book (Session 2.8, Activity 1) and model how to find each answer.

Ensure the learners can read all the words.

Give time for learners to write out matching questions and answers. As you move around the class, check for good letter formation, comfortable pencil grips and good use of basic punctuation: capital letters, question marks or full stops.

> **Differentiation ideas:** Support learners by providing answers on cards for them to match with questions.

Challenge learners to formulate their own questions for others to answer.

Answers:
a 1iv; 2v; 3iii; 4ii; 5i
b–d Learners' own responses

2 Sort pictures for retelling a recount (20–30 minutes)

Learning intention: to sort pictures into the correct order for retelling

Resources: Learner's Book, Session 2.8, Activity 2; *A Trip to a Theme Park* (Learner's Book, Session 2.7); Track 11; Worksheet 2.3; props, such as sunglasses or a bag

Description: Check learners' understanding of the complete recount in Learner's Book, Session 2.7, Activity 1, by asking two confident learners to pretend to be Sal and Polly. You may want props, such as sunglasses or a bag. Change the characters to boys' names if you wish two boys to retell the recount.

Ask the two 'actors' to talk about what Sal and Polly did in the right order. Others in the class may prompt.

The 'actors' might say:

- *We went to a theme park, Cloud Nine, because it was Polly's birthday.*
- *First we saw the dolphins.*
- *Then we went on the big roundabout.*
- *Then we found the Slide and Glide water splash.*
- *Finally we went to the café.*
- *It was a fun day out.*

Return to the Learner's Book (Session 2.8, Activity 2) and ask learners to record the correct order of the pictures to retell the story. You may wish to provide Worksheet 2.3 Sequencing pictures here.

> **Differentiation ideas:** Support learners by providing Worksheet 2.3 Sequencing pictures so they can cut and stick the pictures into the correct order.

Challenge learners to write a sentence for each picture, too.

Answers:
c, f, a, d, e, b

3 Make up actions and act (10–20 minutes)

Learning intention: to add actions to a retelling to enhance meaning

Resources: Learner's Book, Session 2.8, Activities 2 and 3

Description: Repeat the events in Activity 2, but this time work with the actors to act each event. Model this first. While making an appropriate action for each event, ask: *What are we doing?* (See the answers and some suggested actions in square brackets in the Answer section.)

Repeat this role play with different pairs or as a whole class. Encourage learners to come up with their own actions.

> **Differentiation ideas:** Support learners by pairing confident and less confident learners and by providing props. Challenge learners to suggest their own ideas in pairs before working as a class.

Answers:

Learners' own actions, similar to:

- We went to a theme park, Cloud Nine, because it was Polly's birthday. [*They hold hands.*]
- First we saw the dolphins. [*They pretend to look at something exciting.*]
- Then we went on the big roundabout. [*They hold hands and go round in a circle.*]
- Then we found the Slide and Glide water ride. [*They make a slide and splash gesture with their hands.*]
- Finally we went to the café. [*They sit down and look tired, pretending to drink.*]
- It was a fun day out. [*They put their arms round each other's shoulders.*]

Plenary idea

Preferences (5 minutes)

Description: Ask learners to talk about their experiences of theme parks or birthday treats. Can they sort the experiences into different kinds, e.g. rides, water; animals; food. Check they use pronouns correctly as they talk.

CROSS-CURRICULAR LINKS

Science: Identify different sources of sound. Ask learners to listen for all the sounds they can hear from a theme park using an online sound bank.

Homework ideas

Learners complete the Workbook Session 2.8 activities if not completed in class.

They try to find another recount, or a song, about a theme park.

Answers for Workbook

1 correct circling of the word *they* eight times
2 **a** they; **b** she; **c** he; **d** it
3 Learners' own sentence endings. For example:
   a … they liked it.
   b … she splashed Polly and Sal.
   c … he saw the big wheel.
   d … it was fun.

2.9 Exploring words and writing a recount

LEARNING PLAN

Learning objectives		Learning intentions	Success criteria
Main focus	**Also covered**	• To explore plurals.	• Learners can explore plurals.
1Ri.04, 1Ww.04, 1Wc.02, 1Wc.04	1Rw.02, 1Rv.02, 1Rs.01, 1Ww.02, 1Wv.01, 1Wv.02, 1SLg.03	• To explore and use sequencing words. • To plan and write a recount.	• Learners can explore and use sequencing words. • Learners can plan and write a recount.

LANGUAGE SUPPORT

Check learners understand the terminology of *singular* and *plural* if you want to use correct terminology. Learners may like to consolidate learning of plurals by sorting small-world figures of animals and people into sets and then using the correct plural form to describe them, e.g. adding *–s* (*hens*), adding *–es* (*horses*), other (*babies*) or irregular endings (*children*).

The active listening activities will support some learners, but reading the sentences out loud, rather than playing the audio, may be more appropriate for your learners as this will enable you to say the sentences at a slower speed, and possibly also with a clearer emphasis.

Common misconception

Misconception	How to identify	How to overcome
We add *–s* to make irregular plurals.	Ask learners: *Can we say:* *Peoples* like to go to parks. *Childrens* like waterslides. If necessary, clarify that the answer is *no*, because *people* and *children* are irregular plurals. This means we have to remember that they are different.	Make a working wall or hanging display of irregular plurals as a reminder for learners to use when speaking or writing.

Starter idea

Plurals (5–10 minutes)

Resources: Learner's Book, Session 2.9: Getting started

Description: Ask learners to point to different things in class and say the plural, e.g. *pens*, *books*, *chairs*.

See Language support and Common misconception.

Use the Language focus box in the Learner's Book to talk about some initial rules for making plurals.

Work through the examples in Getting started together.

Main teaching ideas

1 Listen for plurals (10–20 minutes)

Learning intention: to identify plurals in sentences

Resources: Sentences from *A Trip to a Theme Park* (Learner's Book, Session 2.9, Activity 1); Track 12; Workbook, Session 2.9

Audioscript: *A Trip to a Theme Park*

Sal and Polly loved theme parks.

They wanted to see the dolphins first.

They stood on boxes at the show so that they could see.

They watched the bumper cars. There were so many crashes!

They watched the Slide and Glide ride. There were so many splashes!

Description: Tell learners they are listening for plurals. When they hear a plural, they should wave if they hear an *–s* ending and clap if they hear an *–es* ending. Note that *–es* sounds like the word *is* at the end of a word. *–s* can sound like /s/ in *parks* or /z/ in *dolphins*. You can use the Workbook Session 2.9 activities for this session now to practise plural endings.

❯ **Differentiation ideas:** Support learners by reading the sentences aloud and stressing the plurals. Challenge learners to make up similar sentences for the class, or a partner.

Answers:
a parks, dolphins, cars; **b** boxes, crashes, splashes

2 Fill the gaps with sequencing words (10–20 minutes)

Learning intention: to use simple time connectives in a recount

Resources: Learner's Book, Session 2.9, Activity 2; *A Trip to a Theme Park* (Learner's Book, Session 2.7); Track 11

Description: Tell learners that some words help us to know the correct order that things happened in, e.g. *first, then, next, at the end of the day.*

Split the class into four groups. Give each group a word or words to listen out for: *first, then, next, at the end of the day.*

Together, re-read the whole story of *A Trip to a Theme Park*. Pause or get the learners to clap or stand up each time they hear any of these words: *first, next, then, at the end of the day.* Discuss how the word *finally* could be used as an alternative to *at the end of the day.*

Ask if they know other words like this that tell the order of things, e.g. *second, third.* Now use the gapped version of the story in Activity 2. Learners supply the missing sequencing words either orally as you read the text aloud, or by reading the text and writing the answers in their notebooks.

> **Differentiation ideas:** Support learners by providing word or phrase cards for them to choose from to fill in the gaps.

Challenge learners to write the sentences in their notebooks filling in the gaps.

Answers:
First, they went to see the dolphins and watched the show.
Next, they saw the big roundabout.
Then, At the end of the day, they found the Slide and Glide.

3 Write a recount (10–20 minutes)

Learning intention: to plan and write a recount

Resources: Learner's Book, Session 2.9, Activity 3; Worksheet 2.4

Description: Explain that you want learners to make up a recount about a picture by using sentences beginning with *first*, *next*, *then* and *finally*.

Use the examples in the Learner's Book and/or use your own pictures of recount scenarios to model the language required. Give learners time to plan their recount. Consider running this activity at speed to see who can provide creative and effective ideas when under time pressure. Accept all creative and fantastical events, but ensure the language used is correct.

Learners write their recount.

> **Differentiation ideas:** Support learners by asking them to work in small groups, or hand out Worksheet 2.4 Using sequencing words, which provides the structure for a specific recount.

Challenge learners to use their own ideas for the four sentences and to include some connectives.

Answers:
Learners' own recounts

Plenary idea

Sort It Out! (10–20 minutes)

Resources: Learners' recounts cut into four sentences

Description: Copy out and cut out a selection of your learners' recounts. Hand out the four sentences for one recount to four learners. Ask them to stand in the correct order to retell the recount. Encourage other learners to agree or disagree on the order. Repeat with other recount sentences.

Homework ideas

Learners complete the Workbook Session 2.9 activities if not completed in class.

They find and explore a book about theme parks in the library or online.

Answers for Workbook

1 ending in –*s*: keys, maps, drinks, bags
ending in –*es*: peaches, foxes, houses, glasses

2 **a** days; **b** zoos; **c** sandwiches; **d** parks **e** dishes

3 Learners' own sentences

4

Add –s	Add –es	Words where you do not add –s or –es
cafés	dishes	people
birthdays	buses	children

2.10 Holiday news!

LEARNING PLAN

Learning objectives		Learning intentions	Success criteria
Main focus	**Also covered**	• To talk about ways to communicate and share news.	• Learners can talk about ways to communicate and share news.
1Ri.03, 1Ri.04, 1Ri.09, 1Ri.13	1Rv.01, 1Rg.02, 1Rg.03, 1Ra.01, 1Ra.04, 1SLp.01	• To explore the features of a postcard.	• Learners explore and identify the features of a postcard.
		• To answer questions to check understanding.	• Learners can answer questions to check understanding.

LANGUAGE SUPPORT

Make a class display titled *We like to tell people what we have done. We use these different ways.* Allow learners to paint their preferred method of communication to add to the display. Add postcards and letters, and photos of learners using technology to the display, too. Use the display at any opportunity to reinforce the vocabulary and language structures of the unit so far.

Check learners' understanding of the word *address*.

Common misconception

Misconception	How to identify	How to overcome
You have to start all over again if you have forgotten to write something when sharing news.	Ask the class if they write letters. Ask what happens if they have finished and then remember something important that they wanted to write. Take learners' ideas. Tell them about the term 'P.S.' (postscript, which means *after writing*), which allows you to add something to a note, postcard or letter after it has been written.	Remind learners of other ways to add information in non-fiction writing: • P.S. in a note, letter or postcard • text in a Tip box • text in a Did you know? / Fact box.

Starter idea

Tell people your news (10–20 minutes)

Resources: Learner's Book, Session 2.10: Getting started; some pictures for learners to describe

Description: Ask learners to share ideas about how they enjoy sending news and recounting their experiences to others. Use the pictures in Getting started as a stimulus or use your own pictures and links.

Ask questions such as:

- *Do we have a class 'show and tell'?*
- *Do we write news books in class?*
- *Does anyone write a diary or a blog?*
- *Who writes letters or sends postcards?*
- *Who likes to talk online?*
- *Who likes to talk on the phone?*

Encourage learners to bring in photos and postcards from home so that they may use these to recount an event to others. See Language support for a display idea.

Main teaching ideas

1 Jared's postcard (20–30 minutes)

Learning intention: to listen to and read a postcard

Resources: *Jared's Postcard* (Learner's Book, Session 2.10, Activity 1); Track 13; examples of postcards

Description: Tell learners that this is a postcard from a boy who is visiting his grandma. Draw their attention to the writing on one side and the address on the other. Together, listen to and then read the postcard.

> **Differentiation ideas:** Support learners by repeating the audio several times. Challenge learners to follow the postcard text with their fingers as they listen. Then ask them to find words ending in –le in the text turtle(s), scramble.

2 Answer questions about the letter (20–30 minutes)

Learning intention: to answer questions to show understanding

Resources: Learner's Book, Session 2.10, Activity 2; *Jared's Postcard* (Learner's Book, Session 2.10); Track 13; question words

Description: Together, read through the questions about Jared's postcard. Ask learners to read (or listen to) the postcard again with these questions in mind.

Encourage learners to answer the questions orally before writing their responses in their notebooks.

> **Differentiation ideas:** Support learners by providing the answers and asking them to match them to the questions. Or ask them to answer just three questions.

Challenge learners to write the answers in full sentences in their notebooks.

Answers:

a   He is writing to his Red Class.

b   Jared is visiting his Grandma.

c   No, there is no date on the postcard.

d   He nearly forgot to tell about the turtles.

e   Learners' own responses, similar to: I think he feels happy and excited.

---

3 Parts of a letter (10–15 minutes)

Learning intention: to identify the beginning and end features of a postcard

Resources: Learner's Book, Session 2.10, Activity 3; Workbook, Session 2.10

Description: Ask learners to again look at the postcard and, in pairs, to find its beginning and end. Ask them how the postcard begins. (*Dear …*) Ask them how it ends. (*See you soon …*) Talk about how we use *See you soon …* if we know the person well. Ask learners if they know how to finish a letter if we do not know the person well (e.g. *Best wishes, from …*).

Talk about the *P.S.* – learners will not know that it means 'postscript', but tell them it is how we can add something we have forgotten to write in a letter. Ask them, in pairs, to find these parts of the letter. Draw their attention to the use of capitals. As you circulate, support all learners to discuss and find the right parts. You can use the Workbook Session 2.10 activities for further practice.

> **Differentiation ideas:** Support learners by working through the points as a class before they work in pairs.

Challenge learners to revisit some of the other parts of the letter as discussed in Activity 2.

Answers:

a Starts with *Dear*, ends with *See you soon*;

b Add something you have forgotten to write in the letter; c Learners' own responses

Plenary idea

Watch online (5–10 minutes)

Resources: a postcard and a letter

Description: Ask learners to say how postcards are different from letters.

Ask them what is the same.

CROSS-CURRICULAR LINKS

Art: Explore and make designs for postage stamps.

Homework ideas

Learners complete the Workbook Session 2.10 activities if not completed in class.

They find out if there are postcards for places near where they live. Why?

Answers for Workbook

1 Learners' own responses
2 Learners tick 1 and 4
3 Learners write a P.S.

2.11 Planning and writing a postcard

LEARNING PLAN

Learning objectives		Learning intentions	Success criteria
Main focus	**Also covered**	• To explore the features of a postcard and a letter.	• Learners can explore the features of a postcard and a letter.
1Ri.03, 1Ri.04, 1Ri.09, 1Ri.13	1Rs.01, 1Rs.02, 1Ri.07, 1Ri.14, 1Wv.01, 1Ww.03, 1Ws.01, 1Ws.02, 1Wc.02, 1Wc.04, 1Wc.05, 1Wp.02, 1Wp.05, 1SLg.04, 1SLp.04	• To talk about additional holiday news ideas.	• Learners can talk about holiday news.
		• To plan a postcard using picture support.	• Learners can plan a postcard using picture support.
		• To write a postcard using key features.	• Learners can write a postcard using key features.

LANGUAGE SUPPORT

Learners will benefit from further recounting experiences they would share on a postcard, e.g. holiday travel or visiting family or a special place.

Practise the use of capital letters to support learners when they come to write their own postcards.

Common misconception

Misconception	How to identify	How to overcome
We only use capital letters at the beginning of a sentence and to begin our names.	Ask learners to find examples of capital letters in Jared's postcard in Session 2.10 and to explain why they are used. For example: *Brighton Park School, Dolphin Street, Seatown, ST2 4ET* *Dear, See, Jared, P.S.*	Practise the formation of capital letters so learners feel confident to use them. Encourage learners to use correct capitals in their own letter or postcard writing.

Starter idea

Postcard features (10–15 minutes)

Resources: Learner's Book, Session 2.11: Getting started

Description: Ask learners to remember all the things they noticed about Jared's postcard.

Share ideas and tell them these things are the letter 'features' and that we can use them in our own writing if we want to.

Show learners the features of letters and postcards in Getting started. Talk about the features together.

Invite learners to think of other ways they might begin or end a postcard to someone they know well. (Hi, Hello!, Love from, Sending hugs, from …)

Main teaching ideas

1 Look at other events (20–30 minutes)

Learning intention: to talk about events to include in a letter or postcard

Resources: Learner's Book, Session 2.11, Activity 1; Workbook, Session 2.11

Description: Tell learners they will now talk with a partner about other things Jared did in Barbados. Ask them to look at the pictures and talk about them.

Ask learners to work in pairs to draw and write any other ideas they have. Ask: *What else might Jared have done in a new city?*

As you circulate, support and challenge learners to be creative.

Ask a few learners to share their ideas.

You can use the Workbook Session 2.11 activities now to practise ordering events.

> **Differentiation ideas:** Support learners by providing the Workbook activities for further practice and/or provide captions for them to match to each picture.

Challenge learners to draw and write captions for additional ideas.

Answers:
a He went body surfing, He played in the sand, He jumped in the pool, He went on his scooter in the dark. (or similar)
b Learners' own ideas

2 Plan to write a postcard (20–30 minutes)

Learning intention: to plan text for a postcard

Resources: Learner's Book, Session 2.11, Activity 2

Description: Tell learners they are going to pretend to be Jared.

Take turns in role playing. Ask learners to sit in the middle of a circle to talk about three special things they did in Barbados whilst visiting Grandma.

Check learners are using the past tense.

Swap a few times so several learners have a go at role playing.

Ask learners to write or draw their ideas in their notebook.

> **Differentiation ideas:** Support learners by inviting them to use their ideas from Activity 1 or by scribing some of their ideas for them.

Challenge learners to use exciting verbs in their recounts.

Answers:
Learners' own responses

3 Write a postcard (20–30 minutes)

Learning intention: to write a postcard

Resources: Learner's Book, Session 2.11, Activity 3; Worksheet 2.5

Description: Tell learners they will now use their three drawings or sentences from Activity 2 to create their own postcard.

You may wish to provide Worksheet 2.5 Writing a postcard as a support and guide.

Circulate in the class to support and challenge learners appropriately. Check correct use of capital letters.

Support learners to stick the two sides of the postcard together so that the picture and the text are the same way up (like a real postcard).

> **Differentiation ideas:** Support learners by allowing them to cut and stick their sentences in the correct order on their postcard.

Challenge learners to copy their sentences onto the Worksheet 2.5 Writing a postcard template, thinking about layout and spacing.

Answers:
Learners' own postcards

Plenary idea

Memory game (5–10 minutes)

Description: Ask learners to sit in a circle or you can work your way around the class as they sit at desks.

Say or chant:

- *I went to see my Grandma and I …*

Each learner completes the sentence.

The next learner must repeat previous sentences before adding their own.

Repeat according to time available.

Ask learners to help each other if they begin to struggle to recall previous sentences.

Homework ideas

Learners complete the Workbook Session 2.11 activities if not completed in class.

They make a list of words that rhyme with *news* (*shoes, whose, views, use, zoos*)

Answers for Workbook

1 Learners' own stamps and arrows, correctly drawn to top right of postcard.

2 Learners' own postcards, including two special things to tell.

3 Learners' own addresses, well-spaced.

2.12 Look back

LEARNING PLAN			
Learning objectives		**Learning intentions**	**Success criteria**
Main focus	**Also covered**	• To check own writing and share postcards. • To talk about the recounts in this unit. • To think about their learning from the unit.	• Learners can check their writing and share their postcards. • Learners can talk about the recounts in this unit. • Learners can think about their learning from the unit.
1Rs.02, 1Rs.04, 1Ri.04, 1Wp.06, 1SLr.01	1Ra.04, 1Ra.05, 1Ra.06, 1Wg.01, 1Wg.03, 1Wp.03, 1SLm.01, 1SLm.02, 1SLg.02, 1SLg.03		

Encourage learners to use the Learner's Book for recall, as well as any posters or displays in the classroom used throughout the unit.

Common misconception

Misconception	How to identify	How to overcome
Using pictures to help us remember things is cheating.	Ask learners what sort of things we do to help us to remember things. Ask: *Is it cheating?*	Encourage learners to use classroom props and resources as well as their own posters or aide-mémoires to help them to embed their learning and remember it.

Starter idea

Spacing (5–10 minutes)

Resources: Learner's Book, Session 2.12: Getting started

Description: Talk to learners about spacing our writing. Ask: *Why do we do it? How does it help readers?*

Look at the samples of learners' writing in Getting started, and ask what they notice about the two versions (one is all unjoined, the other has a digraph joined; they may also comment about other features of the writing, e.g. letter formation, straightness of the phrase).

Agree that spacing is an important part of handwriting and helps people to read our writing. Joining some letters should not make spacing messy.

Main teaching ideas

1 Check writing (10–15 minutes)

Learning intention: to check writing for mistakes and for spacing layout

Resources: Learner's Book, Session 2.12, Activity 1

Description: Discuss the value of making mistakes.

If appropriate for your class, write a sentence on the board that needs correcting. Work together to correct the sentence.

Ask learners to look at the postcard they wrote in Session 2.11. What do they think about the spacing between letters and words? Could they improve it next time? Ask: *Why is spacing important for a letter or a postcard?*

Encourage learners to enjoy reading their postcards and checking their work. Some learners may wish to share their postcards by reading aloud.

Encourage peer feedback, but try to ensure it is kept positive.

> **Differentiation ideas:** Support learners by working with them in a group, when checking their postcard, or selecting a sentence for them to improve.

Challenge learners to spot punctuation errors, too.

2 Look back at the unit recounts (10–15 minutes)

Learning intention: to reflect on recounts and recall their features

Resources: Learner's Book, Session 2.12, Activity 2; Workbook, Session 2.12

Description: Ask learners if they can remember the recounts from the unit using memory as well as class displays that you may have created.

List the recount titles together, encouraging learners to look at the images in the Learner's Book if they cannot remember all of them.

Ask learners to talk about the recounts, asking: *Which did you enjoy most?* Take a class vote.

Ask learners to recall the different types of recount: they were all narratives about experiences, but presented in different ways.

You can use Workbook Session 2.12 here to revisit the content of this unit.

> **Differentiation ideas:** Support learners by using book covers in print or in the Learner's Book, or classroom displays, as reminders of the unit's stories.

Challenge learners to think of other recounts that could have featured in this unit.

3 Skills review (10–15 minutes)

Learning intention: to think about learning in terms of language skills

Resources: Learner's Book, Session 2.12, Activity 3

Description: Remind learners of the terms we use to describe language skills: *reading, writing, spelling, listening and speaking.*

Say each skill one by one and ask learners to put their hand up when you say the skill that they think they are best at. Talk about why.

Ask learners to say or write one thing that helps them with each skill.

These simple learner statements can be extremely useful for informing end-of-term reports.

> **Differentiation ideas:** Support learners to be positive in their skills review, providing models: *I think I am much better at … now.*

Challenge learners to also think of one thing they still need to improve.

Answers:
Learners' own responses

Plenary idea

Lucky Dip review (5–10 minutes)

Resources: assessment sentence starters; a bowl

Description: Put a selection of assessment for learning sentence starters in a bowl to pass round the class, for example:

- *One thing I must remember from this unit is …*
- *Today I have learned …*
- *I still don't understand …*
- *Before this unit, I already knew how to … / about …*
- *I now understand …*

Invite learners to pick one and complete it orally.

Keep passing the statements around until you run out of learners or time.

Homework ideas

Learners complete the Workbook Session 2.12 activities if not completed in class.

They talk to a family member about what they would like to improve about their English work and why.

Answers for Workbook

1 all ticked except **b** a trip to a zoo and **g** a text message

2 **a** We read about a first train trip.
   b I keep a diary.
   c We share our news each day.

3 Learners' own responses

CHECK YOUR PROGRESS

1 It describes or tells us about something that happened.
2 Yesterday (went tells you it was in the past)
3 Learners say or sing the alphabet.
4 Wednesday, Thursday, Friday, Saturday, Sunday.
5 Jared swims every day and next week he is going to try body surfing!
6 Learners' own responses

PROJECT GUIDANCE

These projects build on the reading, writing and understanding learners have developed throughout the unit. The project options here allow learners to extend their work on recounts, either working in a group, as a pair or individually. You may prefer to allocate a project to the class, rather than let them choose.

Group project: Learners set up a class post office to extend the theme of postcards and letters. This post office can be created as a role-play area and learners will need to research the things they need.

Learners will need to use their skills in collaboration and creativity.

Pair project: Provide paper and glue for learners to design and make an envelope by folding a piece of paper. Some learners may write a letter to go inside the envelope.

Solo project: Learners write, or draw, a diary for two weeks. They may like to share it with others.

For more guidance on setting up and assessing projects, see Project guidance at the end of Unit 1.

>3 Rhythm and rhyme

Unit plan

Session	Approximate number of learning hours	Outline of learning content	Resources
3.1 Finger rhymes	1.5	Talk about rhymes. Read and join in with a traditional finger rhyme. Explore rhyming words. Perform a rhyme.	Learner's Book Session 3.1 Workbook Session 3.1 ⬇ Worksheet 3.1 ⬇ Worksheet 3.2 Phonics Workbook A
3.2 Number rhymes	1.5	Explore numbers and number words. Listen to and join in with number rhymes. Explore rhyming words for number words.	Learner's Book Session 3.2 Workbook Session 3.2 ⬇ Worksheet 3.2 ⬇ Language worksheet 3A Phonics Workbooks A and B
3.3 Nonsense rhymes	1.5	Explore the meaning of nonsense. Read a nonsense rhyme. Talk about the sequence of a rhyme. Practise reciting and performing a rhyme.	Learner's Book Session 3.3 Workbook Session 3.3 ⬇ Worksheet 3.3
3.4 Exploring rhythm	2	Listen to a rhyming poem. Read the poem using pictures to work out unfamiliar words. Write sentences to retell the poem.	Learner's Book Session 3.4 Workbook Session 3.4 ⬇ Worksheet 3.4

Session	Approximate number of learning hours	Outline of learning content	Resources
3.5 Planning and writing a poem	2	Explore rhythm and rhyme in a poem. Use own ideas to write a new poem verse.	Learner's Book Session 3.5 Workbook Session 3.5 ⬇ Worksheet 3.5 ⬇ Language worksheet 3B ⬇ Differentiated worksheets 3A–C
3.6 Look back	1	Look back at writing to reflect and edit. Look back on the content of the unit. Review learning.	Learner's Book Session 3.6 Workbook Session 3.6

Cross-unit resources

Learner's Book Check your progress

Learner's Book Projects

BACKGROUND KNOWLEDGE

Before you begin to teach this unit, you may find it helpful to familiarise yourself with:

- the language of poetry: rhythm, rhyme, repeated letter sounds, finger rhymes, number rhymes, nonsense rhymes

- phonics – the language of phonics: name and sound of each letter in the alphabet, long vowel sounds, consonant and vowel digraphs, blending to read, decoding to spell, sound buttons, different spellings of the same phoneme (e.g. *two, to, too*)

- metalanguage: letters, sounds, phrases, sentences, nouns, verbs

- traditional rhymes (English and those in first language)

- poems and picture books that use rhythm and rhyme to represent local, regional, national and international interests and views

- good knowledge of the rhymes featured in this unit – look online for film versions, often with music

- how to listen to, read and then recite or perform poetry.

TEACHING SKILLS FOCUS

Language awareness

In this unit, learners explore a mix of traditional rhymes and rhyming/rhythmic picture books, which provide opportunities to teach and learn explicit knowledge about English letters and sounds, especially in relation to phonics, rhythm and rhyme.

It is important to pass on to learners a passion for poetry and words. We need to develop expert knowledge of children's books including poetry and rhymes. We must share a rich range of poems and rhymes from different cultural backgrounds – including our own. We must be ready to model good reading and writing as well as to guide learners about what else they may read and enjoy.

Challenge 1: For each of the five texts in the unit, find a parallel text that builds on the same language features, to share with learners and place in the class library or make available online.

We need to be confident about our own English skills in order to flag these for learners or provide supported opportunities for them to discover them. We should offer high-quality first teaching and modelling.

Challenge 2: Practise reading *I Got the Rhythm* with rhythm and actions so learners are inspired by you as well as the audio.

At the end of this unit, consider how well you were able to engage learners with a deeper understanding and appreciation of rhythm and rhyme. Use the *Check your progress* questions, but also remember to ask yourself and the learners questions:

- Which poems and rhymes did they most enjoy? Asking learners for their opinion, even from an early age, is an important part of feedback. Ask them to explain their choices and to engage with the language terms.

- Have you provided any audio technology in the classroom that was particularly effective with learners in relation to rhythm and rhyme? If so, what was it and how do you know it enhanced their learning?

- If colleagues came into your classroom, could they tell that learners were engaged in exploring rhythm and rhyme? How would they know?

3.1 Finger rhymes

LEARNING PLAN

Learning objectives		Learning intentions	Success criteria
Main focus	**Also covered**	• To talk about rhymes.	• Learners can talk about rhymes.
1Rv.05, 1Ri.14, 1Ra.02, 1SLm.04, 1SLp.02	1Rw.01, 1Rv.01, 1Rv.02, 1Ri.01, 1Ra.01, 1Ra.04, 1Wv.01, 1Wg.01, 1Wg.04, 1Wp.01, 1SLp.04, 1SLg.01, 1SLg.04	• To join in with words and actions in rhymes. • To explore sounds and words in rhymes.	• Learners can join in with words and actions in rhymes. • Learners can explore sounds and words in rhymes.

Help learners to 'hear' repeated refrains in the rhyme by using exaggerated actions or a different voice tone for those words or phrases. For those who need more practice, use games.

For example, ask learners to clap/jump over a word or phrase written on a card and placed in front of them / leap up from their seat when they hear a word or phrase.

Common misconception

Misconception	How to identify	How to overcome
All learners find it easy to hear rhyme.	Say a word, e.g. *me* Ask learners to say a rhyming word. Note who finds this easy and who struggles.	Play rhyming snap. Hand out word cards to learners that feature words that rhyme but are decodable. Ask learners to find their rhyming partners. Ask them why they are standing together to elicit the discussion about rhyme. Use the Phonics Workbook A, pages 4–5.

Starter ideas

Match the nursery rhymes (10 minutes)

Resources: Learner's Book, Session 1: Getting started

Description: Ask learners if they know any nursery rhymes.

Invite learners to share ideas and to perform if they feel confident. Look out for those learners who need support to build confidence.

Draw on their experiences and use, as a prompt, the pictures in Getting started, which includes representations of *Humpty Dumpty, Little Bo Peep, Twinkle Twinkle Little Star, Jack and Jill, Incy Wincy Spider, The Queen of Hearts, Two Little Dickie Birds, Hey Diddle Diddle*, etc.

Read the rhyme titles in the Learner's Book to help learners match the words to the pictures. Say: *Who can find Jack and Jill? Who can find Incy Wincy Spider?* etc.

Main teaching ideas

1 *Fingers All* (10–15 minutes)

Learning intention: to listen to and join in with a simple finger rhyme

Resources: *Fingers All* (Learner's Book, Session 3.1, Activity 1); Track 14; Worksheet 3.1

Description: Ask learners to show you their hands. Together, name each digit: thumb and Fingers 1, 2, 3, 4. Talk about Finger 1 as the pointing finger, Finger 2 as the tall, middle finger, Finger 3 as the ring finger and Finger 4 as the baby finger.

Together, read or listen to the audio. Do any of the learners know this rhyme or a version of it?

Talk about the names in the rhyme given to each digit. Point out the use of capital letters for names. Get learners to say each name and to clap the syllables.

Tell learners this is an action rhyme, which means they should make actions as they sing! Re-read the rhyme and show the learners how to do the actions. Present each finger at the line *Here I am,* and then bend it, as if bowing, at the line, *How do you do?*

Use Worksheet 3.1 Make a hand puppet to make a hand puppet as a prop to introduce each finger character if you wish.

Re-read the rhyme together, asking the learners to join in where they can with singing and actions.

> **Differentiation ideas:** You may notice some learners struggling with coordination and multi-tasking. Let them practise and enjoy the activity.

Challenge some learners to help you with the actions and guide others.

2 Talk about the rhyme (15–30 minutes;)

Learning intention: to talk about a rhyme's use of language

Resources: Learner's Book, Session 3.1, Activity 2; *Fingers All* (Learner's Book, Session 3.1); Track 14; Workbook, Session 3.1; Phonics Workbook A; Worksheets 3.1 and 3.2

Description: Ask learners to listen for repeated letter sounds and patterns in the rhyme.

Play the audio of the rhyme or read it to learners again.

Talk about each question in the Learner's Book and share ideas. Use Worksheet 3.2 Number rhyming chart here for learners to mark up if helpful.

Ask learners to write their answers in their notebooks.

If using the Workbook in class, use the Workbook Session 3.1 activities now.

Phonics: Phonics Workbook A addresses simple grapheme-phoneme correspondences; see pages 6–7 for words that start with the same letter sound (are alliterative): *th, p, t, r, b* (Theo Thumb, Po-Sin Pointer, Tarak Tall, Ros Ring and Baby Billy).

> **Differentiation ideas:** Support learners by asking them to listen to one question at a time: questions **a, b** and **c**. Repeat the rhyme as often as needed.

Challenge learners to use Worksheet 3.1 Make a hand puppet to make their own *Fingers All* puppet for the rhyme, naming each finger as they wish with repeating letter sounds.

Answers:

a   th, p, t, r, b (Theo Thumb, Po-Sin Pointer, Tarak Tall, Ros Ring and Baby Billy)

b   *Where are you? Here I am.* and *How do you do?*

c   *You* and *do*

d and e   Learners' own answers

3 Perform the rhyme (20 minutes)

Learning intention: to say, sing and perform a rhyme with actions

Resources: Learner's Book, Session 3.1, Activity 3

Description: Invite learners to work in groups of five to practise saying and performing the rhyme.

Learners may sit in a row numbered one to five to represent the thumb and fingers.

The class sings the rhyme, e.g. *Theo Thumb, Theo Thumb, Where are you?*

The learner playing the part of Theo Thumb then jumps up to say: *Here I am, Here I am, How do you do?*

The class can perform the correct actions at the same time. On the last line, all learners, including the performers, jiggle and wave their hands. Repeat so all learners participate.

> **Differentiation ideas:** Support learners who feel shy to perform or speak up, or who find it tricky to sing and perform the actions.

Challenge learners to perform their own versions of *Fingers All* from Activity 2 if they chose to rename the fingers.

Answers:

Learners' performances

Plenary idea

Play an 'exit the classroom' game (10 minutes)

Description: Sing the rhyme using learners' names and ask learners to listen for their name

Sing: *[child's name], Where are you?*

They sing: *Here I am, Here I am, How do you do?* and then leave.

If confident, ask learners to sing to each other to spare your voice!

CROSS-CURRICULAR LINKS

Art: Create finger puppets, using different art techniques.

Homework ideas

Learners complete the Workbook Session 3.1 activities if not completed in class.

They talk to family members about finger rhymes shared in English or their home language when learners were younger, or other rhymes still shared with younger siblings.

Answers for Workbook

1 Learners' own drawings

2 Learners' own verses

3 *Theo* has changed to *Tommy*; *Where are you?* has changed to *How are you?*; *Here I am* has changed to *I am fine*; *How do you do?* has changed to *How about you?*

4 Learners' own questions and answers

3.2 Number rhymes

LEARNING PLAN

Learning objectives		Learning intentions	Success criteria
Main focus	**Also covered**	• To explore numbers and number words.	• Learners can explore numbers and number words.
1Rw.05, 1Rv.05, 1Ri.14, 1Ww.03	1Rw.02, 1Rv.01, 1Rv.02, 1Rs.02, 1Ri.01, 1Ri.12, 1Ri.13, 1Ra.01, 1Ra.02, 1Ww.01, 1Ww.02, 1Ww.05, 1Wp.05, 1SLg.01, 1SLg.04, 1SLm.04, 1SLm.05, 1SLp.02	• To listen to, respond to and read number rhymes. • To find and write rhyming word pairs for number words.	• Learners can listen to, respond to and read number rhymes. • Learners can find and write rhyming word pairs for number words.

LANGUAGE SUPPORT

Make a class number line (you could peg this up as a washing line) for learners to use in class. Ensure the numeral and number word is included. If helpful, provide the number words in home languages, too.

Play Number Bingo to encourage learners to practise number words. Learners have Bingo cards with numbers written on them. They listen for a number to be called out on their card. They cross it out or cover it with a counter when they hear one of their numbers. The winner is the first to cross out or cover all the numbers on their card. To challenge learners, play with numbers on the cards and words on the calling cards or vice versa.

Sing other number rhymes, too.

Common misconception

Misconception	How to identify	How to overcome
to is always spelled with letter *t* and *o*.	Ask learners (or selected learners if coming to write on the board) to write down three short dictated sentences: *I go to the shops.* *I have two hens.* *I have a cat, too.*	Check each sentence and talk about the different spellings of this word. Agree a class code so that each time the word is misspelled, you can say the 'secret code' to alert learners to check the spelling of the word, e.g. two clicks of the fingers or say *Toucan!*

Starter ideas

Count to ten! (5–10 minutes)

Resources: Learner's Book, Session 3.2: Getting started; Phonics Workbooks A and B

Description: Ask learners to count up to ten with you.

Write the words from Getting started on the board and model how to read them. They are not all phonically decodable, but need to be learned and a phonics first approach can be modelled.

- simple and decodable Consonant Vowel Consonant (CVC) words: *six, ten*

- decodable when you know the rules: *three, five, seven, nine*

- tricky: *one, two, eight, four*

Phonics (Phonics Workbooks A and B): you may like to use the additional activities on using a phonics first approach to reading and spelling.

Pair work: encourage the learners to say and read the number words. Check that learners are pronouncing the words correctly.

Main teaching ideas

1   Read number rhymes (30 minutes)

Learning intention: to read, listen to and join in with number rhymes; to say rhyming words

Resources: *One, Two, Buckle My Shoe* and *Oliver Twist* (Learner's Book, Session 3.2, Activity 1); Tracks 15 and 16

Description: Together, talk about number rhymes. You may already sing number rhymes in class or learners may know some from home and in their home language.

Read *One, Two, Buckle My Shoe* and ask the learners to point to the number words as you say them.

Check understanding of the vocabulary: *buckle* and other words you think may be unfamiliar to learners.

Point out that each line of the rhyme features an imperative verb: *buckle, knock, pick up, lay* – except the last! Tell or remind learners that these verbs tell us what to do.

Ask learners what rhymes with *ten* in the rhyme. (*hen*)

Read the rhyme again and invite learners to join in and add actions. For each line you might model an action for the learners to follow.

Now read the second rhyme *Oliver Twist* or again use the audio (the second part of Audio track 14).

Check understanding of the vocabulary; it does not matter if the learners do not know who Oliver Twist or Kevon are – these are just names.

Point out again that each line of the rhyme features an imperative verb: *touch, do, build, go, bang, walk, start.*

Ask them what rhymes with *six* in the rhyme. (*bricks*)

Show learners the word *number* – sound it out to read it. Clap twice to hear the two syllables.

Read the rhyme again and invite learners to join in and add actions. For each line you might model an action for the learners to follow.

> **Differentiation ideas:** Support learners who struggle with coordination and multi-tasking. Let them practise and enjoy the activity.

Challenge learners to say and perform one of the rhymes with their own actions. Invite pairs to perform for the class.

2   Say the rhymes in pairs (20–30 minutes)

Learning intention: to experiment with paired reading aloud and performing

Resources: Learner's Book, Session 3.2, Activity 2; *One, Two, Buckle My Shoe* and *Oliver Twist* (Learner's Book, Session 3.2); Tracks 15 and 16

Description: First, read the instructions in the Learner's Book together.

Ask learners to work in pairs to practise saying and performing one of the rhymes with actions.

Give the pairs time to prepare and perform if possible.

Encourage peer feedback on each performance, modelling how to offer praise and constructive criticism:

- *I thought it was brilliant the way x …*

- *I think x should try to speak a little louder …*

> **Differentiation ideas:** Support learners by arranging different pairings. As their teacher, you will know whether to pair two similar or two dissimilar learners to enable them both to achieve.

Challenge learners to change some of the rhymes if they can, e.g. *Number one – it's such fun!*

3 Find rhyming pairs (20 minutes)

Learning intention: to identify and record rhyming words

Resources: Learner's Book, Session 3.2, Activity 3; Workbook, Session 3.2; Phonics Workbook B; Worksheet 3.2

Description: Share the chart in the Learner's Book with learners to draw their attention to the different words used, as well as the different spellings of words that rhyme.

Find the words orally before asking learners to complete the activity in their notebooks. Use Worksheet 3.2 Number rhyming chart here for learners who will benefit from the structure of the chart.

You can use the Workbook Session 3.2 activities for this as well as Phonics Workbook B activities focusing on different spellings of the same sound (pages 10–19 and 22–25).

> **Differentiation ideas:** Support learners by working in a group to complete the chart together.

Challenge learners to add another word with a different spelling for each number.

Answers:

1	One	–	tongue
2	Two	shoe	shoe
3	Three	–	knee
4	Four	door	floor
5	Five	–	dive
6	Six	sticks	bricks
7	Seven	–	Kevon
8	Eight	straight	gate
9	Nine	–	line
10	Ten	hen	again

Plenary idea

Odd one out (5 minutes)

Resources: lists of three words: two that rhyme, one that does not

Description: Give groups sets of three words and ask them to identify the odd one out (that does not rhyme).

You can vary the difficulty of the words according to reading ability of the group and the challenge you wish to set:

- CVCs: ten, hen, box, fun, sun
- Blends: frogs, bricks, sticks
- Split digraphs: nine, fine, fin
- Tricky words: eight, wait, pin

When they are correct and can explain the odd one out, they may leave the room.

> **Assessment ideas:** Note any learners who cope well with each of the Consonant Vowel Consonant (CVC) words, blended words with adjacent consonants, split digraph words and tricky words. Only CVCs and digraphs may have been explicitly taught.

CROSS-CURRICULAR LINKS

Maths: Explore number words in other languages and create multi-lingual washing lines or class charts; count in twos or threes up to 20 or more; write numerals correctly.

Homework ideas

Learners complete the Workbook Session 3.2 activities if not completed in class.

They can further practise writing the numbers and number words correctly using Language worksheet 3A.

Answers for Workbook

1   Learners' formation of numerals

2   Learners' correct spelling and handwriting of number words

3   and **4** Learners' own rhyme chains – accept nonsense words and spelling attempts

3.3 Nonsense rhymes

LEARNING PLAN

Learning objectives		Learning intentions	Success criteria
Main focus	**Also covered**	• To answer questions about words and meanings.	• Learners can answer questions about words and meanings.
1Rv.05, 1Ri.12, 1SLg.01, 1SLp.02	1Rv.01, 1Rv.02, 1Rg.03, 1Rg.06, 1Rs.01, 1Ri.01, 1Ri.14, 1Ra.01, 1Ra.02, 1Ra.06, 1Ww.03, 1Wg.01, 1Wg.03, 1Wg.04, 1SLs.02, 1SLp.04	• To talk about the order of a rhyme that tells a story. • To say and act a rhyme in a group.	• Learners can talk about the order of a rhyme that tells a story. • Learners can say and act a rhyme in a group.

LANGUAGE SUPPORT

Learners may find the notion of 'nonsense' quite tricky as they battle to make sense of English. We need to ensure that they enjoy and learn from the rhyme in this session. Naming the characters and matching their speech will support learners' understanding, as will acting the rhyme. Providing other examples of simple nonsense rhymes will also help.

Common misconception

Misconception	How to identify	How to overcome
We can only use the verb *to say* when finishing direct speech.	Ask learners to read the sentence: *'Fire! Fire!'* <u>says</u> Obadiah. Ask: *Could we change the word 'says'? What verb could we use instead of* say.	Make a class working wall or hanging display of words to replace *says/said*. When writing, encourage learners to use the wall or display as a word bank.

Starter idea

Find the odd one out (5–10 minutes)

Resources: Learner's Book, Session 3.3: Getting started; Dr. Seuss books (if available) or other available nonsense rhymes

Description: Ask learners to look at the pictures in Getting started. Tell them that there is an 'odd one out'.

Give them two minutes to work in pairs to try to work out which one is the odd one out and why.

Take their ideas – no idea is a bad idea! Try to elicit that the answer is the doctor and boy, and why.

Answers:

It is the picture of the doctor and boy because the others are silly, funny or nonsensical / not real, but the doctor and boy are real.

Main teaching ideas

 1 Listen to and read *Fire!* (10–15 minutes)

Learning intention: to listen to and talk about a nonsense rhyme

Resources: *Fire!* (Learner's Book, Session 3.3, Activity 1); Track 17

Description: Tell learners they are going to hear a nonsense rhyme. Ask them to listen out for what they think is odd or funny.

Take their ideas which might include:

- It has some people with funny names in it.
- They are in a panic because they are trying to put out a fire.
- They are saying silly things – that rhyme.

Ask learners to then to read the rhyme in pairs.

Move around the classroom to find out how learners are reading. Are they pointing to each word as they say it? Are they supporting each other? Are they using phonics for unknown words? Are they using rhyme to prompt them? Offer support or modelling where necessary.

To finish Activity 1, draw learners' attention to the title of the rhyme and the way it is written. Talk about the exclamation mark in *Fire!* and why it is there. They may know or guess that the exclamation mark is used here to show that something is important or urgent.

> **Differentiation ideas:** Support learners by showing the text on a shared screen and modelling how you can track the words with a finger to follow each line of the rhyme. Work with a group who may need support to read the poem after listening.

Challenge learners by asking them to read and pronounce just the unusual names of the characters in the rhyme.

2 Talk about the order of the rhyme (10 minutes)

Learning intention: to match pictures to each line of a rhyme to show its order

Resources: Learner's Book, Session 3.3, Activity 2; Worksheet 3.3

Description: Ask learners to listen to or read the rhyme again.

Ask them to talk about joining the character pictures to each line in the rhyme: *Who said each line and in what order?* They can of course refer to the text to check if they need to.

If you want learners to record the correct sequence, use Worksheet 3.3 Picture sequencing for *Fire!* now so that they can cut and stick the text into the right order.

Ask learners to talk about the idea in the rhyme. Say: *If you do not have a bucket to put water in, can you use your shoe, or is it nonsense?*

> **Differentiation ideas:** Use Worksheet 3.3 Picture sequencing for *Fire!* to support learners who will benefit from physically recreating the sequence of the story in the rhyme.

Challenge learners to find the rhyming pairs in the rhyme. (*fire/Obadiah, where/pear, out/Pout, bucket/MacTucket, shoe/Lou*)

Answers:

a Mr Powt
b Betsy Lou
c Doctor Fox
d Mrs Pear
e Obadiah
f Miss MacTucket

3 Answer questions (20–30 minutes)

Learning intention: to answer and ask questions about a rhyme to show understanding

Resources: Learner's Book, Session 3.3, Activity 3; Workbook, Session 3.3

Description: Ask learners to look at the questions in the Learner's Book.

First, model how to write the answer to each question and then ask the learners to write the answers in their notebooks.

Allow some learners to work alone or in pairs.

Some learners may be able to write questions for partners, or the class, to answer.

As you move around the classroom, check that learners are holding their pencils correctly and forming their letters and numbers correctly, too.

If using the Workbook in class, use it now as a summary for the activities in this session.

> **Differentiation ideas:** Support learners by working with them in a group and/or by providing answers that they could match to the questions.

Challenge learners to write one sentence with a full stop, one with a question mark and one with an exclamation mark. Check correct punctuation.

Answers:

a   Obadiah, Mrs Pear, Doctor Fox, Mr Powt, Miss MacTucket, Betsy Lou

b   Betsy Lou (because she is holding a shoe)

c   Mrs Pear says, 'Where? Where?'

d   no

e   There are 20 capital letters.

4   Act the rhyme (20–30 minutes)

Learning intention: to work in a group to retell the rhyme in character, with actions

Resources: Learner's Book, Session 3.3, Activity 4; empty speech bubbles to write in, or prompt cards; Track 17

Description: Tell learners to listen to the rhyme again. Play the audio or read the rhyme with a different voice for each character. Exaggerate the sense of emergency and shouting!

Split the class into groups (ideally of seven – one for each character, plus a narrator). Ask each group to practise saying and acting the rhyme. Ask them to think about a voice and action for each character.

Some ideas may include:

* Line 1 – arms up in the air in panic
* Line 2 – hand to brow as if looking
* Line 3 – pointing
* Line 4 – flapping hands
* Line 5 – hands out, palms up and shrugging shoulders
* Line 6 – taking a shoe off and offering it!

Ask learners to think about how they can make their performances funny.

Give them time to prepare before bringing them back together to perform for each other.

Use this as an opportunity to encourage peer assessment and to offer positive comments and suggestions for things to improve.

> **Differentiation ideas:** Support learners by setting up groups comprising some learners who would like to be challenged and some learners who would benefit from additional support.

Challenge learners to improvise and use props.

Answers:
Learners' own performances

Plenary idea

Speaking nonsense (5–10 minutes)

Resources: a bank of nonsense sentences and true sentences; a bag or box

Description: An extension of the Learner's Book Getting started activity.

Ask learners to say if a sentence is nonsense or if it makes sense.

Learners pick a sentence out of a bag or box. They read their sentence and ask another learner to say *Nonsense* or *It makes sense.*

Once they have answered correctly, those two learners can leave the classroom.

Keep playing until everyone has read a sentence or responded.

Homework ideas

Learners complete the Workbook Session 3.3 activities if not completed in class.

They research other nonsense rhymes.

Answers for Workbook

1   fire/Obadiah, where/pear, out/shout, bucket/MacTucket, shoe/Lou

2   **a–f** speech as in the rhyme with correct punctuation

3   a   N: The sea is in the sky; Trees grow underground; All cows are round; Fish eat grass.

     b   Learners' own sentences

3.4 Exploring rhythm

LEARNING PLAN			

Learning objectives		Learning intentions	Success criteria
Main focus	**Also covered**	• To listen to and read a poem about rhythm.	• Learners can listen to and read a poem about rhythm.
1Rv.02, 1Rs.01, 1Ra.02, 1Wg.04, 1Wc.03	1Rv.01, 1Rv.05, 1Rg.02, 1Rg.03, 1Rs.02, 1Ri.01, 1Ri.06, 1Ri.14, 1Ra.01, 1Ra.04, 1Ww.02, 1Ww.05, 1Wv.01, 1Wv.03, 1Wg.01, 1Wp.02, 1Wp.05, 1SLm.03, 1SLm.04, 1SLm.05, 1SLs.01, 1SLp.01, 1SLp.02, 1SLp.04, 1SLr.02	• To use pictures to help understand words we do not know. • To write sentences to retell the poem.	• Learners can use pictures to help understand words they do not know. • Learners can write sentences to retell the poem.

LANGUAGE SUPPORT

Check learners know the parts of the body in the rhyme. Check they understand and can use the words in the rhyme that relate to actions, too. It may be necessary to pre-teach these in a small group session. For example:

We think with our mind – think; *We hear with our ears* – beat; *We smell with our nose*– sniff; *We feel with our knees* – knock; *We walk with our feet* – stomp; *We tap with our toes* – tip tap; *We dance with a drum* – beat bop.

Common misconception

Misconception	How to identify	How to overcome
We only use capital letters for names.	Ask learners to read / look at the poem *I Got the Rhythm.* Ask: *How many capital letters can you find?* *How many are for names?* (none)	Discuss with learners how the capital letters are used for emphasis. The capital letters show us the important words in the poem. They are the sound and action words. You may look at other story or rhyme books that use capital letters for different purposes

Starter idea

Me Then You (10–15 minutes)

Resources: Learner's Book, Session 3.4: Getting started

Description: Ask learners to watch and listen to a rhythm you clap or tap. Ask them to copy.

Then extend the activity to moving in a rhythm, e.g. *hop then jump, jump;* or perform a kind of 'heads, shoulders, knees and toes' rhythm.

Try singing a rhythm, e.g. *Boom-cha-cha – boom.*

Try blinking a rhythm!

Make sure learners realise that all of this has happened with very few spoken words.

Ask them to talk about other types of rhythm using the pictures in Getting started as starting ideas.

Main teaching ideas

1 Listen to *I Got the Rhythm* (15–30 minutes)

Learning intention: to listen to a poem and clap the rhythm

Resources: *I Got the Rhythm* (Learner's Book, Session 3.4, Activity 1); Track 18; instruments in a music corner

Description: Tell learners that this next text is a poem that is *about* rhythm and it *has* rhythm!

Ask them to first listen to the poem (with the Learner's Book closed). Play the second part of the audio without the pauses between lines. Ask them to listen and enjoy the rhythm of the poem. Note any learners who feel the need to respond to the rhythm as this tells you that they clearly can recognise rhythm.

Talk about the rhythm. Ask: *What did you hear? What did you notice?* Share ideas and record these if helpful for modelling, list making or mind mapping. They may notice some or all of these things:

- Each first line has a repeated sentence structure.
- Each second line repeats a word.
- At the end there are lots of verbs in pairs – joined by *and.*

Ask them to listen again. This time, play the first part of the audio where there will be pauses so learners can clap the rhythm. Repeat several times

if necessary or for fun. You may, for example, split the class into groups, asking different groups to clap different parts of the poem.

Finally, experiment, if you have the space, with *I say, you say and do.* Invite learners to listen as you read each paired line and then repeat it back and move appropriately, either to the rhythm or with actions to match. Encourage creative physical responses.

> **Differentiation ideas:** Support learners by varying the pace of your reading, e.g. allowing more time for their responses.

Challenge learners to create their own rhythms by providing a music corner for exploration.

Answers:
Learners' own responses

2 Read *I Got the Rhythm* (20–30 minutes;)

Learning intention: to read a rhythmic text in pairs, work out meanings and suggest actions to support the text

Resources: Learner's Book, Session 3.4, Activity 2; *I Got the Rhythm* (Learner's Book, Session 3.4); Track 18

Description: Ask learners to look at the pictures. Ask them to think about how the pictures help with their reading.

Read the poem together. Model reading aloud. Replay the audio or use an online version if you prefer.

Ask learners to follow the poem in the Learner's Book as you read it aloud. Then ask them to read it in pairs.

Talk about what they notice in the poem's structure.

Ask them about the use of capital letters. Ask: *Why has the author done this?* (The action and sound words are in capitals to help stress the rhythm.)

As they read the text, listen to hear how well they are doing. What strategies are they using? How are they reading the words in capitals? Support them as necessary. You may stop the class and share something positive if you see or hear it.

Finally, ask learners if they can read *and* make up actions to accompany their reading. Give them time to practise this and invite some performances of the different rhythms as you re-read the poem with them as a class.

> **Differentiation ideas:** Support learners by asking them to work in pairs where one is a stronger reader than the other. Focus on listening to those pairs who may find the independent reading more difficult.

Challenge learners to record their readings if equipment is easily available. Play it back to the class. Ask: *Have they read with rhythm?*

3 Retell the story in pictures and words (30–40 minutes)

Learning intention: to match pictures to sentences to retell a poem

Resources: Learner's Book, Session 3.4, Activity 3; Workbook, Session 3.4; Worksheet 3.4

Description: Begin the session with a quick recap of parts of the body vocabulary. Say: *Point to your … (mind, ears, eyes,* etc.). This is revisited again in the plenary session.

Talk through the chart in the Learner's Book. Ask learners to match the pictures to the correct sentences and then to suggest the actions or sound words (those in capital letters in the story). Invite them to come up with their own words here if they wish.

Ask learners to complete the chart in their notebooks or use Worksheet 3.4 *I Got the Rhythm* retelling chart. The worksheet invites them to draw their own pictures to match the sentences.

As you pass through the class, check on handwriting and punctuation of each sentence. Check on correct formation of capital letters, too.

> **Differentiation ideas:** Support learners by working through the activity using Worksheet 3.4. If necessary, split the sentences and ask different learners to complete different ones. Then share and come together for a small group retelling using the chart.

Challenge learners to change the verb in each of the sentences, e.g. *I listened to the rhythm with my ears …*

Answers:

a Learners' responses

b Learners' own sentences

c Learners' drawings

d Learners action or sound words in capitals, following the pattern of the poem.

Plenary idea

Simon says … feel the rhythm! (5–10 minutes)

Description: Play Simon Says, but rename the game for the poem *I Got the Rhythm*. We do not know the girl's name, but ask learners to name her.

If you say *X says … show me your …*, then learners should place their hand on that part of their body. If you do not say *X says …* first, then learners should do nothing. If they do, they are out of the game.

Play the game for ears, eyes, nose, mouth, hands, fingers, knees, feet and toes.

Extend the game to use the poem's verbs: *blink your eyes, sniff your nose, snap or click your fingers.*

Extend the body vocabulary if you wish: *shoulders, back, elbows.*

CROSS-CURRICULAR LINKS

Music: Set up a music corner for learners to explore rhythm. Listen to online drum rhythms or similar. Have a class disco and dance to the rhythm!

Homework ideas

Learners complete the Workbook Session activities if not completed in class.

They find a piece of music they enjoy at home and which has a rhythm, and find this online to share at school if possible.

Answers for Workbook

1 a thought; b heard; c smelled; d tapped

2 Learners' own responses, but may include:

a CLICK, BEND; b JUMP, STEP; c WRIGGLE, WRIGGLE; d HEY YEH! HEY YEH!

3 Learners' own responses, e.g. I felt the rhythm with my heart. PUMP PUMP.

3.5 Planning and writing a poem

LEARNING PLAN

Learning objectives		Learning intentions	Success criteria
Main focus	**Also covered**	• To talk about colour.	• Learners can talk about colour.
1Rv.01, 1Ri.09, 1Wv.03, 1Wc.01, 1SLp.02	1Rv.02, 1Rv.05, 1Rg.03, 1Rg.07, 1Rs.02, 1Ri.01, 1Ri.05, 1Ri.12, 1Ri.13, 1Ri.14, 1Ra.01, 1Ra.02, 1Ra.04, 1Wv.01, 1Wc.02, 1SLm.03, 1SLs.02, 1SLg.02, 1SLg.03, 1SLp.01, 1SLp.05	• To talk about and read a poem that has rhythm and rhyme. • To plan and write a new poem using rhythm and rhyme.	• Learners can talk about and read a poem that has rhythm and rhyme. • Learners can plan and write a new poem using rhythm and rhyme.

LANGUAGE SUPPORT

Learners may find a class colour chart useful, especially if used alongside Language worksheet 3B Colour Splat Snap!, which challenges learners to use more than the simplest of colour words.

Sing songs about colours (search online for *I Can Sing a Rainbow*).

Encourage learners to paint with and mix colours so the language is reinforced in real situations.

Worksheet 3.5 *Red is a Dragon* writing framework may be particularly useful as a structure for some learners.

Common misconception

Misconception	How to identify	How to overcome
Red is one colour and one word.	With learners, make a collection of 'red' things from around the classroom. Ask: *If they are all red, why do they look different? Do we know different words that mean 'red' or 'a type of red'?*	Encourage learners to repeat with other colours; to paint with and mix colours of varying shades; to use torn pieces of magazine pages to create 'shades of …' pictures. Make the Colour Splat Snap game using Language worksheet 3B Colour Splat Snap!.

Starter idea

Colour words (25–30 minutes)

Resources: Learner's Book, Session 3.5: Getting started; sets of things in different colours; a class colour chart

Description: Share a collection of objects that are shades of one colour (see Common misconception). Ask learners what colour the things are.

Ask: *How many different colour words do you already know?* Make a class list together.

Ask learners to work with a partner for one minute. Ask: *How many words for blue* (or another colour) *do you know?*

Encourage the use of phrases such as: *It's a bit lighter than /darker than / it looks more* (green).

Ask different learners to find things in the classroom: *Can you find me something that is light blue / a lighter blue than this,* etc.

Look at the colour chart in Getting started. Ask learners to work again with their partner to talk about which colours are their favourites and why.

Invite the pairs to share their partner's ideas so they are reporting on each other's views. Check everyone is listening well and respecting ideas and opinions, and make it clear that you are looking for evidence of this.

Use Language worksheet 3B Colour Splat Snap! to further explore the language of colour.

Main teaching ideas

1 Listen to and read *Red is a Dragon* (15–20 minutes)

Learning intention: to listen to and read a poem about colour; to listen for rhythm and rhyme

Resources: *Red is a Dragon* (Learner's Book, Session 3.5, Activity 1); Track 19

Description: Tell learners that this next poem, like many, has rhythm and rhyme.

Read it aloud or play the audio.

Before a second listening, split the class into three:

• Ask Group 1 to listen out for an example of *rhyme*.

• Ask Group 2 to listen out for an example of *rhythm*.

• Ask Group 3 to listen out for any words they do not understand.

After playing the audio again, share ideas and discuss learners' responses. Include the words *jade* and *firecrackers* in the discussion.

Ask learners to read the poem aloud with you before asking them to read it in pairs or small groups.

> **Differentiation ideas:** Work with any learners to support them in their paired reading or ask some learners to read in groups.

Challenge learners to explain what is meant by *The world is a rainbow for us to explore.*

2 Answer questions (20 minutes)

Learning intention: to answer questions about a poem

Resources: Learner's Book, Session 3.5, Activity 2; Workbook, Session 3.5

Description: You may also choose to use the Workbook at this point.

Talk about the questions in the Learner's Book together.

Check learners know the word *verse*.

Ask learners to read and answer the questions in their notebooks.

> **Differentiation ideas:** Support a group of learners to write their answers in their notebooks. Alternatively, ask them to answer fewer, selected questions.

Challenge learners to write their own questions about the poem for a partner to answer.

Answers:
a six verses; **b** Answers may include: each verse begins with a colour word followed by *is/are*; some verses repeat the colour words, others do not; each verse has rhyming words; each verse has four lines. **c** learners clap; different; **d** drum/come, sand/hand, boots/toots, jade/made, wish/fish, explore/door; **e** Learners' own ideas

3 Complete a planning chart (30–40 minutes)

Learning intention: to plan a new poem based on the structure of *Red is a Dragon*

Resources: Learner's Book, Session 3.5, Activity 3; Differentiated worksheets 3A–C; class word banks or posters of colour words (if available)

Description: Tell learners they are now going to plan their own version of *Red is a Dragon*. They will need to think of new ideas and words to use.

Show them the chart in the Learner's Book, or on the selected worksheet if using the Differentiated worksheet pack.

Remind learners that there are no right or wrong answers here. It is about their own ideas.

Encourage them to use their phonics skills to write their ideas. They may also use class word banks or posters of colour words, if available.

Ask learners to think about a title for their poem, too.

Give them time to work on their ideas. Circulate among them, and support and challenge where necessary.

> **Differentiation ideas:** Support learners to generate ideas by working with a group if necessary. It may be helpful to use banks of pictures or to search online for inspiration if learners need visual support.

Challenge learners to select the right worksheet if using the Differentiated worksheet pack.

Answers:
Learners' own responses

4 Write the colour poem (30–40 minutes)

Learning intention: to use a plan to write a new version of a poem

Resources: Learner's Book, Session 3.5, Activity 4; completed Differentiated worksheets 3A–C; Worksheet 3.5

Description: Using their plans, ask learners to write their own version of the poem.

Remind learners to use the Writing tip about using *is* and *are* correctly.

As you walk around the class, talk to different learners about their ideas and their writing, providing support where necessary.

The room should be industrious and fairly quiet. Any talk should be about the writing, but do encourage learners to help each other and to enjoy their writing.

> **Differentiation ideas:** Support learners by providing Worksheet 3.5 *Red is a Dragon* writing framework, which is a writing template. Some learners may benefit from working in pairs on larger-scale paper before transferring their ideas to Worksheet 3.5.

Challenge learners to work without the writing framework and to think about the layout of their poem and any design features they would like to include, such as illustrations or photos. Ask: *What colours will you use for your text?*

Answers:
Learners' own responses

Plenary idea

Reading aloud (5–10 minutes)

Resources: learners' own writing

Description: Ask learners to share some of their poems – even if not yet finished.

Ask learners to share a problem they have had with their own poem. Ask: *Can anyone help?*

Invite learners to talk about how their planning helped them in their writing. Did they use other resources in the classroom, e.g. posters or working wall displays?

Ask learners if the planning chart made it easier to write their poem.

Art: Mix colour shades; tear and stick torn pieces from magazines to create collage-effect colour spectra; ask learners to create long, narrow strips of one colour. How subtle can they make the changes between one shade and the next? Use language such as: *a little bit lighter, a little bit darker, a bit more* (green), etc.

Science: Encourage learners to ask questions about when and how rainbows occur.

Homework ideas

Learners complete the Workbook Session 3.5 activities if not completed in class.

They learn and sing a colour song at home – and then sing it in class.

Answers for Workbook

1   Learners' own patterns
2   **a** dragon; **b** lemon; **c** starfish; **d** leaf; **e** pool
3   **a** are; **b** are; **c** is; **d** is; **e** are; (learners' own drawings)

3.6 Look back

LEARNING PLAN

Learning objectives		Learning intentions	Success criteria
Main focus	**Also covered**	• To check their writing.	• Learners can check their writing.
1Rv.05, 1Ra.04, 1SLm.03, 1SLm.05, 1SLr.01	1Rs.02, 1Ww.03, 1Wg.01, 1Wg.06, 1Wp.01, 1Wp.02, 1SLm.04	• To share their writing and talk about it. • To think about their learning from the unit.	• Learners can share their writing and talk about it. • Learners can think about their learning from the unit.

LANGUAGE SUPPORT

Use visuals in the Learner's Book or any classroom displays or posters to support learners in the review process of this unit.

Use the *Look what I can do!* statements as a prompt for talking about self-assessment.

Starter idea

What to check (5 minutes)

Resources: Learner's Book, Session 3.6: Getting started

Description: Ask learners what they think they should check when re-reading their poems. What are they checking? Take their ideas and discuss.

Use the Getting started activity as a prompt to ensure that all aspects of writing have been discussed: punctuation, layout, pictures, spelling, ideas and handwriting.

You may dig deeper on any one of these, e.g. for handwriting, ask: *Are you checking your pencil grip, letter formation, spacing, neatness, flow?*

Ask: *Is there anything else that you like to check?*

Main teaching ideas

1   **Look at your ideas (15 minutes)**

Learning intention: to think about and check own writing, share writing and ask for feedback

Resources: Learner's Book, Session 3.6, Activity 1; learners' writing from Session 3.5, Activity 4; coloured pens or sticky notes (optional)

Description: First, ask readers to check their own poems from Session 3.5 Activity 4. They may use a tick list of things from the Session 3.6 Getting started to help them.

It is important to begin to establish the processes of assessment for learning from an early stage. You may prefer in this first term to select a few pieces of work to model the process for learners before asking them to do this more independently.

Ask learners to make any changes, but this should not involve any long rewrites. Devise a class system for edits, e.g. different-coloured pens or sticky notes. Alternatively, agree to update just one sentence in the piece and rewrite that.

Learners can share their poems with a partner.

⟩ **Differentiation ideas:** Support some learners in identifying where their writing needs to be improved/ corrected. Try to identify one thing that learners might focus on for improvement. Help them to find the issue and to make the change.

Challenge learners to work to read their poems to the class and to share feedback ideas.

Answers:
Learners' own responses

2 **Look back at the rhymes and poems shared in Unit 3 (10 minutes)**

Learning intention: to look back and remember the rhymes and poems in Unit 3; to talk about poems that have rhythm and rhyme

Resources: Learner's Book, Session 3.6, Activity 2; Tracks 13–19; Workbook, Session 3.6

Description: Ask learners to identify all the rhymes and poems they have read in the unit, using the pictures in the Learner's Book (Unit 3) to help. You could play all the audio tracks for a celebration of rhymes and poems.

Encourage learners to speak clearly, and ask if they can remember what the focus of each rhyme or poem was. Ask: *What was it about? What did we learn?*

You can use the Workbook Session 3.6 activities now to revisit rhyme, rhythm and handwriting skills.

⟩ **Differentiation ideas:** Support learners by working with them in a small group to find the poems in the book or singing/saying them together.

Challenge learners to list the poems in their notebooks.

Answers:
Learners' own responses

3 **Express preferences about the texts (10 minutes)**

Learning intention: to think and talk about personal preferences

Resources: Learner's Book, Session 3.6, Activity 3

Description: Together, talk about which poems learners liked best and why.

Encourage learners to express their own likes and dislikes in relation to the poems, but ask for explanations.

Encourage others to listen and respect opinions. Do they agree or disagree?

Ask learners to draw or write their answers.

⟩ **Differentiation ideas:** Support learners by working with them in a small group or asking them to work in pairs to talk about preferences. Alternatively, discuss preferences as a class and take some votes on which rhyme or poem they liked best and why.

Challenge learners to write their favourite rhyme or poem in their best handwriting.

Answers:
Learners' own responses

Plenary idea

Check your learning (10–15 minutes)

Description: Ask each learner to think about their learning from this unit.

Ask learners to talk with a partner about three things they liked about this unit.

Ask: *What did you enjoy least? Why?*

Ask: *What would you still like to find out about poems with rhythm and rhyme?*

Homework ideas

Learners complete the Workbook Session 3.6 activities if not completed in class.

Answers for Workbook

1 **a** tea; **b** the; **c** bite; **d** look
2 **a** rainbow/nonsense; **b** ring a ding / sing a song; **c** caterpillar/butterfly; **d** bing bang / boom box
3 Learners' own handwriting

CHECK YOUR PROGRESS

1 May include *dish/fish, hay/pay, bear/fair*
2 May include *box/fox*
3 Learners clap each syllable correctly
4 two, eight

PROJECT GUIDANCE

These projects build on the reading, writing and understanding learners have developed throughout the unit. Since they have just read several rhymes that explore both rhythm and rhyme, the project options here extend the topic and provide opportunities for learners to choose to work in a group, as a pair or alone. It may be that you prefer to allocate a project to the class.

Group project: Learners should make a class poetry book to include more finger rhymes, number rhymes, nonsense rhymes, rhythm poems and poems about colour.

Pair project: Learners should make a number or colour chart that includes words with rhythm or rhyme, e.g. Pink makes us think; Brown bear, brown bear, what do you see? Number Nine, Number Nine what follows you?

Solo project: Learners make a small drum to practise banging rhythms. Encourage them to think creatively about what they could use for this.

For more guidance on setting up and assessing projects, see Project guidance at the end of Unit 1.

>4 Joining-in stories

Unit plan

Session	Approximate number of learning hours	Outline of learning content	Resources
4.1 Off to tell the King	1	Explore characters in traditional tales and the phrases they say. Listen to and read a story, and join in with the repeated refrain.	Learner's Book Session 4.1 Workbook Session 4.1
4.2 Exploring language	1.5	Answer questions about a story. Write sentences using capital letters and full stops. Use *and* to join sentences together.	Learner's Book Session 4.2 Workbook Session 4.2
4.3 Retelling and acting	1.5	Retell a story using pictures and written sentences. Act a story with masks.	Learner's Book Session 4.3 Workbook Session 4.3 ⬇ Worksheet 4.1 ⬇ Worksheet 4.2 Phonics Workbooks A and B
4.4 Run, run as fast as you can	1	Listen to and join in with a story. Listen for and record a story sequence. Write the missing words for a repeated refrain.	Learner's Book Session 4.4 Workbook Session 4.4 Phonics Workbook A
4.5 The pancake rolled on	1.5	Listen to and read Part 1 of a story. Comment on characters and ideas. Link to own experiences. Practise using articles from a story text.	Learner's Book Session 4.5 Workbook Session 4.5 ⬇ Worksheet 4.3

Session	Approximate number of learning hours	Outline of learning content	Resources
4.6 Story endings	1.5	Talk about story endings. Read Part 2 of a story with a surprise ending. Write a story ending.	Learner's Book Session 4.6 Workbook Session 4.6
4.7 Comparing stories	2	Talk about things that are the same and different. Fill in a chart to compare two stories. Talk and write about story choices and likes and dislikes.	Learner's Book Session 4.7 Workbook Session 4.7 ⬇ Worksheet 4.4
4.8 Along skipped a boy with his whirly-twirly toy	1	Listen to, read and talk about Part 1 of a story. Explore language. Answer comprehension questions.	Learner's Book Session 4.8 Workbook Session 4.8 ⬇ Language worksheet 4A
4.9 Out dashed the cat	1.5	Listen, read and talk about Part 2 of a story. Explore verbs ending –ed. Identify true or false statements to show understanding.	Learner's Book Session 4.9 Workbook Session 4.9
4.10 Joining in	1.5	Explore the rhythm of words by clapping syllables. Read a whole story and join in with repeated refrains. Act a story.	Learner's Book Session 4.10 Workbook Session 4.10
4.11 Planning and writing	2	Explore the features of a text. Talk about writing choices. Plan and write a version of a story.	Learner's Book Session 4.11 Workbook Session 4.11 ⬇ Worksheet 4.5 ⬇ Differentiated worksheets 4A–C Phonics Workbooks A and B

Session	Approximate number of learning hours	Outline of learning content	Resources
4.12 Look back	1	Check writing. Talk about the stories in the unit. Talk about preferences.	Learner's Book Session 4.12 Workbook Session 4.12 ⤓ Language worksheet 4B
Cross-unit resources			
Learner's Book Check your progress Learner's Book Projects			

BACKGROUND KNOWLEDGE

Before you begin to teach this unit, you may find it helpful to familiarise yourself with:

Ways to:

- talk about traditional stories including refrains, which are words or phrases in a story that are repeated, e.g. *run, run as fast as you can*
- understand repetition and joining in
- use pictures to support understanding and unfamiliar words

- phonics – letter-to-sound knowledge; adjacent consonants; blending and segmenting words and understanding syllables, e.g. *eu–cal–yp–tus*
- using repetition to support fluency and encourage reading for pleasure
- sequencing
- traditional tales around the world and different versions of them. Note that modern TV and screen adaptions can differ from the original story, e.g. *Mulan*.

TEACHING SKILLS FOCUS

Differentiation

Differentiation is a term to describe adapting your teaching for each learner. Strategies for differentiation vary. Some are fairly simple, e.g. pairing or grouping learners to support each other; others involve more work, e.g. preparing work with different levels of challenge and support.

Which of these types of differentiation have you **not** yet tried?

- By task: give learners different tasks according to ability, but be careful not to limit learning.
- By resource: the same as differentiation by output – vary what you ask learners to produce.
- By grouping: group learners by similar or mixed ability.
- By pace: it is important to vary the pace because sometimes we need in-depth slower

learning to think about something and at other times we need to work more quickly.

- By support: support learners through dialogue and/or scaffolding as necessary. Questioning can help to challenge or guide them, too.
- By questioning: use the full range of question words to promote literal and inferential thinking.

Key features of good differentiation also include marking, feedback and assessment.

At the end of this unit, consider how well you were able to use some of these ideas to offer more effective differentiation in your lessons. What would you need to research further to better implement some of these strategies?

Cambridge Reading Adventures

Learners may enjoy these other fiction titles from Cambridge Reading Adventures that follow the unit theme:

- *Little Tiger Hu Can Roar!* by Gabby Pritchard (Yellow Band)
- *The Lion and the Mouse* by Vivian French (Green Band)
- *The Best Little Bullfrog in the Forest* by Ian Whybrow (Orange Band)

4.1 Off to tell the King

LEARNING PLAN

Learning objectives		Learning intentions	Success criteria
Main focus	**Also covered**	• To talk about story characters and what they say.	• Learners can talk about story characters and what they say.
1Rv.01, 1Ra.02 1Ra.03, 1SLp.01	1RW.05, 1Rv.02, 1Rv.03, 1Rg.02, 1Rg.03, 1Ri.01, 1Wv.01, 1Wv.02, 1Wg.01, 1SLm.01, 1SLm.02, 1SLs.02, 1SLg.03, 1SLg.04, 1SLp.03, 1SLr.01, 1SLr.02	• To listen to a story and point to the matching pictures.	• Learners can listen to a story and point to the matching pictures.
		• To read and join in with parts of a story.	• Learners can read and join in with parts of a story.

Common misconception

Misconception	How to identify	How to overcome
We do not need to notice full stops when reading.	Ask learners to read Chicken Licken's words silently and then out loud. Ask: *What do you notice?*	Remind learners they need to take a tiny pause at the full stop when reading aloud. Provide plenty of read-aloud modelling as well as opportunities for learners to practise. Remind learners to notice the full stops as they read.

Starter idea

Characters in joining-in stories and what they say (10–15 minutes)

Resources: Learner's Book, Session 4.1: Getting started; traditional tale story books

Description: Ask learners to talk about traditional tales or stories and the characters they know.

Explain that this unit is all about traditional tales and stories where we can join in. Ask learners to share their initial ideas and experiences of these kind of stories.

Ask learners to work in pairs to explore and talk about the pictures in Getting started. Then ask them to say what they recognised and were able to name, and whether they could read the speech bubbles.

Ask: *Are there other characters or refrains* (repeated words or phrases) *you would add? Are there some stories or characters that are not familiar to you?* Begin a working-wall class display of favourite traditional tale characters and refrains. Continue to add to it throughout the unit. Allow learners to make it their own.

Main teaching ideas

1 *The Story of Chicken Licken* characters (15–20 minutes)

Learning intention: to talk about story characters; to use pictures in texts to support understanding

Resources: Learner's Book, Session 4.1, Activity 1; pictures of different kinds of birds

Description: Tell learners that the first story in this unit is about a chicken and his bird friends.

Ask them what bird names they know. If necessary, explain that we do not call all birds 'birds'; they have special names that we can learn. Explore the vocabulary options.

Ask learners to talk about any special birds associated with your country, e.g. peacocks in India, cranes in China, Ibis in Cambodia.

Show learners the pictures of the characters in *Chicken Licken*. Read the names together, modelling phonic strategies where necessary, e.g. *D–u–ck L–u–ck*. Establish that this is a story so the characters have storybook names.

Together, describe each character. Ask: *They are all types of farmyard birds, but how are they the same and different?*

> **Differentiation ideas:** Support learners by providing the letters for the character names so they may rebuild them using their phonic skills. Ensure that digraphs are together and not separated, e.g. *ch, ck*.

Challenge learners by asking them to suggest alternative rhyming names that could work, e.g. *Chicken Picken, Hen Ten, Duck Chuck, Turkey Shurkey*.

2 The Story of Chicken Licken (20–30 minutes)

Learning intention: to listen and point to pictures to show comprehension

Resources: *The Story of Chicken Licken* (Learner's Book, Session 4.1, Activity 2); Track 20; Workbook, Session 4.1, Activity 1

Description: Tell learners they will now listen to *The Story of Chicken Licken*. Read the story aloud or play the audio.

Ask learners to listen to how the story begins (*One day …*) and to point to the pictures in Learner's Book as they follow the story.

Talk about the story. Discuss learners' first impressions and ideas. Ask if they have any questions. Draw learners' attention to the tree and what is on the tree (it is an oak tree with acorns).

Ask learners to read the story in pairs.

You can use Workbook Session 4.1 Activity 1 in class now to practise 'who says what'.

> **Differentiation ideas:** Support learners by sitting them in pairs with one stronger reader and/or working with a group to read the story again together.

Challenge learners to point to the words as they listen.

3 Read aloud and join in (10–20 minutes)

Learning intention: to explore a repeated refrain and join in; to copy sentences correctly

Resources: Learner's Book, Session 4.1, Activity 3; *The Story of Chicken Licken* (Learner's Book, Session 4.1); Track 20

Description: Ask learners to look back at the story of Chicken Licken and to find the words in the green speech bubbles.

If not yet established, talk about why they are green. (They are the repeated words)

Work round the class, allowing all learners to take it in turns to read the green words out loud independently. Remind them to take a pause at each full stop.

Ask learners to listen to the story again and to join in with the green words. Read the story aloud or play the audio.

Ask learners to draw a picture of Chicken Licken in their notebooks and to write the green sentences, copying carefully with correct punctuation.

> **Differentiation ideas:** Support learners to write the sentences.

Challenge learners to join two of the sentences with *and*.

Answers:
Learners' own drawings and sentences

Plenary idea

A new story (10–15 minutes)

Resources: a set of picture cards; three pots

Description: Make three sets of simple cards:

- six 'character' cards, e.g. a horse, a goat, a sheep, a donkey, a llama and a dog
- four 'trickster' cards: a tiger, a bear, a giant and a crocodile pictures of things that might fall from the sky, e.g. a star, a cloud, a moon, raindrops and snow.

Place each set of cards in a separate pot.

Choose a picture from each pot to retell *The Story of Chicken Licken* with new characters.

Repeat several times for different combinations.

CROSS-CURRICULAR LINKS

Science: Ask learners if they can name the major parts of an oak tree. Ask: *Do you know what an acorn is?* (a seed)

Homework ideas

Learners complete the Workbook Session 4.1 activities if not completed in class.

They find out what shape an acorn is and draw it. Ask: *What would you make with it or how would you decorate it?*

Answers for Workbook

1 a The sun fell on me. / I will go and tell the King!

   b Come with us.   c I can take you to the king.

   d The sun fell on me. / I will go and tell the King!

2 a I am resting under this tree.   b I am going to tell the King.

3 Learners' own sentences, but may be similar to: Don't be silly! The sun cannot fall on you.

4.2 Exploring language

LEARNING PLAN

Learning objectives		Learning intentions	Success criteria
Main focus	**Also covered**	• To answer questions about a story.	• Learners can answer questions about a story.
1Rg.03, 1Rg.04, 1Ri.13, 1Wg.01, 1Wg.05	1Rg.02, 1Rg.05, 1Rs.02, 1Rs.04, 1Ri.09, 1Ri.11, 1Ra.06, 1Wv.01, 1Wg.03, 1Wg.05, 1SLg.01, 1SLg.04	• To write sentences about a story. • To use *and* to join sentences.	• Learners can write sentences about a story. • Learners can use *and* to join sentences.

LANGUAGE SUPPORT

Learners will benefit from recalling and then retelling *The Story of Chicken Licken*. The repetition of phrases and sentences will be helpful as a structure for some learners.

Where possible, provide non-fiction books showing different kinds of birds so learners can explore how fiction and non-fiction books are different.

Common misconception

Misconception	How to identify	How to overcome
Answers to questions are always in the words of the story.	Ask learners: • *What do the words tell us about what fell on Chicken Licken?* (The sun fell.) • *What does the picture show us?* (It was an acorn.) • *What does it tell us about Chicken Licken* (He's a bit silly.)	Explain that words *and* pictures can give us answers to questions.

Starter idea

Fiction and non-fiction (10–15 minutes)

Resources: Learner's Book, Session: 4.2: Getting started

Description: Show learners the pictures in Getting started and the photos in other parts of the Learner's Book, e.g. the children in Unit 3.

What can learners tell you about the differences between the two types of pictures and when we would use each type? Try to elicit the response that we use artwork for stories and photos for non-fiction or information books. Can learners tell you why?

Working in pairs, ask learners to match the pictures to the speech bubbles in the Getting started activity.

Check the matched pairs as a class, and read through the labels and speech bubbles together.

You may also wish to talk about what sounds these birds make.

Challenge learners to find other stories and non-fiction texts that are about the same or similar topics. Make a small class display. See also the homework ideas later.

Main teaching ideas

1   Check comprehension (20–30 minutes)

Learning intention: to read, say and write answers to questions to show understanding

Resources: Learner's Book, Session 4.2, Activity 1; *The Story of Chicken Licken* (Learner's Book, Session 4.1); Track 20

Description: Ask learners to listen again to *The Story of Chicken Licken,* or to briefly retell the story from the last session.

Ask learners to read and talk about the questions in pairs.

Encourage learners to share their responses so you can check them.

Ask them to write the answers in their notebooks.

As they do so, walk round to check that they are remembering their sentence punctuation.

> **Differentiation ideas:** Support learners by providing them with answers to the questions and asking them to match them up before copying them.

Challenge learners by asking them to write some of their own questions.

Answers:
a   He was shocked because he thought the sun had fallen on his head. (or similar).
b   An acorn fell on his head.
c   Fox Lox tricked Chicken Licken and his friends. / He ate them up. (or similar).

2   Sentence sequencing (15–30 minutes)

Learning intention: to sequence words and phrases to build a sentence for meaning

Resources: Learner's Book, Session 4.2, Activity 2; Workbook, Session 4.2

Description: Write a mixed-up sentence from *The Story of Chicken Licken* on the board,

e.g. *he On met the Hen Len. way* (On the way he met Hen Len.)

Ask learners to work in pairs to sort the words into a sentence that makes sense.

Then, together, agree on the correct sequence.

Draw learners' attention to the Language focus box in the Learner's Book.

Next, ask learners to create and write three sentences using the words in the boxes.

You can use Workbook Session 4.2 in class now for further practice.

> **Differentiation ideas:** Support learners by providing the different parts of the sentences cut up so they can re-sequence them and stick them into their notebooks.

Challenge learners to make their own muddled sentences to be sorted.

Answers:

Learners' own sentences, but may include: Hen Len went with Chicken Licken; Chicken Licken was resting under a tree; Fox Lox tricked Chicken Licken and his friends.

3   Use *and* to join phrases or sentences (10–15 minutes)

Learning intention: to use *and* to retell and exaggerate the sequence of a story

Resources: Learner's Book, Session 4.2, Activity 3; *and* written on a large word card; long strips of paper (one for each group)

Description: Write the word *and* on the board. Ask: *Who can read this?* If necessary, use phonics to blend the letters. Ask learners to provide an example of *and* used in a sentence.

Remind learners that we can use this word to join words or phrases together, e.g. *Chickens and ducks*

Ask for volunteers to play each of the characters in *The Story of Chicken Licken.* Get them to stand in a line.

Ask a different learner to hold the *and* word card.

Ask: *Who went to see the King?*

Learners should respond with: *Chicken Licken **and** Hen Len **and** Cock Lock*, etc. Encourage the learner holding the *and* card to bob up between each of the characters as the words are said, to make the learning active and fun.

Show learners the example of how *and* is used in the Language focus box in the Learner's Book. Ask them to practise putting the characters together in pairs to answer the question. Model how the repetition of *and* can be used for dramatic effect. (In reality, we would usually replace lots of *and*s with commas.)

Ask learners to work in groups on very long strips of paper to write the very long sentence with lots of *and*s.

⟩ **Differentiation ideas:** The game using long strips of paper will support learners in understanding the use of the word *and*.

Challenge learners to use a comma instead of repeating *and* each time.

Answers:
Learners' verbal responses, correctly using *and*.

Plenary idea

The new story revisited (5–10 minutes)

Resources: a set of picture cards as in Learner's Book Session 4.1 Plenary activity

Description: Repeat the game from Learner's Book Session 4.1 Plenary activity using picture cards of characters.

This time, learners use the cards to retell the story but use the word *and* to create a chain of characters as they have practised in Activity 3.

CROSS-CURRICULAR LINKS

Science: Ask learners to think about living things in the story and other living things in their local environment, e.g. ask: *How is a fox the same or different to a bird? How are chickens and eagles the same or different?*

Homework ideas

Learners complete the Workbook Session 4.2 activities if not completed in class.

They bring in examples from home of storybooks (in print or online) and non-fiction texts (newspaper articles, books or online articles) with similar types of content that can be added to the class display (see Starter activity).

Answers for Workbook

1
   a   Chicken Licken;

   b   Hen Len;

   c   Cock Lock. (Pictures and names should be correctly joined.)

2
   a   Chicken Licken was resting under a tree.

   b   Hen Len and Chicken Licken and Cock Lock met Duck Luck.

   c   Fox Lox did not take them to the King.

3   Any words that rhyme with the first word of the name. Ensure learners avoid expletives.

4.3 Retelling and acting

LEARNING PLAN

Learning objectives		Learning intentions	Success criteria
Main focus	**Also covered**	• To talk about ways to retell a story.	• Learners can talk about ways to retell a story.
1Rs.01, 1Ri.06, 1Ws.01, 1Wc.02, 1SLp.04	1Rw.02, 1Ww.01, 1Ww.05, 1Wv.01, 1Wv.02, 1Wc.01, 1Wp.06, 1SLm.04, 1SLg.01, 1SLg.04, 1SLp.01, 1SLr.02	• To say and write sentences for pictures to retell a story. • To act a story using masks.	• Learners can say and write sentences for pictures to retell a story. • Learners can act a story using masks.

LANGUAGE SUPPORT

Learners may benefit from being able to play in a role-play area to explore ways of retelling stories. Where possible, provide a rich range of props.

Common misconception

Misconception	How to identify	How to overcome
Verbs ending in –ed all sound like /d/	Ask learners to read the verb *gobbled*, which ends with a /d/ sound. Repeat with the word *shocked*. Learners may say the word ending in /g/, but explain that there are two digraphs (*sh*, *ck*) and that the –ed ending is spelled *ed* but pronounced /t/.	Remind learners of the different ways to pronounce *ed* when they encounter them in their reading. Play games to sort verbs ending in –ed by sound. You may also wish to introduce the /id/ pronunciation, too, e.g. *sorted*.

Starter idea

Help at home (5–10 minutes)

Resources: Learner's Book, Session 4.3: Getting started

Description: Ask learners to talk about different ways they know of retelling a story. (They will have participated in role play and used puppets in previous units.) List learners' ideas. Talk about the pictures in Getting started to further stimulate discussion. Discuss what each picture shows, adding to the list of learners' ideas as necessary.

You may wish to create a classroom puppet theatre so learners can experience how retelling stories using puppets is different from retelling stories using masks.

Main teaching ideas

1 Retell a story using pictures (10–20 minutes)

Learning intention: to retell a familiar story using pictures

Resources: Learner's Book, Session 4.3, Activity 1

Description: By now, the story of Chicken Licken should be familiar to learners.

Tell learners they are going work in pairs and use the pictures of Chicken Licken in Activity 1 to retell the story. Point out the examples in the speech bubbles.

As you circulate round the classroom, listen in to learners' retellings and support, check and advise as necessary.

Invite volunteer pairs to share their retellings.

Invite peer comment and feedback, and add your own comments. Try to ensure focus on good use of:

- sentences, repetition and sequencing
- choice of vocabulary
- expression and pace
- confidence in speaking aloud.

> **Differentiation ideas:** Support learners by working with a group or specific pairs.

Challenge some learners to use more expression and different ways to engage listeners.

2 In-role retelling (20–30 minutes)

Learning intention: to write sentences to match pictures and to retell a story

Resources: Learner's Book, Session 4.3, Activity 2; Workbook, Session 4.3; Phonics Workbooks A and B; Worksheet 4.1

Description: Ask learners to write their own sentences for each picture in the Learner's Book retell the story of Chicken Licken.

If you wish to remind learners about using phonics for their spellings, draw their attention to the Writing tip in the Learner's Book, which reminds them about digraphs.

Phonics: you may like to use Phonics Workbook A, pages 36–37, Phonics Workbook B, pages 4–5, and/ or the Workbook Session 4.3 activities now for further practice.

Give learners time to use the pictures from Activity 1 as a guide to their sentences.

Circulate to support and encourage learners' writing, both in terms of content and presentation.

> **Differentiation ideas:** Support learners to use Worksheet 4.1 Writing sentences to retell a story, which will allow them to write directly under each

picture, or to work in pairs to cut and stick and create a story board using the pictures.

Challenge learners by asking them to write more sentences (to reflect their oral retellings in Activity 1) and to talk to a partner about their writing.

Answers:
Learners' own sentences

3 Make and use masks for retelling (30–60 minutes)

Learning intention: to retell a story in a group, using masks

Resources: Learner's Book, Session 4.3, Activity 3; Worksheet 4.2

Description: Ask learners to work in groups of six.

In their groups, agree who will play each role and support learners to make masks for their character. You can use Worksheet 4.2 Mask template here.

Give groups time to make their masks and then to use these as they practise their retellings.

As learners practise, support them to develop speaking confidence by encouraging them to stand tall and speak loudly and clearly.

> **Differentiation ideas:** Support learners by using mixed-ability groupings. Wearing masks can sometimes support less confident learners to speak up in character.

Challenge learners to add their own ideas for speech to the story or to elaborate on the story in some other way, borrowing from their oral retellings and/ or written sentences in earlier sessions.

Plenary idea

Perform (5–10 minutes)

Description: Invite further performances to share with the class or another class if you ran out of time in Activity 3.

If everyone performed in the session, talk to learners about which performance was the best and why. Invite peer feedback.

Ask: *What did you learn about retelling with masks? How do masks make the audience feel?*

CROSS-CURRICULAR LINKS

Art: Make a finger puppet.

Science: Discuss which materials can be used to make puppets and why they are most suitable.

Homework ideas

Learners complete the Workbook Session 4.3 activities if not completed in class.

They provide lists of words that feature digraphs. Ask learners to write these in sentences. Differentiate the list based on your learners' needs: by the number of words and/or the difficulty of the words. (Refer to Teaching skills focus at the beginning of this unit for further information on differentiation.)

Answers for Workbook

1   *ck* circled in each name

2   **a** Ch, ck, ck, tt, ng, er, ee; **b** Th; ll, sh, ck; **c** ay, ee, th, ng, ck, ck

3   **a** hen (no *ll*); **b** turkey (no *ck*); **c** fox (no *ay*); **d** he (no *ee*)

4.4 Run, run as fast as you can

LEARNING PLAN

Learning objectives		Learning intentions	Success criteria
Main focus	**Also covered**	• To listen to a story, identifying and joining in with the repeated words. • To talk about the story sequence. • To explore words ending or beginning in two consonants.	• Learners can listen to a story, identifying and joining in with the repeated words. • Learners can talk about the story sequence. • Learners can explore words ending or beginning in two consonants.
1Rw.03, 1Rv.01, 1Rv.05, 1Rg.03, 1Ri.14, 1Ww.02	1Rw.04, 1Rw.05, 1Rv.03, 1Rs.01, 1Rs.02, 1Ri.01, 1Ri.02, 1Ra.01, 1Ra.02, 1Ra.06, 1Ww.03, 1Ww.05, 1Wp.03, 1Wp.05, 1SLm03, 1SLs.02, 1SLg.04, 1SLp.05		

LANGUAGE SUPPORT

Learners will benefit from familiarity with the story of *The Gingerbread Man* as it shares a similar refrain as *The Runaway Chapatti*. They will also be supported by seeing the story pictures, as they listen (see Learner's Book Session 4.4 Activity 1). Picture cards of the characters will help learners to sequence the story as they listen.

Common misconception

Misconception	How to identify	How to overcome
We always say two sounds for two consonants together in a word.	Write the word *flicked* from the story on the board. Ask learners to identify the two pairs of consonants (*fl* and *ck*). Ask them to say how we say each e.g. *f-l-* not /fl/ and /k/ not /k//k/	Practise showing learners digraph cards and asking them to respond at speed by saying one sound e.g. *ch*: /ch/ or two sounds e.g. *sp*: /s/ /p/. Write a sentence from the story on the board: *The clever tiger flicked The Chapatti Man up in the air.* Ask learners to find any examples of two consonants together. e.g. *th, fl, ck, ch, tt* Ask them to say each word and sort the digraphs into two sets: • two letters, but one sound: *th, ck, ch, tt* • two letters, two sounds: *cl, fl*

Starter idea

Bread Man rhyme (5–10 minutes)

Resources: *Bread Man* (Learner's Book, Session 4.4: Getting started); Track 21

Description: Read the rhyme in Getting started together.

The rhyme mentions three types of bread: *roti, nans* and *toast.*

Talk about bread and the words we use for different kinds of bread.

Discuss the questions together.

Do learners know other rhymes about bread? (*The Muffin Man*)

Main teaching ideas

1 *The Runaway Chapatti* (10–15 minutes)

Learning intention: to listen to and follow a story using pictures; to join in with a repeated refrain

Resources: *The Runaway Chapatti* (Learner's Book, Session 4.4, Activity 1); Track 22

Description: Tell learners they will now listen to a story about a different kind of bread man – a pretend man made of bread.

Ask learners to listen as you read the text aloud or play the audio.

Before you begin, ask them to name the characters in Activity 1. (They will say *girl* rather than *Little Anya* at this stage.)

Ask learners to point to each character as they hear their name in the story.

Ask them, also, or on a repeated listen, to identify and join in with the repeated refrain. (Some may recognise it if they know the story of *The Gingerbread Man.*)

Talk about the story and check how much learners have followed and understood by asking simple questions, e.g. *What is the girl's name? What is she making? What happens?*

Identify how the context and events of the story are similar or different from real life.

⟩ **Differentiation ideas:** Support learners by allowing them to listen more than once and by pairing them with stronger readers who can model following a text by pointing.

Challenge learners to make parallels with *The Gingerbread Man* or other stories in which there are cumulative groups of characters, e.g. *The Enormous Turnip*.

Answers:
Learners point to pictures and join in with the repeated refrain of the story.

---

2 **Listen and record characters in sequence (15–30 minutes)**

Learning intention: to listen and record information in a chart

Resources: Learner's Book, Session 4.4, Activity 2; *The Runaway Chapatti* (Learner's Book, Session 4.4); Track 22

Description: Ask learners to listen to the story again and, working in pairs, record the sequence of characters in their notebooks.

Ask learners to draw and label each character in the order they hear them.

As learners work, move around the classroom and check their pencil grips, letter formation and correct use of punctuation.

If you only want learners to respond orally, check they are responding with clear spoken language and correct sentence structures and tenses.

⟩ **Differentiation ideas:** Support learners by working with them in a group. Provide pictures of the characters with text labels and ask pairs of listeners to listen out for their character and/or ask learners to stand in line in the correct order to reinforce the sequence.

Challenge learners to name each character and write these names with capital letters, e.g. *Terrible Tiger*.

Answers:
Learner's drawings, in order: Little Anya, dog, monkey, crocodile, tiger

---

3 **Write words with adjacent consonants (10–15 minutes)**

Learning intention: to read words with adjacent consonant and to find examples of them in a text

Resources: Learner's Book, Session 4.4, Activity 3; Workbook, Session 4.4; Phonics Workbook A

Description: Remind learners what the The Chapatti Man says each time he runs away.

Look at the cloze sentences in the Learner's Book or write it on the board. Ask learners what the missing words are.

Write: *fast, stop.* Ask learners: *What is the same about these words?* Answers may include: they both have four letters, they are both about speed and they both have *st* in them. The word *fast* has letters *st* at the end and the word *stop* has letters *st* at the beginning.

You may wish to model how letter *a* in *fast* has an /ar/ sound

Ask learners to draw The Chapatti Man in their notebooks and write this full sentence in a speech bubble with the words *fast* and *stop*.

You can use Workbook Session 4.4 in class now for further practice of adjacent consonants, as well as Phonics Workbook A, pages 34–36.

Challenge learners to practise their handwriting, joining the adjacent consonants.

⟩ **Differentiation ideas:** Support learners by providing a large speech bubble for them to write in, rather than writing in their notebooks.

Challenge learners to think of other words with the same or different adjacent consonants, e.g. *still, first* or *speedy, wasp.* Challenge learners to join whole words in their handwriting, but watch carefully for correct letter formation.

Answers:
Run, run as <u>fast</u> as you can. You can't <u>stop</u> me – I'm The Chapatti Man!

Plenary idea

Two letters: one sound or two?
(5–10 minutes)

Resources: sets of letter cards with digraphs to show at speed: *ch, ng, nk, th, sh, st, sp, lp, sm, bb, dd, ff, fr, lt*

Description: Show learners the cards one at a time, at speed, and ask them to respond by saying the sound (phoneme) or the letter sounds.

You may like to support them by saying: *One sound or two?* Then ask them to say the sound.

Ensure all learners have the opportunity to respond.

If learners answer correctly, they may leave the classroom. If learners answer incorrectly, they have to have wait for another turn.

Continue until everyone has left.

CROSS-CURRICULAR LINKS

Maths: Work on fraction challenges using chapattis or other round foods.

Homework ideas

Learners complete the Workbook Session 4.4 activities if not completed in class.

They ask their family members how the bread they eat at home is made or where it is bought from.

Answers for Workbook

1 **a** salt; **b** flipped; **c** jumped; **d** want; **e** fast

2 double consonants circled in each word and pronounced correctly

3 **a** t/oa/<u>s/t</u>

   b j/u/<u>m/p</u>

   c a/<u>c/r</u>/o/<u>ss</u>

   d f/a/<u>s/t</u>

   e <u>s/t</u>/ay

4 Learners' own answers, but may include:

   a coast, roast, post, stop, stay, stand

   b lump, pump, bump

   c boss, toss or crop, crisp

   d mast, past or still, stop

   e stop; stand

4.5 The pancake rolled on

LEARNING PLAN

Learning objectives		Learning intentions	Success criteria
Main focus	**Also covered**	• To listen to and read a story independently.	• Learners can listen to and read a story independently.
1Rv.02, 1Rg.07, 1Ri.07, 1Ra.03, 1Wg.06	1Rw.05, 1Rv.01, 1Rv.05, 1Rg.04, 1Rs.01, 1Rs.02, 1Rs.04, 1Ri.01, 1Ri.05, 1Ri.13, 1Ri.14, 1Ra.01, 1Ra.02, 1Wv.01, 1SLg.02, 1SLp.02, 1SLp.04, 1SLp.05	• To talk about the story characters and ideas. • To use *the*, *a* and *an* in sentences.	• Learners can talk about the story characters and ideas. • Learners can use *the*, *a* and *an* in sentences.

LANGUAGE SUPPORT

With learners, make story picture cards to include the pancake and each of the other characters. Use these cards to help learners to sequence the events in the story, either in words or by acting.

If the print book of *The Big Pancake* is available, encourage learners to revisit and re-read the story repeatedly.

Make pancakes! Practical experiences such as this will support the development of new vocabulary.

Common misconception

Misconception	How to identify	How to overcome
There is no difference between *a*, *an* and *the*.	Write three words on the board, preceded by a gap: ____ *teacher* (in general) ____ *child* (particular child) ____ *children*. Ask learners to fill the gaps with *a*, *an* or *the* and talk about why. (A teacher, the child, the children)	Explicitly teach this content and provide practice using Learner's Book Session 4.5 Activity 3 and the accompanying Workbook activities. **A** is used for things in general. **The** is used for things in particular and plurals. **An** is used before general things that begin with a vowel.

Starter idea

A pancake rhyme (15–20 minutes)

Resources: *Mix a Pancake* (Learner's Book, Session 4.5: Getting started); Track 23

Description: Talk to the learners about what songs they know about food.

Listen to, sing or say the rhyme about pancakes in the Getting started activity.

Together, create actions to match the imperatives: *mix, stir, put, fry, flip* and *catch*.

Talk about pancakes.

If there is time, you might like to make a class song and rhyme book with the theme of food.

Main teaching ideas

1 *The Big Pancake,* Part 1 (30–45 minutes)

Learning intention: to listen to story for understanding and repeated words; to read a simple text with some independence using phonic skills, repetition and pictures

Resources: *The Big Pancake,* Part 1 (Learner's Book, Session 4.5, Activity 1); Track 24

Description: Tell learners they are going to listen to a story about a big pancake. Explain that they might think it is a bit like *The Gingerbread Man* or *The Runaway Chapatti,* but they should still listen carefully.

Ask learners to listen out for the words: *The pancake rolled …* and to count how many times they hear it (four). This may require a second listening.

Discuss the story with learners, before asking them to read the text independently or in pairs. You may want to set up guided reading groups for this text with some groups.

Draw their attention to the Reading tip in Activity 2. As you circulate and listen in to their reading, remind them of the reading strategies: to use their phonics and to make use of the language patterns in the story and also the pictures.

> **Differentiation ideas:** Support learners by working with a group for guided reading or pairing more confident readers with less confident readers.

Challenge learners by asking them to read aloud to the class, and to talk about words they found

difficult to read and which strategies they used to read these words.

2 Match questions to answers (20–30 minutes)

Learning intention: to read and match answers to questions to show understanding

Resources: Learner's Book, Session 4.5, Activity 2; Worksheet 4.3; cards with questions from Activity 2

Description: Choose 10 learners. Give half of them the questions from Activity 2 and half of them the answers.

One by one, ask those holding the questions to read their question aloud.

Ask those holding the answers to pair up with the learner holding the question that they think matches their answer. Ask them to read their answer and see if the rest of the class agree with their choice.

Ask learners to then write the questions and matching answers in their notebooks, remembering to use capital letters and full stops or question marks.

Together discuss why the cook was making a pancake and encourage different opinions and reasoning.

> **Differentiation ideas:** Support learners by giving them the question cards from Activity 2 and asking them to match them or, using Worksheet 4.3 Questions and answers, to cut and stick the matching questions and answers together.

Challenge learners to write their own versions of this matching game, creating their own charts with different questions and answers.

Answers:

a

1 What did the cook say about the pancake?	C It's the biggest pancake I have ever seen.
2 How did the pancake help the lady?	E He let the lady land on him when she jumped out of the window.

3 How did the pancake help the boy?	A He lay on top of the big hole in the road so the goats did not fall into it.
4 How did the pancake help the girl?	B He floated in the water for the girl to climb on
5 Why did the pancake keep rolling on?	D Because he thought they all wanted to eat him.

b   Possible answer: The cook was probably making a pancake to eat for himself or for someone else. Perhaps he changed his mind when he saw how helpful the pancake was.

3   **Choose *a*, *an* or *the* (15–20 minutes)**

Learning intention: to use articles correctly

Resources: Learner's Book, Session 4.5, Activity 3; Workbook, Session 4.5

Description: See Common misconception and remind learners of the rules about using articles.

Practise with sentences from the story in Activity 1, reading them without the article and asking learners to say which word is missing: *a*, *an* or *the*.

Then ask learners to complete Activity 3, filling in the gaps as they write the sentences into their notebooks.

You can use the Workbook Session 4.5 activities for this session in class now for further practice.

> **Differentiation ideas:** Support learners by working with specific groups and modelling the answers together before asking learners to write them independently.

Challenge learners to write a sentence that has *a*, *an* and *the* in it.

Answers:
a   a
b   the
c   the. Sentences correctly written with capital letters and full stops.

Plenary idea

Make pancake statements (5–10 minutes)

Resources: *Mix a Pancake* (Learner's Book, Session 4.5)

Description: Return to the Getting started rhyme. Sing or say it again.

Pretend you are tasting the pancake and say: *Mmmmmm. It's the sweetest pancake in the world.*

Point to other learners and ask them to say a similar sentence (or invite ideas), e.g. *Mmmmmm. It's the biggest, roundest, stickiest, smallest, spiciest, messiest, smelliest, tastiest pancake in the world.*

See how long you can keep going with the superlative descriptions.

CROSS-CURRICULAR LINKS

Maths: Talk about the shape of pancakes and other foods.

Science: Find out how to make pancakes and make them!

Art: make a pancake (and/or a chapatti) or a gingerbread man/woman model with dough or in paintings.

Homework ideas

Learners complete Workbook Session 4.5 activities if not completed in class.

They retell the story of *The Big Pancake* to a family member.

Answers for Workbook

1   The cook made a big pancake. But the pancake jumped out of the pan and rolled away.

'Come back,' said the cook. The big pancake rolled on.

2   The pancake came to a house. 'Help me!' said a lady. 'Jump! I'll catch you!' said the pancake. The pancake rolled on.

3   The cook and the lady ran after the pancake. The pancake came to an enormous hole in the road. 'Help! My goats will fall in to the big hole!' said the boy. 'I can help you!' said the pancake. The pancake rolled on.

4.6 Story endings

LEARNING PLAN

Learning objectives		Learning intentions	Success criteria
Main focus	**Also covered**	• To talk about story endings.	• Learners can talk about story endings.
1Rs.01, 1Ri.02, 1Ri.07, 1Ri.10, 1Wg.04	1Rg.02, 1Rg.03, 1Ri.05, 1Ri.11, 1Ra.01, 1Ra.03, 1Wg.01, 1Ws.01, 1Wc.01, 1Wc.04, 1SLm.03, 1SLg.02, 1SLg.04, 1SLp.01, 1SLp.03	• To read the end of a story that has a surprise. • To choose and write their own story endings.	• Learners can read the end of a story that has a surprise. • Learners can choose and write their own story endings.

LANGUAGE SUPPORT

If the print book of *The Big Pancake* is available, learners will benefit from revisiting the story to support understanding.

Check learners are familiar with as many other traditional story texts as possible so they can draw

on the language of story endings, e.g. *And they all lived happily ever after; And that was that!; And they were never seen again.*

Common misconception

Misconception	How to identify	How to overcome
Traditional stories always begin with *Once upon a time* and end with *And they all lived happily ever after.*	Note what beginnings and endings learners are using in their own stories – either written or verbal.	Ask learners to try to recall some of the ways traditional tales begin and end. Explore the language together: *Long, long ago* *One fine day.* *Back in time when animals could talk …* *In a land far, far away* *And that was the end of the …* *And that is how the story ends.* *And from that day to this …* *And the x was never seen again.*

Starter idea

Story endings (10–15 minutes)

Resources: Learner's Book, Session 4.6: Getting started

Description: Find out what learners already know about story endings.

Look at the pictures in Getting started to see what they can remember of the stories they have met so far, as well as others they may know.

Provide other examples of traditional stories from your own country that learners will be familiar with.

Talk about happy and sad endings. Ask: *Are there other types of endings, e.g. endings that leave you unsure about how the story ends?*

Refer to Common misconception earlier and, together, create a class display or working wall of story beginnings and endings, if time allows.

Main teaching ideas

1   **Talk about story endings for *The Big Pancake* (20–30 minutes)**

Learning intention: to take turns in listening to others; to give an opinion

Resources: Learner's Book, Session 4.6, Activity 1; *The Big Pancake*, Part 1 (Learner's Book, Session 4.5) Track 24

Description: Ask one of your learners to summarise the story of *The Big Pancake* so far (as in Learner's Book Session 4.5 Activity 1), if necessary. What was the last thing that happened? (The pancake saved the girl in the river and rolled on.)

Where do learners think the pancake rolled to next and how do they think the story will end? Encourage learners to take turns to express their opinions about the ending. Take all ideas.

Together, read the story ending ideas in Learner's Book Session 4.6 Activity 1 and discuss them.

Take a class vote to see which ending is the most popular and record the results. Tell learners that in the next activity they will find out how the story ends.

 2   **Read *The Big Pancake* ending (20–30 minutes)**

Learning intention: to read the ending of a simple text with some independence using phonic skills and pictures for support

Resources: Learner's Book, Session 4.6, Activity 2; Track 24

Description: Tell learners to read Part 2 of the story alone, or in pairs. Ask them to read quietly and, when they find out the ending, to fold their arms.

When all learners have indicated that they have read the ending, read the story aloud to check that all learners are supported. Ask for some reactions to the ending.

Look at the results of the class vote. Ask: *Did you predict the ending correctly?*

Make sure learners understand that the surprise ending is even a surprise for the main character – the big pancake – who is sure that the others want to eat him.

Ask learners to reflect on what helped them to make predictions about the ending. Did they rely on their knowledge of other similar stories where the character is usually tricked and eaten, e.g. *The Gingerbread Man* and *The Runaway Chapatti*?

> **Differentiation ideas:** Support learners by working with a group, or reading the ending aloud with them, modelling how to:

- run your finger under each word
- stop and use phonics on some decodable words
- refer to the pictures.

Challenge learners to read the ending alone and to make a list of words they are not sure about, and where they were able or unable to use phonics. Discuss those words with those learners to model how to tackle those words. Ask: *Can you think of other stories that have a surprise ending?*

3   **Draw and write new endings (15–20 minutes;)**

Learning intention: to write a new story ending

Resources: Learner's Book, Session 4.6, Activity 3

Description: Remind learners of the stories listed in Getting started, and how they end.

Talk to learners about how the endings for those stories could be different. Create some ideas together.

For additional stimulus, use the pictures in Activity 3.

Ask learners to choose an idea and draw and write a new story ending for each of the three pictures.

Model writing a story ending together if this work needs scaffolding for your class.

> **Differentiation ideas:** Support learners by working out some sentences together, for them to select from before copying one or two, rather than all.

Challenge learners to go beyond the Activity 3 ideas to create and record their own.

Answers:

Possible endings include:

The Story of Chicken Licken: Fox took Chicken Licken and friends to see the king. The king made sure that the sun was put back in the sky.

The Runaway Chapatti: The tiger helped the chapatti to cross the river and they became friends.

Don't Spill the Milk!: Penda and her Daddy walked back home together.

Plenary idea

Leave in pairs (5–10 minutes)

Resources: printed sentences from Part 2 of *The Big Pancake* in Activity 2; bag or box

Description: Type and print sentences from Part 2 of *The Big Pancake* in Activity 2 to match the number of learners in your class.

Cut the sentences in half (e.g. *You will just / have to eat me.; We don't / want to eat you!*) and put the beginnings in one bag or box.

Hand out the sentence endings to learners.

Mix up the sentence beginnings and read them out, one by one, asking learners to claim the one that matches their ending.

Once they do so, they may leave.

CROSS-CURRICULAR LINKS

Science: Explore, talk about and describe the movement of familiar objects. What else could roll down a hill?

Maths: Display the results of your class vote on story endings in a block graph or pictogram.

Homework ideas

Learners complete Workbook Session 4.6 activities if not completed in class.

They read a favourite storybook at home and make up a different ending.

Answers for Workbook

1. a The cook made a big pancake.
   b The pancake rolled away.
   c The cook wants to eat me.
   d The pancake came to a river.
   e I can help you.

2. a They all ran after the pancake.
   b The pancake came to a hill.
   c I can't roll up the hill.
   d You will just have to eat me.
   e We want to say thank you.

3. Learners' own endings

4.7 Comparing stories

Learning objectives		Learning intentions	Success criteria
Main focus	**Also covered**	• To talk and write about things that are the same and different in stories.	• Learners can talk and write about things that are the same and different in stories.
1Rs.02, 1Ri.01, 1Ri.02, 1Ra.04, 1Wp.05	1Rv.05, 1Rg.04, 1Ra.05, 1Ra.06, 1Ws.02, 1Wc.02, 1SLp.02, 1SLp.05	• To fill in a chart to compare stories. • To show information in different ways.	• Learners can fill in a chart to compare stories. • Learners can show information in different ways.

LANGUAGE SUPPORT

Learners will benefit from revisiting *Chicken Licken*, *The Big Pancake* and especially the listening text *The Runaway Chapatti*.

They will also benefit from playing Spot the Difference games and other simple games where they have to respond to the question: *Are these the same or different?*

Practise language structures to describe differences and similarities. Say: *They both have ...; This one has ..., but that one does not.*

Common misconception

Misconception	How to identify	How to overcome
Traditional stories are always about characters joining each other one by one on a journey.	Ask learners if all traditional stories are about adding characters one by one.	Share other traditional stories that do not involve adding characters on a journey.

Starter idea

Sing a song (10–15 minutes)

Resources: *Roll Over!* (Learner's Book, Session 4.7: Getting started); Track 26

Description: Learners will need to count down from ten to one. Practise doing this together.

Sing the story song *Roll Over!* together as a class. You can play the audio if you wish:

Audioscript: *Roll Over!*

There were ten in the bed

And the little one said, 'Roll over! Roll over!'

So they all rolled over

And one fell out!

(Keep singing with 9, 8, 7, 6, 5, 4, 3, 2 in the bed until ...)

There was one in the bed and he said, 'Where is everyone else?'

Ask learners how this story song is similar and different to the stories they have read so far in this unit. (The stories they have read add characters whereas this song loses characters one by one.)

If you have time, role play having ten characters and one sitting down each time.

Ask learners if they know other stories or songs where characters or things are added or taken away?

Main teaching ideas

1 Sort things (20–30 minutes)

Learning intention: to think about different ways to sort stories

Resources: Learner's Book, Session 4.7, Activity 1; piles of books to sort

Description: Talk about sorting things. Explain that we can sort things by thinking about what is the same and different about them. Draw comparisons with other sorting activities learners may have done in other lessons, e.g. maths or science.

Show learners a pile of books. Talk about how we can sort them by:

- size, colour, format (hard cover, soft cover, online)
- photos or illustrations
- fiction or non-fiction
- content – real story, pretend story, stories about …
- author.

If time, give groups piles of books and ask for their ideas about how to sort them.

Remind learners that they have now read or heard three stories.

Ask them how we could sort those stories, drawing their attention to the ideas in Activity 1.

Make sure they understand what is meant by 'story events'.

Take their ideas and explanations.

Tell them that in this session they will be working out what is the same and different about the stories they have read and listened to.

> **Differentiation ideas:** Support learners by having physical copies of the books or stories in this unit or traditional tales in general.

Challenge learners to think of other ways to sort the stories, e.g. good characters or bad characters.

2 Fill in a chart (30–40 minutes)

Learning intention: to fill in a chart with information about stories

Resources: Learner's Book, Session 4.7, Activity 2; Workbook Session 4.7; Worksheet 4.4; large pieces of paper; pens

Description: Tell learners they are now going to work in groups to think about what is the same and what is different about the stories read so far in Unit 4.

Show them the chart in Activity 2. Together, talk through the 'things to look out for' so learners understand what they mean. Then talk about each story and model how to fill the chart in.

You can provide Worksheet 4.4. Comparing stories here so learners do not have to copy the chart into their notebooks, or you may prefer to provide large pieces of paper for learners to recreate and fill out the chart.

Give learners time to discuss and complete the activity in their groups.

Bring the class together and discuss ideas.

You can use the Workbook Session 4.7 activities now for further practice of making comparisons.

> **Differentiation ideas:** Support learners by setting up mixed groups and/or asking them to work on just one or two things to look out for.

Challenge learners to add further things to look out for and to present their charts to the class.

Answers:

Sorting stories	The Story of Chicken Licken	The Runaway Chapatti	The Big Pancake
By character	*Animals – birds and a fox*	*A person, animals and a pretend thing* (The Chapatti man)	*Some people and a pretend thing* (a big pancake)

By story beginning	Something falls on Chicken Licken's head and he sets off to tell the king.	Little Anya is making a chapatti when it jumps up and runs away.	The cook made the pancake and it rolled away.
By story events	The birds join Chicken Licken one by one.	People and animals chase the chapatti one by one.	People chase the pancake one by one.
By story ending	Fox Lox eats all the birds.	A tiger eats The Chapatti Man.	The people do not eat the pancake

3 Share charts (30–40 minutes)

Learning intention: to re-present information in different ways

Resources: Learner's Book, Session 4.7, Activity 3

Description: Ask learners to use their charts to talk about things in the story that are the same or different. Share ideas.

Choose two of the stories from the charts and ask learners to write sentences to show two things that are the same and two things that are different.

As you circulate, check learners are using *same* and *different* correctly.

> **Differentiation ideas:** Support learners by working with a group and providing a sentence structure for them to copy into their notebooks, e.g. two things that are the same/different in the stories (list the things).

Challenge learners to add additional ideas to their charts, e.g. repeated words or phrases in the stories.

Answers:
Learners' own responses

Plenary idea

Sort ourselves into sets (5–10 minutes)

Description: Ask groups of learners to sort themselves into sets.

Say: *Stand in this part of the classroom if you are a boy and over there if you are a girl.*

Say: *Stand in this part of the classroom if you are wearing blue and over there if you are wearing brown. Stand in the middle if you are wearing both! And sit if you are wearing neither.*

Repeat with different examples.

CROSS-CURRICULAR LINKS

Maths: Counting up to ten and back again; sorting things into sets.

Homework ideas

Learners complete the Workbook Session 4.7 activities if not completed in class.

They find a book at home or another traditional story that has something the same or different to these stories.

Answers for Workbook

1 and **2** Learners' own drawings

3 Learners' own answers, but may include:

    a Same: each character is a type of food; each character is pretend / jumps up and runs away and is chased / can talk / is round.

    b Different: each character is made differently; The Chapatti Man is eaten but the Runaway Pancake is not; one is helpful, one is not.

4 Learners' own answers

4.8 Along skipped a boy with his whirly-twirly toy

LEARNING PLAN

Learning objectives		Learning intentions	Success criteria
Main focus	**Also covered**	• To explore words and language.	• Learners can explore words and language.
1Rv.03, 1Rv.05, 1Ri.12, 1Ri.13	1Rv.01, 1Ri.01, 1Ri.07, 1Ri.10, 1Ra.01, 1Ww.04, 1Wv.01, 1Wv.02, 1SLg.04	• To listen to and read Part 1 of a story.	• Learners can listen to and read Part 1 of a story.
		• To answer questions about the story to show they understand.	• Learners can answer questions about the story to show they understand.

LANGUAGE SUPPORT

Pre-teach any vocabulary or language structures you think learners may not know, e.g. *eucalyptus*, *scare in the air*, *shade*.

Check learners know that *tummy* is a colloquial word for *stomach*.

Reading aloud and omitting these key words or phrases for learners to say will reinforce enjoyment and meaning.

Common misconception

Misconception	How to identify	How to overcome
We always have to use the correct name for things in our writing.	Ask learners to listen to the opening of the story: *One day in the leaves of the eucalyptus tree hung a* **scare in the air** *where no eye could see, …* What do they think the 'scare in the air' is? (It's the snake.)	Create a class resource of fun phrases like this: *A fright in the night* (a night creature) *An eye in the sky* (a bird)

Starter idea

Describe things in a fun way
(10–20 minutes)

Resources: Learner's Book, Session 4.8: Getting started; a small collection of toys as shown in the Getting started activity

Description: Show learners the pictures in Getting started. Ask them to name each of the toys.

Now encourage learners to come up with funny words to describe each of the toys. Model how to do this by saying: *How could we describe a windmill in a fun way using rhyming words? What does the toy do? It moves round / it whirls and it twirls: it's a whirly–twirly toy!*

Learners' ideas may not always rhyme and that does not matter at this stage. You can use the Workbook Session 4.8 activities for this session in class, now, for further practice of making plural nouns.

You can use Language worksheet 4A here, too. You may also draw learners' attentions to the mascot which reminds them about adding –s to make plural nouns: toy/toys.

Answers:
May include: shaky-wakey toy, rocky-tocky toy, stacky-whacky toy, floaty-boaty toy

Main teaching ideas

1 *One Day in the Eucalyptus, Eucalyptus Tree*, Part 1 (20–30 minutes)

Learning intention: to listen to a story and for a specific phrase; to point to pictures to indicate following a text

Resources: *One Day in the Eucalyptus, Eucalyptus Tree,* Part 1 (Learner's Book, Session 4.8, Activity 1); Track 27

Description: Tell learners they will listen to Part 1 of a story about a boy with a 'whirly-twirly toy'.

Ask them to just listen and you point to the pictures in Activity 1 as they do so. If necessary, model how you will do this first. Then repeat, asking learners to point to the pictures in their books.

On the repeat listen, ask learners to listen for the phrase *whirly-twirly toy*. Ask them to raise their hands when they hear it. (It appears twice.)

Give learners time to share ideas about the story with each other and with you.

Ask learners if anyone knows the title of the story. (*One Day in the Eucalyptus, Eucalyptus Tree*)

Check learners' understanding of *eucalyptus tree* (This is followed up in subsequent units, too.)

> **Differentiation ideas:** Support learners in their understanding of the story by pausing the audio, discussing and asking questions as prompts, e.g. *What could be hanging in the air up in the tree? What happens to the boy with the toy?*

Challenge learners to read sections of the story aloud for the class.

2 Answer questions (20–30 minutes; longer if role playing answers)

Learning intention: to check understanding of texts; to hear rhyming words

Resources: Learner's Book, Session 4.8, Activity 2; *One Day in the Eucalyptus, Eucalyptus Tree,* Part 1 (Learner's Book, Session 4.8); Track 26

Description: If learners need more time to discuss the story, revisit some of the ideas in the text, saying, e.g. *The boy thinks quickly from inside the snake's dark and deep tummy.* Ask: *Why does he tempt the snake to eat more? Does he have a plan?*

Can learners find or hear rhyming pairs, e.g. (*scare / air, tree / see, boy / toy*)?

Ask learners to listen again, or read the story, and then to work through the questions in pairs.

Share answers as a class.

> **Differentiation ideas:** Support learners by working with a group to answer the questions together.

Challenge learners to work independently to write their own question about the story.

Answers:
a skipping; b in the tree; c the boy and the toy; d a bird cheeping

3 Explore words and phrases (10–15 minutes)

Learning intention: to find and explore specific words and phrases in the story

Resources: Learner's Book, Session 4.8, Activity 3

Description: Ask learners what sort of worm the snake ate (an *ooey-gooey* one). Ask them what else we might describe as *ooey-gooey*, e.g. sticky toffee, the feeling when you put your hands in play dough or goo.

Then ask learners to work in pairs to talk about the other two language examples in Activity 3, e.g. *sneaky-slidey* could describe a fox on ice, or a crocodile in a muddy river, *dark and deep* could also describe a cave, a hole, down your throat!

Ask learners to write and draw the phrases and their matching pictures in their notebooks, or consider making a class display of them.

⟩ **Differentiation ideas:** Support learners by giving them just one phrase to work on.

Challenge learners to think of more examples for each phrase or more descriptions.

Answers:
Learners' own responses

Plenary idea

What next? (10 minutes)

Resources: Learner's Book, Session 4.8, Activity 1; online animated version of *One Day in the Eucalyptus, Eucalyptus Tree*

Description: If possible, play an online animated version of Part 1 of the story read by the author, Daniel Bernstrom. This will further stimulate learners' thoughts about what happens next.

Ask learners what they think the snake might do in the next part of the story.

Encourage them to explain their thinking.

Note learners who are able to make logical predictions based on Part 1.

CROSS-CURRICULAR LINKS
Design and Technology: find out how to make a hand-held windmill and how to make it whirl and twirl. **Science:** Explore, talk about and describe the movement of familiar objects. Explore a range of toys with moving parts.

Homework ideas

Learners complete the Workbook Session 4.8 activities if not completed in class.

They retell Part 1 of the session story to someone at home.

Answers for Workbook

1. **a** trees; **b** boys; **c** days; **d** snakes; **e** birds; **f** worms
2. **a** Foxes; **b** stories; **c** wishes
3. Learners' own sentences using **a** leaves; **b** tummies; **c** mummies; **d** lives.

4.9 Out dashed the cat

LEARNING PLAN

Learning objectives		Learning intentions	Success criteria
Main focus	**Also covered**	• To explore verbs. • To listen to and read Part 2 of a story. • To say if sentences are true or false to show they understand.	• Learners can explore verbs. • Learners can listen to and read Part 2 of a story. • Learners can say if sentences are true or false to show they understand.
1Rv.01, 1Rv.03, 1Ri.12, 1Rg.06	1Rw.07, 1Rv.05, 1Ri.01, 1Ri.07, 1Ri.10, 1Ra.01, 1Wv.01, 1Ww.03, 1SLm.01, 1SLg.01, 1SLg.03		

Some learners may be less familiar with the sounds animals make in English texts. Support them by providing options for them to choose from. Explore how these animals sound in learners' first language, as well as in other languages.

The very structured language patterns in this text will support learners, and using non-verbal communication (hand actions or facial expressions) for some phrases will help, e.g. *under-over (slid the snake)*.

Common misconception

Misconception	How to identify	How to overcome
Listening for rhyme does not help our reading and spelling.	Ask learners to read with you and fill in a simple cloze written on the board. *'Do you think,' said the snake* *to the boy with the _____,* *'that there's room for something yummy* *with you inside my _____?'* Show how *boy/toy* and *yummy/tummy* share spelling patterns.	Practise phonic games and provide further simple dictations where learners must use one spelling pattern to write another word. Note that the spelling patterns will not always be the same for rhyming words, e.g. *The snake had a tummy ache!*

Starter idea

Animal check (10–15 minutes)

Resources: Learner's Book, Session 4.9: Getting started; Workbook, Session 4.9

Description: Ask learners to remember the story so far. Ask: *What happened?*

Ask how the snake knew the bird with the ooey-gooey worm was in the tree. (it cheeped)

Ask learners what other animal sounds they know.

Together, look at the pictures in Getting started and discuss.

Ask learners to name the animals in the pictures. (snake, bird, ape, bear and fly). Together, suggest words to describe the sounds they might make (snake: hiss, silence; bird: tweet, chirp, cheep, sing, twitter; ape: gibber; grunt; bear: growl, grunt, munch; fly: buzz, etc.). Write down these words for use in the next activity.

Main teaching ideas

1 *One Day in the Eucalyptus, Eucalyptus Tree*, Part 2 (20–30 minutes)

Learning intention: to listen to a story and for events; to point to pictures to indicate following a text

Resources: *One Day in the Eucalyptus, Eucalyptus Tree*, Part 2 (Learner's Book, Session 4.9, Activity 1); Track 28

Description: Tell learners to listen to Part 2 of the story.

As before, ask them to first listen and point to the pictures in Activity 1 to follow the story and text.

Then, on a repeat listen, ask learners to listen out for what the snake did next and compare this with their predictions in Learner's Book 4.8 Activity 3. (*He ate a cat, an ape and a bear. Then he burst because he was so full ... and then out they all jumped leaving the snake with a tummy ache).*

Ask learners to also compare the animal sound words from the class list created in Getting started, with the words in the text.

Give learners time to share ideas about the story with each other and with you. Ask: *What did you like / not like? What surprised you? Why?*

> **Differentiation ideas:** Support learners by pausing the audio, discussing the events and asking questions as prompts, e.g. *What do you think qually-wally hair is?* (silly hair); *Why was the snake's tummy gurgling and blurbling?* (he had eaten too much).

Challenge learners to read sections of the story aloud to the class.

2 Explore verbs (15–20 minutes;)

Learning intention: to find, list and sort verbs into regular (ending *–ed*) and irregular

Resources: Learner's Book, Session 4.9, Activity 2; *One Day in the Eucalyptus, Eucalyptus Tree,* Part 2 (Learner's Book, Session 4.9); Track 28; Workbook, Session 4.9

Description: Tell learners they are going to be verb detectives, listening out for any verbs in the past tense ending *–ed*.

Remind them that, usually, we add *–ed* for verbs in the past tense, e.g. gobble/gobbled: *The snake gobbled up ...*

Read the story aloud. Ask learners to stand up or clap when they hear a verb in the past tense ending *–ed*.

Ask them to work in pairs to create a list of these past tense verbs.

Set them to work alone, or in pairs, to find the words they just listened for in the story text in Activity 1.

Explain that some other verbs do not follow the *–ed* pattern, e.g. say/said: *The boy said, 'I'll bet that you're still very hungry ...'.*

Ask them to find and write a list of the other (irregular) verbs, not ending in *–ed*.

You can use Workbook Session 4.9 Activity 2 in class, now, for further consolidation of verbs ending *–ed*.

> **Differentiation ideas:** Support learners by repeating the listening game in a smaller group and/ or by providing the verbs ending *–ed* on separate cards so they can mix and match them.

Challenge learners to change the verbs in the last section of the story beginning *Out ran the bear ...,* e.g. *Out sprinted the bear ...*

Answers:

Ending in *–ed*: gobbled, snaked, dashed, skipped

Not ending in *–ed* / irregular verbs: bent, went, ran, swung, flew

3 True or false? (20–30 minutes)

Learning intention: to check understanding of texts; to discuss ideas and listen well

Resources: Learner's Book, Session 4.9, Activity 3

Description: If time was short in the previous activity, learners may need more time to discuss the story and revisit some of the meanings in the text. Check that learners can see the patterns of repetition.

Ask: *Can you explain why the boy is tempting the snake to eat more each time?*

Ask learners to listen again, or read the story and give them time to work through the true/false statements in pairs.

Share answers. Draw learners' attention to the Listening tip and ensure that they are taking it in turns to speak and that they are listening well.

> **Differentiation ideas:** Support learners by working with a group and working through the statements together with YES or NO cards (rather than true or false), which they must show as you read each statement.

Challenge learners to work independently to write a similar true/false quiz about the story.

Answers: a false; **b** true; **c** true; **d** false

Plenary idea

Simple dictations (10–15 minutes)

Resources: simple cloze sentences

Description: As in Common misconception, provide groups of learners with simple cloze sentences and ask them to write correct spellings for the missing words, using rhyme as a clue. For example:

* 'What shall I wear?' said the (bear).
* What will the (snake) take?
* Grapes in a bunch! That is what I'll have for (lunch).
* Can you see a eucalyptus (tree)?

The team with the most correct spellings are the winners.

CROSS-CURRICULAR LINKS

Maths: Use familiar language to describe length, including: *long, longer, longest, thin, thinner, thinnest, short, shorter, shortest, tall, taller* and *tallest*. Talk about the different characters in the story. Ask: *How can you compare them using mathematical vocabulary?*

Maths: Use familiar language to describe sequences of objects. Create and describe shape patterns for the skin of a snake.

Art: Make snake puppets from old socks. Stick on features and patterns.

Homework ideas

Learners complete the Workbook Session 4.9 activities if not completed in class.

They find out if there is a similar story in their own country, e.g. *There was an old lady who swallowed a fly.* Encourage them to ask family members.

Answers for Workbook

1 **a** cat: purr, purr **b** ape: slurp, burp **c** bear: munch, munch **d** bird: cheep cheep **e** snake: gurgle, gurgle

2 **a** slurped, burped **b** Sniffed, sniffed. Gulped. **c** Purred, purred **d** Gurgled-gurgled **e** Cheeped, cheeped **f** Munched, munched

3 Out <u>ran</u> the bear and out <u>swung</u> the ape,

Out **dashed** the cat and out <u>flew</u> the bird with the ooey-gooey worm,

And out **skipped** the boy with the whirly-twirly toy …

one day in the eucalyptus, eucalyptus tree.

4.10 Joining in

LEARNING PLAN

Learning objectives		Learning intentions	Success criteria
Main focus	**Also covered**	• To clap the rhythm of words and phrases. • To read a whole story and join in with some parts. • To act a story as a class.	• Learners can clap the rhythm of words and phrases. • Learners can read a whole story and join in with some parts. • Learners can act a story as a class.
1Rv.05, 1Rg.03, 1Ri.14, 1Ra.02, 1SLm.04, 1SLp.04	1Rs.01, 1Ri.02, 1Ri.06, 1Ri.07, 1Ra.03, 1SLm.05, 1SLg.01, 1SLr.02		

Learners will benefit from having words, such as *eucalyptus*, written on long strips of paper so they can cut them up into syllables and then add the sound dots. A sound dot (like a large full stop) should be added under each letter or letters representing a phoneme, e.g. chick = ch –i–ck • • •

Manage learner groupings so those who are less confident in speaking aloud and acting are paired with learners who are more confident in this area.

Common misconception

Misconception	How to identify	How to overcome
Clapping syllables is the same as clapping phonemes / letter sounds.	Ask learners to clap the word *skipped*. (one clap) Ask them to clap the phonemes: /s/ /k/ /i/ /pp/ /ed/ (five claps) Repeat with several other words: *sniff* (one clap), *gobble* (two claps), *animal* (three claps).	Repeat these games frequently. Ask learners to use this strategy in their writing work to help them work out how many and which letters to use. Use the Starter idea.

Starter idea

Clap syllables for pronunciation and speech fluency (5–10 minutes;)

Resources: Learner's Book, Session 4.10: Getting started; Workbook, Session 4.10

Description: Ask learners to listen and clap.

Say: *eucalyptus*. Then model how to clap this in syllables as shown in Getting started.

Ask learners to copy you.

Repeat this process for each phrase of increasing length in the Learner's Book. (You can also use this activity to build awareness of noun phrases.)

Split the class into two groups. Ask one group to say the words and phrases and the other group to respond in claps.

Repeat with several other phrases – ideally from the story or with other story titles.

You can use the Workbook Session 4.10 activities here.

Main teaching ideas

1 Group chanting (20–30 minutes)

Learning intention: to join in with key repetitive refrains from a story

Resources: Learner's Book, Session 4.10, Activity 1; audio recording equipment, if available

Description: Tell learners they are going to read or listen to *One Day in the Eucalyptus, Eucalyptus Tree* together.

Split the class into three groups for the repeated refrains of the boy, the snake and the book title. You will need to read the narrator's voice (text in brackets).

Boy	Snake	Book title
'I'll bet,' (said the boy, in the belly dark and deep,) 'that you're still very hungry And there's more you can eat.'	'Do you think,' (said the snake to the boy with the toy), 'that there's room for something yummy with you inside my tummy?'	One Day in the Eucalyptus, Eucalyptus Tree

Read the story and ask learners to join in with their group repeated refrain, each time. Then read to the end of the story.

Encourage learner involvement by allowing time for learners to suggest changes to the groupings so the story can be read in different ways.

If possible, record the chanting/reading aloud so learners can listen back and begin to self-assess.

> **Differentiation ideas:** Support learners by pointing to their group when it is their turn to chant.

Challenge learners to suggest different groupings to create new parts for joining in. Invite two confident readers to read the narrator's part (creating a fourth group).

2 Act the story (30–60 minutes)

Learning intention: to retell a story with actions and story book language

Resources: Learner's Book, Session 4.10, Activity 2; props as necessary

Description: Decide if you want learners to work in small groups of eight (to include a narrator) or to act the story as a class and repeat several times with different learners participating.

First, model how the story can be retold:

- Create a circle using a skipping rope or similar on the floor (to represent the snake's tummy).

- Choose characters for the boy and the snake.

- Choose characters for the bird, cat, ape, bear and fly.

Tell or read the story, encouraging learners to respond to the text, saying: *We want to see the snake sneaking and sliding towards his prey, and the prey jumping inside the snake's 'tummy' as they are eaten.*

Set up groups for learners to prepare their own plays using similar techniques.

Depending on time available, allow learners to perform to each other or to another class.

> **Differentiation ideas:** Support learners by setting up groups so that learners with different strengths are working together to help each other.

Challenge learners to be creative about using non-verbal communication in their acting as well as thinking of imaginative ideas for props.

Plenary idea

Leave the classroom in a … way (5–10 minutes)

Description: Group by group, ask learners to leave the classroom in different ways, (without touching other people or furniture). For example:

- in a whirly-twirly way
- in a sneaky-slidey way
- in a under-over way
- in a twisty-twisty way
- in a stretchy-stretchy way.

Homework ideas

Learners complete Workbook Session 4.10 activities if not completed in class.

They make a set of simple finger puppets to retell the story at home.

Answers for Workbook

1 tree; munchy grapes; Ooey-gooey worm
2 twist-twist; under-over; gurgle-gurgle
3 Learners' own responses

4.11 Planning and writing

Learning objectives		Learning intentions	Success criteria
Main focus	**Also covered**	• To explore the structure of a story they know.	• Learners can explore the structure of a story they know.
1Rs.01, 1Ri.02, 1Wv.02, 1Ws.01, 1Wc.01, 1Wc.02	1Rw.07, 1Ri.04, 1Ww.06, 1Wv.01, 1Wv.03, 1Wg.04, 1SLg.04	• To talk about choices they make when writing a story.	• Learners can talk about choices they make when writing a story.
		• To plan and write a similar story.	• Learners can plan and write a similar story.

LANGUAGE SUPPORT

One Day in the Eucalyptus, Eucalyptus Tree should now be very familiar to learners, but they may benefit from using the planning worksheets (Worksheet 4.5 Planning our story; Differentiated worksheets 4A–C) to support their writing outcome.

The repeated structures of this story should support learners in their writing. Work in groups to write a new story if necessary.

Common misconception

Misconception	How to identify	How to overcome
We can use phonics to decode all words.	Ask learners to read these words: *can, toy, slurp, the, said.* Ask how they worked out how to read these words. They probably used phonics for /c/ /a/ /n/, /t/ /oy/, /s/ /l/ /ur/ /p/, but may have found it difficult for *the* and *said*.	Talk about high-frequency or tricky words, and how sometimes we have to use phonics as our first approach and then try other ways to work out a word if phonics cannot help us get all the way there. Encourage learners to use phonics first and then, if necessary, use other strategies to work out a word. Explain that for high-frequency words, we sometimes just have to learn to recognise them, e.g. *the, said.*

Common misconception (continued)

Misconception	How to identify	How to overcome
		Use the Phonics Workbooks for on-going practice of both high-frequency and tricky words.
		Phonics Workbook A: pages 13, 15, 19, 25, 29, 31, 43, 45, 49, 51 and 53.
		Phonics Workbook B: pages 11, 13, 17, 19, 21, 25, 27, 29, 31, 35, 37, 45 and 53.

Starter idea

Eucalyptus trees (15–20 minutes)

Resources: Learner's Book, Session 4.11: Getting started; online research into eucalyptus trees

Description: Ask learners to say all the things they already know about eucalyptus trees from the story. Remind them that it is story so perhaps not everything is true.

This is a good opportunity to talk about the difference between stories (fiction) and information books (non-fiction).

Share ideas and then tell learners that you have further information about the eucalyptus tree.

Show them the pictures in Getting started. Talk about them together, asking: *What does the tree look like? What animals like to visit the tree?*

The animal vocabulary in the Learner's Book may be quite challenging for some learners, so explore it together.

Ask learners to write any questions they have about the eucalyptus tree. For example:

- Where does it grow?
- How big does it get?
- What sort of weather does it like?
- What sort of leaves and flowers does it have?

Agree a class list of questions. (These can be used later for homework.)

Main teaching ideas

1 Change the story (20–30 minutes)

Learning intention: to start planning a new story by changing characters

Resources: Learner's Book, Session 4.11, Activity 1; Worksheet 4.5

Description: Tell learners they will now be working in pairs to think about what new characters they want to include in their own version of *One Day in the Eucalyptus, Eucalyptus Tree*.

Establish that they are going to keep the boy (or it could be a girl) and the snake. They are only changing the things the snake eats.

Ask them to work in pairs to copy and complete the chart in Activity 1 or to fill in Worksheet 4.5 Planning our story.

As you circulate, support and challenge learners to be creative and to draw on the information they gathered in Getting started. Some learners may want to include other animals, or things that do not feature in Getting started. Allow them freedom to make their own choices.

Ask a few learners to share their completed charts as good models.

> **Differentiation ideas:** Support learners by providing Worksheet 4.5 Planning our story and/or by providing options to choose from for each character in the chart.

Challenge learners to be creative in their choices of new characters, even if they are pretend.

Answers:
Learners' own ideas, but many will select animals from those listed in Getting started

2 Questions as a framework for writing (20–30 minutes)

Learning intention: to answer questions to create a new story text

Resources: Learner's Book, Session 4.11, Activity 2; Workbook, Session 4.11; Differentiated worksheets 4A–C

Description: Tell learners they will now use their planning chart from the last session and the questions in Activity 2 to complete their own stories.

Support learners to read and answer the questions in Activity 2. Remind them to use the planning charts from Activity 1, too.

You can use Differentiated worksheets 4A–C now to help scaffold learners' story writing.

You can use the Workbook Session 4.11 activities in class now, for further practice of high-frequency words in this text.

> **Differentiation ideas:** Support learners in creating a group story by answering questions as a group and then asking each learner to copy one of the responses to cumulatively form their own story version. Alternatively, allow some learners to continue to work in pairs.

Challenge learners to add sentences to their own story versions if they remember them from the original story text. Ask learners to check and re-check their spelling, punctuation and handwriting.

Answers:
Learners' own answers

3 Presentation (30–60 minutes)

Learning intention: to develop stories further using pictures and speech bubbles

Resources: Learner's Book, Session 4.11, Activity 3; poster-sized pieces of paper; scissors and glue if appropriate

Description: Talk to learners about how to present their stories as a poster. Take their ideas about what they can add to make their stories more interesting for the reader, e.g. by adding:

- pictures
- speech bubbles
- decoration.

Ask learners to work in pairs to recreate their story (or one of their stories) on a large, poster-sized piece of paper.

They will need 11 boxes or spaces on their paper – show them how to fold it to create the 11 boxes.

Ask them to write their title story in the first box.

They should then copy their answer to each question from Activity 2 into the next 10 boxes:

- Box 2: Where was the snake?
- Box 3: Who came skipping along?
- Box 4: What did the snake do?
- Box 5: What did the snake see and hear next? What did he do?
- Box 6: What did the snake see and hear next? What did he do?
- Box 7: What did the snake see and hear next? What did he do?
- Box 8: What did the snake see and hear next? What did he do?
- Box 9: What did the snake see and hear next? What did he do?
- Box 10: What did the snake do because his tummy was so full?
- Box 11: What came out of the snake's tummy?

Ask learners to add more detail to their story posters, using pictures and speech bubbles.

Make a class display of learners' story posters.

> **Differentiation ideas:** Support learners by folding the poster for them to create the 12 boxes and cutting their question answers so they can stick each into a box.

Challenge learners to add further words or details to their posters and to present them to the class / other classes.

Answers:
Learners' own posters

Plenary idea

Other changes (5–10 minutes)

Description: Ask learners what they changed about the story. (its characters)

Ask them to quickly say what else they could have changed:

- The main characters: the boy and the snake
- The setting: the shade of a tree
- The type of tree

| CROSS-CURRICULAR LINKS |

Science: Together, identify the different parts of a eucalyptus tree.

Art: Make paintings of eucalyptus trees, leaves or flowers, ideally after a study of real samples. If not, use a bank of pictures as stimulus.

Homework ideas

Learners complete the Workbook Session 4.11 activities if not completed in class.

They revisit the list of questions posed about the eucalyptus tree from Getting started and invite learners to try to find out some of the answers with their family members.

Answers for Workbook

1 One, of, tree, the, no
2 snake, from, up, with, day
3 said, and, you're / you are, you, Do, with, for, with (or any similar words that make sense)

4.12 Look back

LEARNING PLAN

Learning objectives		Learning intentions	Success criteria
Main focus	**Also covered**	• To share stories, asking and answering questions.	• Learners can share stories, asking and answering questions.
1Ra.04, 1Ra.05, 1Wp.06, 1SLm.01, 1SLr.01, 1SLp.05	1Ri.07, 1Wp.03, 1SLm.02, 1SLm.03, 2SLs.02, 1SLg.01, 1SLg.02, 1SLg.03, 1SLg.04,	• To check and improve their writing.	• Learners can check and improve their writing.
		• To talk about the stories and their learning in this unit.	• Learners can talk about the stories and their learning in this unit.

LANGUAGE SUPPORT

Use the Language worksheet 4B to check knowledge and understanding of the unit vocabulary, and to practise spelling.

CAMBRIDGE PRIMARY ENGLISH 1 TEACHER'S RESOURCE

Common misconception

Misconception	How to identify	How to overcome
When handwriting, we need to join all the letters in a word.	Ask learners to try to write the word *eucalyptus* with some joined letters.	Ask learners how they might join the word *eucalyptus*. Ask learners to try joining the whole word, but to stop at the *y* (we do not loop *y*, so we have to take a break). Ask learners how else we could join words: • by syllables joining *eu–cal–ypt–us* (but still not the *y*) • by phonemes: this is probably easier to demonstrate with a simpler word, e.g. *boy b–oy, tree t–r–ee.*

Starter idea

Ask and answer questions (5–10 minutes)

Resources: Learner's Book, Session 4.12: Getting started; learners' story posters from Session 4.11

Description: Ask learners to tell you what words we can use to begin a question. (*Why, what, how, when, where, who, which*)

Draw their attention to the question starters in Getting started and model the creation of good questions using these. Questions may relate to poster content, layout, design, etc.

Select some of the story posters from Session 4.11 and invite learners to question each other about their posters. Celebrate their work and encourage positive and constructive peer feedback.

Main teaching ideas

1 Check writing (10–15 minutes)

   Learning intention: to start learning how to check writing for mistakes

   Resources: Learner's Book, Session 4.12, Activity 1

   Description: Remind learners of the value of mistakes, saying: *We learn from mistakes.*

   If appropriate, choose an example of text that needs correcting. Write it on the board and discuss it together.

Then ask learners to look at their story posters. Can they find:

• one spelling mistake and one word that they could write more neatly?

• a word that has a digraph or trigraph which they could practise joining?

• something they would prefer to change if they could?

Encourage peer feedback, but try to keep it positive.

> **Differentiation ideas:** Support learners by working with them in a group or selecting a sentence for them to improve.

Challenge learners to spot punctuation errors, too.

Answers:
Learners' own responses

2 The unit stories (10–15 minutes)

   Learning intention: to reflect on the unit's stories and recall features

   Resources: Learner's Book, Session 4.12, Activity 2; Workbook, Session 4.12; Language worksheet 4B

   Description: Ask learners if they can recall the poems and stories from the unit, using memory as well as any class displays you may have created.

   List them together and then look at the pictures in the Learner's Book for further prompts.

Ask learners to talk about the stories and poems, saying: *Which did you enjoy most? Why?*

Ask learners to recall the characters and which they liked the best and the least, explaining why.

You can use the Workbook Session 4.12 activities in class now for further practice.

Ask learners which poems or stories they would like to read again.

You can use Language worksheet 4B here to encourage learners to create a personal wordbank for the unit that they can revisit and use in their writing.

> **Differentiation ideas:** Support learners by using the pictures in earlier sessions of Unit 4, or classroom displays as reminders of the unit texts.

Challenge learners to find other versions of stories they have enjoyed, or stories with similar themes, and to record as a log of books read.

Answers:
Learners' own responses

3   Skill review (10–15 minutes)

Learning intention: to think about learning in terms of language skills

Resources: Learner's Book, Session 4.12, Activity 3

Description: Remind learners of the vocabulary we use to describe language skills: reading, writing, spelling, listening and speaking.

Say each skill in turn and ask learners to put their hand up if they think they are good at it.

Now ask learners to say or write one thing from this unit that helped them with these skills.

These simple learner statements can be extremely useful for informing end-of-term reports.

> **Differentiation ideas:** Support learners to be positive in their skill review by providing oral models, e.g. *I think you are much better at … now.*

Challenge learners to also think of one thing they still need to improve.

Answers:
Learners' own responses

Plenary idea

Taster (5–10 minutes)

Resources: other traditional tales to inspire reading for pleasure

Description: Share a collection of other traditional tales and read just the opening pages to include the repeated refrain.

Books may be in print or online and may include:

*   *Goldilocks*
*   *The Three Billy Goats Gruff*
*   *The Enormous Turnip*
*   *Mulan*
*   any favourites from your country.

Ask learners which they would like to read next and why.

Homework ideas

Learners complete the Workbook Session 4.12 activities if not completed in class.

They find an official version of one of the stories from Unit 4 online and watch it with someone at home.

Answers for Workbook

1   Learners correctly join characters to speech bubbles:
    a   Chicken Licken
    b   Chapatti man
    c   boy with toy
2   Learners' own choices, but may include:
    *   Snake: Do you think there is room for something yummy with you inside my tummy?
    *   The cook: Come back!
3   Learners' own choices of characters and repetitive refrains

CHECK YOUR PROGRESS

1 We have been reading 'joining-in' stories in this unit.

2 Run, run as fast as you can. You can't stop me, I'm The Chapatti Man. (with or without speech marks is acceptable).

3 Possible answers: All the stories had repeated words / had talking animals (or similar).

4 Learners' own answers

5 boys, foxes

6 The Chapatti Man jumped up and (he) ran away.

PROJECT GUIDANCE

Group project: Support learners to make some pancakes, chapatti or gingerbread men (real with ingredients or pretend with modelling clay or similar).

Pair project: Learners can design and make a storytelling card game. Ask them to draw their story pictures on pieces of card and then to place the cards in order as they tell the story.

Solo project: Provide materials for learners to design and make a bookmark that explores the content of this unit in some way. Encourage learners to use their bookmark to show their place in their reading books.

For more guidance on setting up and assessing projects, see Project guidance at the end of Unit 1.

>5 Do it like this!

Unit plan

Session	Approximate number of learning hours	Outline of learning content	Resources
5.1 Information all around us	1.5	Talk about different forms of information. Read labels and signs to check understanding.	Learner's Book Session 5.1 Workbook Session 5.1 ⬇ Worksheet 5.1
5.2 Writing labels and signs	1.5	Find out about and discuss why signs are written in capitals. Create signs.	Learner's Book Session 5.2 Workbook Session 5.2 ⬇ Worksheet 5.2
5.3 How to mix colours	1	Talk about colours and find some in the classroom. Listen to and read an instructional text about mixing colours.	Learner's Book Session 5.3 Workbook Session 5.3
5.4 Checking understanding	1	Answer questions about a text to check understanding. Explore digraphs.	Learner's Book Session 5.4 Workbook Session 5.4 Phonics Workbooks A and B
5.5 Making a poster	1.5	Explore the features of an instructional text. Plan and write an instructional poster.	Learner's Book Session 5.5 Workbook Session 5.5
5.6 Listening – from fiction to non-fiction	1.5	Explore a fictional story that includes an instructional text. Talk about fiction and non-fiction texts.	Learner's Book Session 5.6 Workbook Session 5.6 ⬇ Differentiated worksheets 5A–C

Session	Approximate number of learning hours	Outline of learning content	Resources
5.7 How to make a ladybird	1.5	Read and follow instructions to make an origami ladybird.	Learner's Book Session 5.7 Workbook Session 5.7
5.8 Writing and sorting instructions	1.5	Write simple instructions. Match instructions to pictures and sequence these.	Learner's Book Session 5.8 Workbook Session 5.8
5.9 Instructions for cooking	1	Talk about ingredients and equipment for a recipe. Listen to and read a recipe, exploring the use of full stops.	Learner's Book Session 5.9 Workbook Session 5.9 ⬇ Worksheet 5.3
5.10 Checking sequence	1.5	Talk about the importance of order in instructions. Answer questions to check understanding.	Learner's Book Session 5.10 Workbook Session 5.10 ⬇ Language worksheet 5A ⬇ Language worksheet 5B
5.11 Planning and writing a recipe	1.5	Identify the features of a recipe. Write a recipe based on a model provided.	Learner's Book Session 5.11 Workbook Session 5.11 ⬇ Worksheet 5.4 ⬇ Differentiated worksheets 5A–C
5.12 Look back	1	Check instruction writing. Talk about the instructional texts in the unit. Think about learning.	Learner's Book Session 5.12 Workbook Session 5.12
Cross-unit resources			
Learner's Book Check your progress Learner's Book Projects			

BACKGROUND KNOWLEDGE

Before you begin to teach this unit, you may find it helpful to:

- prepare to talk with learners about instructions. You could prepare some examples to share such as labels, signs, posters, pictures and recipes. Familiarise yourself with the language of instructions, e.g. requests and commands and how numbers can be used to sequence them.

- familiarise yourself with the phonics and grammar elements in this unit, including:

  - phonics - letter to sound correspondence, consonant and vowel diagraphs, words with adjacent consonants, blending and segmenting words

  - sequencing words, pictures and events using time adverbials such as *first, then* and *next*

  - using capital letters for emphasis.

TEACHING SKILLS FOCUS

Assessment for Learning

Assessment for Learning (AfL) is a very powerful tool to support teaching and learning. It gives teachers insight into learners' own perceptions of their learning and allows us to use that information to focus teaching.

How can you teach your Stage 1 learners to engage with AfL?

In different teaching sessions, try out ideas and identify which ideas work most effectively for your different learners. For example:

- *Sharing learning intentions* so that learners know what the focus of their learning for this lesson is. Throughout this resource, learning intentions are provided in the Learning plans for each session. One key learning intention is provided in the Learner's Book for each session and is clearly linked to framework objectives.

- *Sharing and negotiating success criteria.* Sample success criteria, derived from the learning intentions, are also included in the

Learning plans for each session, but you and your learners may wish to modify these to reflect their strengths and weaknesses.

- *Giving feedback* to learners both tells them how to improve their work and models what feedback looks like.

- *Making opportunities for peer and self-assessment* encourages learners to assess and evaluate their own and others' work. Initially, you may wish to encourage learners simply to say something they are proud of in their own work and to tell a partner what they can be proud of. As learners become more confident and discriminating, invite them to suggest one improvement.

- *Effective questioning* can be used to scaffold learning by one question leading to a harder question, to encourage reflection and to give learners the chance to explore, explain and develop their thinking.

Cambridge Reading Adventures

Learners may enjoy other fiction titles from Cambridge Reading Adventures that follow the unit theme:

- *On the Track* by Claire Llewellyn (Blue Band)
- *How Chocolate is Made* by Claire Llewellyn (Turquoise Band)
- *Draw the World* by Catherine Chambers (Turquoise Band)

5.1 Information all around us

LEARNING PLAN

Learning objectives		Learning intentions	Success criteria
Main focus	**Also covered**	• To talk about, listen to and read information around them.	• Learners can talk about, listen to and read information around them.
1Rv.02, 1Rs.02, 1Rs.04, 1Ri.08	1Ri.03, 1Ri.04, 1Ri.09, 1Ra.01, 1Ra.04, 1Ww.05, 1Wv.01, 1SLm.01, 1SLg.03, 1SLp.05, 1Ws.01	• To understand picture signs and their meanings.	• Learners can understand picture signs and their meanings.
		• To draw signs and write labels.	• Learners can draw signs and write labels.

LANGUAGE SUPPORT

Learners will benefit from a 'walk-about' in school, or the local community, to discover and talk about signs and labels (see Homework ideas).

Practise language structures such as *What does this sign say / tell us to do?* and *Where do we see signs like this?*

Common misconception

Misconception	How to identify	How to overcome
We always have to say every letter sound in a word.	Write the word *sign* on the board. Ask learners to say the sounds and blend them to read the word. They may say: /s/ /i/ /g/ /n/ and wonder how the letter sounds help us to read the word. Explain to learners that we always start by using phonics to sound out words, but sometimes we have to try out other letter sound possibilities to sound the word correctly. Model saying /s//igh/ /n/ and talk through how to try using a long /igh/ rather than a short /i/ and then how to jump over the silent *g*.	Find different examples of words with tricky letters or unstressed vowels but linked to the topic, e.g. *labels* (unstressed *e*); *ice* (*c* as /s/). Remind learners, when they are struggling with a word, that they might need to try other letter sound possibilities.

Starter idea

Information all around us (10–15 minutes)

Resources: *How to make chocolate-chip muffins* (Learner's Book, Session 5.1: Getting started); Track 29; further pictures or photos of different kinds of instructions

Description: Explain that this unit is about giving and following instructions. Say: *Instructions tell us to do something and often how to do it.*

Ask learners to talk about what they know about instructions and to share their experiences. Introduce some of the vocabulary and key content from the unit.

Ask learners to explore and talk about the pictures in Getting started, in pairs. Then ask them to share what they recognised or can name.

Encourage the use of vocabulary such as: *labels, signs, recipes, actions, instructions to make things*, etc.

Ask: *Do the pictures show any instructions that are not familiar to you? Are there other instructions you would add?*

Play the audio or read the text about how to make chocolate-chip muffins.

Main teaching ideas

1 Read labels and signs on a map (10–15 minutes)

Learning intention: to talk about labels and signs on a map and explore meanings

Resources: Learner's Book, Session 5.1, Activity 1

Description: Tell learners that for this activity they are going to explore information on a map. Check they understand the word *map*.

Ask learners what signs they see on their way to school. Give learners time, in pairs, to explore the map in Activity 1 and its labels and signs. Ask them what they noticed and read.

Draw learners' attention to the use of pictures and words. Ask them to point to different labelled features, e.g. forest or car park.

Invite their comments and interpretations of the information. Discuss what else could be labelled, e.g. campsite, mountains, a roundabout.

If possible, arrange for learners to go out to record signs nearby, or to create their own play mat map (see Projects at the end of this unit).

> **Differentiation ideas:** Support learners by pairing them with learners who have different reading strengths.

Challenge learners to say what is missing in the map

2 What do signs mean? (15–30 minutes')

Learning intention: to talk about what picture or symbol signs mean and to add them to a map in the correct place

Resources: Learner's Book, Session 5.1, Activity 2; Worksheet 5.1; map from Activity 1

Description: Show a collection of sign images if available. Ask learners if they know what various pictures or symbols mean.

Show learners the signs in Activity 2.

In pairs, ask learners to name and explain each sign before finding it on the map in Activity 1. (For each sign, give learners a few minutes to locate an example before asking for responses.) Ask if there is more than one place to find or put each sign.

Ask learners to use Worksheet 5.1 Labels and signs to record their responses.

> **Differentiation ideas:** Support learners by enlarging the map in Worksheet 5.1 Labels and signs and completing it as a group.

Challenge learners to draw each sign and write a sentence about what each sign means. Some learners may enjoy drawing and labelling the map without the worksheet, so suggest large pieces of paper and felt tip pens for those wanting to do this.

Answers:
a zebra crossing means it is safe to cross here; sharp bend; roundabout; snow or ice on the road; campsite; no parking

3 Draw other signs (15–30 minutes)

Learning intention: to draw signs to add to the map

Resources: Learner's Book, Session 5.1, Activity 3; learners' ideas from Activity 1; large pieces of paper and felt tip pens or paints (optional)

Description: Revisit learners' earlier ideas in Activity 1 for other signs that might be added to the map.

Show learners the two signs in Activity 3 as examples. Discuss the shape, colour and pictures or symbols on the two signs:

- diamond shape, yellow and black, duck and ducklings
- circle, red and black, a diagonal line, a camera.

Give learners three minutes to work in pairs to say what other information they would like to give people who are using the map, and what signs they would like to add.

Circulate and encourage creativity. Then ask for learners' ideas.

Ask learners to draw and explain two of their new sign ideas. You may wish them to do this in their notebooks or to draw or paint them on larger pieces of paper. Either way, ensure they have written a sentence to explain what their sign means.

> **Differentiation ideas:** Support learners by encouraging them to change the signs in the activity, e.g. change ducklings to hedgehogs/turtles (*Look out for hedgehogs/turtles!*) and the phone to a car (*No cars*).

Challenge learners to create more than two of their own newly designed signs with explanations. This might make an attractive class display.

Answers:
Learners' own drawings and ideas

Plenary idea

1 Quick-fire signs (5 minutes)

Resources: online images of signs

Description: Show a selection of online sign images.

Ask learners to view and identify the instruction for each sign you show, at speed!

This may be played as a team game in which you ask each group to respond to a sign. If they answer incorrectly, they are out of the game.

Homework ideas

Learners complete the Workbook Session 5.1 activities for this session if not completed in class.

They record any signs they see on their way home from school and describe them the next day.

Answers for Workbook

Answers might include:

1 **a** stop; **b** angry; **c** sad; **d** you can't go this way / no right turn; **e** zoo; **f** school

2 Learners write appropriate missing labels (e.g. pen pot, jug, sink) and join all labels to the correct pictures.

3 Learners' own labels and responses

5.2 Writing labels and signs

LEARNING PLAN

Learning objectives		Learning intentions	Success criteria
Main focus	**Also covered**	• To explore non-verbal communication.	• Learners can explore non-verbal communication.
1Wc.05, 1Wp.02, 1SLm.04, 1SLr.02	1Rv.03, 1Rs.02, 1Rs.04, 1Ri.03, 1Ri.04, 1Ri.08, 1Ri.09, 1Wc.04, 1Wp.01, 1Wp.05, 1SLm.01, 1SLm.03, 1SLm.05, 1SLg.04, 1SLp.05	• To use capital letters to write a sign. • To describe a sign.	• Learners can use capital letters to write a sign. • Learners can describe a sign.

LANGUAGE SUPPORT

All learners will benefit from the non-verbal communication strategies in this unit: using our faces and bodies to make signs.

Provide gross and fine motor skill activities to support those who struggle to write letters small. Letter formation in a variety of media will also support handwriting, e.g. in sand and paint.

Common misconception

Misconception	How to identify	How to overcome
Capital letters are just bigger versions of lower-case letters.	Ask learners to look at a sign written in lower-case letters and one written in capitals. Ask: *What do you notice?* Highlight letters that are the same: *s* and *S*, *w* and *W*, *p* and *P* What do they notice about other letters, such as: *b* and *B*, *h* and *H*?	Provide a class frieze for learners to use when they are unsure how to write a letter in either case. Allow peer-assessment time: Encourage learners to choose a word from their writing and talk about it with a partner. They should check for correct letter size, comparative sizing and correct use of lower-case and capital letters.

Starter idea

Non-verbal communication (15–20 minutes;)

Resources: Learner's Book, Session 5.2: Getting started; emoticons

Description: Stand in front of the class and do not speak. Give some simple instructions using hand gestures, facial expressions and actions. Continue for a while and try to get learners to respond.

After a while (and some fun!), ask learners what they know about communicating without words.

Together, look at the photos in Getting started. Ask learners to say what each child is 'saying' (especially if none of these instructions has arisen so far in discussion).

Give learners a few minutes to think of their own signs to act and to try out some of their ideas in pairs. Then ask learners to share their ideas in pairs or groups.

Be mindful if you have learners from different countries, since some gestures that are acceptable in your culture may be considered offensive in others.

Main teaching ideas

1 Talk about signs (20–30 minutes)

Learning intention: to explore capital letters on signs

Resources: Learner's Book, Session 5.2, Activity 1; Workbook, Session 5.2; stickers; capital letters

Description: Review the signs you have already explored in and out of the classroom. If you have begun a display or collection of signs, review it together.

Ask learners if they can see, or remember seeing, any signs in capital letters.

Discuss why capital letters might be used sometimes. (To make a strong point, to get someone's attention or to tell us that something is serious or dangerous.)

Ask learners to read the signs in Activity 1 and to answer the questions.

Give them a few minutes to work on these with a partner before asking for responses.

You can use the Workbook Session 5.2 activities here for further practice of capital letters.

> **Differentiation ideas:** Support learners with mixed-ability pairings or work with them in a group.

Challenge learners by asking them to think of other examples of places each sign might be.

Answers:
a–c The signs are written in capital letters; KEEP OUT and DO NOT ENTER: near somewhere where you should not enter (like a top secret room or a building site); DANGER: near something that is dangerous (like a cliff edge); CLOSED: on a shop door, to tell you a shop is closed.

2 Design and write a sign with capital letters (20–30 minutes)

Learning intention: to design and write a sign using capital letters

Resources: Learner's Book, Session 5.2, Activity 2; Worksheet 5.2

Description: Tell learners they are going to design and make their own signs with capital letters.

Learners can work in pairs or individually. Consider allowing them to choose how they create their final sign (e.g. paint, coloured pencils, collage).

Draw their attention to the planning chart in Activity 2 and discuss the different design options they should think about, and the questions.

Ask learners to share their ideas with a partner or, if working alone, to write notes and draw sketches. You can provide Worksheet 5.2 Design a sign now to help learners structure their thought processes.

Ask learners to create their signs and check that their capital letters are correctly formed.

> **Differentiation ideas:** Support learners by helping them to practise drawing their sign, ready to copy into their notebook or onto their piece of paper. They may also benefit from practising letter formation on the table top, or in a sand tray, if they are feeling unsure about letter formation.

Challenge learners to self-assess or peer assess the effectiveness of their sign.

Answers:
Learners' own designs

3 Describe a sign (10–15 minutes)

Learning intention: to present to the class

Resources: Learner's Book, Session 5.2, Activity 3

Description: Remind learners how important is it to speak clearly when we are speaking to others.

What tips do they know about speaking out loud? (e.g. Standing tall, smiling, using a big, clear voice, looking at the people you are talking to.) You may wish to draw learners' attention to the Speaking tip.

Ask learners to prepare to talk about their signs, either in their pairs or independently.

They should say:

- where their sign is for
- what it shows or tells us
- what shape and colour it is.
- what word is written in capital letters
- where they will display it and why.

Allow time for learners to prepare, and circulate in the classroom to offer support.

Ask for volunteers to present their signs using a loud, clear voice. Ask the audience to give feedback on the presenter. Provide some sentence starters: *I liked the way …; I thought … (it was a very useful sign because …); I think he/she used a very strong voice …*, etc.

> **Differentiation ideas:** Support learners by providing fewer discussion prompts for their signs, or by prompting them with questions when they present them.

Challenge learners to add more detail in their presentation and to invite audience participation.

Answers:
Learners' presentations of their signs

Plenary idea

Non-verbal exit game (5–10 minutes)

Description: Give learners instructions to do things using non-verbal communication

See how long you can keep going.

Eventually use non-verbal communication to ask them to leave in different ways, e.g. hop, skip, clap as they go out of the classroom.

Keep asking learners to leave in different ways until all have left.

CROSS-CURRICULAR LINKS

Maths: Explore the number of sides of 2D shapes used to create signs

PSED: Research other ways that people communicate without words, e.g. Makaton or other sign languages.

Art: Paint creative pictures using capital letter shapes as inspiration.

Homework ideas

Learners complete the Workbook Session 5.2 activities if not completed in class.

They record or take photos of signs in the environment that use capital letters and share them with the class.

Answers for Workbook

1. Learners copy the lower-case letters with correct letter formation, and then self-assess.

2. Learners copy the capital letters with correct letter formation, and then self-assess.

3. Learners write words in capital letters for each sign with correct letter formation, and then self-assess.
    a STOP; **b** SCHOOL; **c** ONE WAY; **d** CLOSED

4. Learners write words in capital letters for each sign with correct letter formation, and then self-assess.
    a CROSSING; **b** ROUNDABOUT; **c** SNOW/ICE; **d** CAMPSITE

5.3 How to mix colours

LEARNING PLAN

Learning objectives		Learning intentions	Success criteria
Main focus	**Also covered**	• To talk about colours.	• Learners can talk about colours.
1Ri.03, 1Ws.02, 1Wp.04, 1SLs.01	1Rw.07, 1Rs.02, 1Ri.04, 1Ri.08, 1Ri.09, 1Ra.01, 1Ra.03, 1Ra.04, 1Ww.02	• To write a list and record information in a chart. • To listen to and read instructions for how to mix colours.	• Learners can write a list and record information in a chart. • Learners can listen to and read instructions for how to mix colours.

LANGUAGE SUPPORT

Play games and undertake activities to reinforce the language of colour. Learners may benefit from physically experimenting with mixing colours to reinforce correct language. Try mixing a 'class colour', or creating a colour mixing chart or frieze for display.

Common misconception

Misconception	How to identify	How to overcome
It is tricky to listen and read at the same time.	Ask learners to think about different language skills. Ask them to listen to a sentence. Ask them to read a different sentence. Ask them to listen to and follow a sentence at the same time. Ask: *Which was easiest? Hardest? Why?*	Give learners systematic practice of both reading and listening, but also of asking them to listen, then listen and read, then read, in order to scaffold skills.

Starter idea

Play a game (5–10 minutes)

Resources: Learner's Book, Session 5.3: Getting started; class colour chart or frieze (if available)

Description: Quickly check learners know their colours be asking: *Can you bring me something yellow?, Can you touch something red?,* etc.

Explain to learners that they are going to play a colour game. Ask them to listen carefully to the instructions and to respond.

Say: *Stand up if up are wearing* [colour]. *Hop if you are wearing* [colour]. *Jump up if you are wearing* [colour] *Show me if you are wearing* [colour]. Refer to a class colour chart if you have one.

You might like to link to phonics here by playing this game using sound talk, e.g. *Stand up if you are wearing r-e-d. Find me something that is b-r-ow-n,* etc.

Play other colour games that learners know.

Main teaching ideas

1 Name the colours (15–20 minutes)

Learning intention: to explore colour names with paint

Resources: Learner's Book, Session 5.3, Activity 1; class colour chart or frieze (if available); paint and paint brushes

Description: Introduce colours again using your classroom colour frieze or display if you have one. (Make sure the chart and its labels are low enough in your classroom so that learners can see it clearly to check colour spellings.)

Consider using paint and paint brushes to demonstrate a practical version of Activity 1 with the class.

When learners have practised, look at pictures in the Learner's Book together and ask learners to draw the different-coloured paint brushes and label them in their notebooks.

> **Differentiation ideas:** Support learners with labels for them to match to the colours.

Challenge some learners to include other colours, e.g. *turquoise.*

Answers:
Learners' own responses

2 Look for colours (15–30 minutes;)

Learning intention: to identify and record colours

Resources: Learner's Book, Session 5.3, Activity 2; Workbook, Session 5.3

Description: Tell learners they are going to create a colour chart.

Model how to do this using the picture in the book.

- Write the names of five colours.
- Find something that has the first colour.
- Tick the colour.
- Draw and label the thing you find.
- Repeat for the other colours.

You can use the Workbook Session 5.3 activities now.

> **Differentiation ideas:** Support learners by allowing them to work in pairs and/or by providing a chart layout.

Challenge learners by asking them to find more than one thing to draw and label for each colour, or to list more than five colours.

Answers:
Learners' own responses

3 Read the instructions (10–15 minutes)

Learning intention: to read and listen to instructions

Resources: *How to Make Colours* (Learner's Book, Session 5.3, Activity 3); Track 30; paint and paint brushes

Description: Tell learners they are going to listen to instructions about how to mix paints to make new colours.

Ask what they already know about colour mixing: *Do you know how to do this?* You might like to demonstrate with two colours.

Now, ask learners to follow the text as they listen. Play the audio or read the text again.

Ask learners to read the text in pairs.

> **Differentiation ideas:** Support learners by asking them to only listen for how to make green.

Challenge learners to read the text aloud for the class.

Plenary idea

Colour mixing (5–10 minutes)

Description: Provide learners with colour-mix challenges for a group discussion, e.g. *How do you make black paint into grey paint? How do you make light blue into dark blue?*

Encourage creative responses.

CROSS-CURRICULAR LINKS
Art: Explore what happens when you mix two, three and even four colours together.
Music: Sing songs about colours.

Homework ideas

Learners complete the Workbook Session 5.3 activities if not completed in class

They create a mood board of one colour to show how one colour can vary in its tones. They may tear up magazines pages to create this rather like a mosaic.

Answers for Workbook

1   Learners colour correctly and write their own colour words.

2   Paint brushes, paper

3   **a** Mix; **b** red; **c** make; **d** purple; **e** green

4   Missing labels: orange and green.

5.4 Checking understanding

LEARNING PLAN

Learning objectives		Learning intentions	Success criteria
Main focus	**Also covered**	• To answer questions to show understanding.	• Learners can answer questions to show understanding.
1Rw.02, 1Rw.05, 1Rw.07, 1Ww.02, 1Ww.06	1Rw.03, 1Rw.06, 1Ri.13, 1Ra.03, 1Ww.05, 1Wp.04, 1SLs.02	• To fill word gaps to show understanding and to spell common words.	• Learners can fill word gaps to show understanding and to spell common words.
		• To sort words by vowel digraphs.	• Learners can sort words by vowel digraphs.

LANGUAGE SUPPORT

Learners may benefit from phonic games and activities, including those in the Phonics Workbooks, to practise blending and segmenting words that feature digraphs. See Phonics Workbook A, pages 36–51, and Phonics Workbook B, pages 4–23.

Play games of Bingo or Snap to reinforce recognition of common words, e.g. *to, and, the, make, need.*

Common misconception

Misconception	How to identify	How to overcome
Seeing –le at the end of a word means we say luh.	Write some words ending in –le on the board, e.g. *purple*, *bottle*, *juggle*, *giggle*. Ask learners to read them. Model how to sound them out to demonstrate that –le is two letters but one sound /l/.	Create a –le word bank for learners to use when writing. Remind learners how to respond to words ending in –le when reading.

Starter idea

Play a game (10–15 minutes)

Resources: Learner's Book Session 5.4: Getting started; colour cards (orange, red, yellow, green, blue, purple); plus and equals sign cards

Description: Check that learners can identify colours, including purple, green and orange.

Hand out the colour cards (for the colours in Getting started, but you may include other colours if you wish).

Ask learners to stand up when they hear their name and colour. Say: *If X is red* (learner stands up) *and Y is yellow* (learner stands up) *and they mix together, what colour will they make?*

Ask learners for a response: *They make orange* (orange stands up).

Play several times with different learners holding different colour cards.

Main teaching ideas

1 Answer questions (10–20 minutes)

Learning intention: to answer questions to check understanding

Resources: Learner's Book, Session 5.4, Activity 1; *How to Make Colours* (Learner's Book, Session 5.3); Track 30

Description: Tell learners to re-read the text in Learner's Book Session 5.3 Activity 3.

Ask a few learners to read the text aloud a few times to the class.

Explain that they are going to answer questions about the text to show they understand it. This activity could be set up as a competition. Explain that they will get one point for each correct answer and one bonus point for each correct answer written as part of a sentence.

Give learners time to work in pairs or in a group. Ask them to write their answers in their notebooks.

Swap with a partner to score their answers.

> **Differentiation ideas:** Support learners by using mixed-ability pairs or groups.

Challenge learners to write some bonus questions.

Answers:
a It's a paint brush. (correct spelling only to win point); b You need it for painting. c No, you don't. / You don't need blue to make orange; d Yes, you do. / You do need red to make purple. e You mix yellow and blue to make green. f You get pink if you add white to red. g Learners' own questions

2 Fill in the gaps (15–20 minutes)

Learning intention: to check understanding by filling in the gaps

Resources: Learner's Book, Session 5.4, Activity 2; *How to Make Colours* (Learner's Book, Session 5.3); Track 30

Description: Read the text in Learner's Book Session 5.3 Session 3 aloud a few times. Leave different words out each time. Ask learners to listen and supply the missing words.

Ask learners to copy the text from Learner's Book Session 5.4 Activity 2 and fill in the missing common words.

Remind learners to use their phonics, where they can, to correctly spell the words.

> **Differentiation ideas:** Support learners by providing the missing words as word cards.

Challenge learners by asking them to challenge each other with their own versions of this activity.

Answers:
to, need, make, to, to, Mix, make, and

3 Copy the chart (10–15 minutes)

Learning intention: to explore digraphs

Resources: Learner's Book, Session 5.4, Activity 3; Workbook, Session 5.4; Phonics Workbooks A and B

Description: Write the following colour words on the board: *green, yellow, purple, blue*. Ask learners to blend the sounds to read the words.

Talk about the digraphs in each word: *ee, ow, ur* and *ue*.

Together, look at the words before the chart in Activity 3. Read one of the words. Ask learners to find a word with a matching sound e.g. *turn* matches *purple*.

Ask learners to work in pairs to complete the chart in the Learner's Book.

You can use the Workbook Session 5.4 activities here, for further practice.

Phonics: you may like to use Phonics Workbook A, pages 40–41 and 50–51, and Phonics Workbook B, pages 18–21, here for further practice of specified digraphs.

> **Differentiation ideas:** Support learners by providing the words on cards, to be sorted into sets.

Challenge learners to add more words to each set.

Answers:
green: need, seen; yellow: flow, show; purple: turn, curl; blue: glue, true. (Note, *bean* has the same sound but different letters, and *how* has the same letters but a different sound.)

Plenary idea

Digraph Bingo (5–10 minutes)

Resources: blank Bingo cards (3x3, one for each pair); bag

Description: Ask learners to work in pairs to write nine words that feature vowel digraphs on their Bingo cards and also in a list. Ask them to cut up the words in the list.

Put the cut-up list of words from each pair in a bag and mix them up.

Then ask learners to swap their card with another pair.

Pick out words and call them out.

Learners cross out words on their card.

The winners are the pair who cross out all their words first.

CROSS-CURRICULAR LINKS

Art: Continue to explore colour mixing. If possible, show how speed or splatter painting can create colour merging and interesting effects.

Homework ideas

Learners complete the Workbook Session 5.4 activities if not completed in class.

They find more words like *purple* that end in *–le* and add them to the class list.

Answers for Workbook

1 green: screen/been; yellow: pillow/show; purple: fur/turtle; blue: true/clue

2 green: mean/theme; yellow: toe/boat; white: night/I; blue: two/too; red: bread/said

3 Learners' own responses

5.5 Making a poster

LEARNING PLAN

Learning objectives		Learning intentions	Success criteria
Main focus	**Also covered**	• To explore the features of an instructional text.	• Learners can explore the features of an instructional text.
1Rs.01, 1Rsi.04, 1Wc.04, 1Wc.05, 1Wp.05	1Rs.02, 1Rs.04, 1Ri.03, 1Ri.04, 1Ri.08, 1Ri.09, 1Ra.01, 1Ra.04, 1Ws.01, 1Ws.02, 1Wp.04, 1SLg.01, 1SLg.02, 1SLg.03, 1SLg.04	• To listen to instructions and match to pictures in order. • To plan and write a poster for the classroom.	• Learners can listen to instructions and match to pictures in order. • Learners can plan and write a poster for the classroom.

LANGUAGE SUPPORT

Continue to reinforce the language of instructional texts explored so far, including labels, signs and *how to …* texts.

Provide opportunities to revisit number names and formation.

Provide opportunities to talk about and sequence common daily routines, e.g. asking learners to stand in the correct order with cards or pictures.

Common misconception

Misconception	How to identify	How to overcome
Listening to a series of instructions is difficult.	• Ask learners to follow a series of simple instructions, e.g. *stand up, sit down, put your arms on your head and close your eyes.* • Ask them what they are doing to understand and follow your instructions. • Ask: *What makes listening difficult?* (e.g. background noise)	Prepare learners well for listening tasks, e.g. tell them in advance and give a sign; ask them to prepare by sitting still and focusing on what they hear; ask them to be confident in their responses. Regular practice will help.

Starter idea

Features (10–15 minutes)

Resources: Learner's Book, Session 5.5: Getting started; *How to Make Colours* (Learner's Book, Session 5.3); Track 30

Description: Ask learners to list the features of the *How to make colours* text in Session 5.3 Activity 3. The text should be familiar to them now, but they may need to look back at it.

See how many features they can recall, before looking at the examples in Getting started.

Ask learners to tell you about each feature to reinforce the learning.

Draw their attention to the speech bubble text. They may decide that arrows or numbers would help people to know what order to mix the colours in.

Tell them that in this session they are going to explore picture instructions.

Main teaching ideas

1 Listen and point (10–15 minutes;)

Learning intention: to listen to instructions and point to pictures in sequence

Resources: *How to wash your hands before you eat* (Learner's Book, Session 5.5, Activity 1); Track 31

Description: Ask learners how they wash their hands. Give them a few minutes to work in pairs or small groups to discuss and to come up with instructions for how to wash hands.

Ask one or two groups to share their ideas.

Ask other learners if the instructions given were clear. Discuss why, or why not.

Tell learners they are going listen to some instructions for how to wash hands.

Draw learners' attention to the Listening tip, which will help them in subsequent activities.

⟩ **Differentiation ideas:** Support learners by working with them as a group.

Challenge learners by asking them to retell the sequence using numbers or words (*first, then, next*, etc.).

Audioscript: *How to wash your hands before you eat*

How to wash your hands before you eat.

1 Put some water in a bowl and wet your hands.
2 Put some soap in your hands.
3 Rub the soap into your hands.
4 Rinse the soap off your hands.
5 Dry your hands.
6 Sit down to eat.

Answers:

Learners point to the pictures in the following order:

3 Put some water in the bowl and wet your hands.
5 Put some soap in your hands.
1 Rub the soap into your hands.
6 Rinse the soap off your hands.
2 Dry your hands.
4 Sit down to eat.

---

2 Look at and talk about posters (15–20 minutes)

Learning intention: to plan a poster

Resources: Learner's Book, Session 5.5, Activity 2; Workbook, Session 5.5; instructional posters, if you have any to share; large pieces of paper

Description: Show learners your instructional posters or share those in Activity 2.

Ask learners to identify the heading and the sub-headings. Read them together.

You can use the Workbook Session 5.5 activities now.

Ask learners to work in pairs or groups to choose one of the posters and to plan it. Ask them to make notes on a large piece of paper.

Talk about how notes do not have to be full sentences; they can just be words. They do not have to be in best handwriting; they are just to support writing later.

Give learners five minutes to plan their posters.

Before inviting learners to share their plans, draw their attention to the Speaking tip to encourage good listening.

Encourage feedback, and encourage learners to check their plans against the features list in Getting started.

> **Differentiation ideas:** Support learners by providing the headings and working as a group with them.

Challenge learners to think about design and layout.

Answers:
Learners' own ideas for instructional posters

3   Make a poster (30–40 minutes)

Learning intention: to make and write an instructional poster

Resources: Learner's Book, Session 5.5, Activity 3; Learners' plans from Activity 2; large pieces of poster-sized paper; pens/paint

Description: Ask learners to now write their posters using their plans from Activity 2. Provide large pieces of paper, felt tips or paints. Give them plenty of time to create their posters.

As you move about the classroom, encourage learners to work creatively and industriously. Point out any areas that learners need to think about or correct. Check for use of capital letters and full stops/question marks, etc.

Share the posters and display them where they will be helpful to people to reinforce the instructional (useful) nature of these texts.

> **Differentiation ideas:** Support learners by helping them with layout in pencil before they begin to work in pen.

Challenge learners to check their handwriting and punctuation, too.

Answers:
Learners' own posters

Plenary idea

Sing a song about common routines and how we do things (5–10 minutes)

Resources: *This is the way we …* song or other songs

Description: Together, sing the song, adding in lyrics for how we do different things, e.g. *This is the way we tidy up / mix the paint.*

Encourage the use of actions for each of the verses.

Homework ideas

Learners complete the Workbook Session 5.5 activities if not completed in class.

They ask someone at home how they do something, e.g. *How do you find a programme on TV? How do you load the dishwasher?*

Answers for Workbook

1   Learners match instructions to pictures.

2   Learners' correctly copied sentences

3   Learners' own written instructions, numbered and with imperatives

4   Learners' own drawings and written instructions, numbered and with imperatives

5.6 Listening – from fiction to non-fiction

LEARNING PLAN

Learning objectives		Learning intentions	Success criteria
Main focus	**Also covered**	• To talk about and identify fiction and non-fiction books. • To listen to a story and follow the pictures. • To answer questions to show understanding.	• Learners can talk about and identify fiction and non-fiction books. • Learners can listen to a story and follow the pictures. • Learners can answer questions to show understanding.
1Rv.02, 1Rs.03, 1Ra.04, 1Ra.06, 1Wp.04	1Rv.01, 1Rv.03, 1Rg.01, 1Rg.03, 1Ri.02, 1Ri.03, 1Ri.04, 1Ra.01, 1Ra.05, 1SLm.02, 1SLs.01, 1SLs.02, 1SLg.04, 1SLr.02		

LANGUAGE SUPPORT

Learners will benefit from handling a range of fiction, non-fiction and poetry books from the school or class library.

Pre-teach any vocabulary from the listening activity, including: *to fold, to flip, to pull, a crane* (the bird),

origami, napkins, pyramids, fans, crowns, fancy, crisp (adjective).

Common misconception

Misconception	How to identify	How to overcome
There is only one type of book.	Ask learners in small groups to talk about books you provide for them, e.g. a story book, a poetry book, an annual, stories and recipes. Ask what sort of books they have.	Invite learners to find other books that include more than one type of content, e.g. anthologies, poems and puzzles. Show learners that books are varied and exciting. When they go to a library to choose a book, they should remember this.

Starter idea

Sorting books (10–20 minutes)

Resources: Learner's Book, Session 5.6: Getting started; selection of books

Description: Show learners a selection of books and ask them to help you sort them into three piles: stories/fiction, poems and non-fiction.

Draw on learners' experiences and reinforce their knowledge of book language: *cover, title, back cover*, etc.

Invite learners, in small groups, to find another book of each kind in the library, if you have one. Can they add their book to the correct pile?

Back in the classroom, ask learners to look at the pictures in Getting started and ask them to sort those books in the same way, explaining how they made their decisions.

Ask which book they would most like to read and why.

Main teaching ideas

1 Listen to part 1 of *More-igami* (15–20 minutes)

Learning intention: to listen to a story text and answer questions about it

Resources: *More-igami,* Part 1 (Learner's Book, Session 5.6, Activity 1); Track 32; an origami model (if possible)

Description: Tell learners they are going to listen to a text about a boy who likes to fold things.

On a first listen, ask them to listen and point to the pictures to follow the story.

On a second listen, ask them to try to write any words they hear that are interesting or that they do not understand.

Discuss learners' thoughts and explore any words they have heard – including *origami,* which is explained in the character's speech bubble.

If possible, show learners some origami (something you have made earlier) so they can see how paper folding works.

> **Differentiation ideas:** Support learners by sitting with a group and modelling how to point to the pictures to follow the story.

Challenge learners to use their phonics to write words or phrases they hear.

Audioscript: *More-igami,* **Part 1**

Joey loved things that folded.

One day, Sarah Takimoto's mother came to school.

She took a plain piece of paper.

She folded it, and flipped it, and pulled it, until it became …

a crane.

Mrs Takimoto called it origami.

Joey wanted to make origami.

Mrs Takimoto told him you need practice and patience to become an origami master.

Joey practised his folding with every bit of paper he found and then got told off for even using his mum's money!

He went to tell his friend, Mr Lopez who ran a Mexican restaurant. Mr Lopez let Joey practise folding the napkins in the restaurant.

Joey folded pyramids, fans and crowns. It made the tables look fancy.

Finally, he was ready to try the most difficult fold of all.

He took a crisp napkin. He folded. He flipped. He pulled.

It worked. He made a crane.

Dori Kleber

2 Answer questions (20–30 minutes;)

Learning intention: to answer questions to show understanding of a listening text

Resources: Learner's Book, Session 5.6, Activity 2; Workbook, Session 5.6

Description: Together, read the questions in Activity 2.

See how many questions learners can answer from memory (from the story they heard in Activity 1).

Discuss widely and share ideas.

If necessary, listen to the audio again to answer any remaining questions.

You can use the Workbook Session 5.6 activities now, for further practice.

> **Differentiation ideas:** Support learners by asking them to answer fewer questions so they have to listen for less.

Challenge learners to answer all the questions and to ask their own, too.

Answers:
Similar to: **a** Folding things; **b** She folded it and flipped it, and pulled it, until it became a crane. **c** Joey practised folding because he wanted to be an origami master. **d** At the Mexican restaurant / Muy Mexicana; **e** He made pyramids and then a crane. **f** We can see how Joey feels by looking at his face and his body actions. **g** Learners' own questions

3 **Talk about *More-igami* and categorise it (5–10 minutes)**

Learning intention: to categorise a book

Resources: Learner's Book, Session 5.6, Activity 3; examples of books that have more than one text type within

Description: Ask learners what sort of book they have been looking at in Activities 1 and 2, and to explain their thoughts.

Ask them to look at and describe *More-igami*, Part 2. Establish it is an instructional text about how to make another origami model.

Do learners know other books that have more than one text type within?

> **Differentiation ideas:** Use Differentiated worksheets 5A–C.

Answers:
a It is part fiction and part non-fiction.

b It is a story book with an instruction at the back.

c Learners' own responses

Plenary idea

Listen again (5–10 minutes)

Resources: *More-igami,* Part 1 (Learner's Book, Session 5.6); Track 32

Description: Ask learners to listen again to the story part of the audio.

Ask them to identify one part they really liked – a word, a sentence or something that is described.

Invite their comments providing models such as: *I like the bit where …; I like the word …*

Homework ideas

Learners complete the Workbook Session 5.6 activities if not completed in class.

They notice that the word *crane* can be a bird or a machine that lifts heavy things, see that the word *crisp* has two meanings, too, and find two meanings for each of these words: *lift*, *nails* and *bark*.

Answers for Workbook

1   Learners' own ideas, but may include: clothes, card, sheets, a (fold-up) bed, arms.

2   Joey loved things that folded; Joey wanted to make origami; Joey folded pyramids, fans and crowns.

3   A person: Joey; A place: a restaurant; A shape: a pyramid; A bird: a crane.

5.7 How to make a ladybird

LEARNING PLAN

Learning objectives		Learning intentions	Success criteria
Main focus	**Also covered**	• To explore and talk about shapes.	• Learners can explore and talk about shapes.
1Rv.01, 1Rg.05, 1Rg.06, 1Wv.03	1Rs.02, 1Ri.03, 1Ri.04, 1Ri.08, 1Ri.09, 1Ra.01, 1Ra.04, 1Wp.04, 1SLg.01, 1SLr.01	• To listen to, read and follow instructions to make an origami ladybird.	• Learners can listen to, read and follow instructions to make an origami ladybird.
		• To identify and list imperatives from a text.	• Learners can identify and list imperatives from a text.

LANGUAGE SUPPORT

Make sure learners know what a ladybird is.

Pre-teach shape vocabulary and provide books and pictures about shapes to support vocabulary and comprehension of the topic.

Making shapes for a class display will help to support learners further.

Common misconception

Misconception	How to identify	How to overcome
Two words cannot make one word with a different meaning.	Ask learners to read these words: Lady Bird ladybird Ask: *How are the meanings different?*	List other compound words together, e.g. *windmill, keyboard, sunflower, butterfly.*

Starter idea

Look at shapes (10–15 minutes;)

Resources: Learner's Book, Session 5.7: Getting started; some 2D and 3D shapes (or pictures of them)

Description: Ask learners to name a collection of shapes or pictures of shapes. Include a square, circle, star, triangle and heart as a minimum. If you wish, extend to a discussion about 2D and 3D shapes, using the correct terminology.

Ask learners to work in pairs to count the shapes in Getting started and record the numbers in their notebooks.

Compare answers at the end to check counting skills!

Tell learners that in this session they will need to listen and follow instructions that use some of these shape words.

Answers:
squares: 6; circles: 9; stars: 4; triangles: 5; hearts: 6

Main teaching ideas

 1 Listen to and read Part 2 of *More-igami* (10–20 minutes)

Learning intention: to listen to and read an instructional text

Resources: *More-Igami,* Part 2 (Learner's Book, Session 5.8, Activity 1); Track 33

Description: Tell learners they will first listen to and then read instructions about how to make an origami ladybird.

Show and discuss the pictures in Activity 1. Discuss what features are giving the instructions e.g. labels, dotted lines and arrows.

Play the audio, stopping after each section to model how to listen and point to the matching picture in the Learner's Book.

Replay the audio, inviting learners in pairs to listen and point.

Finally, ask learners to try to read the text in pairs or groups.

You may link to phonics here by showing learners words with

- adjacent consonants: *fold*; *start*; *spots, flip,* etc.
- digraphs: *ir* in *bird*; *ee* in *keep*; *igh* in *right*; *ow* in *down,* etc.

> **Differentiation ideas:** Support learners by pairing less confident readers with more confident readers.

Challenge learners to find examples of words with split digraphs, e.g. *make, same*.

2 Write instructional verbs (10–15 minutes)

Learning intention: to find instructional verbs

Resources: Learner's Book, Session 5.7, Activity 2; Workbook, Session 5.7

Description: If necessary, revisit the instructions from Activity 1.

Give pairs a limited time to see how many instructional verbs they can list. Invite them to share. Try to make this activity fast-paced.

As you circulate, encourage learners to use their phonics knowledge to check spellings.

Ask them say how many different verbs there are (seven).

You can use the Workbook Session 5.7 activities now, to further explore imperative verbs.

> **Differentiation ideas:** Support learners by providing a list of the verbs to find and tick off.

Challenge learners to think about how they might change the verbs, but retain the meaning, e.g. *begin* instead of *start*.

Answers:
start, fold, make, fold, press, make, open, fold, make, add

3 Make an origami ladybird (20–30 minutes)

Learning intention: to try to follow instructions using words and pictures

Resources: Learner's Book, Session 5.7, Activity 3; origami squares of paper; additional, adult help (if available)

Description: Tell learners they are going to try to make an origami ladybird.

Remind them that the numbers, verbs and pictures will help them to know what to do and in what order.

You may wish to practise first, before you ask learners to try.

Establish pairs or small groups. You may need an extra adult for support, too.

Hand out the squares of paper.

Circulate and support as learners attempt the folding. Remind them to keep practising. It does not matter if their folding goes wrong, as the key learning is to try to follow the instructions.

Celebrate the models and discuss how easy or difficult the activity was.

> **Differentiation ideas:** Support learners by working as a group to make one model.

Challenge learners to work independently to create their own models.

Plenary idea

Find your partner (5–10 minutes)

Resources: imperative word cards with similar meanings and cut into two

Description: Talk about the verbs *begin* and *start* (see Differentiation ideas for Activity 2). Can learners understand that these verbs have similar meanings?

Ask learners to pick one of the word cards and then find their partner who has a verb with a similar meaning.

Ask learners to line up in pairs so they may present their two verbs before they leave.

CROSS-CURRICULAR LINKS

Maths: Explore and identify 2D shapes and their number of sides.

Maths: Differentiate between 2D and 3D shapes.

Homework ideas

Learners complete the Workbook Session 5.7 activities if not completed in class.

They fold a square of paper to make a pattern or a model and/or give instructions to a family member to make an origami model.

Answers for Workbook

1 Numbers correctly copied with correct formation

2 a <u>Start</u> with a square of paper.

 b <u>Keep</u> practising!

 c <u>Fold</u> the triangle in half.

 d <u>Press</u> down hard to make a crease.

3 Possible answers include: **a** Fold, Create; **b** Turn; **c** press; **d** Draw

5.8 Writing and sorting instructions

LEARNING PLAN

Learning objectives		Learning intentions	Success criteria
Main focus	**Also covered**	• To follow and describe pictorial instructions.	• Learners can follow and describe pictorial instructions.
1Rs.04, 1Ri.08, 1Ws.01, 1Wc.02, 1Wc.04, 1SLs.01	1Rv.01, 1Rg.05, 1Rg.06, 1Ri.03, 1Wv.03, 1Wg.01, 1Wg.04, 1Wg.05, 1Wg.06, 1Ws.02, 1Wc.05, 1Wp.05, 1SLs.02, 1SLg.01	• To write instructions. • To match and sequence written instructions to pictures.	• Learners can write instructions. • Learners can match and sequence written instructions to pictures.

LANGUAGE SUPPORT

Revisit instruction symbols and pre-teach how we can use arrows in instructions. Talk about what the arrows in the penguin instructions might mean.

Pre-teach directional vocabulary, e.g. *up, down, turn over/flip, top, middle, corner, turn around*.

Encourage learners to orally rehearse instructions before trying to write them.

Common misconception

Misconception	How to identify	How to overcome
Finding small words within words is just a fun thing to do.	Ask learners to read these words and find other words in them: *Square/are* (Knowing *are* does not help us read *square*.) *Penguin/pen/in* (Knowing *pen* and *in* helps us to read *penguin*.)	Remind learners to try this technique when they are trying to work out an unknown word using their phonics. Sometimes it may be helpful.

Starter idea

Origami models (10–15 minutes)

Resources: Learner's Book, Session 5.8: Getting started; learners' ladybird models from Session 5.7, Activity 3; origami models or pictures online

Description: Share any origami models or folded paper patterns that you or the learners have made, including their ladybird from Session 5.7 Activity 3. Alternatively, share pictures online, or use the pictures in Getting started.

Name each model and invite learners to talk about which they would like to make.

What do they think would be easy or very difficult, and why?

What advice would they give to others just beginning to learn paper folding?

Main teaching ideas

1   Talk about picture instructions
    (20–30 minutes)

   Learning intention: to explore and say instructions to match pictures

Resources: Learner's Book, Session 5.8, Activity 1

Description: Together, look at the pictorial instructions for how to make a penguin model. Agree on a sentence for each, using instructional verbs and shape vocabulary.

Ask: *What do the arrows mean?* (fold to the right, left, up or down) *What does the looped arrow mean?* (turn or flip the paper over)

Make this a discussion rather than expecting definitive answers, so that learners feel confident to experiment with their responses.

> **Differentiation ideas:** Support learners by giving them options, e.g. *Does this mean* fold up *or* fold down?

Challenge learners to explain their responses.

Answers:
Learners' own responses

---

2 Match instructions to correct pictures (20–30 minutes)

Learning intention: to match written instructions to pictorial instructions

Resources: Learner's Book, Session 5.8, Activity 2

Description: Tell learners they are going to read some of the written instructions for how to make a penguin and then match them to the correct pictures.

Together, read the instructions. Check understanding of the words: *fold, square, top to bottom, sides, beak.*

Together, work out which instruction matches which of the pictures and discuss how the words and pictures help.

> **Differentiation ideas:** Support learners by working with them as a group.

Challenge learners to check their punctuation and to draw some of the pictures to accompany their sequenced instructions.

Answers:
a 1; b 5; c 9

3 Write instructions (15–20 minutes)

Learning intention: to write instructions

Resources: Learner's Book, Session 5.8, Activity 3; Workbook, Session 5.8

Description: Ask learners to focus on the instructions in Activity 2 for steps 1 and 3.

Ask learners to write the instructions for these two steps.

> **Differentiation ideas:** Support learners by working with them as a group.

Challenge learners to write an instruction for another step.

Together, discuss what the penguin will look like once folded and ask the learners to draw the penguin.

Plenary idea

Assess the instructions (5 minutes)

Description: Talk about sorting the instructions. Ask: *What was difficult? What was easy?*

Ask learners to reflect on what might have made it easier to sort the instructions.

Do they now love to make origami models, or do they find it too difficult? What could they do to improve their origami models?

CROSS-CURRICULAR LINKS

Maths: Fold paper shapes in half to explore simple fractions. Use paper shapes and folding to explore equivalence in fractions.

Homework ideas

Learners complete the Workbook Session activities if not completed in class.

They try to find instructions to make other examples of origami.

Answers for Workbook

1 a How to fold a bird; **b** How to fold a tree; **c** How to fold a boat

2 1 Fold a piece of paper into pleats.
   2 Hold and stick one end of the pleats with sticky tape.
   3 Hold the end and fan yourself to keep cool.

3 Learners' own instructions, using numbers and imperatives

5.9 Instructions for cooking

LEARNING PLAN

Learning objectives		Learning intentions	Success criteria
Main focus	**Also covered**		
1Rg.02, 1Rg.04, 1Rs.02, 1Ra.04, 1Wg.01, 1Wg.05	1Rg.03, 1Rg.07, 1Rs.04, 1Ri.03, 1Ri.04, 1Ri.08, 1Ri.09, 1Ra.01, 1Ra.03, 1Wg.06, 1Ws.01, 1SLm.02, 1SLg.04, 1SLp.01, 1SLp.03	• To explore the language of recipes. • To listen to and read a recipe. • To explore the use of *and* and full stops.	• Learners can explore the language of recipes. • Learners can listen to and read a recipe. • Learners can explore the use of *and* and full stops.

LANGUAGE SUPPORT

Check that learners understand the vocabulary of cooking and pre-teach this, where necessary, looking at Getting started for examples.

Where possible, follow the instructions to make muffins as part of a practical class activity.

Set up a role-play kitchen so learners can use appropriate language, handle equipment and act cooking scenarios with other learners to reinforce their understanding.

Common misconception

Misconception	How to identify	How to overcome
We have to repeat the whole of the second sentence when we use *and*.	Show learners the two sentences: *Put in the eggs.* *Put in the oil.* Ask learners to join the two sentences with the word *and*. Some learners will say: *Put in the eggs and put in the oil.* Show learners that you can make the sentence shorter by saying: *Put in the eggs and oil.*	When you hear or see examples like this in learners' speech or writing, remind them of how to shorten the sentence, providing the example here as a model.

Starter idea

The language of cooking (10–15 minutes)

Resources: Learner's Book, Session 5.9: Getting started; Worksheet 5.3

Description: Ask learners to look at the photos in Getting started. Do learners know what all these things could be used to make? Elicit the response of *baking a cake*.

Find out what learners already know about cooking.

Pre-teach vocabulary where necessary (see Language support).

Look at the photos again. This time, discuss each picture and label it.

Use this an opportunity to revisit the use of determiners *a, an, the* and *some*.

Take the opportunity to show learners that *teaspoon* may become shortened to *tsp.* (with a full stop); this is referred to later in this session.

Together, sort the items into the two sets: food and equipment. You can provide Worksheet 5.3 Sorting ingredients and equipment to help structure learners' responses to this sorting activity.

Main teaching ideas

1 Listen and read (10–15 minutes)

Learning intention: to listen and then read a recipe

Resources: *How to make muffins* (Learner's Book, Session 5.9, Activity 1); Track 34; Workbook, Session 5.9

Description: Tell learners they are going to listen to some cooking instructions. Explain that we call this kind of instruction a recipe. Point learners to the character's speech bubble which gives guidance on the unusual pronunciation of the word *recipes*.

Tell learners to first listen. Ask them to listen for how many steps there are in these instructions. (seven)

Then repeat, this time asking them to point to the instructions in Learner's Book Session 5.9 Activity 1 as they listen.

Discuss anything they notice about the recipe, before finally asking them to read the recipe aloud in pairs. Point out the Reading tip: to ask for help from a partner if they get stuck.

You can use the Workbook Session 5.9 activities now.

> **Differentiation ideas:** Support learners by working with them as they listen and point, so you can guide them, or by pairing learners with different reading strengths, so they can help each other.

Challenge learners to read the text aloud for the class.

2 Add the word *and* (10–15 minutes)

Learning intention: to use *and* to join two short sentences together

Resources: Learner's Book, Session 5.9, Activity 2

Description: Ask learners to work in pairs and to look at Step 3 in the recipe.

Give them one minute to work out how they could change this to make one sentence. Then ask for ideas to elicit the answer: *Put in the milk **and** mix.*

Ask learners to do the same for Steps 4 and 5, writing the sentences in their notebooks.

Ask them to reflect on which version (one sentence or two) is clearer and to say why. Instructions tend to be short to avoid confusion. So two sentences may be clearer to understand.

> **Differentiation ideas:** Support learners by providing an *and* word card for them to use as a prompt and, if necessary, physically make one sentence with several word cards as they have done before.

Challenge learners to write their response to whether instructions are clearer as one sentence or two.

Answers:
3 Put in the milk and mix. 4 Put in the sugar and whisk. 5 Put in the flour and baking powder and mix.

3 Using full stops (10–15 minutes)

Learning intention: to notice the use of full stops

Resources: Learner's Book, Session 5.9, Activity 3; Workbook, Session 5.10

Description: Ask learners when we use a full stop. Share ideas.

Draw their attention to the Language focus box. Did learners mention all these reasons?

Give learners time to re-read the recipe, looking for full stops, and then share ideas about where they are used.

You can use the Workbook Session 5.9 activities now for further practice.

> **Differentiation ideas:** Support learners by providing word and punctuation cards for learners to hold so they can build sentences and punctuate them. Ask learners to arrange themselves in order and re-read to check each sentence.

Challenge learners to self-assess a piece of their writing to check for correct use of full stops.

Answers:
Responses should include: At the end of sentences; to show a word is shortened.

Plenary idea

Be a capital letter and a full stop (5–10 minutes)

Resources: instructional sentences written as word cards and cut up

Description: Hand out the word cards to a matching number of learners.

Ask them to stand in line in the correct order.

Ask some learners to be a capital letter and others to be a full stop.

Ask: *Where should you stand to punctuate the instruction?* (You may need two full stops if numbers are included in the instruction.)

Ask others in the class to check if the capital letter and full stop(s) are in the correct place.

Repeat with a different instruction if time allows.

CROSS-CURRICULAR LINKS

Maths: Explore the capacity of different spoon and cup measures.

Science: Explore the properties of baking powder in baking. Ask learners to make predictions about what they think will happen.

Homework ideas

Learners complete the Workbook Session 5.9 activities if not completed in class.

They make a list of cooking equipment they can find at home, with help from an adult.

Make sure learners understand they should never handle cooking equipment without permission from an adult. Some learners may bring in unusual pieces of equipment to show and tell.

Answers for Workbook

1   Learners correctly match pictures to words: flour, butter, milk, sugar, eggs.

2   Learners list all the ingredients (in any order), for example:

   1 butter

   2 flour

   3 eggs

   4 milk

   5 sugar

3   **a** Put in the eggs.

   b Put in the oil.

   c Put in the milk. Mix.

   d Put in a tsp. of salt.

4   Learners' own responses

5.10 Checking sequence

LEARNING PLAN

Learning objectives		Learning intentions	Success criteria
Main focus	**Also covered**	• To talk about correct order in instructions. • To check understanding. • To explore the verbs in instructions.	• Learners can talk about correct order in instructions. • Learners can check understanding. • Learners can explore the verbs in instructions.
1Rg.05, 1Rs.01, 1Ri.05, 1Ri.13	1Rv.01, 1Rg.03, 1Rg.06, 1Ri.08, 1Wv.01, 1Wv.03, 1Wc.04, 1Wp.04, 1SLm.04, 1SLs.01, 1SLs.02, 1SLg.01, 1SLp.04		

LANGUAGE SUPPORT

Play the game in Getting started to support the idea of order and reinforce recipe vocabulary. Extend the game for making other things.

Encourage learners, where possible, to play in sand or water with some of the equipment so that they can work out what these things do.

Ask questions to encourage problem solving: *How can we use a colander or sieve? What do we use a jug for? What sort of spoon is this?*

Ensure learners are familiar with the vocabulary *before* and *after*.

Common misconception

Misconception	How to identify	How to overcome
We can only use numbers to show the correct order of instructions.	Ask learners to recall what they have learned about how to show the correct order of instructions. They will probably say: *We use numbers*. Ask learners if there is another way to show order, e.g. arrows connecting boxes, showing something in a flow chart or as a circle, adding letters a, b, c, etc.	Remind learners to always think about the best features to use when showing the correct order of instructions.

Starter idea

Play Jump in the Bowl (10–15 minutes)

Resources: Learner's Book, Session 5.10: Getting started; Workbook, Session 5.10; Language worksheet 5A; ingredient labels, badges or pictures; a large space; skipping rope

Description: Ask learners if they can remember how to make muffins. Recap the recipe instructions in Session 5.9 Activity 1 if necessary.

Put a skipping rope on the floor in a circle and pretend it is a mixing bowl.

Give out labels, badges or pictures of the ingredients from the muffin recipe in Session 5.9 and invite some learners to be each ingredient.

Ask those watching to tell learners to jump in the bowl in the correct order to make the muffins.

Get them to role play 'mixing' the ingredients. Have some fun!

Invite learners to make up some new recipes with different sets of learners.

You can use Language worksheet 5A here, to further practise ordering.

Main teaching ideas

1 Answer questions (20–30 minutes)

Learning intention: to answer questions to show understanding

Resources: Learner's Book, Session 5.10, Activity 1

Description: Give learners some time to re-read the muffin recipe (Session 5.9 Activity 1) and then ask them some quick-fire quiz-style questions about it, e.g. *Who can remember …, Tell me …*

After a while, read the questions together in Activity 1. Model how to answer the questions orally.

Then ask learners to read and write their responses to the questions in their notebooks.

You may wish to check learners are secure in reading the recipe words using their phonic skills first.

⟩ **Differentiation ideas:** Support learners by working with them as a group or by providing answers for them to match with questions.

Challenge learners to write additional questions to test each other.

Answers:
a Ingredients; **b** It is a jug and it is for keeping/pouring/measuring liquid; **c** Yes; **d** Put in the eggs; **e** Bake the muffins in the oven; **f** Wash hands, put on an apron.

Learners' own questions

2 Read and find instructional verbs (15–20 minutes)

Learning intention: to identify commands in a text and to explore alternatives

Resources: Learner's Book, Session 5.10, Activity 2; Language worksheet 5B

Description: Together, read the recipe again. Ask learners to stand up each time they hear an instructional verb: *put, mix, whisk* and *bake*.

Talk about possible alternatives for these instructional verbs, asking: *Which different verbs would work as well?*

The Writing tip provides some ideas for learners to explore.

Share ideas, ensuring that everyone understands the meanings of *tip, add, pour* and *crack,* and any other verbs suggested.

You can provide Language worksheet 5B now, for further practice.

⟩ **Differentiation ideas:** Support learners by providing the alternative verbs as word cards for them to consider.

Challenge learners to explain their choices, e.g. *Does* whisk *really mean the same as* beat? *Do you need to add any extra information,* e.g. *beat/mix* with a fork?

Answers:
a put, mix, whisk, bake
b Similar to:
  * Crack the eggs and tip them in.
  * Pour in the oil.
  * Pour in the milk. Stir.
  * Tip in the sugar. Beat.
  * Tip in the flour and baking powder. Stir.
  * Add the choc-chips.
  * Cook the muffins in the oven.

3 Write instructions (15–25 minutes)

Learning intention: to write new sentences with alternative verbs

Resources: Learner's Book, Session 5.10, Activity 3

Description: Ask learners to now rewrite the recipe using their new verbs.

As you circulate, support all learners to discuss and use the best instructional verbs.

Also support them with handwriting and punctuation.

> **Differentiation ideas:** Support learners by asking them to work in pairs, or copy the sentences created with the verb cards in the Session 5.9 Plenary idea.

Challenge learners to peer assess their work to check for sense, as well as punctuation and handwriting.

Answers:
Learners' own instructions similar to answers for Activity 2b

Plenary idea

Watch or read recipes (5–10 minutes)

Resources: online access

Description: Search online for recipe examples or look at recipe books.

As a class, talk about the order and the clarity of the instructions.

Share and enjoy!

CROSS-CURRICULAR LINKS

Science: Explore cooking equipment and its role/function. Show learners how to use equipment appropriately, e.g. a garlic press.

Homework ideas

Learners complete the Workbook Session 5.10 activities if not completed in class.

They ask learners to design a class cooking apron.

Answers for Workbook

1   **b** eggs; **c** milk; **d** flour; **e** butter
2   **a** put; **b** mix; **c** whisk; **d** bake
3   Learners' own cooking verbs
4   **a**   Play the game *Jump in the Bowl!*
     b   How do numbers help us in instructions?
     c   Make up another question for a partner.
5   Learners' own sentences

5.11 Planning and writing a recipe

LEARNING PLAN

Learning objectives		Learning intentions	Success criteria
Main focus	**Also covered**	• To explore the features of a recipe and create a chart.	• Learners can explore the features of a recipe and create a chart.
1Ri.04, 1Ws.01, 1Wc.01, 1Wc.02, 1Wc.04	1Rs.02, 1Rs.04, 1Ri.03, 1Ww.05, 1Ww.06, 1Ww.07, 1Wv.01, 1Wv.03, 1Wg.01, 1Ws.02, 1Wc.05, 1Wp.04, 1Wp.05, 1SLg.01, 1SLg.02	• To change a recipe. • To plan and write a recipe using a model.	• Learners can change a recipe. • Learners can plan and write a recipe using a model.

LANGUAGE SUPPORT

Learners will enjoy reading a variety of recipes, looking at the pictures and tasting the outcomes.

Revisit the language of ingredients and equipment that are common in your locality.

Encourage learners to continue to enjoy any food-based role-play area set up in class.

Common misconception

Misconception	How to identify	How to overcome
We can call all instructions recipes.	Show learners a recipe and ask them what it is called. Show them different instructions from the unit and ask them whether we can call them recipes. Establish that the word *recipe* only applies to cooking instructions.	Reinforce the meaning of the word *recipe*.

Starter idea

Recipe features (10–15 minutes)

Resources: Learner's Book, Session 5.11: Getting started; Worksheet 5.4

Description: Ask learners to remember all the things they noticed about the muffin recipe in Session 5.9 and its features.

Share ideas and tell them these things are the recipe 'features' and that we can use them in our own writing if we want to. You might like to remind them that they did this in the last non-fiction unit about recounts/letters (Unit 2).

Show learners the chart in Getting started. Talk about it together. Ask learners to point to the chart together and to agree *yes* or *no* for each feature listed.

Do learners want to add anything else to this chart of features?

You can use Worksheet 5.4 Features of a recipe or Description in Activity 1.

Answers:
Learners' observations may include: All rows can be answered with *yes*, except: *Begin with Dear …?* (like a letter) and *Give instructions in the past tense.* (Instructions are written in the present tense and use the imperative verb form.)

Other features for a recipe include: the use of abbreviations, e.g. tsp., measurements (e.g. cup), and short sentences.

Main teaching ideas

1 Write a features chart (20–30 minutes)

Learning intention: to create a features chart and list the features of a recipe

Resources: Learner's Book, Session 5.11, Activity 1; Worksheets 5.4 and 5.11

Description: Tell learners they will now write their own features chart for a recipe.

They should pretend they are telling someone how to write a recipe.

Ask them to work in pairs to draw and write other ideas, too.

As you circulate, support and challenge learners.

Ask a few learners to share their ideas.

You can use Worksheet 5.4 Features of a recipe now.

> **Differentiation ideas:** Provide learners with Worksheet 5.4 Features of a recipe for support with drawing the chart.

Challenge learners to write a features chart, as in Getting started, that has some false statements and then ask them to share with the class.

Answers:
Learners' charts containing a similar list of content to the chart in Getting started, plus some of learners' own ideas

2 Change the muffin recipe (15–20 minutes)

Learning intention: to change a recipe

Resources: Learner's Book, Session 5.11, Activity 2, Workbook, Session 5.11

Description: Tell learners they are going to change the muffin recipe to use a different flavour/ingredient they like!

Ask: *What other sot of muffin do you know? What could replace the choc-chips?* Show them the examples in Learner's Book Session 5.11 Activity 2 (cherries; honey and apple).

Encourage creative responses and sharing of ideas.

You can use the Workbook Session 5.11 activities now. Ask learners to write their idea for a different muffin in their notebooks.

> **Differentiation ideas:** Support learners by providing pictures of ingredient/flavour options with matching word cards.

Challenge learners to change something else in the recipe.

Answers:
Learners' own ideas

3 Plan a recipe (15–20 minutes)

Learning intention: to plan a recipe

Resources: Learner's Book, Session 5.11, Activity 3

Description: Tell learners they now need to plan their recipe.

Ask them what headings they will need to use.

Draw their attention to the headings in Activity 3.

Give learners time to work on their plan.

> **Differentiation ideas:** Support learners by working with them in a group or asking them to work in pairs. Encourage them to be creative and to record their ideas in any way that works for them.

Challenge learners by asking them to add extra details to their plans.

Answers:
Learners' own plans

4 Write a recipe (20–30 minutes)

Learning intention: to write a recipe

Resources: Learner's Book, Session 5.11, Activity 4; Differentiated worksheets 5A–C; learners' plans from Activity 3

Description: Tell learners they will now use their plans from the last activity to complete their own recipe.

Draw their attention to the Writing tip, which reminds them to use their phonics or classroom resources, or to ask for help if they do not know how to spell a word.

You may wish learners to use Differentiated worksheets 5A–C for support and guidance. Circulate in the class to support and challenge learners appropriately.

> **Differentiation ideas:** Support and challenge learners using Differentiated worksheets 5A–C.

Answers:
Learners' own written recipes

Plenary idea

Poems (5–10 minutes)

Resources: poems or songs about food or a recipe

Description: Share and enjoy a range of poems or songs about food or recipes.

Ask learners if they know any others. Repeat according to time available.

CROSS-CURRICULAR LINKS

Science: Talk about our senses and which ones we use when we are cooking and eating.

Homework ideas

Learners complete the Workbook Session 5.11 activities if not completed in class.

They make a list of ingredients for a favourite recipe and write it like a shopping list.

Answers for Workbook

1   Learners' own drawings.

2   Learners' own responses

3   Learners' own drawings

4   Learners' own responses

5 and 6 Learners completed charts, written correctly, showing popular things family and friends like to cook with the most popular food

5.12 Look back

LEARNING PLAN

Learning objectives		Learning intentions	Success criteria
Main focus	**Also covered**	• To check their writing and to share recipes.	• Learners can check their writing and share their recipes.
1Rs.04, 1Ri.04, 1Ra.04, 1Wp.06, 1SLp.05, 1SLr.01	1Ra.05, 1Ra.06, 1SLm.01, 1SLg.02, 1SLg.03, 1SLp.03	• To talk about the instructions in this unit.	• Learners can talk about the instructions in this unit.
		• To think about their learning from the unit.	• Learners can think about their learning from the unit.

LANGUAGE SUPPORT

When recalling features of instructional texts, encourage learners to use the Learner's Book as well as any posters or displays in the classroom used throughout the unit.

Common misconception

Misconception	How to identify	How to overcome
Instructions sound rude and bossy.	Ask learners to tell you how to do something. They may sit: *Sit down!* or *Drink your cup of tea!* or similar. Ask them to ask you again, this time politely. Talk about how adding *please* can sound more polite when we are talking to someone we know. Check that this is true in our texts in the unit.	Check with learners, when they are saying or writing instructions, whether they feel they should add *please* or not. It will help them to consider audience and purpose.

Starter idea

Talk about instructional texts (5–10 minutes)

Resources: Learner's Book, Session 5.12: Getting started

Description: Talk to learners about different kinds of instructions.

Show them the examples in Getting started, or examples of other instructional texts in this unit.

Ask what they notice about the different texts to revisit typical features in general.

Encourage learners to share ideas and establish who likes to read and follow these kinds of texts and who prefers fiction – explore when and why.

Main teaching ideas

1 Check your writing (10–15 minutes)

Learning intention: to check writing for layout and correct use of features

Resources: Learner's Book, Session 5.12, Activity 1; Workbook, Session 5.12; learner's recipes from Session 5.11, Activity 3

Description: Discuss the importance of layout and neatness of work.

If appropriate, choose an example of a sentence or instructional text that needs correcting in terms of spacing or use of features. Write it on the board and work on this together first.

Model how to stop at full stops when reading aloud.

Then ask learners to look at the recipe they wrote in Session 5.11 Activity 3. Ask: *What do you think about it?* They can use the chart in Session 5.11 Getting started to check its features.

Ask them to enjoy reading their recipes and checking their work. Some learners may wish to share their recipes by reading aloud.

Encourage peer feedback, but, as usual, try to ensure it is kept positive.

> **Differentiation ideas:** Support learners by working with them in a group, when checking their recipe or selecting an aspect of it for them to improve.

Challenge learners to spot punctuation errors, too; especially the use of full stops at the end of sentences and after numbers or abbreviations, e.g. tsp. for teaspoon.

2 The unit instructional texts (10–15 minutes)

Learning intention: to reflect on all instructions and recall the features that are similar or different

Resources: Learner's Book, Session 5.12, Activity 2; Workbook, Session 5.12

Description: Ask learners if they can remember the instructional texts from the unit, using memory as well as any class displays that you may have created.

List the instructions or their titles together, encouraging learners to look at the images in Activity 2 if they cannot remember all of them.

Ask learners to talk about the instructions and which they enjoyed finding out about most. Take a class vote.

You can use the Workbook Session 5.12 activities here.

> **Differentiation ideas:** Support learners by using book covers from printed books or pictures in the Learner's Book, or classroom displays as reminders.

Challenge learners to think of other instructions that could have featured in this unit.

3 Skills review (10–15 minutes)

Learning intention: to think about learning in terms of language skills

Resources: Learner's Book, Session 5.12, Activity 3

Description: Remind learners of the words we use to describe language skills: reading, writing, spelling, listening and speaking.

Say each skill, one by one, and ask learners to put their hand up when you say the skill they think they are best at.

Now ask learners to say or write one thing from this unit that helped them with these skills.

These simple learner statements can be extremely useful for informing end-of-term reports.

> **Differentiation ideas:** Support learners to be positive in their skills review, providing models: *I think you are much better at … now.*

Challenge learners to also think of one thing they still need to improve.

Plenary idea

Lucky Dip review (5–10 minutes)

Resources: assessment sentence starters; a bowl

Description: Put a selection of Assessment for Learning (AfL) sentence starters in a bowl to pass round the class, for example:

- *One thing I must remember from this unit is …*
- *I still don't understand …*
- *Before this unit, I already knew how to … / about …*
- *I now understand …*
- *I would now do x differently …*

Invite learners to pick a sentence starter and complete the sentence.

Keep passing the sentence starters around until you run out of learners or time.

Homework ideas

Learners complete the Workbook Session 5.12 activities if not completed in class.

They talk to someone at home about what they would like to improve in their learning and why.

Answers for Workbook

1   Learners read and write common words.

2   Do you know how to make cakes?

3   Learners' own jumbled sentences

CHECK YOUR PROGRESS

1   Numbers can help to make instructions clear.

2   Learners' own signs

3   Turn, wash (off)

4   Stand it up and pull out the side corners, and refold them so they stick out.

5   Any of the following ingredients: sugar, milk, baking powder, flour, eggs, oil, choc-chips (or other flavours)

6   Learners' own responses, but may include: a label is a written word to tell you what something is; origami is paper-folding to make models; equipment is things you need to do a job; a recipe tells you how to cook or bake something.

PROJECT GUIDANCE

These projects build on the reading, writing and understanding learners have developed throughout the unit. Since learners have just read several different kinds of instructional texts, the project options here extend the focus and provide opportunities for the learners to choose to work in a group, as a pair or alone. You might prefer to allocate a project to the class.

Group project: Support learners to set up a cooking club. They will need to plan and research the things they need. In this project, learners will need to use collaboration and practical skills to collect and follow recipes, and prepare food.

Pair project: Learners design and make a road play mat from cardboard and populate it with buildings and signs. Help them to source the equipment and resources they need.

Solo project: Learners research, choose and follow instructions to make another origami model. Provide some guidance here so that their choice is achievable. Learners should review the clarity of the instructions and how they could be improved.

For more guidance on setting up and assessing projects, see Project guidance at the end of Unit 1.

>6 Rhyme time

Unit plan

Session	Approximate number of learning hours	Outline of learning content	Resources
6.1 Our senses	1.5	Talk about the senses and match to body parts. Join in with a poem. Explore verb use. Play I Spy / I Hear.	Learner's Book Session 6.1 Workbook Session 6.1 ⬇ Worksheet 6.1 Phonics Workbook A
6.2 Touch	1.5	Talk about the sense of touch. Listen to and join in with poems about touch to explore rhyme and non-rhyme. Write a sentence.	Learner's Book Session 6.2 Workbook Session 6.2
6.3 Feeling sad	2	Talk about feelings and how it feels to be sad. Explore a poem about feeling unwell and read it aloud, pausing at full stops. Create a class A–Z of feelings.	Learner's Book Session 6.3 Workbook Session 6.3 ⬇ Worksheet 6.2
6.4 Feeling happy	2	Talk about happy times and feelings. Play with the language of a happy birthday rhyme and then explore and perform a new poem.	Learner's Book Session 6.4 Workbook Session 6.4 ⬇ Worksheet 6.3 ⬇ Worksheet 6.4 ⬇ Language worksheet 6B ⬇ Differentiated worksheets 6A–C

Session	Approximate number of learning hours	Outline of learning content	Resources
6.5 Planning and writing a rhyme	2	Sing a days of the week rhyme and talk about what makes a good or bad day. Listen to and read a poem. Answer questions. Write a poem.	Learner's Book Session 6.5 Workbook Session 6.5 ⬇ Worksheet 6.5 ⬇ Language worksheet 6A
6.6 Look back	1	Look back at writing to reflect and edit. Look back at the content of the unit and review learning.	Learner's Book Session 6.6 Workbook Session 6.6
Cross-unit resources			
Learner's Book Check your progress Learner's Book Projects			

BACKGROUND KNOWLEDGE

Before you begin to teach this unit, you may find it helpful to:

- familiarise yourself with the poetry in this unit – you may be able to find film versions with music that you can share with your class. Prepare ways to talk with your learners about:
  - the language of poetry: rhythm, rhyme, repeated letter sounds, lines and verses
  - poems and picture books that use rhyme to represent local, regional, national and international interests and views
  - how to listen to, read and then recite or perform poetry

- familiarise yourself with the phonics and grammar elements in this unit, including:
  - phonics – the language of phonics: consonant and vowel diagraphs, long vowel sounds, trigraphs, blending to read, decoding to spell, sound buttons, different spellings of the same phoneme (I, eye) and rhyming words with the same spellings (walk, talk)
  - metalanguage letters, sounds, phrases, sentences, nouns, verbs, endings and adjectives.

TEACHING SKILLS FOCUS

Active learning – performance

In this unit, learners explore rhymes around the theme of the senses and feelings. There are natural opportunities for both formal and informal performance.

Challenge yourself to find different ways to support learners to perform for different outcomes:

- making and using puppets: stick, hand, glove
- devising actions to use alongside rhymes
- making oral recordings
- acting in character with and without props
- performing for each other and for a larger audience.

Provide opportunities to share performances, either in class or between classes, to develop learners' confidence in speaking aloud and reciting.

At the end of this unit, consider which techniques were regularly used by the learners and ask yourself and them the following questions:

- Learner voice: *Which poems did the learners most enjoy? Why? Why not? What ideas were they able to contribute?*
- Techniques: *What did not work well? Should you consider changing some techniques in response? What worked really well?*
- The environment: *Where did most learning take place? What change have you made to accommodate active learning, e.g. a practice area, a make-shift stage or performance area?*
- Evidence: *If colleagues came into your classroom, could they tell that learners were engaged in active English learning?*

6.1 Our senses

LEARNING PLAN

Learning objectives		Learning intentions	Success criteria
Main focus	**Also covered**	• To talk about our senses.	• Learners can talk about their senses.
1Rv.01, 1Rv.05, 1Ri.14, 1Ra.02, 1SLm.01, 1SLp.02	1Rw.02, 1Rv.03, 1Rg.02, 1Rg.06, 1Ri.01, 1Ra.01, 1Ra.04, Ww.02, 1Wv.01, 1Wv.03, 1Wp.01, 1Wp.02, 1Wp.03, 1SLm 02, 1SLm 03, 1SLm 04, 1SLm 05	• To join in with words and actions in rhymes. • To explore sounds and words in rhymes.	• Learners can join in with words and actions in rhymes. • Learners can explore sounds and words in rhymes.

Prepare learners with the vocabulary they will need for this session: the senses and matching parts of the body. Make a poster together and display it so that learners have it as a reference to use during activities. Exaggerate the saying of rhymes with matching actions, too.

Use the audios of the rhymes or think about reading the rhymes so that you can control the speed for some learners.

Common misconception

Misconception	How to identify	How to overcome
We join from capital letters.	Ask one or all learners to copy and join a sentence from the rhyme in this session beginning with *My …*. Check they are beginning with a capital letter and ending with a full stop. Check they are not joining from the capital *M*.	Use the Workbook Session 6.1 activities for joining practice. Create a class dangle to hang from a washing line: *WE NEVER JOIN TO OR FROM CAPITAL LETTERS*.

Starter idea

The senses (10 minutes)

Resources: Learner's Book, Session 6.1: Getting started

Description: Ask learners what they know about their five senses. Give them a few minutes to talk in pairs and then share their ideas. Be sensitive to any learners in class who have disabilities. Incorporate discussion about those who may not be able to see or hear into your discussions.

Consider singing the traditional song *Heads, Shoulders, Knees and Toes* to reinforce vocabulary through active learning.

Draw on learners' experiences and use the pictures in Getting started as prompts.

For each picture ask: *What are they doing?* (e.g. using their nose to smell.) Ask: *What else can we use our nose and sense of smell for?*

Main teaching *ideas*

1   Match pictures to words
    (10–15 minutes)

   Learning intention: to match pictures with words

   Resources: Learner's Book, Session 6.1, Activity 1; Workbook, Session 6.1; Phonics Workbook A; Worksheet 6.1

Description: Ask learners to write the words: *eyes, mouth, ears, feet, nose, teeth, eyebrows* and *hands*. Encourage them to do this in pairs or in a group, and then invite them to the board to share their spelling ideas.

Talk about the ideas in the poem *My Eyes Can See* to ensure that everyone knows what each action is (*hear, smell, wiggle, touch, bite, walk, talk, see*).

Ask learners to work in pairs to match the body parts to the correct verb and then to write their answers in their notebook. Some learners may find it easier to use Worksheet 6.1 What can my body do?

You can use the Workbook Session 6.1 activities now for handwriting practice of topic vocabulary. They include joining practice of digraphs.

Phonics (Phonics Workbook A, pages 26–27, 36–37 and 40–41): link to phonics by asking learners to notice that *feet* and *teeth* and *see* all contain /ee/. Ask: *What other double letters / digraphs can you see?* (*th* in *teeth*, *ll* in *smell*, *gg* in *wiggle*) You may discuss the irregularity of the word *eye* and point out how different it is from the word *I*.

> **Differentiation ideas:** Support learners by working with them in a group to complete Worksheet 6.1 What can my body do?

Challenge learners to find the rhyming words in the rhyme in Activity 1 (*talk*/*walk*).

Answers:
a eyes – see; **b** mouth – talk; **c** ears – hear
d feet – walk; **e** nose – smell; **f** teeth – bite;
g eyebrows – wiggle; **h** hand – touch

---

 2   *My Eyes Can See* (10–15 minutes)

Learning intention: to listen to and join in with a simple action rhyme

Resources: *My Eyes Can See* (Learner's Book, Session 6.1, Activity 2); Track 35

Description: Tell learners they are going to hear a rhyme about how we use our bodies to sense the world.

Together, read or listen to the rhyme *My Eyes Can See*.

Repeat the rhyme with actions. Check that learners are pointing to parts of their body as they sing. Repeat again, missing out the verb and asking learners to supply it each time, e.g. *My eyes can _____*.

Before moving on, allow time for learners to read and sing the rhyme.

> **Differentiation ideas:** If some learners struggle with coordination and multi-tasking, let them practise and enjoy the activity.

Challenge some learners to help you with the actions and guide others, too. Some may like to perform the rhyme alone or in pairs.

3   Extending vocabulary: verbs (15–30 minutes)

Learning intention: to extend vocabulary and to build a class word bank of verbs

Resources: Learner's Book, Session 6.1, Activity 3; large pieces of paper/wallpaper; sticky notes / small pieces of paper; sticky putty or glue

Description: Draw round one of the learners and display the drawing on the wall.

Invite learners to explore other vocabulary choices for what each body part does. Ask: *What else can our eyes/ears/mouths/feet/teeth/eyebrows/hands do?*

Give learners time to write their ideas on sticky notes, if possible. If sticky notes are not available, use pieces of paper with sticky putty or glue.

Invite different learners to stick their words onto the body outline.

Keep and use this as a class word bank of verbs relating to the body.

> **Differentiation ideas:** Support learners by asking them to work in mixed-ability groups.

Challenge learners to attempt spellings by using their phonics knowledge and to try again if they make incorrect (even though viable) spelling choices, e.g. *eyebrows can skoul* (scowl).

Answers:
Learners' own responses

---

4   Play a game of *I Spy* (10–15 minutes)

Learning intention: to say letters and sounds for word beginnings

Resources: *I Spy* and *I Hear* (Learner's Book, Session 6.1, Activity 4); Tracks 36 and 37; sunglasses; headphones; music

Description: Play an adapted game of *I Spy*.

Ask learners to sit in a circle and pass round two objects: a pair of sunglasses and a pair of headphones.

Play music. When the music stops:

*   the learner holding the sunglasses should say: *I spy with my little eye something beginning with … [letter]*
*   the learner holding the headphones should say: *I hear with my little ear something beginning with … [letter]*
*   Other learners must guess the correct answers.

Start the music again and repeat to ensure all learners have the opportunity to spy or hear.

> **Differentiation ideas:** Support learners by modelling examples of each of the types of statements for the game.

Challenge learners to make bold statements, e.g. using statements to include digraphs – words that have a particular letter sound in them such as /oo/.

Plenary idea

Pass It On (10 minutes)

Description: Choose ten learners at a time to stand at the front.

Whisper a sentence or phrase to the first learner and ask them to pass it on quietly to the next person. They must whisper it so no one else can hear it and they may only say it once.

The last person in the line must say the sentence or phrase out loud.

Compare what you said to the first learner with what this last learner says. It can be very funny if the message changed quite a bit as learners passed it along.

The moral of the game is that we need to speak clearly and listen well.

CROSS-CURRICULAR LINKS

Art: Create pictures of body parts that contain the written word, e.g. a picture of an eye that features the word eye as part of the artwork.

Homework ideas

Learners complete the Workbook Session 6.1 activities if not completed in class.

They find out more about games that involve using or not using one of the senses, e.g. Blindfold Bluff where a player must wear a blindfold and catch other players, using only their hearing.

Answers for Workbook

1   Correctly formed letters for each word plus horizontal join for *ou* and diagonal join to ascender for *th*

2   Joins: *ee, ear, ou, ll*

3   **a–e**   Correct joins for words as shown

6.2 Touch

LEARNING PLAN

Learning objectives		Learning intentions	Success criteria
Main focus	**Also covered**	• To explore words and rhymes about touch.	• Learners can explore words and rhymes about touch.
1Rv.05, 1Ri.14, 1Wv.01, 1Wv.03, 1SLm.03	1Rw.03, 1Rs.02, 1Ri.01, 1Ri.12, 1Ri.13, 1Ra.01, 1Ra.02, 1Ra.03, 1Ra.04, 1Ww.02, 1Ww.05, 1Wg.01, 1Wg.03, 1Ws.01, 1Wc.01, 1SLs.01, 1SLs.02, 1SLg.02, 1SLg.04, 1SLp.05	• To hear when a poem does not rhyme. • To write a sentence about sand.	• Learners can hear when a poem does not rhyme. • Learners can write a sentence about sand.

LANGUAGE SUPPORT

Make a class Touch Box. Play some music and ask learners to stand up and shake their hands to it. When the music stops, the last one to sit down must put a hand in the box and describe and identify the object inside. This will build learners' confidence and develop their vocabulary. Change the object in the box between rounds.

Provide a sand tray for sand play. Allow learners, especially those who may not have experience of it, to feel sand (wet, dry, gritty, soft, etc.) to support their vocabulary development.

Play Rhyme Snap. Search online for rhyming cards and ask learners to match the rhymes picture to picture, picture to word or word to word depending on the level of challenge required. This will support learners to hear rhymes and non-rhymes. You may use Language worksheet 6B here.

Common misconception

Misconception	How to identify	How to overcome
Long words are hard to read.	Ask learners to read the longer words in the poem *Sand in …*: *fingernails* *earholes* *sandwiches* *everywhere* Talk about how they worked out how to read them.	Create a class tip list for working out longer words and encourage learners to use it: 1 Is the long word made up of two words? 2 Can you split the letters or sounds? 3 Read the sentence for meaning.

Starter idea

Listening activity (5–10 minutes)

Resources: *Hands Up* (Learner's Book, Session 6.2, Getting started); Track 38

> **Audioscript: *Hands Up***
>
> Hands up to the ceiling,
>
> Hands touch the floor,
>
> Reach up again,
>
> Let's do some more,
>
> Now touch your head,
>
> Then touch your knee,
>
> Then touch your shoulder,
>
> Just like me.
>
> Hands up to the ceiling,
>
> Hands touch the floor,
>
> That's it for now, goodbye!
>
> There isn't any more.
>
> *Anonymous*

Description: Ask learners to tell you the name of the sense represented by our hands. (touch) Check learners understand the vocabulary *floor* and *ceiling* before introducing the new rhyme: *Hands Up*.

Ask learners to listen as you read the rhyme aloud or play the audio. Repeat and ask them to listen for the word *touch* (it is used five times). Repeat and ask them to join in with the actions. Note that *touch* is a

tricky word to read: /t/ /ou/ /ch/ with *ou* representing the /u/ sound.

Main teaching ideas

1 **Listen to and read a rhyme (15 minutes)**

Learning intention: to read, listen to and join in with a rhyme

Resources: *Sand in...* (Learner's Book, Session 6.2, Activity 1); Track 39

Description: Together, talk about sand and how it feels to touch it. Share experiences and find out what learners already know about sand and what vocabulary they already have.

Ask learners to listen to the poem *Sand in …*. Read the poem and ask learners to jump up each time they hear the word *sand*. Use the audio if you prefer.

Ask learners what they notice about the structure of the poem. (It repeats the word *sand* at the beginning of each line.)

Ask them what rhymes with *toes*, *bananas* and *hair*. This is picked up again in the Activity 2 differentiation ideas.

Read the rhyme again and invite learners to join in and add actions. For each line you might model an action for the learners to follow.

❯ **Differentiation ideas:** Support learners with any unfamiliar vocabulary, e.g. *fingernails*, *earholes*, *sandwiches*, *pyjamas*.

Challenge learners to perform the poem for each other in pairs.

2 Answer questions (20 minutes)

Learning intention: to answer questions about the features of a poem

Resources: Learner's Book, Session 6.2, Activity 2; Workbook, Session 6.2

Description: Ask learners to read the questions and write the answers in their notebooks.

As they work, circulate in the classroom to offer support and to check spelling and handwriting.

You can use the Workbook Session 6.2 activities now.

⟩ Differentiation ideas: Support learners by arranging different pairings or sit with a group to help them.

Challenge learners to write another word to rhyme with each of *toes*, *bananas* and *hair*.

Answers:
a Sand and touch; **b** 12 times and 13 if you count sand in *sandwiches*; **c** toes/nose, bananas/pyjamas, hair/everywhere

3 Rhyming pairs (20 minutes)

Learning intention: to identify a non-rhyming poem

Resources: *Sand* (Learner's Book, Session 6.2, Activity 3); Track 40; *Sand in...* (Learner's Book, Session 6.2); Track 39

Description: Tell learners they will hear another poem about *sand*. You may re-read *Sand in ...* in Activity 1 before asking them to listen as you read *Sand* or play the audio.

Ask them to think about what is the same about the poems and then listen again to find out what is different about each poem. (Possible answers: One poem is longer than the other; one begins with the word *sand* in each verse while the other begins with a different word in most lines; one poem makes sand sound like a nuisance, whereas the Shirley Hughes poem is about liking sand; one rhymes and one does not.)

Establish that this poem does not rhyme. There are no rhyming words.

Discuss the Reading tip. Ask: *Does anyone in class have a hyphenated name, e.g. Rose-Anne or Kal-El?* Model how to read each phrase to make it sound like one long joined-up word.

⟩ Differentiation ideas: Support learners by asking them to find the rhyming words in the Shirley

Hughes poem (so when they cannot, they realise it is not a rhyming poem).

Challenge learners to list another similarity and difference between the poems.

4 Write a sentence (10 minutes)

Learning intention: to write a sentence expressing a preference; to punctuate a sentence correctly

Resources: Learner's Book, Session 6.2, Activity 4

Description: Revisit the Reading tip in Activity 3.

Tell learners they will write their own sentence about what kind of sand they like best. They may use hyphens if they like.

If you have set up a sand tray in class, incorporate hands-on experience.

Together, create a word bank of adjectives to describe sand, e.g. *sticky, wet, muddy, fine, silvery, yellow, gritty.*

Share descriptive words and model how to join words together using the hyphen:

- *The stuck-under-your-fingernails kind*
- *The mix-it-with-water kind*
- *The pat-it-into-a-castle kind*
- *The sprinkle-it-through-a sieve kind.*

Ask learners to choose a phrase and write it in their notebooks.

⟩ Differentiation ideas: Support learners by putting their chosen phrases in front of them so they can copy without looking up to the word bank.

Challenge learners to make up their own phrases.

Answers:
Learners' own sentences

Plenary idea

Which poem? (5 minutes)

Resources: *Sand in...* and *Sand* (Learner's Book, Session 6.2); Tracks 39 and 40

Description: Together, re-read both poems in Session 6.2 or listen to them again.

Which poem is most popular? Ask learners to vote by standing up for the poem they like best.

Ask a few learners why they have chosen one poem rather than the other.

Encourage all learners to listen well and respect the opinions of others.

CROSS-CURRICULAR LINKS

Art: Play with sand to explore how it feels and make patterns. Make sand pictures with black paper and glue.

Science: Ask questions about sand: *Why does sand stick to our hands and feet? What is sand made of? How can you make sand dry?*

Homework ideas

Learners complete the Workbook Session 6.2 activities if not completed in class.

They draw around their hand and fill it with words and pictures about the sense 'touch'. Make a class display of their hands.

Answers for Workbook

1   **a** in; **b** between; **c** in; **d** up

2   **b** bananas; **c** night; **d** pyjamas.

3   Learners' own responses

6.3 Feeling sad

LEARNING PLAN			

Learning objectives		Learning intentions	Success criteria
Main focus	**Also covered**	• To explore words and rhymes about feelings.	• Learners can explore words and rhymes about feelings.
1Rw.01, 1Rv.04, 1Ri.14, 1Wv.03, 1SLm.03, 1SLg.01	1Rw.02, 1Rw.05, 1Rv.01, 1Rv.02, 1Rv.03, 1Rv.05, 1Rg.03, 1Rg.06, 1Rs.02, 1Ri.01, 1Ri.11, 1Ri.13, 1Ra.01, 1Ra.04, 1Ww.03, 1Wv.01, 1SLm.04, 1SLg.03, 1SLr.02	• To answer questions about 'sad' rhymes. • To work together to create an A–Z of feelings.	• Learners can answer questions about 'sad' rhymes. • Learners can work together to make an A–Z of feelings.

LANGUAGE SUPPORT	

Learners may need support to remember the synonyms for the different feelings in this session. The A–Z class bunting (paper flags made in Activity 4) will help with this, so encourage learners to continue to add to it and to use it.

Alternatively, encourage learners to make their own banks of words and pictures about feelings. The Workbook activities will help with this, too.

Worksheets of the poems, which may be marked up with a highlighter pen, may help learners when they are looking for words. Use different-coloured pens, for example to find the words in different rhyming sets as in Activity 2.

Common misconception

Misconception	How to identify	How to overcome
The alphabet is just a sequence of letters that we have to learn how to say.	Ask learners to say the alphabet together as a class. Then ask if anyone can sing the alphabet in a song. Then ask: *What else can we do with the alphabet? What else does it help us to do?*	Make a class A–Z of feelings. Continue to add words to each letter flag as you work through this unit. Learners will realise that the alphabet is helpful for creating fun displays that can then help them with their reading and writing.

Starter idea

Feelings (10–15 minutes)

Resources: Learner's Book, Session 6.3: Getting started; camera (if available)

Description: Ask learners: *How are you feeling today? What do they say?* (*Fine, thank you.; I'm well, thank you.; I don't feel very well today.; I'm tired today.*)

Give learners two minutes to work in pairs to ask each other how they are feeling.

Then ask them the question again. Invite pairs to share their own questions and answers.

Draw three basic emojis on the board: happy, sad and neutral. Ask learners what they know about these 'signs'.

Then ask learners to look at the pictures in Getting started.

Talk together about which words they can use to say how the girl is feeling. Not all the words provided will be used, but they provide a rich word bank for exploring new vocabulary with learners.

If you have time, take some photos of learners' expressions that reflect how they are feeling. Share the photos as a plenary to this session or print them to create a class display.

Main teaching ideas

1 Listen to and read *Sad Today* and *Sick* (15–30 minutes)

Learning intention: to listen, read and talk about two short rhyming poems to identify how the poet is feeling

Resources: *Sad Today* and *Sick* (Learner's Book, Session 6.3, Activity 1); Tracks 41 and 42

Description: Tell learners they are going to hear you read two poems. Ask them to listen carefully and decide what feelings the poems are about.

Take their ideas. They might say the poems are about feeling sad/unwell/unhappy/unsure.

Ask learners to share their experiences of feeling sad. Deal sensitively with any issues that arise. (This topic is picked up again in Session 6.5 Activity 1 in the rhyming story, *Bad Day, Good Day.*)

Ask learners to share experiences of feeling unwell, using some of the words and phrases from the poem, *Sick*, e.g. *tummy ache, headache, sore finger, sore leg, feeling very hot, itchy, tired, upset* and *bored.* Ask: *Does anyone enjoy feeling unwell? Why?*

Then ask learners to read the poems in pairs or as a class together.

You could use the Phonics Workbooks for further practice of using phonics for reading and spelling.

> **Differentiation ideas:** Support learners by showing the text on a shared screen and modelling how you can track the words with a finger to follow each line of the rhyme. Work with a group who may need support to read the poem after listening.

Challenge learners by asking them to find words in the poem with tricky spellings and to say what they notice, e.g. the *ch* in *aching* as /k/; the *ea* in *heavy* as /e/; the *w* in *wrinkles* as a silent letter; the *c* in *medicine* as /s/; the *ou* in *soup* as long /oo/. Ask them to reflect on how they can remember these tricky words.

2 Rhyming words (15–30 minutes)

Learning intention: to identify and sort the rhyming words in poems; to notice the spelling of rhyming words

Resources: Learner's Book, Session 6.3, Activity 2; *Sad Today and Sick* (Learner's Book, Session 6.3); Tracks 41 and 42; Worksheet 6.2

Description: Ask learners to listen to or read the poems in Activity 1 again.

Ask them to work in pairs to find the rhyming words in each poem. You can provide Worksheet 6.2 Feeling sad here for learners to annotate.

> **Differentiation ideas:** Support learners who will benefit from physically marking up, and even colour coding the different rhyme sets, by providing Worksheet 6.2 Feeling sad. Some learners may like to cut out the rhyming words and stick them in sets.

Challenge learners to add a rhyming word to each set.

Answers:
day: today, say, away, okay; sad: bad, glad; bed: head; up: cup; feet: sheet

3   Questions (20–30 minutes)

Learning intention: to answer and ask questions about a rhyme; to find words and show understanding

Resources: Learner's Book, Session 6.3, Activity 3; *Sick* (Learner's Book, Session 6.3); Track 42; Worksheet 6.2

Description: Ask learners to read the poem *Sick* again and look at the questions in the Activity 3.

First, model how to write the answer to each question and then ask learners to write the answers in their notebooks.

Allow some learners to work alone and some in pairs. You may decide to work with a group for additional support. Use Worksheet 6.2 Feeling sad again if helpful for annotations.

Some learners may be able to write questions for partners or the class to answer.

As you move around the classroom, check that learners are holding their pencils correctly and forming their letters and numbers correctly, too.

> **Differentiation ideas:** Challenge learners to write about a time when they felt sick.

Support learners by working with them in a group and/or by providing answers that they could match to the questions.

Answers:
a Hot, cross, aching head; **b** Prickly, tickly and itchy; **c** Books, toys and puzzles; **d** She is sick of them; **e** She wants to feel better and get up.

4   A–Z of feelings (15–30 minutes, but ongoing)

Learning intention: to work in a group to create an alphabetical collection of feelings

Resources: Learner's Book, Session 6.3, Activity 4; Workbook, Session 6.3; bunting template (search online or make from A4 sheets of paper)

Description: Ask learners to say the alphabet (letter names not sounds). Can they sing it, too?

Split the class into six groups: four groups can prepare four bunting flags each and two groups can prepare five flags each.

Each group should:

*   cut out the bunting flag and write the letter of the alphabet in capital letters

*   write words for feelings beginning with that letter on the reverse side of the flag – for tricky letters they will need to be creative, e.g. v: *very*; x: *eXcited*; y: *yucky*; z: *zany*.

Give groups time to prepare before bringing them back together to share their flags and words.

Use this as an opportunity to encourage peer assessment, to offer positive comments and to add further words to each flag. Also reflect on how these words may be useful to them.

String up the flags for your class display. Once strung up, new words are best added on a sticky note.

You can use the activities in Workbook Session 6.3 in class now.

> **Differentiation ideas:** Challenge learners to find out what additional words might mean, e.g. *adventurous, zealous*.

Support learners by setting up mixed-ability groups. Encourage the use of games to reinforce the vocabulary explored in this unit, e.g. Guess the Feeling; Feelings Bingo; Feelings board game (if you land on a feeling word you have to say a time when you felt like that).

Plenary idea

Guess the Feeling (5–10 minutes)

Resources: word cards featuring feeling words

Description: Whisper a feeling to a learner or give them a word card featuring a 'feeling' word. Ask them to act this feeling.

Others must guess the word from the actions.

The person who guesses correctly picks the next card.

Homework ideas

Learners complete the Workbook Session 6.3 activities if not completed in class.

They find other poems about feeling sad or unwell.

Answers for Workbook

1 Learners' own drawings to reflect happy, sad and angry

2 **a** sleepy; **b** excited; **c** shy/worried

3 Learners' own drawings and words

6.4 Feeling happy

LEARNING PLAN

Learning objectives		Learning intentions	Success criteria
Main focus	**Also covered**	• To explore words and rhymes about feeling happy.	• Learners can explore words and rhymes about feeling happy.
1Rw.04, 1Ri.14, 1SLp.01, 1SLp.02, 1SLp.04	1Rw.02, 1Rw.05, 1Rv.05, 1Rg.02, 1Rg.03, 1Rs.01, 1Rs.02, 1Ri.01, 1Ri.06, 1Ra.01, 1Ra.02, 1Ww.01, 1Wv.01, 1Wc.02,03, 1SLg.01 1SLp.02, 1SLp.03	• To read and write verbs ending –s, –ed and –ing. • To read and perform a poem.	• Learners can read and write verbs ending –s, –ed and –ing. • Learners can read and perform a poem.

LANGUAGE SUPPORT

Learners may need support to explore synonyms for *happy*. Use the A–Z class bunting from Session 6.3 Activity 4, and add to it if you can. Encourage learners to continue to use it as a word bank.

Explore onomatopoeic words we use for *laughter* in English and home languages, too, e.g. *giggle,*

snigger, howl, guffaw. Challenge learners with vocabulary choices.

Worksheet 6.3 Feeling happy can be marked up with a highlighter pen and may help learners when they are working with the text for performance.

Common misconception

Misconception	How to identify	How to overcome
When we add *–s, -ed* or *–ing*, there is no change to the spelling of the root verb.	Ask learners to look at sets of verbs you write on the board: *laugh, cheer* (no change with verb endings) *smile, dance* (drop e with verb endings) *grin, chat* (double consonant with verb endings) Ask them to work quickly in pairs or groups to add the verb endings to each. Ask: *What do you notice?*	Discuss with learners how they might remember to check their spellings when adding the verb endings. You could create a class poster for learners to use as they write.

Starter idea

Parties and birthdays (15–20 minutes)

Resources: Learner's Book, Session 6.4: Getting started

Description: Ask learners what makes them feel happy. Share ideas and activate prior knowledge of experiences and vocabulary.

Ask them to look at the pictures in Getting started and, together, explore the questions. Ask: *Does anyone have a birthday this week? How do you celebrate birthdays in school or class?* Be sensitive if there are learners in your class who do not specifically celebrate birthdays – they may celebrate other special times.

Sing any Happy Birthday songs you might know.

Look at the questions in Getting started together. Encourage learners to answer them and share their ideas.

Revisit the rules of punctuation for questions and demonstrate how to ask questions.

Main teaching ideas

1   Listen to *Laughing Time* (15–30 minutes)

Learning intention: to listen to a poem and discuss its features

Resources: *Laughing Time* (Learner's Book, Session 6.4; Activity 1); Track 43; Worksheet 6.3; Differentiated worksheets 6A–C

Description: Tell learners they are going to listen to a new poem.

Ask them to first listen to the poem *Laughing Time* and to tell you whether it is about feeling happy or sad.

Play the audio of the poem or read the poem aloud for learners.

Talk about learners' views on the poem. Ask: *What did you hear? What did you notice?* Share ideas. They may notice some or all of these things:

*   It is about animals laughing. It is a poem about happy feelings.

*   Each verse of the poem has three lines.

*   The final line of each verse has funny laughing words written in *italics*.

*   The ending repeats all the funny laughing words.

Ask them to listen again. This time, ask them to think about how they listen well, drawing their attention to the How are we doing? feature.

You can use Differentiated worksheets 6A–C here to focus on listening for or reading for words, sentences and phrases in the poem.

You can use Language worksheet 6A here to talk about the use of capital letters for the names of the animals.

> **Differentiation ideas:** Support learners by varying the pace of your reading. Encourage them to work in pairs or groups to talk about the features of the poem. Provide Worksheet 6.3 Feeling happy if helpful for marking up what they notice.

Challenge learners to talk about other words they use for *laughter*, in English and/or their own language.

2 Verb endings –s, –ing and –ing (20–30 minutes)

Learning intention: to explore verb endings –s,–ing and –ed

Resources: Learner's Book, Session 6.4, Activity 2; Workbook, Session 6.4

Description: Refer to Common misconception.

Draw learners' attention to the Language focus box in the Learner's Book. Talk about the rules for adding these endings to verbs.

• –s for third person present (things that usually happen)

• –ing for present continuous (things that are happening)

• –ed for past tense (things that have happened)

Show them that if a verb ends in *e* we can add *s* with no change, but we may have to drop the *e* before adding –ing or –ed.

Ask them to look at the sentences and work through the answers in pairs or individually.

You can use the Workbook Session 6.4 activities now.

〉 **Differentiation ideas:** Challenge learners to record their answers in sentences, working alone or in pairs.

Support learners by asking them to work in pairs where one is a stronger reader than the other. Ask them to just write the correct verb form.

Answers:
a chattering; **b** swinging; **c** croaked; **d** holding, dancing; **e** smiled

3 Put the pictures in order to retell the poem's story (20–30 minutes)

Learning intention: to sequence pictures and use them to retell the story of a poem

Resources: Learner's Book, Session 6.4, Activity 3; *Laughing Time* (Learner's Book, Session 6.4); Track 43; Worksheet 6.4; Language worksheet 6B

Description: If possible, begin the activity by quickly re-reading the poem in Activity 1 aloud.

Ask learners to create masks to represent the different animals in the poem, using Worksheet 6.4 Mask template.

Now ask six learners to hold or wear a mask for each animal and get themselves into the correct order as they appear in the poem.

Once the learners in masks are in order, use them as a prompt to model how to retell the story.

Ask learners to then work in pairs at their desks to repeat the activity. They can draw the illustrations in the correct order in their notebooks and use these to orally rehearse the retelling.

Then use the language of the poem or make up simple sentences to match each animal, e.g. *The Giraffe laughed first like this: Ha! Ha! Then the Chimpanzee laughed like this: Hee! Hee!* etc.

Use Language worksheet 6B to explore the long vowel phoneme rhymes in the poem if helpful for the retelling or as a challenge for learners.

〉 **Differentiation ideas:** Challenge learners to write captions for the illustrations. Some may even make a zig-zag book for this. Use Language worksheet 6B here to explore rhyming long vowel phonemes as a challenge.

Answers:
Learners sequence the pictures in the order:
c Giraffe **f** Chimpanzee **d** Crow **a** Bear **e** Donkey **b** Moon

Support learners by working through the sequencing again in a smaller group.

4 Read and perform *Laughing Time* (30–60 minutes)

Learning intention: to recite and perform a poem

Resources: Learner's Book, Session 6.4, Activity 4; *Laughing Time* (Learner's Book, Session 6.4); Track 43; Worksheets 6.3 and 6.4

Description: Organise learners into groups of five.

Hand out Worksheet 6.3 Feeling happy, and Worksheet 6.4 Mask template if required.

Draw learners' attention to the Speaking tip to remind them how to speak confidently.

Ask learners to work in their groups to practise their recitals. Encourage creative responses to the laughter words.

Provide time for practice and for performance.

You could perform as a class by grouping together learners who took the same part, e.g. all those who played the Giraffe in their small groups form a group; those who were the Chimpanzee form a group and so on.

> **Differentiation ideas:** Challenge learners to learn the poem in full.

Support learners by setting up mixed groups and pairings. Some learners will gain confidence to perform when hiding behind a mask.

Plenary idea

Sing a song (5–10 minutes)

Resources: 'If you're happy and you know it' audio song.

Description: Listen to and join in with the song: 'If you're happy and you know it'. You can search for lyrics online if necessary.

Invite learners to add actions to the song.

CROSS-CURRICULAR LINKS

Technology: Search online sound banks for the sound of animals laughing or their cries or calls that sound like a laugh to us.

Maths: Make a class block chart or pictogram to show how many learners have birthdays in each month of the year.

Art: Make patterns and pictures with the shape of the question mark.

Homework ideas

Learners complete the Workbook Session 6.4 activities.

They practise singing the song: 'If you're happy and you know it' for their families.

Answers for Workbook

1 laughing; lifted; dancing; waltzed

2 chattering/chatters/chattered; jumping/jumps/ jumped; smiling/smiles/smiled; giggling/ giggles/ giggled

3 swinging; croaking; waltzing; taking; going; having; smiling; starting

6.5 Planning and writing a rhyme

LEARNING PLAN

Learning objectives		Learning intentions	Success criteria
Main focus	**Also covered**	• To talk about the days of the week.	• Learners can talk about the days of the week.
1Rv.05, 1Rs.01, 1Rs.02, 1Wv.01, 1Wc.01, 1Wc.02	1Rv.01, 1Rv.03, 1Rg.02, 1Ri.01, 1Ri.07, 1Ri.13, 1Ri.14, 1Ra.01, 1Ra.02, 1Ra.06, 1Ww.05, 1Ww.07, 1Wv.03, 1Wg.01, 1Wg.03, 1Ws.01, 1Wc.03, 1Wp.02, 1Wp.03, 1SLm.03, 1SLg.02, 1SLg.04, 1SLp.05, 1SLr.02	• To explore a rhyme about good days and bad days. • To plan and write a new rhyme about days.	• Learners can explore a rhyme about good days and bad days. • Learners can plan and write a new rhyme about days.

LANGUAGE SUPPORT

Learners may find a class Days of the week chart useful. Create a Months of the Year chart, too.

Sing songs about the days of the week (search online for *Days of the week songs*).

Encourage learners to paint with and mix colours so the language is being reinforced in real situations.

Worksheet 6.5 Writing framework for *Bad Day, Good Day* may be particularly useful as a structure for some learners.

Common misconception

Misconception	How to identify	How to overcome
We always have to pronounce every letter in a word.	Write the word *Wednesday* on the board. Say it in two ways and ask learners which is correct: *Wed-nes-day* *Wensday* Use this as an example. Then select other words that feature silent letters or unstressed syllables, e.g. *surprise*, pronounced *su'prise*.	Encourage learners to play 'I say, you say'-type games in which they must repeat correct pronunciation, or games that ask them to select the correct pronunciation. Reading aloud will also help with this.

Starter idea

Days of the week (15–20 minutes)

Resources: Learner's Book, Session 6.5: Getting started; Workbook, Session 6.5; a days of the week song

Description: If you know a days of the week song, then begin the session with this. Sing together.

Ask learners to say the days of the week with you and then invite individuals or pairs to say the days. Learners may know other days of the week rhymes that they can share.

Ask learners what today is. Ask them how they feel today. Then say: *Ah, so today is a good day. It's a [go-to-tea-with-a friend-day]* or similar.

Talk about what makes a good day or a bad day, and together make two lists on a shared board.

You can use the Workbook Session 6.5 activities here to focus on writing the days of the week and joining some letters or the whole word.

Work round the class, encouraging a chain reaction of 'good day' experiences, with learners saying *It's a good day when …* and then repeating with 'bad day' experiences.

Encourage learners to think about how they can show feelings without using words, e.g. with expressions or gestures.

Main teaching ideas

1 Listen to and read *Bad Day, Good Day* (15–20 minutes)

Learning intention: to listen to and read a rhyming poem

Resources: *Bad Day, Good Day* (Learner's Book, Session 6.5, Activity 1); Track 44; Language worksheet 6A

Description: Tell learners that this next rhyme includes the days of the week.

Read it aloud or play the audio.

On a second listening, ask learners to point to each day of the week in Activity 1 as they hear it.

Talk about what is happening in the rhyme. Ask: *Is it quite like real life?*

Talk about the language features of the rhyme:

- Each verse ends in the word *day*.

- Just as in the poem *Sand* in Session 6.2, the hyphen is used to join words together in a fun way, e.g. *kit-day; sit-day*.

- Draw learners' attention to the How are we doing? question and discuss. (Joining the words creates a pattern and rhythm that helps with reading aloud.)

- Notice the use of capital letters for the days of the week. Use Language worksheet 6A if you wish to elaborate on this point.

Ask learners to read the rhyme aloud with you before asking them to read it in pairs or small groups.

> **Differentiation ideas:** Work with any learners to support them in their paired reading, or ask some learners to read in groups.

Challenge learners to explain what is meant by *Lost my kit-day. Had to sit-day.* (It means that she did not have her sports kit/clothes so could not join in but had to watch others.)

2 Answer questions (20 minutes)

Learning intention: to answer questions about a poem

Resources: Learner's Book, Session 6.5, Activity 2; *Bad Day, Good Day* (Learner's Book, Session 6.5); Track 44; Language worksheet 6A

Description: Work through the questions orally, with learners reading the question aloud and modelling answers together.

Ask learners to read and answer the questions in their notebooks.

Remind them about the use of full stops and capital letters in their sentences. If using Language worksheet 6A, use here. If not, remind learners that they need to use capital letters for the days of the week as well as at the beginning of each sentence.

As you circulate, check learners are writing their responses with correct punctuation.

> **Differentiation ideas:** Support learners to write their answers in their notebooks. Alternatively, ask them to answer fewer, selected questions.

Challenge learners to write their own question about the poem for a partner to answer. Check the formation of the question mark.

Answers:

a A girl. (We can see from the pictures.)

b A sad day

c She was late, she had to run and she dropped her bun.

d On Sunday she felt happy because it was her birthday.

e Learners' own questions

3 Complete a planning chart (30–40 minutes)

Learning intention: to plan a new poem based on the structure of *Bad Day, Good Day*

Resources: Learner's Book, Session 6.5, Activity 3; Worksheet 6.5

Description: Tell learners they are now going to plan their own version of *Bad Day, Good Day*. They will need to think of new ideas and words to use instead of the underlined words.

Show learners the chart in Activity 3, or Worksheet 6.5 Writing framework for *Bad Day, Good Day* if using.

Remind learners that there are no right or wrong answers here. It is about their own ideas.

Encourage them to use their phonics to write their ideas. They may also use class word banks such as the A–Z of feelings started in Session 6.3.

Give them time to work on their ideas. Circulate among them, and support and challenge where necessary.

> **Differentiation ideas:** Challenge learners to mix ''' 'good day' with 'bad day' ideas.

Support learners to generate ideas by working with a group if necessary. It may be helpful to use banks of pictures or to search online for inspiration if learners need visual support.

Answers:
Learners' own responses

4 Write a new rhyme (30–40 minutes)

Learning intention: to use a plan to write a new version of a rhyme

Resources: Learner's Book, Session 6.5, Activity 4; Worksheet 6.5

Description: Using their plans from Activity 3, ask learners to write their own version of the rhyme for each day of the week.

Remind learners to use a capital letter for each day of the week.

As you walk around the class, talk to different learners about their ideas and their writing, adding support where necessary.

The room should be industrious, but encourage learners to help each other and to enjoy their writing.

Once finished, the rhymes could be collated into a class book of poems.

> **Differentiation ideas:** Support learners by providing Worksheet 6.5 Writing framework for *Bad Day, Good Day*, which is a chart / writing template. Some learners may benefit from working in pairs on a larger piece of paper before transferring their ideas to the worksheet.

Challenge learners not to use the writing framework but to think about the layout of their poem and any design features they would like to include such as pictures or photos. Ask: *What colours will you use?*

Answers:
Learners' own rhymes

Plenary idea

How was your day? (5–10 minutes)

Resources: a large inflatable ball

Description: Ask learners to pass or lightly throw the ball to each other asking: *How was your day/lesson today?*

Learners respond in various ways (*It was a tough/sad/fun/brilliant/funny day/lesson*).

To challenge learners, ask: *Why?*

Homework ideas

Learners complete the Workbook Session 6.5 activities.

They make and keep a diary for a week

Answers for Workbook

1 Days of the week written in the correct order: Monday, Tuesday, Wednesday, Thursday, Friday, Saturday, Sunday.

2 Joins as requested.

3 Joins as requested.

6.6 Look back

LEARNING PLAN

Learning objectives		Learning intentions	Success criteria
Main focus	**Also covered**	• To check our writing.	• Learners can check their writing.
1Rv.05, 1Rs.02, 1Ra.04, 1Wp,06, 1SLp.05, 1SLr.01	1Ww.03, 1Wg.01, 1Wg.06, 1Wp.01, 1Wp.02, 1SLm.03, 1SLm.04	• To share our writing and talk about it. • To think about our learning from the unit.	• Learners can share their writing and talk about it. • Learners can think about their learning from the unit.

LANGUAGE SUPPORT

Use the pictures in the Learner's Book or any classroom displays or posters to support learners in the review process.

Starter idea

What to check (10 minutes)

Resources: Learner's Book, Session 6.6: Getting started

Description: Ask learners to talk about how they might be able to work together to help each other with their writing.

First, draw their attention to the flow chart in Getting started to establish a sequence they could follow:

• Read your rhyme aloud. Ask: *How did it sound?*

• Then listen to your partner reading aloud. Tell them how it sounded.

• Swap rhymes. Read the rhymes and say one thing you thought was done well and one thing you think could have been done better.

Ask: *Is there anything else that you would like to add to the process of helping each other?*

If useful, consider making a class poster of this for future use.

Main teaching ideas

1 Check our writing (15–30 minutes)

Learning intention: to think about and check own writing; to share writing and ask for feedback

Resources: Learner's Book, Session 6.6, Activity 1; flow chart in Getting started

Description: Choose a pair of learners and ask them to model how they will work together using the flow chart in Getting started.

Invite discussion as the pair proceeds, and ask questions of the other learners:

• *Are they listening well?*

• *Are the ideas they are exchanging helpful to each other?*

• *Are their ideas kind?*

• *Are they speaking clearly so their ideas are clear?*

• *Are their ideas useful for improving the rhyme? Why? How?*

Ask learners to then do the same in their pairs in the remaining time.

The two learners who have modelled the process may now consider which changes to make or not.

⟩ Differentiation ideas: Some learners will need support in framing responses to their partner's work. Devise two simple cards to support them with this, e.g. one with a smiling mouth and one with a straight-line mouth, or ask them to choose just one thing they thought was good and one thing that could be better. Consider working with a group to repeat the modelling of the process.

Challenge learners to add stages to the flow chart process after they have worked together.

2 Look back at rhymes and poems (10 minutes)

Learning intention: to recall rhymes and poems; to enjoy re-reading, saying or singing rhymes and poems

Resources: Learner's Book, Session 6.6, Activity 2; Workbook, Session 6.6; all poems from Unit 6

Description: Ask learners to identify all the rhymes and poems they have read in Unit 6, using the pictures in Activity 2 to help.

Encourage learners to speak up clearly, and ask if they can remember the main focus of the rhyme or poem. Ask: *What was it about? What did we learn?*

You can use the Workbook Session 6.6 activities now to check some of the key vocabulary and learning from the unit.

⟩ Differentiation ideas: Support learners by working in a small group to find the rhymes and poems in the book or sing/say them together.

Challenge learners to list the rhymes and poems in their notebooks.

3 Speaking, listening, reading and writing rhymes and poems (10–15 minutes)

Learning intention: to explore the differences between the four key literacy skills; to express preferences

Resources: Learner's Book, Session 6.6, Activity 3

Description: Together, talk about which rhymes and poems learners liked best, and why, for each of the four literacy skills.

Remind learners that each literacy skill links back to a sense as explored in the early sessions of Unit 6.

Encourage learners to express their own likes and dislikes in relation to the rhymes and poems, but ask for explanations.

Encourage others to listen and respect opinions. Ask: *Do you agree or disagree?*

Ask learners to draw or write their answers.

You can use the Workbook Session 6.6 activities now.

⟩ Differentiation ideas: Support learners by working in a small group, or asking them to work in pairs, to talk about preferences. Alternatively, discuss preferences as a class and take some votes on which rhyme or poem learners liked best and why.

Challenge learners to memorise one of their favourite rhymes or poems.

Plenary idea

Happy as a ..., Sad as a ... (10–15 minutes)

Description: Ask learners to think of two ideas to complete each sentence: *Happy as a ... and Sad as a ....* For example:

- happy as a rainbow / a guitar / a birthday / the sun
- sad as a broken wing / a drooping flower / a lonely thing

Once each learner or pair has thought of their sentences, set up a chain reaction around the class and invite the sharing of the sentences.

CROSS-CURRICULAR LINKS

Maths: Create class bar charts to show which poems learners liked best in each of the literacy skills.

Homework ideas

Learners complete the Workbook Session 6.6 activities if not completed in class.

Answers for Workbook

1 **a** jump (not a sense)

   b touch feel (do not rhyme)

   c in (not a part of the body)

   d fruit (not a feeling)

2 **a** felt (does not end in –*ing*)

   b laugh (is not a laughing word with an exclamation mark)

   c tiger (is not a name with a capital letter)

   d March (is not a day of the week)

3 Answers similar to:

   fun (describes something nice)

   bad (the others are about feeling good)

   laughing (you have to drop the *e* before adding –*ing* on the others) or possibly dancing (not a facial action)

   Hee-haw (joined with a hyphen and does not have exclamation marks)

CHECK YOUR PROGRESS

1 See, hear, touch, smell, taste

2 May include: spy, tie, why, buy, eye

3 Learners' own rhyming sounds

4 Learners' own sentences

PROJECT GUIDANCE

These projects build on the reading, writing and understanding learners have developed throughout Unit 6. Since they have just read several poems about feelings, the project options here extend the topic and provide opportunities for learners to choose to work in a group, as a pair or alone. It may be that you prefer to allocate a project to the class.

Group project: Learners record all the rhymes in this unit to make an audio resource for the listening corner. They will need recording equipment and space to make their recordings.

Pair project: Learners make a simple board game about being sad or happy. They will need card for the game base or an empty board game template as well as a die to throw.

Solo project: Learners learn a poem by heart and say it to their family or class. Learners may need access to a selection of poetry books from which they may choose.

For more guidance on setting up and assessing projects, see Project guidance at the end of Unit 1.

> 7 You'll never believe it!

Unit plan

Session	Approximate number of learning hours	Outline of learning content	Resources
7.1 Let's pretend	1.5	Share what is known about pretend and real places. Listen to and read a fantasy story and answer questions about it. Create a map of a pretend land.	Learner's Book Session 7.1 Workbook Session 7.1
7.2 *The Grass House*	1.5	Talk about quiet places. Listen to a poem which includes a list. Write a list of experiences in a quiet place. Practise using common words. Compare photos and illustrations.	Learner's Book Session 7.2 Workbook Session 7.2 ⬇ Worksheet 7.1 ⬇ Language Worksheet 7A Phonics workbook B
7.3 *How to Catch a Star*	1	Share ideas about real and pretend things in the sky. Listen to a story about catching a star. Practise using *a, an* or *the*.	Learner's Book Session 7.3 Workbook Session 7.3
7.4 Checking understanding	1.5	Re-read a story. Complete comprehension activities to check understanding.	Learner's Book Session 7.4 Workbook Session 7.4 ⬇ Language worksheet 7B ⬇ Differentiated worksheets 7A–C Phonics Workbook B

Session	Approximate number of learning hours	Outline of learning content	Resources
7.5 Exploring new ideas	1.5	Use imagination to explore new ideas for a story. Writing ideas for a class display.	Learner's Book Session 7.5 Workbook Session 7.5 Phonics Workbook B
7.6 *We're Going on a Bear Hunt*	1	Talk about journeys. Listen, join in with and read a story about a difficult journey. Talk about the story ending. Respond to questions in character.	Learner's Book Session 7.6 Workbook Session 7.6 ⬇ Worksheet 7.2
7.7 Sequencing and retelling	2	Talk about verbs and settings used in a story. Create a story trail to sequence the story. Retell and act the story.	Learner's Book Session 7.7 Workbook Session 7.7 ⬇ Worksheet 7.3
7.8 *Bedtime for Monsters*	1	Talk about pretend characters. Listen to and read a funny scary story. Make predictions for the story ending.	Learner's Book Session 7.8 Workbook Session 7.8 Phonics Workbooks A and B
7.9 Comparing story settings	1.5	Read the end of the story to check predictions. Answer questions to show understanding. Create a chart to compare story settings. Explore word order in sentences.	Learner's Book Session 7.9 Workbook Session 7.9 ⬇ Worksheet 7.4
7.10 Retelling in different ways	2	Explore emotions and expressions. Sequence pictures to retell a story. Retell a story in a different way.	Learner's Book Session 7.10 Workbook Session 7.10

Session	Approximate number of learning hours	Outline of learning content	Resources
7.11 Planning and writing	1.5	Explore the features of a text. Write a pretend scary story using a storyboard format.	Learner's Book Session 7.11 Workbook Session 7.11 ⤓ Worksheet 7.5
7.12 Look back	1	Talk about punctuation marks. Check storyboard writing for correct punctuation. Talk about the stories in the unit and think about learning.	Learner's Book Session 7.12 Workbook Session 7.12

Cross-unit resources

Learner's Book Check your progress

Learner's Book Projects

BACKGROUND KNOWLEDGE

Before you begin to teach this unit, you may find it helpful to:

- familiarise yourself with the stories in this unit. Prepare ways to talk with your learners about:
  - fantasy settings and the idea of pretending
  - feelings and responses to stories
- familiarise yourself with the phonics and grammar elements in this unit, including:
  - phonics - letter to sound correspondence; words with adjacent consonants; blending

and segmenting words and understanding compound words

- punctuation: capital letters and end-of-sentence punctuation marks
- using rhyme to support spelling
- the different uses of capital letters
- prepare examples of sequencing, e.g. a sequence of pictures to tell a story or a sequence of words in a sentence.

TEACHING SKILLS FOCUS

Differentiation

Differentiation is a term to describe adapting your teaching for each learner. Strategies for differentiation vary.

Which of these types of differentiation have you *not* yet tried?

- By task: give learners different tasks according to ability, but be careful not to limit learning.

- By resource (differentiation by output): vary what you ask learners to produce.

- By grouping: group learners by similar or different ability.

- By pace: it is important to vary the pace because sometimes we need slower, in-depth learning to think about something and at other times we need to work more quickly.

- By support: support learners through dialogue and/or scaffolding as necessary. Questioning can help to challenge or guide them, too.

- By questioning: use the full range of question words to promote literal and inferential thinking.

Key features of good differentiation also include marking, feedback and assessment.

At the end of this unit, consider how well you were able to use some of these ideas to offer more effective differentiation in your lessons. Consider: What would you need to research further in your professional development to better implement some of these strategies?

7.1 Let's pretend

LEARNING PLAN

Learning objectives		Learning intentions	Success criteria
Main focus	**Also covered**	• To talk about places that are real or pretend.	• Learners can talk about places that are real or pretend.
1RV.02, 1Rv.03, 1Ra.06, 1Wv.01, 1Wp.04	1Rv.05, 1Ra.01, 1Ra.02, 1Ww.03, 1Ww.05, 1Wv.02, 1Wv.03, 1Ws.02, 1Wc.04, 1Wp.05, 1SLg.01	• To listen to and read a story set in a pretend place. • To record answers to questions in a list.	• Learners can listen to and read a story set in a pretend place. • Learners can record answers to questions in a list.

LANGUAGE SUPPORT

Learners will benefit from several retellings of the story, using fingers or finger puppets to reinforce numbers and sequence. They may also enjoy acting the story.

Reinforce letter sounds of the places the dragons visit, e.g. *Marvellous Mountains, Golden Castle.* Change the names of places that do not have alliteration so that they do, e.g. *Cold Castle.*

Common misconception

Misconception	How to identify	How to overcome
Lists are just for reminding us of things to do or what to buy at the shops.	Ask half the class to talk with partners about the places the dragons visit. Ask the other half of the class to talk about how the dragons fly in the story. As they provide answers, write them in a list.	Talk about how writing lists can help us to make notes or to remember things.

Starter idea

Places we know (10–15 minutes)

Resources: Learner's Book, Session 7.1: Getting started

Description: Ask learners to talk about pretend places or fantasy settings. Use the term most suited to your class.

Ask learners to explore and talk about the pictures in Getting started with you. They are all pretend settings. Ask: *What other pretend places do you know?*

Explain that this unit is all about pretend stories.

Main teaching ideas

1 *Dragon Land* (15–20 minutes)

Learning intention: to listen to a story and then read it together

Resources: *Dragon Land* (Learner's Book, Session 7.1, Activity 1); Track 45

Description: Tell learners they are going to first listen to a story about a place called Dragon Land. Ask them to listen for how many baby dragons there are. (Five) Read the story aloud or play the audio.

Discuss the story and whether the place is real or pretend. Ask: *How do you know?*

Play the audio (again) and ask learners to follow and/or read aloud with you, pointing to the words as you go.

Share ideas about the story.

> **Differentiation ideas:** Support learners by pairing them with stronger readers and/or working with a group to read the story again together, modelling how to track words with your finger as you hear them.

Challenge learners by asking them to read the text in pairs. Ask them to think about how they tackle the longer words, e.g. *marvellous*. Ask: *Can you explain what you do?*

2 Write and draw lists (15–20 minutes)

Learning intention: to recall detail from a story; to write responses in a list

Resources: Learner's Book, Session 7.1, Activity 2

Description: Ask learners where each of the five little dragons visited in Dragon Land.

On the board, write a full response for the first two dragons:

- *Dragon 1 swooped over the Golden Castle.*
- *Dragon 2 zoomed over the Enchanted Forest.*

Then show learners how you could make a list to answer the question:

- *Golden Castle*
- *Enchanted Forest,* etc.

Ask learners to finish writing the list in pairs.

Then ask them to list *how* the dragons flew.

> **Differentiation ideas:** Support learners by providing the locations on word cards for them to create a visual list.

Challenge learners to write lists in different ways, e.g. horizontal with commas, or vertically.

Answers:

a   the Golden Castle, the Enchanted Forest, the Land of the Giants, the Marvellous Mountains

b   swooped, zoomed, soared, glided, rode/climbed on board his mother

3   Draw a map (30–60 minutes)

Learning intention: to work in a group and create a map of a pretend land

Resources: Learner's Book, Session 7.1, Activity 3; map from Activity 1; large sheets of paper and coloured marker pens/paints

Description: Ask learners to look back to the map of Dragon Land in Activity 1.

Ask learners to work in small groups to plan and create a map of their own pretend land and give it a fun name.

Encourage learners to think about how to plan their pretend land before they draw and write on the large pieces of paper.

> **Differentiation ideas:** Support learners to share and draw their ideas on a piece of rough paper first.

Challenge learners to add detail and additional labels to their map, and to experiment with different lettering.

Answers:
Learners' own maps

Plenary idea

Play What Can You Do, Little Dragons? (5 minutes)

Description: Tell learners they are going to leave the classroom in small groups, pretending to be little dragons. Give learners two minutes to decide *how* they will show this.

Ask each group in turn: *What can you do, Little Dragons?*

Each group chants: *Look what we can do. We can …* (*soar, fly, flap, breathe fire,* etc.)

The group may then leave the classroom in the manner they have described.

> CROSS-CURRICULAR LINKS

Geography: Look at a country or word map and find places with the word *land* in them, e.g. *Greenland, Iceland, Finland, England.*

Homework ideas

Learners complete the Workbook Session 7.1 activities if not completed in class.

They find another story book about dragons.

Answers for Workbook

1   Following words underlined with learners' drawings: **a** sky/by; **b** rocket/pocket; **c** moon/spoon; **d** loop/swoop

2   **a** hoop; **b** boom; **c** roar; **d** ride; **e** drive

3   Learners' own responses

7.2 *The Grass House*

LEARNING PLAN

Learning objectives		Learning intentions	Success criteria
Main focus	**Also covered**		
1Rv.05, 1Ri.11, 1Ri.12, 1Ww.06, 1SLp.04	1Rw.02, 1Rw.05, 1Rw.06, 1Rv.03, 1Rs.02, 1Rs.04, 1Ri.01, 1Ri.13, 1Ri.14, 1Ra.01, 1Ww.03, 1Ww.05, 1Ww.07, 1Wv.01, 1Wv.03, 1SLp.02	• To listen to a poem about a quiet place. • To write responses in a list. • To spell common words.	• Learners can listen to a poem about a quiet place. • Learners can write responses in a list. • Learners can spell common words.

LANGUAGE SUPPORT

Learners will benefit from some pre-teaching of vocabulary for the poem. Show them either real seeds, weeds, stalks and pods, or pictures.

Role play sitting in a grass house and using the senses to support the experience. This will also help learners to use simple language structures, e.g. *I can see …, I feel …* (Worksheet 7.1).

Provide a small range of fiction and non-fiction books on similar content. Ask learners to match up the corresponding fiction and non-fiction titles to support their understanding of pictures and photographs.

Common misconception

Misconception	How to identify	How to overcome
Illustrations are of things that are not real and photos are of things that are real.	Show learners an illustration of something real, e.g. an apple, and a photo of something pretend, e.g. a boy flying. Ask: *Which is real and which is pretend?*	Find different examples of illustrations and photos to explore their use. Use Learner's Book Session 7.2 Activity 3.

Starter idea

Quiet places (10–15 minutes)

Resources: Learner's Book, Session 7.2: Getting started

Description: Ask learners to give some examples of quiet and noisy places they know.

It is important here to stress *quietness*, rather than *secrecy*, which we would not wish to encourage. Stress that if they have a private place like this, they should always tell parents or friends (someone they trust) where they are going. Treat this subject with delicacy.

Look at the pictures in Getting started and, together, decide if each place is quiet or noisy (quiet places: girl in tree, girl in bed, boy under bed).

Talk about learners' favourite quiet places. Take all their ideas and develop the discussion about what they like to do there. Again, use the pictures to prompt this, e.g. reading in bed, under the covers; thinking in a tree house.

Main teaching ideas

1   Listen to a poem (20–30 minutes)

Learning intention: to listen to a poem about a quiet place and identify a list in it

Resources: *The Grass House* (Learner's Book, Session 7.2, Activity 1); Track 46; Phonics Workbook B; Language worksheet 7A

Description: Introduce the learners to the poem *The Grass House*. Tell them it is about a boy who likes to sit in deep grass. Explain that it is written by Shirley Hughes; she is the poet.

Phonics (Phonics Workbook B, pages 22–23): there is an opportunity here to focus on the title of the poem and the phonics within it. Notice the /ow/ phoneme is spelled as *ou*.

Read the poem or play the audio. Ask learners to listen out for the things the boy lists that he can see. (seeds, weeds, stalks, pods, tiny little flowers)

Check learners' understanding of *feathery plumes*. Get them to say the words and wave their arms like feathery plumes as they do so.

Re-read the poem in a quiet whispery voice and encourage the learners to join in.

You can use Language worksheet 7A here for further practice of singular and plural nouns.

⟩ **Differentiation ideas:** Support learners by sharing the picture in the Learner's Book and asking them

to point to the pictures of the things in the list. You may also like to provide picture cards for learners to sort as they hear each thing in the list.

Challenge learners to write a list of what the boys sees.

Audioscript: *The Grass House*

The grass house

Is my private place.

Nobody can see me

In the grass house.

Feathery plumes

Meet over my head.

Down here,

In the green, there are:

Seeds

Weeds

Stalks

Pods

And tiny little flowers.

Only the cat

And some busy, hurrying ants

Know where my grass house is.

Shirley Hughes

---

2   Pretend to sit in the grass house (10–15 minutes)

Learning intention: to sequence and retell a story by pictures

Resources: Learner's Book, Session 7.2, Activity 2

Description: Ask learners to close their eyes and have some quiet time for just a minute.

Ask them to imagine they are sitting in the grass house or their own quiet place.

Then ask them to open their eyes and share their thoughts. Ask: *Did you enjoy being quiet? How did you feel? What did you think about?*

Ask what they could see, hear, taste, touch and smell, and ask them to record these things as a list.

> **Differentiation ideas:** Support learners by asking them to draw their list.

Challenge learners to draw and write their list.

3 Pictures and photos (20–30 minutes)

Learning intention: to talk about the use of illustrations and photographs in fiction and non-fiction

Resources: Learner's Book, Session 7.2, Activity 4; examples of story books that use photos, and non-fiction books that use illustrations

Description: Ask learners what an illustration is and what a photograph is. Ask: *Can you show me one of each from the class library?*

Use the Common misconception 'real and pretend' activity.

Talk about when we use illustrations and photos, before showing learners the examples in Activity 4. Explain that we most often see illustrations in story books (fiction) and photos in non-fiction, but not always.

If you have some exceptions, then share them with learners now to stimulate further discussion.

Ask learners to work in pairs to match the illustrations and the photos in Activity 4.

> **Differentiation ideas:** Support learners with concrete examples of books that use different illustration styles and include illustrations and photos.

Challenge learners to find further examples of illustration and photo use in books, magazines or online.

Answers:
Learners' responses, correctly matched

4 Spell common words – gap fill (20–30 minutes)

Learning intention: to listen to a story and write the missing common words

Resources: Learner's Book, Session 7.2, Activity 3; Track 46; Workbook, Session 7.2

Description: Ask learners to look at the sentences in Activity 3 with the missing words.

Ask learners to listen to the story in Activity 1 again; this time they should listen for the missing words.

Pause the audio where necessary, if using, to allow learners to write the missing words for each of the four sentences.

Use the Workbook activitis now for further practice of spelling common words.

Answers:
a house; **b** me, the; **c** my; **d** some

Plenary idea

Pass the Book (5–10 minutes)

Resources: a pile of books; music

Description: Ask learners to sit in a circle. Put a pile of books in the middle.

Play some music while learners pass round one of the books.

When the music stops, the learner holding the book must look at it and describe it as fiction or non-fiction with photos or illustrations.

Ask everyone to agree if they are correct.

That learner then chooses another book and the music and passing continues.

CROSS-CURRICULAR LINKS

Science: Explore different grasses in your local area. Encourage learners to draw and label their different parts.

Homework ideas

Learners complete the Workbook Session 7.2 activities if not completed in class.

They collect examples of photo books and illustrated books.

Answers for Workbook

1 see, me, meet, green, seeds, weeds
2 Learners' own drawings and labels
3 Learners' own poems

7.3 *How to Catch a Star*

LEARNING PLAN

Learning objectives		Learning intentions	Success criteria
Main focus	**Also covered**	• To listen to and join in with a story about trying to do something impossible.	• Learners can listen to and join in with a story about trying to do something impossible.
1Rg.01, 1Rg.07, 1Ra.06, 1Wg.06	1Rw.06, 1Rv.02, 1Ri.07, 1Ra.01	• To read a story and pause at full stops.	• Learners can read a story and pause at full stops.
		• To write *a*, *an* or *the* correctly in sentences.	• Learners can write *a*, *an* or *the* correctly in sentences.

LANGUAGE SUPPORT

Some pre-teaching of vocabulary may be useful: *plane, sky, castle, rainbow, star, moon.*

If available, a printed copy of *How to Catch a Star* by Oliver Jeffers will enable learners to revisit the complete story before, during and after this session.

Common misconception

Misconception	How to identify	How to overcome
Full stops do not tell us what to do.	Ask learners to read a small extract: *The boy thought he would never catch a star.* *Just then he noticed something floating in the water.* *It was the prettiest star he had ever seen. Just a baby star.* Ask them how many full stops they can see (four). Ask them what full stops are for. (They might tell you that they show the end of sentence / they tell you to pause/breathe.)	Draw learners' attention to the other full stops in the full text. Remind learners what full stops tell us in their one-to-one reading aloud sessions.

Starter idea

What's in the sky? (10–15 minutes)

Resources: Learner's Book, Session 7.3: Getting started

Description: Ask learners to talk about what they might see in the sky, either in the day or at night. They may base their answer on reality or what they have seen in books.

Ask learners to then look at and talk about the pictures in Getting started. Give them time to share their ideas before asking them to write their responses in their notebook using the language structure provided: *I can see … in the sky.*

Main teaching ideas

1 *How to Catch a Star* (20–30 minutes)

Learning intention: to listen to and follow a story using pictures

Resources: *How to Catch a Star* (Learner's Book, Session 7.3, Activity 1); Track 47

Description: Tell learners that this story is about a boy who wants to do something that seems impossible. He wants to catch a star to have for himself – a bit like a pet!

Ask learners why they think the boy wants a star, e.g. *Is he lonely? Is he spoilt? Does he just love the way a star twinkles?* Encourage creative responses here.

Give learners some independent time to look through the pictures before asking them to listen to the story as you read the text or play the audio.

Talk about their first impressions after the first listening.

- Do they notice that the boy is never given a proper name?

- Did anyone notice the use of ellipsis (…)? What do learners' think the three dots mean? (Something is missing but the text continues.)

- Did they notice the expression: *to fish [something] out?* Tell them this has nothing to do with the creature 'fish', but means to get something out of something else.

Ask them to listen again, but this time to point to the words and join in where they can. Model how we pause at a full stop.

Finally, ask learners to read the text in pairs, supporting each other. As you circulate round the class, listen in to check who is using phonic strategies to read some words where necessary.

⟩ **Differentiation ideas:** Support learners listening by asking them to stand up or clap each time they hear the word *star*. This would work well as a small-group follow-up activity, but could be fun for the whole class, too!

Challenge some learners to share their blending of letters to read some words, as a model for others. Provide words for them to model if necessary, e.g. *s-t-ar; b-ea-ch; a-pp-ear.*

2 Use *a, an* or *the* (10–15 minutes)

Learning intention: to use *a*, *an* and *the* correctly in sentences

Resources: Learner's Book, Session 7.3, Activity 2; Workbook, Session 7.3

Description: Draw learners' attention to the Language focus box. Write some examples on the board and encourage learners to fill the gap:

> *a star*   *an amazing star*   *the boy*
> (from the story)

Ask learners to copy and complete the sentences from Activity 2.

You can use the Workbook Session 7.3 activities here for further practice of articles.

⟩ **Differentiation ideas:** Support groups of learners by reading the sentences aloud and then working with them to say their responses orally.

Challenge learners by asking them to write their own sentences for a similar activity in their notebooks.

Answers:
a a, the; **b** The, an

Plenary idea

Problem solving (5–10 minutes)

Description: Ask learners to reflect on how the boy in the story solves a problem and encourage them to talk about how they solve problems.

Challenge learners with some impossible tasks, e.g. sliding down a rainbow or speaking Star language. Ask: *How would you solve those problems?*

CROSS-CURRICULAR LINKS

Science: Talk about what we see in the sky in the day/at night. Make the connection between the sun and other stars.

Art: Create a class display of things in the sky in the day/at night.

Homework ideas

Learners complete the Workbook Session 7.3 activities if not completed in class.

They look at the night sky, draw a picture or take a photo and say how it makes them feel.

Answers for Workbook

1 Learners circle all the full stops.

2 Learners circle all instances of a, an and the.

3 Learners' own sentences, but similar to: **a** The boy is looking at a star. **b** The star is on the beach. **c** The boy tries to reach the star. **d** The boy is in a rocket. **e** The boy is holding hands with the star.

7.4 Checking understanding

LEARNING PLAN

Learning objectives		Learning intentions	Success criteria
Main focus	**Also covered**	• To explore words and sentences in a story to show understanding.	• Learners can explore words and sentences in a story to show understanding.
1Rv.03, 1Ri.13, 1Ra.04, 1Ws.01, 1Sls.02	1RS.01, 1Ri.01, 1Ri.07, 1Ri.09, 1Ri.11, 1Ri.12, 1Ra.01, 1Ra.03, 1Ra.06, 1Wg.01, 1Wc.02, 1Wp.04	• To answer and ask questions about the story in different ways.	• Learners can answer and ask questions about the story in different ways.
		• To sequence sentences in a story using adverbs like *once, at first, then* and *so*.	• Learners can sequence sentences in a story using adverbs like *once, at first, then* and *so*.

LANGUAGE SUPPORT

Provide games to support the use of compound words, e.g. compound word jigsaws or dominoes.

Create a class display or table mats of question words so learners have them to hand as support for Activity 2.

Common misconception

Misconception	How to identify	How to overcome
We only answer questions with *yes* or *no*.	Ask learners a series of closed questions: *Do/Did you …?; Can/could you …?; Are/Were you …?* What do they notice about their responses, (They are all *yes* or *no*.) Then ask them a few open questions, using question words: *why, how, what,* etc. Now what do they notice about their responses? (They do not feature *yes* or *no*.)	Help learners to be aware of their questions and their responses in talk sessions. Remind them as opportunities arise. You may wish to use the terms *open* and *closed questions* if appropriate for your class.

Starter idea

Star game (10–20 minutes)

Resources: Learner's Book, Session 7.4: Getting started; Phonics Workbook B; Language worksheet 7B; star shape with the word *star* written on it; small whiteboards or blank word cards

Description: Ask one learner to stand with a star-shaped word card, labelled with the word *star*.

Phonics (Phonics Workbook B, pages 20–21 and 50–51): revise the /ar/ sound with learners.

Invite learners to think of words that join the word *star* to make a new word.

Give them two minutes to work with a partner and then share ideas. (*superstar, starfish, stardust, stargaze, megastar, starship, starlight,* etc.)

Write the additional words (*super, fish, mega,* etc.) on small whiteboards or blank word cards and hand these out. Invite learners, one by one, to stand next to the learner holding the *star* word card to physically build the compound words.

Look at the pictures in Getting started. Ask: *Did you make a starfish, starlight, a superstar?*

Use Language worksheet 7B now for further practice of compound words.

Main teaching ideas

1 Answer *yes* or *no* (15–20 minutes)

Learning intention: to answer closed questions about a story

Resources: Learner's Book, Session 7.4, Activity 1

Description: Tell learners that one way to check our understanding is to ask and answer questions.

Ask a few questions that require a *yes* or *no* answer, e.g. *Is the story about a girl? Is the story about catching a star?*

Together, read the questions and ask learners to listen again (if necessary) with these questions in mind.

They should write *Y* or *Yes* or *N* or *No* for each question.

At the end of the listening, share ideas and explanations.

> **Differentiation ideas:** Support learners by working with them in a smaller group to answer the questions.

Challenge some learners to write their response more fully (see bracketed responses earlier).

Answers:

a   Yes (he liked stars very much); No (just before the sun was about to go away/sunset); No (he wanted to catch a star)

b   Learners' own questions

2 Match questions to answers (15–30 minutes)

Learning intention: to match questions to answers

Resources: Learner's Book, Session 7.4, Activity 2

Description: Show learners how this works using some examples on the board.

Read each question with learners and discuss the answers as a class.

If you want learners to respond orally, check they are responding with clear spoken language and correct sentence structures and tenses.

> **Differentiation ideas:** Support learners by providing them with the questions and answers on strips and asking them to find the matching pairs. Then, read the pairs to check they are correct. Support learners to create a question in groups or pairs and answer it (as a group or pairs), as an example.

Challenge learners to write the questions and answers in their notebooks and then to work independently to write their own example.

Answers:

a   He wanted a star of his very own.

b   He thought the star would be tired.

c   He climbed to the top of a tree.

d   He tried to fish it out with his hands.

3 Write sentences in order, using adverbs (15–30 minutes)

Learning intention: to sequence sentences and then write them using adverbs

Resources: Learner's Book, Session 7.4, Activity 3; Differentiated worksheets 7A–C; sentences from Activity 3 written on separate sentence cards

Description: Read the sentences that follow, asking learners to listen out for and clap in response to hearing the words *once, at first, then, so, finally* and *later*.

- *Once the boy wanted a star of his own.*
- *So, he tried to catch a star.*
- *At first, he saw a star in the sky.*
- *Then he saw a star in the sea.*
- *Later, he found a star on the beach.*
- *Finally, the boy had a star of his very own.*

In pairs, ask learners to look at the sentences in the Learner's Book and sequence them.

Then ask them to use the adverbs to strengthen the sequence. (They have rehearsed this orally, but now they will need to work it out independently.)

Use Differentiated worksheets 7A–C to support learners at different levels of challenge for further practice of exploring sentences and sequencing.

> **Differentiation ideas:** Support learners in a group by giving them sentence strips to sequence and adverb word cards to insert in the correct position.

Challenge learners to write the sentences in the correct order with adverbs.

Answers:
d; b; c; a; e; and f as bullets above

Plenary idea

Yes or No panel game (10–15 minutes)

Resources: three word cards with *YES!* on one side and *NO!* on the other side

Description: Choose a panel of three learners to sit at the front of the class on chairs.

Give the three learners a *YES!/NO!* word card each.

The other learners ask questions and each time a question is asked, the panel must show the correct side of their card.

If they get an answer wrong, they swap with another learner who wants to try sitting on the panel.

CROSS-CURRICULAR LINKS

Maths: Explore star shapes with different numbers of points. Count the number of sides for each.

Art: Explore star-shaped patterns.

Homework ideas

Learners complete the Workbook Session 7.4 activities if not completed in class.

They draw or write a list of star-shaped things at home or on the way home from school.

Answers for Workbook

1   **a** no; **b** no; **c** yes; **d** no; **e** yes/no

2   **a** You can look for stars in the sky. **b** The boy was looking for a star. **c** He was looking for a star because he wanted one of his very own. **d** He looked for a star every night. **e** He found a star on the beach.

3   Answers may include:
   a Why are you looking at the moon?
   b Where is the moon?
   c When can you see the moon shining?
   d Who did you go out with to look for the moon?

7.5 Exploring new ideas

<table>
<tr><td colspan="5">LEARNING PLAN</td></tr>
<tr><td colspan="2">**Learning objectives**</td><td>**Learning intentions**</td><td>**Success criteria**</td></tr>
<tr><td>**Main focus**</td><td>**Also covered**</td><td rowspan="2">
<ul>
<li>To sing a song and say the rhyming words.</li>
<li>To use their imaginations to explore new ideas about a story.</li>
<li>To use capital letter *I*, to denote self, correctly.</li>
</ul>
</td><td rowspan="2">
<ul>
<li>Learners can sing a song and say the rhyming words.</li>
<li>Learners can use their imaginations to explore new ideas about a story.</li>
<li>Learners can use capital letter *I*, to denote self, correctly.</li>
</ul>
</td></tr>
<tr><td>**1Ri.02, 1Wv.02, 1Wv.03, 1Wg.03, 1Wp.05**</td><td>1Rw.02, 1Rw.05, 1Rw.06, 1Rv.03, 1Rs.01, 1Ww.06, 1Ww.07, 1Wv.01, 1Wg.04, 1SLm.03, 1SLs.01, 1SLg.04, 1SLp.01</td></tr>
</table>

LANGUAGE SUPPORT

Singing *Twinkle, twinkle, little star* will allow learners to familiarise themselves with the language structure of the song, before they undertake the Workbook writing activity (*like a … in the sky*) in Workbook Session 7.5.

Learners will need support to express their imaginative ideas, so encourage them to draw first and then scribe for them as appropriate.

Common misconception

Misconception	How to identify	How to overcome
We only use capital letter *I* at the beginning of a sentence.	Show learners a sentence: *Twinkle, twinkle little star,* *How I/i wonder what you are.* Ask: *Which I/i is correct? Why?* (We always use a capital letter for *I* when we talk about ourselves even in the middle of a sentence.)	When learners are writing their own sentences and stories, remind them that *I* should always be a capital letter.

Starter idea

Sing a song (5–10 minutes)

Resources: *Twinkle, Twinkle, Little Star* (Learner's Book, Session 7.5: Getting started); Track 48; Workbook, Session 7.5; Phonics Workbook B; story maps (posters or online), if available

Description: Ask learners if they know any songs about stars.

Use the words in Getting Started to sing the song, *Twinkle, twinkle, little star*.

Can learners tell you what the rhyming words are? (*star/are*; *high/sky*) Use this opportunity to remind learners about the different spellings of phonemes and link to Phonics Workbook B, pages 10–19, if helpful.

You can use the Workbook Session 7.5 activities here for further practice of rhyming words and also the use of repeated language structures.

Main teaching ideas

1   Pretend to own a star (20–30 minutes)

Learning intention: to express creative, pretend ideas about owning a star

Resources: Learner's Book, Session 7.5, Activity 1; a version of the song *Catch a Falling Star*, if available

Description: If possible, sing the song and use it as a stimulus for this activity.

What do learners think the boy did with his star?

Encourage learners to share ideas for what they would do with a star of their very own.

*   Make a list of up to about ten ideas
*   Take a class vote on which is the best idea.

Look at the picture in Activity 1 and talk about it, modelling the language learners could use to explain what they would do, e.g. *I would take my star for a walk;*
I would travel with my star to reach other stars;
I would put my star in a photo frame on the wall;
I would hang up my star on a piece of string.

Encourage learners to draw and write their own best idea. Remind learners that when we write *I* to talk about ourselves, it must be a capital letter wherever it appears in a sentence. (See Common misconception.)

⟩ **Differentiation ideas:** Support learners by encouraging them to draw their ideas and use the language structure: *I would* …. Scribe for learners to copy where necessary.

Challenge learners by asking them to write their own sentences about their star using *and*.

Answers:
Learners' own written ideas

2   Pretend to catch something (30–40 minutes)

Learning intention: to apply language patterns of a text to new ideas in pictures and writing

Resources: Learner's Book, Session 7.5, Activity 2

Description: Ask learners, in pairs, to think about other pretend/impossible things they might like to try to catch.

Give them time and then gather and share ideas.

Orally rehearse the language structure: *I would like to catch a … because* ….

Challenge learners to say *how* they would catch the thing. Rehearse the language pattern:

This is how I would do it:

- *First, I would …*
- *Then I would …, etc.*

Together, look at Activity 2 and note whether anyone mentions these ideas: *cloud, rainbow, moon*. You may use the picture in Activity 3 as prompts.

Encourage learners to write their ideas and then share them.

⟩ **Differentiation ideas:** Support learners by asking them to write what they would choose and one sentence about how they would catch it.

Challenge learners to write more extensively about their choice and to use adverbs to describe what they would do, and in what order, to catch it.

Answers:
Learners' own ideas based on the given structure

3   **Draw and write on shapes**
    (15–20 minutes)

Learning intention: to write creative ideas for a classroom display

Resources: Learner's Book, Session 7.5, Activity 3; paper and scissors; string (and anything else needed to hang the shapes)

Description: Ask learners to draw a shape of their chosen thing on a piece of paper and then cut it out.

Ask learners to write their ideas about what they would do with the thing they have caught, on the paper shape.

Remind learners to think about the space they have to fill with their writing and to use the pronoun *I*.

Involve learners in the problem-solving process of where and how to hang the shapes for a class display, e.g. a washing line, coat hangers, from a beam ….

⟩ **Differentiation ideas:** Support learners by adding writing lines to their shape template so they know how to space their work.

Challenge learners to create and share a layout plan for their shape with a partner before they begin their writing.

Answers:
Learners' own responses

Plenary idea

Sing the songs of the session (5–10 minutes)

Resources: a version of the songs *Catch a Falling Star* and *Twinkle, Twinkle, Little Star,* plus any other songs about stars that learners know

Description: Sing the songs about stars as a class.

Encourage actions where appropriate or known.

CROSS-CURRICULAR LINKS

Music: Search for online music about the planets or stars, e.g. *Waltz of the Rising Star*. Encourage learners to draw pictures as they listen and are inspired. You may also invite them to respond in movement.

Homework ideas

Learners complete the Workbook Session 7.5 activities if not completed in class.

They research online, with family members, other examples of music about the night sky.

Answers for Workbook

1   Learners' own responses

2   Learners' own responses using a capital letter for *I*

3   Learners' own drawings and descriptions: The star: shiny, pointed, bright; The rainbow: bright, coloured, curved; learners' other ideas.

7.6 *We're Going on a Bear Hunt*

LEARNING PLAN

Learning objectives		Learning intentions	Success criteria
Main focus	**Also covered**	• To listen for repeated parts of a story.	• Learners can listen for repeated parts of a story.
1Rv.05, 1Rg.03, 1Ri.07, 1Ri.11, 1Ri.14, 1SLp.04	1Rv.01, 1Rv.02; 1Rs.02, 1Ri.02, 1Ri.09, 1Ri.12, 1Ri.13, 1Ra.02, 1Wv.01, 1Wv.02, 1Wv.03, 1Wg.04, 1Ws.02, 1Wp.05, 1SLm.03, 1SLs.02, 1SLr.02	• To read a story about a difficult journey. • To talk about a story ending in character.	• Learners can read a story about a difficult journey. • Learners can talk about a story ending in character.

LANGUAGE SUPPORT

Learners will benefit from looking at the print book of *We're Going on a Bear Hunt* to support understanding, if at all possible. Many online versions are available, too, including a reading by the author Michael Rosen. (Note: the version in Learner's Book Session 7.6 is an extract.)

Check learners understand the vocabulary of *grass*, *river*, *forest* and *cave*.

Common misconception

Misconception	How to identify	How to overcome
We can only use one adjective to describe something.	Look at the photos in Learner's Book Session 7.6 Getting started. Ask learners to describe each photo. If they respond with just one adjective, e.g. *tall grass*, ask: *How else can we describe the grass?* e.g. *Feathery, long, tall grass ...*	Remind learners that in their speech and writing they can use two or three adjectives to describe something to make it more accurate and interesting, e.g. *a big, dark forest* or *a big, deep, dark forest*. (See Plenary activity.) If appropriate for your learners draw their attention to the use of the comma.

Starter idea

Match descriptions to photos
(10–20 minutes)

Resources: Learner's Book, Session 7.6: Getting started

Description: Talk about journeys and things that can stop your progress. Encourage learners to share their experiences, e.g. flat tyres, delayed flights ....

Ask them about stories they know about journeys: remind them of Penda's journey in Unit 4, for example.

(She didn't let anything get in her way of taking the milk to her daddy.)

Draw learners' attention to the photos in Getting started and then ask learners to read and match the descriptions to the photos.

Talk about what they might do if faced with these obstacles.

Tell learners that this session is about a long, difficult family journey to find … a bear! Some learners may know the story already as it is very popular.

Main teaching ideas

1 *We're Going on a Bear Hunt*
   (20–30 minutes)

Learning intention: to listen for repeated parts of a story

Resources: *We're Going on a Bear Hunt* (Learner's Book, Session 7.6, Activities 1 and 2); Track 49

Description: Tell learners that this story is about a family who go on a pretend journey to find a bear.

Ask if any learners already know the story, *We're Going on a Bear Hunt*.

Ask learners to first listen to the story and to notice when words are repeated. Talk about the story afterwards and the stages along the way: the grass, river, forest and cave.

Ask for learners' ideas about actions they could perform for each part of the journey.

Listen again and invite learners to join in with words and actions.

Finally, open the Learner's Book and look at Activity 1, and ask learners to read the text in pairs. You may wish to draw their attention to *Uh-uh!* and how to say it, as well as the words in capital letters.

> **Differentiation ideas:** Support learners with several re-readings and actions.

Challenge learners to read the story aloud in parts after the paired readings.

2 The story ending (30 minutes)

Learning intention: to respond to questions in character

Resources: Learner's Book, Session 7.6, Activity 3; Worksheet 7.2 Mask template; scissors, string

Description: You can provide Worksheet 7.2 Mask template now, which enables learners to make a bear mask.

You may want learners to make their own individual mask or to work together to create one mask per group.

Ask groups to take it in turns to choose someone to be the bear and wear the mask.

Other members of the group ask the bear the questions from Activity 3. The bear must answer in character.

Repeat the activity, so several learners have the chance to be the bear.

> **Differentiation ideas:** Support learners by asking simple closed questions, e.g. *Are you sad?*, rather than open questions such as *How did you feel?*

Challenge learners to give further explanation in their answers.

Answers:
Learners' responses. Answers may include:

a   I was excited to see some people; I chased them because I wanted to be friends;

b   No, I don't see many people so I get excited when I do!

Plenary idea

Adjectives (5–10 minutes; longer if using Workbook 7.6)

Resources: lists of nouns relevant to the story; Workbook, Session 7.6

Description: You may wish to use the Workbook activities for this session first, to explore descriptions before you begin this activity.

Say a noun such as *grass*, *river*, *forest*, *cave* or *nose*

Ask learners to work in pairs to add at least two adjectives to the noun, e.g. *long*, *wavy grass*; *shiny*, *wet nose*. (See Common misconception.)

Once each pair of learners has responded, they may leave. Continue until everyone has left the room.

CROSS-CURRICULAR LINKS

Science: Explore how animals need air, water and suitable food to survive. Find out where bears like to live and what they like to eat.

Homework ideas

Learners complete the Workbook Session 7.6 activities if not completed in class.

They find an official version of *We're Going on a Bear Hunt* online and share with a family member.

Answers for Workbook

1 Learners' correctly labelled bear face

2 Learners' own sentences, but similar to:

   a This is a panda bear and it is black and white.

   b This is a polar bear and it has white fur.

3 Possible responses: a I think this bear feels shy.
   b This bear feels happy. c This bear feels angry.
   d This bear feels sad. I can tell from the bear's face/actions.

7.7 Sequencing and retelling

LEARNING PLAN

Learning objectives		Learning intentions	Success criteria
Main focus	**Also covered**	• To identify verbs and match them to actions and sounds.	• Learners can identify verbs and match them to actions and sounds.
1Rg.06, 1Rs.01, 1Ri.06, 1Wv.03, 1Wc.03, 1Wp.05, 1SLm.04	1Rv.03, 1Rg.03, 1Rg.05, 1RS.02, 1Ri.07, 1Ri.14, 1Ra.03, 1Ra.04, 1Ww.07, 1Wv.01, 1Wg.01, 1Ws.01, 1Wc.01, 1Wc.02, 1Wc.04, 1SLs.01, 1SLg.01, 1SLp.04, 1SLr.02	• To add a setting to a story. • To sequence a story and explore retellings.	• Learners can add a setting to a story. • Learners can sequence a story and explore retellings.

LANGUAGE SUPPORT

Learners may need support with the richer onomatopoeic vocabulary in this session, e.g. stumble-trip, but the active learning suggestions should support them well.

Create some class displays of synonyms that learners may refer to when writing, e.g. falling: *fall over, stumble, trip, crash*; to walk carefully: *tiptoe, creep*; etc.

Common misconception

Misconception	How to identify	How to overcome
Letter q has the sound /kyoo/	Ask learners to tell you the letter name for Qq (letter Q). Ask them for its letter sound. Explain that it has no sound on its own – it must have the letter u with it: qu makes the sound /kwu/ as in queen or quiz. Ask learners to read some words that feature qu, e.g. squeeze, squelch, squish.	Remind learners when they are reading aloud or spelling that if there is a q there will also be a u and we say /kwu/. Also mention that many words begin with squ ....

Starter idea

Verbs (10–15 minutes)

Resources: Learner's Book, Session 7.7: Getting started; *We're Going on a Bear Hunt* (Learner's Book, Session 7.6); Track 49; Workbook, Session 7.7

Description: Remind learners of the story of *We're Going on a Bear Hunt*, if necessary. You may ask them to recall it, read it aloud or listen to the audio again.

Ask volunteers to show an action for a stumble, a trip, a swish and a splash. Learners may have used these actions in Learner's Book Session 7.6 Activity 3, but repeat the ideas and enrich the learning.

Share ideas about where we might stumble, trip, swish or splash.

Tell learners they will be exploring the language in *We're Going on a Bear Hunt*.

You can use the Workbook Session 7.7 activities here for further practice of nouns and verbs.

Main teaching ideas

1 Add a setting to the story (20–30 minutes)

Learning intention: to choose a new setting and write a sentence about it using descriptive language

Resources: Learner's Book, Session 7.7, Activity 1; pictures of other settings, if possible

Description: Tell learners they can choose a new setting for the bear hunt.

What else could get in their way along the journey? What sounds and actions would they make to get through it?

Together, look at the pictures in Activity 1 for stimulus and modelling of sentences. For example:

> Uh oh! A swamp. A sticky, muddy swamp. Sink-squelch, sink-squelch!

Ask learners to work in pairs to choose a new setting and to write a sentence for it in their notebooks.

Select a few pairs to share their settings and sentences.

> **Differentiation ideas:** Support learners by providing the structure of the story text and asking them to replace the underlined words. They might work in a group to do this.

> Uh-uh! *A forest!*
> *A big dark forest.*
> *Stumble trip!*

Challenge learners to add two new settings and to check their spellings of the sound words in particular (see Common misconception for words with *qu*).

Answers:
b Learners' own sentences

2 Make a story trail (30–60 minutes)

Learning intention: to sequence a story as a storyboard using words and pictures

Resources: Learner's Book, Session 7.7, Activity 2; Worksheet 7.3 Story trail or large sheets of paper

Description: Tell learners that now they are going to create a story trail of the journey to the bear and back again, to include their extra setting(s).

Ask learners to work in small groups. Provide large sheets of paper or Worksheet 7.3 Story trail as a guide to the layout.

Ask each group to draw and then write a sentence for each step of the journey.

If working without the worksheet, direct learners to the Activity 2 prompts (images set out in boxes), which learners may use as guidance.

As you circulate, encourage learners to use their phonics skills to spell words they are unsure about.

> **Differentiation ideas:** Support learners by using guidance in Worksheet 7.3 Story trail or by arranging mixed groups where learners can support each other.

Challenge learners to plan their own story-trail layout on a large piece of paper.

Answers:
Learners' own responses

3 Retell the story (30–40 minutes)

Learning intention: to retell a story in different ways in a group

Resources: Learner's Book, Session 7.7, Activity 3

Description: Talk about the different ways that learners can retell the story, referring to Activity 3.

Allocate a retelling focus to each group or ask learners to choose one.

You may wish to model these different ways with one group or the whole class first.

Give groups time to practise their retellings using their story trails from Activity 2 for support. Circulate to support learners in organising their group (who does what) and also in their retelling focus.

Allow time for each group (or at least four groups, each with a different focus) to perform.

Ask learners to talk about how they used their story trail: Which was the best retelling and why.

> **Differentiation ideas:** Support learners by considering groupings carefully.

Challenge learners to think about the best way to ensure all learners are fully involved in the group.

4 Act the story (30–60 minutes)

Learning intention: to act out a story as a class

Resources: Learner's Book, Session 7.7, Activity 4; list of what worked best in the paired retellings; large space for performances and large play equipment, if available

Description: You may wish to carry out this activity in a large space, if available, so that you can plot the journey with large play equipment.

Remind learners of what worked well in the retellings.

Tell them they are going to act the story as a whole class.

Agree on which new and additional settings to add on the way to find the bear.

You will need:

- actors to play the hunters and the bear
- actors to make the sound words for each setting
- narrators for each step of the journey
- musical instrument players, if appropriate.

Rehearse the play and, if possible, perform to another class.

> **Differentiation ideas:** Support learners by choosing roles carefully and sensitively.

Challenge learners to ensure all the retelling features are included in the performance and, especially, to play with speed and volume.

Plenary idea

List other stories about bears (5–10 minutes)

Resources: story books about bears in the class library, if possible

Description: Ask learners to talk with a partner about other stories that feature bears.

You could ask some learners to search the class library for such books.

Together, create a list.

Geography: Find out where there are swamps in the world and what animals live in or near them.

Homework ideas

Learners complete the Workbook Session 7.7 activities if not completed in class.

They tell their story to a family member, using their story trail.

Answers for Workbook

1   a swish; b splash; c stumble; d tiptoe

2   Learners' own sentences

3   Learners' own verbs, but similar to: a jump; b dance; c struggle; d trip-trap

4   Learners' own drawings

7.8 Bedtime for Monsters

LEARNING PLAN

Learning objectives		Learning intentions	Success criteria
Main focus	**Also covered**		
1Ri.10, 1Ra.04, 1SLm.03, 1SLg.04, 1SLp.05	1Rw.06, 1Rw.07, 1Ra.03, 1Ww.06, 1Wv.01, 1Wg.02, 1Wg.04, 1Wg.05, 1Ws.02, 1SLg.02, 1SLg.03	• To talk about pretend story characters. • To listen to and read a funny, scary story with expression. • To predict what a pretend character does next.	• Learners can talk about pretend story characters. • Learners can listen to and read a funny, scary story with expression. • Learners can predict what a pretend character does next.

LANGUAGE SUPPORT

Revisit any vocabulary that learners have met in *We're Going on a Bear Hunt* in Sessions 7.6 and 7.7, e.g. *swamp* and *forest*, and opposites such as *up* and *down*, *high* and *low*.

Ask learners to practise licking their lips and thinking about something in an 'eating-it-up kind of way'. Ask: *What does that look like?*

Starter idea

Wondering (10–15 minutes)

Resources: Learner's Book, Session 7.8: Getting started

Description: Tell learners that the story in this unit begins like this:

Do you ever wonder if somewhere, not too far away, there might be ...

MONSTERS?

Ask them if they do! Then ask them what else they wonder.

Together, look at the speech bubbles in Getting Started and discuss them. They include other imaginary creatures: unicorns, dragons and mermaids.

Ask learners to say how they feel about those things, especially if they are near!

Be sensitive to those who are less confident about exploring fear, even in a pretend way. Say: *This is scary book, but it's just pretend.*

Main teaching ideas

50 1 *Bedtime for Monsters*, Part 1
(20–30 minutes)

Learning intention: to listen carefully and respond in a way that demonstrates comprehension and/or imagination

Resources: *Bedtime for Monsters*, Part 1 (Learner's Book, Session 7.8, Activity 1); Track 50; Workbook, Session 7.8

Description: Tell learners that this story is about a pretend monster on a journey to find US!

Ask if any learners already know this story, *Bedtime for Monsters*.

Ask learners to first listen to the story. Play the audio or read the story aloud.

Ask learners to notice when words are louder or emphasised in other ways, e.g. with fearful intonation and pauses, or different types of voice.

Talk about the story afterwards and the fact that we are left wondering what this monster is going to do to us.

Listen again and invite learners to join in saying some of the words in the different ways.

Talk about how we can use actions to show intentions; see Language support earlier. Ask: *What does 'thinking about something in an eating-it-up kind of way' look like?* Practise this.

Finally, ask learners to read the text in Activity 1 in pairs. You may wish to draw their attention to the words in capital letters.

You can use the Workbook Session 7.8 activities here, and the Phonics Workbooks, for further practice of spelling common words if helpful:

Phonics Workbook A: pages 13, 15, 19, 25, 29, 31, 43, 45, 49, 51 and 53.

Phonics Workbook B: pages 11, 13, 17, 19, 21, 25, 27, 29, 31, 35, 37, 45 and 53.

> **Differentiation ideas:** Support learners with several re-readings, including actions.

Challenge learners to read the story aloud for the class to model how to 'build fear'.

2 Predict (20–30 minutes)

Learning intention: to talk about and write what a character does next

Resources: Learner's Book, Session 7.8, Activity 2; *Bedtime for Monsters*, Part 1 (Learner's Book, Session 7.8); Track 49; large pieces of paper

Description: Play the audio again and ask listeners to work in pairs to say what they think the monster is going to do. Talk about prediction, if appropriate to your class.

Model a response: *I think the monster finds us in our beds and eats us up! / I think the monster finds us and wants to play – just like the bear in* We're Going on a Bear Hunt.

Continue the discussion and sharing of ideas.

Ask learners to draw a monster shape on a piece of paper, and then write their prediction inside the shape. Create a class display of these predictions to refer back to at the beginning of the next session.

> **Differentiation ideas:** Support learners by providing some prediction options they can choose from to copy.

Challenge learners to work independently to write a prediction and to explain it.

Answers:
Learners' own predictions including the word *and*

Plenary idea

I'm wondering if there is/are ... (5 minutes)

Description: Ask learners to close their eyes and 'wonder' as they did at the beginning of Session 7.8.

Ask them to each say a sentence about what they are wondering, and then to extend their response, e.g. *I'm wondering if there is a monster outside the classroom; I'm wondering if there are giants in the playground.*

Encourage the idea of pretending, but be sensitive to those learners who feel unsure. In such cases, accept other statements, e.g. *I'm wondering if my mum has cooked rice for tea.* Once learners have said a sentence, they may leave the classroom.

CROSS-CURRICULAR LINKS

Science: Make predictions about what learners think will happen. Provide opportunities for them to make predictions in simple science experiments.

Science: Search online for a gloopy slime recipe. Make some slime and explore its characteristics, choosing words to describe it.

Homework ideas

Learners complete the Workbook Session 7.8 activities if not completed in class.

They make a monster puppet from an old sock, with help from a family member.

Answers for Workbook

1   you; not; that; his; of

2   Learners' own drawings

3   **a** through; **b** the; **c** up; **d** high, low, down

4   *Through/the*; *low/down*

5   Do; because; no; than; This.

6   Learners' own sentence endings

7   Possible answers: *th* in *think/that* or *s* in *he's/lips*

7.9 Comparing story settings

LEARNING PLAN

Learning objectives		Learning intentions	Success criteria
Main focus	**Also covered**	• To check predictions and their understanding of a story.	• Learners can check predictions and their understanding of a story.
1Rg.01, 1Rg.02, 1Rg.05, 1Rs.02, 1Ra.05	1Rv.03, 1Rs.01, 1Rs.03, 1Rs.04, 1Ri.04, 1Ri.06, 1Ri.13, 1SLm.03, 1SLm.05, 1SLg.01, 1SLg.02, 1SLg.04, 1SLp.01, 1SLp.03, 1SLp.05	• To compare story settings.	• Learners can compare story settings.
		• To sort words into the correct order in a sentence.	• Learners can sort words into the correct order in a sentence.

LANGUAGE SUPPORT

Learners may need support with *same* and *different,* but the visual nature of the comparing settings activity (using a chart) will help this.

Common misconception

Misconception	How to identify	How to overcome
Words in a sentence can be in any order.	Ask learners to read a jumbled sentence. Ask them if it makes sense and to say why. Ask them to sort the words into the correct order. Ask: *How do they know what order to put the words in?*	Remind learners that a sentence must make sense when you read it back. If it does not, then you have to re-order the words. Explain that we can use the capital letter and a full stop as clues in this type of activity.

Starter idea

Talk about settings (10 minutes)

Resources: Learner's Book, Session 7.9: Getting started; *Bedtime for Monsters,* Part 1 (Learner's Book, Session 7.8); Track 50

Description: Remind learners about the journey the monster took in Session 7.8. If necessary, re-read the text out loud.

Ask learners to talk in pairs about where the monster went. Remind them that these places are called *settings*.

Bring the class back together and share ideas (forest, swamp, snowy mountain, town, etc.).

What other settings can learners think of? Ask: *How are these settings similar? How are they different?*

Main teaching ideas

1 *Bedtime for Monsters*, Part 2 (10–15 minutes)

Learning intention: to check predictions

Resources: *Bedtime for Monsters,* Part 2 (Learner's Book, Session 7.9, Activity 1); Track 51; *Bedtime for Monsters,* Part 1 (Learner's Book, Session 7.8); Track 50

Description: Remind learners that we still do not know, after the last session, what the monster wants to do! Ask them to listen to the end of the story as you read it aloud.

After they hear the funny ending, ask for their reactions:

- *Who predicted correctly?*
- *Who thought that we'd be eaten?*
- *Were you really scared, or did you know the story was meant to be fun?*

You could handle the topic of fear, and in particular night-time fear, here, if appropriate to your learners.

Reflect on what helped learners to predict, as well as what helps them to overcome fear.

Do they know other scary stories like this? (Lots of fairy stories are quite scary.)

2 Answer questions about settings (10–20 minutes)

Learning intention: to explore, find and use words in a story

Resources: Learner's Book, Session 7.9, Activity 2

Description: Ask learners to talk about and answer the questions in Activity 2 about the settings in *Bedtime for Monsters*: the forest, the swamp and the mountains.

Ask them to then write about each setting in their notebooks.

> **Differentiation ideas:** Support learners by providing captions for them to match to each setting picture they have drawn.

Challenge learners to use their own rich vocabulary, drawing on other stories they know and writing more than one sentence.

Answers:

a   Learners' own responses, but may include the words from the story: *The forest is dark and terrible. The swamp is gloopy, schloopy. The mountains are cold and snowy.*

b   Learners' own sentences using their own words

3 Comparing stories (10–20 minutes)

Learning intention: to compare story settings.

Resources: Learner's Book, Session 7.9, Activity 3; *We're Going on a Bear Hunt* (Learner's Book, Session 7.6); Track 49; *Bedtime for Monsters,* Parts 1 and 2 (Learner's Book, Session 7.8); Tracks 50 and 51; Workbook, Session 7.9; Worksheet 7.4

Description: Remind learners that this is the second story in Unit 7 about a journey.

Revisit *We're Going on a Bear Hunt* (Session 7.6) and *Bedtime for Monsters* (Sessions 7.8 and 7.9), if necessary, and stop along the way to describe similarities and differences, e.g. *Uh-uh! A forest! A big, dark forest … Wait a minute! We had a forest in the monster story too – it was a dark and terrible forest … do you remember?*

Invite learners to tell you about similarities and differences between the stories in general and also with a focus on settings.

Ask them to work in pairs to copy and complete the chart in Activity 3 to help them to compare the settings of the two stories, or provide Worksheet 7.4 Comparing stories.

When they have completed the chart, discuss again what they have noticed about the two stories.

> **Differentiation ideas:** Support learners by working with a group to complete the chart.

Challenge learners to copy and/or to complete the chart independently. Ask them if there are any similarities or differences in things other than the setting, e.g. character, picture style, use of capital letters.

Answers:

Setting	1	2	3	4	5
We're Going on a Bear Hunt	grass	river	forest	cave	*house*
Bedtime for Monsters	*cave*	*forest*	swamp	mountains	town

4 Word order in a sentence (10–20 minutes)

Learning intention: to sequence words in a sentence for meaning

Resources: Learner's Book, Session 7.9, Activity 4; word cards

Description: Remind learners that as well as sequencing pictures to retell a story, we can sort letters in words or words in sentences, too.

Model how to sort letters in a word. Invite a learner to unscramble letters for: *monster*, *bear* and *forest*.

Model how to sort words in a sentence. Hand out word cards with the words of a sentence to individual learners, e.g. *The monster bicycled through a forest.*

Ask learners to rearrange themselves in the correct sentence order. Ask others to read the sentence to check for meaning.

Ask learners to do the same thing with the scrambled sentences in Activity 4. Explain that the sentences might be from either of the two stories.

> **Differentiation ideas:** Support learners by giving them sentences to cut up into the individual words so they can physically re-sequence them.

Challenge learners to create their own scrambled sentences and to swap with another learner to sequence them.

Answers:
a   We're going to catch a big one.
b   We're not scared.
c   He's licking his lips.

Plenary idea

Sing a song (10–20 minutes)

Resources: text and tune for *The Bear Went Over the Mountain* song

Description: Search online for the words and tune to *The Bear Went Over the Mountain* or another song about a bear or monster.

Sing the song together as a class.

CROSS-CURRICULAR LINKS

Science: Sort and group objects, materials and living things based on observations of the similarities and differences between them: Use the vocabulary of *same* and *different* in science teaching.

Homework ideas

Learners complete the Workbook Session 7.9 activities if not completed in class.

They make a Spot the Difference game for a friend to play.

Answers for Workbook

1   Learners' own drawings and sentences
2   Learners' own responses, based on the pictures
3   Learners' own responses, e.g. *They are both about bears. This one is a story book. This one is an information book.*

7.10 Retelling in different ways

LEARNING PLAN

Learning objectives		Learning intentions	Success criteria
Main focus	**Also covered**	• To describe feelings and emotions.	• Learners can describe feelings and emotions.
1Rs.01, 1Ri.02, 1Ri.06, 1Wc.02, 1Wp.03, 1SLp.04	1Rv.01, 1Rg.01, 1Rg.02, 1Rs.02, 1Wv.02, 1Ws.01, 1Wc.03, 1Wp.01, 1Wp.02, 1SLm.02, 1SLm.03, 1SLm.04, 1SLm.05, 1SLs.02, 1SLg.01, 1SLp.01, 1SLp.03, 1SLr.02	• To sequence and retell a story in different ways. • To recognise humour in a story text.	• Learners can sequence and retell a story in different ways. • Learners can recognise humour in a story text.

LANGUAGE SUPPORT

Support learners by acting the different actions and emotions of the three different monsters in Getting Started.

The vocabulary of the settings should now be familiar to learners, but the subtlety of the humour and using a scary voice may need extra practice.

Use the structure of the text and, in particular, the questions to support learners' ideas, e.g. *Do you think … (he's smiling because he remembered how tasty children in Class X will be)?*

See Common misconception, too.

Common misconception

Misconception	How to identify	How to overcome
A story is usually set in one place only.	Ask learners where the story *Bedtime for Monsters* is set.	Encourage learners to identify the settings: forest, bedroom, swamp, cave, town and mountains.

Starter idea

Monsters (10–20 minutes)

Resources: Learner's Book, Session 7.10: Getting started

Look at the pictures in Getting Started and talk about the monsters' emotions.

Invite learners to act a variety of emotions. Ask: *How can you show you are angry, sad, surprised etc.?*

You may play this as a game of charades, asking: *What sort of monster am I?* or *How do I feel?*

Encourage learners to think about facial expression, body actions or stance and voice.

Main teaching ideas

1 **Sequence pictures and write captions (20–30 minutes)**

   Learning intention: to sequence pictures and write captions to retell a story

   Resources: Learner's Book, Session 7.10, Activity 1; Workbook, Session 7.10

Description: Tell learners they are now going to sequence some pictures of *Bedtime for Monsters* to retell the story.

If helpful, make simple picture cards of a cave, forest, swamp, mountains, town and bedroom to hand out to learners so they may organise themselves into the correct order while others retell the story verbally.

When this has been rehearsed a few times, if necessary, ask learners to work in their notebooks to draw each setting, in the correct order, and then to write a sentence as a caption for each story to retell the story in words.

Ask learners to think about their handwriting in this activity. As you circulate, check letter formation, any joining of letters and use of capital letters for storytelling effect.

You can use the Workbook Session 7.10 activities now for further handwriting practice if helpful.

› **Differentiation ideas:** Support learners by repeating the whole-class exercise of sorting the pictures into the correct order before working with them to agree captions for each picture.

Challenge learners to write more than one sentence in their captions, as well as to make good use of humour and capital letters for storytelling effect.

Answers:
Learners' own sentences, but pictures in the order of: **d** monster cave; **a** forest; **c** swamp; **f** mountains; **e** town; **b** bedroom.

---

2   Retell the story (20–30 minutes)

Learning intention: to read aloud own writing to retell a story

Resources: Learner's Book, Session 7.10, Activity 2; learners' picture strips from Activity 1

Description: Learners will have had the story modelled enough times by now to be able to bring their own personality to the retelling.

Select or invite different learners to retell the story using their pictures and captions.

Remind learners to speak clearly when reading aloud and not to rush. Encourage them to use their voice in different ways to make the story scary.

› **Differentiation ideas:** Support learners by allowing them to present the retelling in pairs.

Challenge learners to ensure that their humour and use of capital letters is obvious to the class audience.

Answers:
Learners' own retellings

Plenary idea

Watch online (5–10 minutes)

Resources: online access

Description: Search online for an official reading of *Bedtime for Monsters*.

Talk about how the reader(s) make it scary and funny at the same time.

CROSS-CURRICULAR LINKS

Art: Explore different lettering and fonts to create 'scary' sentences, e.g.

Homework ideas

Learners complete the Workbook Session 7.10 activities if not completed in class. They write a scary word in scary letters, e.g. slimy dripping letters, letters with a scary face.

Answers for Workbook

1   Learners' accurate and correct copying of the sentence

2   Learners' accurate and correct copying of the sentence

3   Correct joins for *ow, ou* and *ai*.

4   Learners' accurate and correct copying of the sentence

5   Correct joins for *au, or* and *ers*.

7.11 Planning and writing

LEARNING PLAN

Learning objectives		Learning intentions	Success criteria
Main focus	**Also covered**	• To describe the features of a story we know. • To plan and write a pretend scary story. • To create a storyboard and annotate it.	• Learners can describe the features of a story we know. • Learners can plan and write a pretend scary story. • Learners can create a storyboard and annotate it.
1Rs.02, 1Ws.02, 1Wc.01, 1Wc.02, 1Wc.04, 1Wp.05	1Rs.01, 1Ri.02, 1Ra.04, 1Wv.01, 1Wv.03, 1Wg.02, 1Wg.04, 1Wp.01		

LANGUAGE SUPPORT

Learners will benefit from using Language worksheets 7A and 7B, and Worksheet 7.5 Storyboard template to support their writing outcome.

The list of language features and questions should support learners in their writing. If necessary, work with a group of learners to create a group story.

Common misconception

Misconception	How to identify	How to overcome
We only use capital letters at the beginning of a sentence and for our names.	Ask learners to look again at the end of *Bedtime for Monsters* in Learner's Book Session 7.9 Activity 1. Ask: *Where are capital letters used?*	Learners notice that capital letters are used for emphasis. Read the text again with emphasis on the words written in capital letters.

Starter idea

Story features (10–15 minutes)

Resources: Learner's Book, Session 7.11: Getting started; *Bedtime for Monsters*, Parts 1 and 2 (Learner's Book, Session 7.8); Tracks 50 and 51

Description: Ask learners to remember all the things they noticed about the story *Bedtime for Monsters* in Learner's Book Sessions 7.8 and 7.9.

Share ideas and tell them these things are the story 'features' and that we can use them in our own writing if we want to; we can borrow these good ideas.

Show learners the list of features in Getting started. Talk about it together and ask learners to give examples of each feature from the story.

Ask learners if there were any other things they noticed or liked about these stories, e.g. the use of questions to make it funny and scary at the same time, or funny pictures (not photos).

Main teaching ideas

1 Answer questions to plan a story (10–15 minutes)

Learning intention: to use story features to plan a new story

Resources: Learner's Book, Session 7.11, Activity 1; Workbook, Session 7.11; learners' charts from Learner's Book Session 7.9 Activity 3

Description: Tell learners they will now think about what features they want to borrow from *Bedtime for Monsters* to plan their own version of the story. What will they keep and/or change?

Read the questions in Activity 1 together as a class so there are no access issues.

Model how learners can plan their own story by choosing a pretend scary character, four settings (they can refer to their chart of settings from Learner's Book Session 7.9 Activity 3 here), some funny words and an ending.

You can use the Workbook Session 7.11 activities to support new ideas, too.

Ask them to work in pairs to make their choices and to make a note of them or to draw them in rough.

As you circulate, support and challenge learners to be creative.

> **Differentiation ideas:** Support learners by providing Workbook Session 7.11 as a way to structure initial ideas, or work with a group to make a group story.

Challenge learners to work independently on their own story if they wish.

Answers:
Learners' own ideas

2 Draw a storyboard (30–50 minutes)

Learning intention: to use verbal plans to write a storyboard

Resources: Learner's Book, Session 7.11, Activity 2; Worksheet 7.5

Description: Tell learners they will now use their ideas from the last activity to complete their own storyboards.

You can provide Worksheet 7.5 Storyboard template now as guide if you wish.

In the same pairs, encourage learners to transfer their verbal ideas onto the storyboard. They should start by drawing a picture for each story step.

Support them to write a sentence for each picture.

> **Differentiation ideas:** Support learners by numbering their ideas from Session 7.11 Activity 1 and the six boxes on Worksheet 7.5 Storyboard template so they know how to match their responses to the space available.

Challenge learners to write more than one sentence for each picture in their story. Ask learners to check, and check again, their spelling, punctuation and handwriting.

Answers:
Learners' own storyboards

3 Annotate the storyboard (30–40 minutes)

Learning intention: to create an annotated storyboard

Resources: Learner's Book, Session 7.11, Activity 3; learners' storyboards from Activity 2; large pieces of paper; glue and coloured pens

Description: Show learners how they can stick their storyboard onto a larger piece of paper so they have room to annotate their story further.

Provide large pieces of paper and coloured pens, glue, etc., so the storyboard becomes a creative piece of work.

Encourage learners to add questions, different fonts, asides and instructions.

As you circulate, encourage learners to be bold in their choices and to see the fun in planning a story in this way. Remind them to add a story title.

Make a class display of their stories.

> **Differentiation ideas:** Support learners by helping them with their annotation ideas. Mixed pairings can also help to support learners in this activity.

Challenge learners to present their storyboards to the class.

Plenary idea

Story features (5–10 minutes)

Resources: another story book for each group

Description: Show learners other story books that use a range of techniques to make them more interesting. (Story books by Lauren Child are good for this.)

Provide groups of learners with a different story book each. Ask learners to work in their groups to quickly say what features they notice about their book.

Before they leave the classroom, they must share the features they have noticed.

Homework ideas

Learners complete the Workbook Session 7.11 activities if not completed in class

They search online with an adult for an official retelling of a Lauren Child book – *Is it scary or funny? Which do you prefer?*

Answers for Workbook

1   Learners' own drawings and responses

2   Learners' correctly matched pictures and sentences

3   Learners' own responses, but similar to:

How does the monster …	My funny words
cross the swamp?	Trudge, squelch
climb up the mountains?	Huff, puff-puff
search all over town?	High and spy

7.12 Look back

LEARNING PLAN

Learning objectives		Learning intentions	Success criteria
Main focus	**Also covered**	• To check their writing and share our stories. • To talk about the stories in the unit. • To think about their learning from the unit.	• Learners can check their writing and share their stories. • Learners can talk about the stories in the unit. • Learners can think about their learning from the unit.
1Ra.04, 1Ra.05, 1WP.06, 1SLg.02, 1SLp.01, 1SLr.01	1Rg.01, 1Wv.01, 1Wg.01, 1SLm.01, 1SLm.05, 1SLp.03		

LANGUAGE SUPPORT

Use classroom punctuation mats or posters to remind learners of the punctuation marks we use.

Share any print or online versions of stories in this unit, as well as the Learner's Book and any

resources made by learners throughout the unit so they can revisit, recall and reflect on the stories with visual prompts.

Common misconception

Misconception	How to identify	How to overcome
Mistakes are bad.	Ask learners if they can remember a time when they made a mistake. Ask them how they felt. Ask: *Did you learn from it?* Have a sensitive class discussion about the value of mistakes.	Establish a classroom culture where mistakes are welcomed as opportunities to learn.

Starter idea

Punctuation marks (5–10 minutes)

Resources: Learner's Book, Session 7.12: Getting started

Description: Write a sentence on the board without end punctuation.

Ask learners to add the correct end punctuation and to name it (full stop).

Ask learners to look in their notebooks to find examples of where they have used fullstops correctly and where they may have forgotten to use one!

Main teaching ideas

1 Check the storyboard writing and annotations (10–15 minutes)

Learning intention: to check writing for correct punctuation

Resources: Learner's Book, Session 7.12, Activity 1; Workbook, Session 7.12; learners' storyboards from Session 7.11 Activity 2

Description: Discuss the value of mistakes. (see Common misconception.)

If appropriate, choose an example of a sentence that needs correcting. Write it on the board and work on this together first.

Then ask learners to look at their storyboards. Ask: *Can you find one punctuation mistake and one word that you could write more neatly?*

Ask them to enjoy reading their stories and checking their work with other pairs.

Remind them that the storyboard is a plan. They can correct any errors when they write up their story in their notebooks (if that is what they go on

to do). Encourage peer feedback, but try to ensure it is kept positive.

You can use Workbook Session 7.12 activities here for further self-correcting practice.

> **Differentiation ideas:** Support learners by working with them in a group when checking their storyboards or selecting a sentence for them to improve.

Challenge learners to reflect on what they would do differently next time and on the benefits of working alone or with a partner.

2 The stories in the unit (10–15 minutes)

Learning intention: to reflect on stories and recall their characters and settings

Resources: Learner's Book, Session 7.12, Activity 2; class displays of stories in the unit; stories in earlier sessions or printed copies of the stories

Description: Ask learners if they can remember the stories from the unit using memory as well as class displays that you may have created.

List the story titles together, encouraging learners to look at the images in the Learner's Book if they cannot remember all of them.

Ask learners to talk about the stories: *Which did you enjoy most?* Take a class vote.

Ask learners to recall the characters and settings for each of the stories and to revisit the unit focus of pretending in stories.

> **Differentiation ideas:** Support learners by using book covers in print or in the Learner's Book, or classroom displays as reminders.

Challenge learners to think of other story settings or characters that could have featured in this unit.

3 Skill review (10–15 minutes)

Learning intention: to think about learning in terms of language skills

Resources: Learner's Book, Session 7.12, Activity 3

Description: Remind learners of the language we use to describe language skills: reading, writing, spelling, listening and speaking.

Say each skill one by one, and ask learners to put their hand up when you say the skill they think they are best at.

Now ask learners to say or write one thing from this unit that helped them with these skills.

These simple learner statements can be extremely useful for informing end-of-term reports.

⟩ **Differentiation ideas:** Support learners to be positive in their skills review, providing models: *I think you are much better at … now.*

Challenge learners to also think of one thing they still need to improve.

Plenary idea

Pick a card (5–10 minutes)

Resources: a set of challenge cards, with challenges such as: *Talk for 30 seconds about what you have learned in this unit; Tell us three things you liked in this unit; Spell 'dragon', Clap this sentence; Say … in a scary way*; music; selection of light objects (ball, tiny toy monster, etc.)

Description: Play some music. Pass a light object (ball, tiny toy monster, etc.) around the classroom.

The learner holding the ball when the music stops must pick a challenge card and perform that challenge.

Keep going until you run out of time or all learners have had a challenge.

Homework ideas

Learners complete the Workbook Session Session 7.12 activities if not completed in class.

They make a unit mat (like a visual summary) to remind them of the content or learning from Unit 7.

Answers for Workbook

1   Learners' responses should:

a add full stop; **b** add capital letter *T*; **c** add full stop after *Grass*.

2   **a** *Dragon Land*; **b** *How to Catch a Star*; **c** *We're Going on a Bear Hunt*

3   Following words circled and corrected: **a** my; **b** watched; **c** bear; **d** licking

4   **a** *Dragon Land*; **b** *How to Catch a Star*; **c** *We're Going on a Bear Hunt*; **d** *Bedtime for Monsters*

5   **a** But Mother, I can't swoop or zoom. I can't soar or glide.

b   He tried to fish the star out with his hands.

c   What a beautiful day!

d   You're not scared, are you?

6   **a** *Dragon Land*; **b** *How to Catch a Star*; **c** *We're Going on a Bear Hunt*; **d** *Bedtime for Monsters*

CHECK YOUR PROGRESS

1 It is the place where a story happens, even if it is pretend.
2 today/away, dragons/hills
3 We read stories about pretend places.
4 The *boy* waited and waited to see *a/the* star.
5 Learners' own compound words
6 Learners' own responses

PROJECT GUIDANCE

These projects build on the reading, writing and understanding learners have developed throughout the unit. Since they have just read several stories that explore fantasy or pretend settings, the project options here extend this focus and provide opportunities for learners to choose to work in a group, as a pair or alone. It may be that you prefer to allocate a project to the class.

Group project: Learners design and create a class quiet place. This can be designed as a plan on paper (what is needed, where it would go, how it is to be built, etc.) and then created as an actual place. Learners can create rules about when and how it is to be used.

Pair project: Learners design and build a 3D model of a pretend world. They may like to refer back to their maps of their pretend lands in Session 7.1 Activity 3. They may need construction blocks, junk modelling or PE equipment, depending on their ideas.

Solo project: Learners design and create a miniature world in a box. They must use their imagination to populate the tiny world.

For more guidance on setting up and assessing projects, see Project guidance at the end of Unit 1.

>8 Finding out

Unit plan

Session	Approximate number of learning hours	Outline of learning content	Resources
8.1 Finding out: what and how?	1.5	Talk about book covers and label the parts. Choose a topic and explore what is known about it.	Learner's Book Session 8.1 Workbook Session 8.1
8.2 Exploring a chart	1.5	Talk about a topic. Explore a chart that helps to organise information into groups.	Learner's Book Session 8.2 Workbook Session 8.2
8.3 Exploring contents information	1.5	Talk about book and screen contents, and how they help us to find information.	Learner's Book Session 8.3 Workbook Session 8.3
8.4 Writing a contents page	1.5	Write a book contents page based on a model. Design a cover for a class display.	Learner's Book Session 8.4 Workbook Session 8.4
8.5 Exploring pictures and captions	1.5	Explore the use of pictures and captions in information texts. Write captions.	Learner's Book Session 8.5 Workbook Session 8.5 Phonics Workbook B
8.6 Exploring topic words	1.5	Explore topic words. Understand how icons can help with understanding.	Learner's Book Session 8.6 Workbook Session 8.6
8.7 Exploring a glossary	1.5	Explore a simple picture and word glossary.	Learner's Book Session 8.7 Workbook Session 8.7 Worksheets 8.1
8.8 Exploring a dictionary	1.5	Revisit the alphabet. Explore a simple picture dictionary. Write a dictionary page.	Learner's Book Session 8.8 Workbook Session 8.8 Worksheet 8.2 Phonics Workbook A

Session	Approximate number of learning hours	Outline of learning content	Resources
8.9 Exploring a fact file	1.5	Talk about a fact file and explore its features. Create a fact file.	Learner's Book Session 8.9 Workbook Session 8.9 ⬇ Worksheet 8.3 ⬇ Unit 8 Language worksheets
8.10 Exploring a report	1	Talk about a report and explore its features. Answer questions to check understanding.	Learner's Book Session 8.10 Workbook Session 8.10 ⬇ Differentiated worksheets 8A–C
8.11 Planning and writing a report	1.5	Plan and write a report.	Learner's Book Session 8.11 Workbook Session 8.11 ⬇ Worksheet 8.4
8.12 Look back	1	Check report writing. Revisit information about book features explored in the unit. Reflect on learning.	Learner's Book Session 8.12 Workbook Session 8.12
Cross-unit resources			
Learner's Book Check your progress Learner's Book Projects			

BACKGROUND KNOWLEDGE

Before you begin to teach this unit, you may find it helpful to:

- Prepare to talk about facts: learners will be encouraged to identify what they know already and what they want to know or find out more about.
- prepare examples of how information can be found and used in different ways, including in:
  - parts of a book
  - parts of a website
  - pictures, photos and captions
  - lists, labels and and fact boxes
  - glossaries and dictionaries

- reports
- fact files
- familiarise yourself with the phonics and grammar elements in this unit, including:
  - phonics – letter to sound correspondence, consonant and vowel digraphs, words with adjacent consonants, blending and segmenting words, verb endings, e.g. *s, ing* and *-ed*
  - grammatical links between words in sentences (to avoid repetition), e.g. ***The visitors*** *shouted to the penguins, but the penguins slid away from* ***them***.
  - using headings and sub-headings.

TEACHING SKILLS FOCUS

Cross-curricular learning

Cross-curricular learning demands that you exploit opportunities to teach knowledge and skills associated with more than one subject. In this unit, learners explore different ways to read for information and the uniting theme throughout is animals.

In this unit, challenge yourself to find different ways to support and challenge learners to identify connections with other subject areas:

- Make cross-curricular learning explicit for learners – go beyond a simple link to explain specific subject knowledge.

- Create opportunities for them to think, do and talk alongside reading and writing.

- Create cross-curricular displays and book collections with learners.

- Explore innovative ways to display their thinking, e.g. a curriculum web for a topic or subject so they begin to identify cross-curricular links themselves.

- Make explicit links to poetry, music, art and drama, too, e.g. *How does what you know about a jelly fish change the way you might move in PE when asked to move like a jelly fish?*

At the end of this unit, consider which aspects of cross-curricular learning were most effective for the learners and then consider why and how. Ask yourself and the learners questions about:

- Learner voice: Were the subject, knowledge and skills links clear to learners?

- Techniques: Where did most learning take place? Did you consistently go back to English as your main focus? Did having one uniting topic help you with planning and learners with learning?

- Moving on: What will you try next? How can you challenge learners to always identify cross-curricular links and/or to question a topic in new and exciting ways?

- The environment: Does your classroom support cross-curricular learning opportunities, e.g. Are there active wall displays to show links? Are there book displays to support links, too? Is there access to technology? Is there a thinking zone?

- Evidence: If colleagues came into your classroom, could they tell that learners were engaged in cross-curricular learning with a focus on English?

Cambridge Reading Adventures

Learners may enjoy these other non-fiction information titles from Cambridge Reading Adventures that follow the unit theme:

- *Animal Homes* by Lauri Kabuitsile (Pink A Band)

- *In the Sea* by Claire Llewellyn (Red Band)

- *Crabs* by Ralph Hall and Andy Belcher (Blue Band) (includes a picture glossary)

8.1 Finding out: what and how?

LEARNING PLAN

Learning objectives		Learning intentions	Success criteria
Main focus	**Also covered**	• To explore what you know and how to find out more.	• Learners can explore what they know and how to find out more.
1Rs.03, 1Rs.04, 1Ra.04, 1Ra.05, 1SLp.05	1Rv.02, 1Rg.04, 1Ri.03, 1Ri.08, 1Ri.09, 1Ri.13, 1Wv.03, 1Wg.05, 1Wc.05, 1Wp.03, 1SLm.03, 1SLs.02, 1SLg.04	• To talk about the information on a book cover.	• Learners can talk about the information on a book cover.
		• To choose a topic and say why it is interesting.	• Learners can choose a topic and say why it is interesting.

LANGUAGE SUPPORT

Review the difference between statements and questions, including punctuation. Practise asking questions and play games with question words, e.g. learners pick a card that features a question word and then ask a question using that word.

Make sure all learners have at least one thing they can say they know and one thing they want to find out.

Common misconception

Misconception	How to identify	How to overcome
It is best to choose a book from the front-cover information.	Ask learners to look at a book in small groups. Ask: *What does the front cover tell you?* *What does the back cover tell you?*	Talk about using all the information on a book cover to gauge what the book is about and whether learners want to read it.

Starter idea

What we know (10–15 minutes)

Resources: Learner's Book, Session 8.1: Getting started

Description: Explain that this unit is about different ways of finding out information and using tools to help us.

Ask learners to explore and talk about the questions in Getting started, together in pairs. Then ask them to give feedback on different ways to find information (e.g. look online, use an information book, ask an expert, watch a film or television programme, look in a dictionary). Encourage the use of appropriate vocabulary.

Ask: *Are there some processes or tools that are not familiar to you? Are there others you would add?*

Main teaching ideas

1 Information books (15–30 minutes)

Learning intention: to talk about information books and covers

Resources: Learner's Book, Session 8.1, Activity 1; examples of information books

Description: Tell learners that in this session they are going to explore information books.

Discuss the covers and questions in Activity 1 and share views.

Now provide a few clear examples of information books to different groups and ask them to:

- discuss what the book is about and how they know
- think about the role of pictures on the front cover
- consider the information on the back cover, too.

Ask groups to present their books and observations to the class.

If possible, begin a class library display of information books that the class have selected as 'interesting'.

> **Differentiation ideas:** Support learners by setting up groups comprising some learners who would like to be challenged and some learners who would benefit from additional support.

Challenge learners to present an information book on their own.

Answers:

a   marine life transport, football, nature

b and c   Learners' own responses

2 Match pictures to information books (15–30 minutes)

Learning intention: to talk about content and match it to a book

Resources: Learner's Book, Session 8.1, Activity 2

Description: Ask learners if they know what to expect in different information books, e.g. a book of transport will probably give information about cars, bikes, etc. Ask: *Will it tell us about new and old cars or taxis around the world?*

Show learners the pictures in Activity 2.

In pairs, ask learners to match the pictures to the books in Activity 1. As you circulate, ask learners to explain their reasons when they match an image to a book.

Ask a few learners to share their ideas.

> **Differentiation ideas:** Support learners by asking them to work in pairs or work with a group to help them match correctly.

Challenge learners to list other things they would expect to find in the books.

Answers:

All Kinds of Plants: tree and shark image; Things that go!: tuk tuk image; My First Football Handbook: football image, Sea World: shark image

3 Choosing a topic (15–30 minutes)

Learning intention: to choose a topic and write a sentence about it, giving reasons

Resources: Learner's Book, Session 8.1, Activity 3; Workbook, Session 8.1; large pieces of paper (optional)

Description: Revisit the book covers and the photos of information in Activities 1 and 2. Ask: *Which topic would you like to find out more about?*

Draw learners' attention to the Language focus (Activity 3). Model how to use *because* when giving reasons for our choices (after the question *Why?*). Model how to use *and* to talk about more than one thing (e.g. *whales* and *sharks*).

Work round the classroom, practising the language structure *I want to find out more about … because …* to explore learners' choices.

Ask learners to draw and explain their topic choice. You may wish them to do this in their notebooks or to draw or paint it on larger pieces of paper. Either way, ensure they have written a sentence to explain their choice.

You can use Workbook Session 8.1 in class now to practise the use of *and* and *because*.

> **Differentiation ideas:** Support learners by providing the sentence structure for them to fill in the gaps:

I want to find out more about _____ because _____.

Challenge learners to not just repeat *because I am interested in* [the topic]. Encourage them to use an adapted language structure.

Answers:
Learners' own responses

Plenary idea

Quick-fire Topics (5–10 minutes)

Resources: topic images or word cards; a bag; music

Description: Ask learners to sit in a circle. Play music.

Pass a bag round that contains the topic cards.

Stop the music. The learner holding the bag picks a card. That learner must say if they are interested in finding out more about the topic on the card, and the reasons why.

Start the game again and repeat.

> ### CROSS-CURRICULAR LINKS
>
> **Art:** Provide the opportunity for learners to consider book covers when making decisions about useful sources of information in other subject areas.

Homework ideas

Learners complete the Workbook Session 8.1 activities if not completed in class.

They share any information books they enjoy at home and build a class display of favourites for a 'show and tell' session.

Answers for Workbook

Answers might include:

1. a I like reading about dinosaurs and monsters.
   b I know that cars and bikes are called transport.
   c I'm interested in sharks and other sea creatures.
   d The back cover and the front cover give us information.

2. Learners' own responses, e.g. In *All Kinds of Plants*, I think I will learn about trees and flowers. In *Stars*, I think I will learn about planets and space travel.

3. Learners' own responses, e.g. In *Things That Go*, I think I will learn about all different kinds of transport, and information about travel. I would choose *My First Football Handbook* because I'm more interested in football than transport.

8.2 Exploring a chart

LEARNING PLAN

Learning objectives		Learning intentions	Success criteria
Main focus	**Also covered**	• To organise ideas for a topic.	• Learners can organise ideas within a topic.
1Rv.02, 1Rs.04, 1Ri.08, 1Ws.02, 1SLm.02	1Rv.03, 1Rs.02, 1Ri.03, 1Ri.04, 1Ri.13, 1Wv.01, 1Wg.01, 1Wc.04, 1Wc.05, 1Wp.04, Wp.05, 1SLm.05, 1SLs.02, 1SLg.01, 1SLp.04	• To understand information in a chart. • To describe animals by group and appearance.	• Learners can understand information in chart form. • Learners can describe animals by group and appearance.

Common misconception

Misconception	How to identify	How to overcome
Questions always begin with a question word.	Ask learners to ask questions about an animal. Do they only use question words? e.g. *What?, Why?, When?* Can they ask a question that does not begin with a question word? e.g. *Is it a mammal? Does it swim fast?*	Talk about the difference between open questions (those that need a fuller answer and start with questions words) and closed questions (those that need a *yes/no* answer). Encourage learners to use both types of question in their speech and writing.

Starter idea

Organising animal ideas (10–15 minutes)

Resources: Learner's Book, Session 8.2: Getting started; animal pictures, if available

Description: Talk about animals using the pictures in Learner's Book Session 8.2 Activity 1 or provide your own.

Ask: *How many animals can you name?* Create a list together.

Talk about learners' favourite animals and ask why they have chosen them.

Ask learners to quickly work with a partner to choose an animal or an animal group, and to write:

- three things they know
- three things they want to know.

Draw their attention to the Writing tip about using a question mark at the end of the question.

Give learners a few minutes to write their questions.

Together, share the questions.

Main teaching ideas

1 Talk about a chart (20–30 minutes)

Learning intention: to find out how to read the information in a chart

Resources: Learner's Book, Session 8.2, Activity 1; Workbook, Session 8.2; large pieces of paper or plastic hoops; animal pictures or small model animals

Description: Remind learners about the work they have already completed on information books and that the information topic in this unit is animals.

Recreate the chart in Activity 1 to show how it can help us to organise animals into groups.

Ask learners to sit in a circle on the floor. Put three big pieces of paper or three hoops in the centre to make a floor chart. Label the three areas as in the chart in the Learner's Book.

Put the animal pictures or small model animals in a big pile.

Invite learners to sort and group the animals using the floor chart.

Check what learners think their chart is showing them. Ask them to name more animals for each group and to think about animals that fit into more than group.

You can use the Workbook Session 8.2 activities here to talk about other types of chart.

› **Differentiation ideas:** Support learners by providing animal pictures or small animal models for them to talk about and practise naming.

Challenge learners by asking them to use animal group names: mammals, reptiles, insects and spiders, birds, amphibians and fish.

Answers:
a The chart shows a way to group different kinds of animals; b Learners' own responses; c amphibians (frogs toads, etc.) can live in water or on land, for example

2 Draw a chart (20–30 minutes)

Learning intention: to draw and write on a chart to sort animals into groups

Resources: Learner's Book, Session 8.2, Activity 2; large pieces of paper or plastic hoops; animal pictures or small model animals

Description: Tell learners they are going to draw and write on their own chart in their notebooks. Decide if you want them to work in pairs or individually.

Draw their attention to the animal pictures and labels in Activity 2, and check understanding of vocabulary.

You may wish to orally rehearse the animal groups from Activity 1 before learners create the chart in their notebooks.

When completed, compare the sorting decisions. Discuss what learners did when an animal could be placed in more than one group. Ask: *Which animals were these?*

Ask: *Can you add any more animals to the chart?*

> **Differentiation ideas:** Support learners by providing small model animals (or animal pictures) and asking them as a group to sort them.

Challenge learners to work out how to draw a circle in their notebooks, e.g. finding something to draw round to help them. Ask them to add more animals to each group and to label them.

Answers:
Learners' own drawings and labels, correctly grouped:

Animals that can fly: barn owl, golden eagle, dragonfly

Animals that live on land: lion, elephant, monkey, (crocodile, green turtle, frog)

Animals that live in water: (crocodile, green turtle, frog), seahorse, shark

Animals that are in more than one group: crocodile, frog, green turtle

3 Describing game (10–15 minutes)

Learning intention: to describe animals by groups or features

Resources: Learner's Book, Session 8.2, Activity 3

Description: Model how to describe an animal without saying its name. Ask learners to guess the animal you are thinking of.

Allow time for learners to choose an animal and to think about how they will describe it.

Ask a learner to describe their animal to the class. The learner who guesses correctly then thinks of another animal and describes it.

Play until everyone has had a turn or you run out of time.

> **Differentiation ideas:** Support learners by providing pictures of the animals for them to use as a reminder when describing and/or allowing them to speak in pairs

Challenge learners to use the correct animal groups terminology as rehearsed in Activity 1 Differentiation ideas, e.g. *My animal is an amphibian. That means it can live in water and on land.*

Plenary idea

My favourite animal is … (5–10 minutes)

Description: Work round the class, encouraging learners to state their favourite animal and say which group it is in.

Then they may leave the classroom.

CROSS-CURRICULAR LINKS
Maths: Explore other charts used in maths, e.g. pictograms or block charts.

Homework ideas

Learners complete the Workbook Session 8.2 activities if not completed in class.

They share any animal games they know from home.

Answers for Workbook

1 and **2** Learners sort pictures into topic headings plus learners' own pictures. Animals: elephant, shark; Hobbies: football, ballet; Transport: bus; Weather: lightning, wind.

3 **a** Seven; **b** Five; **c** hippos

4 Three children like elephants.

5 Learners' own sentences or similar to: This chart gives us information about transport. / It tells us that the children saw more cars than other types of transport in ten minutes. / It tells us they saw only two lorries.

6 Learners' own titles, similar to: Chart to show transport passing the school in 10 minutes.

8.3 Exploring contents information

LEARNING PLAN

Learning objectives		Learning intentions	Success criteria
Main focus	**Also covered**	• To explore contents information.	• Learners can explore contents information.
1Rv.03, 1Rs.03, 1Rs.04, 1Ri.04, 1Ri.12	1Rw.06, 1Rv.01, 1Rv.02, 1Rs.02, 1Ri.03, 1Ri.05, 1Ri.08, 1Ra.05, 1Wv.01, 1Wv.03, 1Wp.04, 1SLg.01, 1SLg.02, 1SLg.03, 1SLg.04	• To answer questions to show understanding. • To compare contents information in books and web pages.	• Learners can answer questions to show understanding. • Learners can compare contents information in books and web pages.

LANGUAGE SUPPORT

Model how to use a contents page when working with groups.

Check knowledge and vocabulary of sea creatures and bugs, and pre-teach if necessary.

Check numbers 1–25.

Common misconception

Misconception	How to identify	How to overcome
You do not find contents pages in story books; they are only found in non-fiction books.	Tell learners that information books usually have contents pages. Have a story book anthology and poetry anthology to share with learners. Ask: *Do you think these books – one with stories and one with poems – have a contents page?*	Show learners that sometimes books that have collections of stories or poems may have a contents page to help us choose the right page. Tell them that usually it is a feature of information books (but not always!).

Starter idea

Explore a contents page (10–15 minutes)

Resources: Learner's Book, Session 8.3: Getting started

Description: Quickly check that learners can count to 25 and recognise numbers 1–25.

Show a contents page from an information book.

Remind learners what they already know about books: that the covers can tell us quite a bit about what is in a book, for example.

Ask learners to talk about contents pages and what they may include (the book's title, headings, sub-headings, lists of contents, page numbers, the publisher's information).

Ask them to work in pairs to discuss the questions in Getting started:

- The contents page is telling us the book title, the animals that are included in the book, the page numbers, the author's name and the publisher's information.
- It is to help us find the correct page for the information we are looking for.
- It gives us page numbers.

If possible, ask groups of three to find an information book in the class or school library and to present its contents page.

Main teaching ideas

1 Read a contents page (15–20 minutes)

Learning intention: to read and talk about a contents page

Resources: Learner's Book, Session 8.3, Activity 1

Description: Introduce the contents page in Activity 1 and ask learners to talk about it in pairs or groups.

Give them time and then ask which words or numbers they found easy or difficult to read.

Revisit the idea of using pictures to support reading.

Read the contents page out loud to provide a model of good reading. Encourage learners to read with you.

> **Differentiation ideas:** Support learners by working with a group to support their reading.

Challenge learners to model how they worked out how to read some of the words they found difficult.

2 Answer questions about a contents page (15–30 minutes)

Learning intention: to demonstrate understanding of a contents page

Resources: Learner's Book, Session 8.3, Activity 2; Workbook, Session 8.3

Description: Tell learners they are going to answer questions about the contents page.

Answer the first question together as a class, and then ask learners to look at the other questions.

Ask learners to write their answers in their notebooks.

Encourage them to share and check their answers.

You can use the Workbook Session 8.3 activities now.

> **Differentiation ideas:** Support learners by working with them as a group or by organising mixed-ability groupings so they may help each other.

Challenge learners by asking them to write more questions for a partner to answer.

Answers:
a Page 16; b Animals that can fly; c Monkeys; d They fit into more than one group/two groups.

3 Webpage contents (15–30 minutes)

Learning intention: to explore the contents page of a website and compare it with a printed contents page

Resources: Learner's Book, Session 8.3, Activity 3; examples of online contents screens of age-appropriate animal websites

Description: Tell learners they are going to talk about how a book contents page is different from an online webpage.

If possible, have groups looking at different animal websites suitable for young learners. Alternatively, explore websites together as a class to share ideas about similarities and differences. For example:

- more images
- no page numbers
- clicking a link takes you to more information
- can scroll across or down.

Collate ideas.

Ask learners to look at the example in Activity 3 or at another animal webpage online. Ask: *Do you find any new similarities or differences?*

⟩ **Differentiation ideas:** Support learners by working with them to discuss a website.

Challenge learners to write their similarities and differences in a chart and to share their ideas with the class.

Plenary idea

What 'caught your eye'? (5–10 minutes)

Description: Explain to learners that if something catches your eye, it means you noticed it and found it interesting.

Ask learners to think for a minute about something that caught their eye in one of the contents pages they have been reading (print or online).

Encourage creative responses.

Science: Encourage learners to group living things, including animals, based on their similarities and differences.

Homework ideas

Learners complete the Workbook Session 8.3 activities if not completed in class.

They work with a family member to find a website about animals that they really like. Ask them to report back on why they liked it.

Answers for Workbook

1   **a** page 4; **b** page 14; **c** no

2   **a** 15; **b** tarantula spiders; **c** A big bug chart; **d** Learners' own responses

3   Learners' own questions

8.4 Writing a contents page

LEARNING PLAN

Learning objectives		Learning intentions	Success criteria
Main focus	**Also covered**	• To name parts of a book.	• Learners can name parts of a book.
1Rs.02, 1Rs.03, 1Wv.01,1Ws.02, 1Wc,04, 1Wp.05	1Rs.04, 1Ri.03, 1Ri.04, 1Ra.05, 1Ww.07, 1Wv.03, 1Wg.06, 1SLm.01, 1SLm.04	• To plan and write a contents page for a chosen topic. • To design a book cover.	• Learners can plan and write a contents page for a chosen topic. • Learners can design a book cover and create a class display.

LANGUAGE SUPPORT

Learners will benefit from handling books to reinforce the language of book features.

Show me … is a useful phrase to practise (See Getting started).

Check knowledge of useful vocabulary in this session: *jungle*, *desert* and *mountains*, and pre-teach if necessary.

Common misconception

Misconception	How to identify	How to overcome
Desert and *dessert* are pronounced the same and mean the same.	Write both words on the board. Ask learners: *Which is the place with sand?* (*desert*) *Which is the sweet thing you eat after dinner?* (*dessert*)	Model how to say both words with the stress falling either at the beginning or the end of the word: desert: **des**-ert dessert: dess-**ert** Model the use of each word in a sentence: *What is for dessert today?* *Did you choose the desert as your topic?*

Starter idea

Point to the parts of a book (10–15 minutes)

Resources: Learner's Book, Session 8.4: Getting started

Description: Ask learners to each hold a book and to listen.

Say: *Show me the … outside front cover / inside front cover / outside back cover / contents page / title,* etc.

As you do so, encourage learners to point to each feature.

Now ask learners to play the game again, in pairs.

Main teaching ideas

1 **Choose a topic for a contents page (10–15 minutes)**

   Learning intention: to choose a topic for a contents page

   Resources: Learner's Book, Session 8.4, Activity 1; large pieces of paper

   Description: Tell learners to re-read the contents page in Activity 1.

   Ask: *What other topic could you choose for a contents page? In the … jungle/desert/mountains/ forest/air?*

   Model how to create a mind map of words that link to a topic. Explain that these words could be used in a contents page for an information book about the topic.

Discuss different ways to organise the ideas for a contents list. For example:

- Jungle: *trees, plants, animals, dangers,* etc. or *monkeys, tigers, crocodiles,* etc.

- Desert: *sand, things that grow, animals,* etc. or *desert rats, camels, lizards, foxes,* etc.

- Mountains: *rocks, things that grow, temperature, animals,* etc. or *goats, snow leopards, sheep, marmots,* etc.

Working in pairs or groups, ask learners to choose a topic and write their list of words as you have done. They may wish to do this on a large piece of paper.

⟩ **Differentiation ideas:** Support learners by mixing up the pairs or groups.

Challenge some learners to choose their own topic.

Answers:
see Description

2 **Write and draw a contents page (20–30 minutes)**

   Learning intention: to write a contents page

   Resources: Learner's Book, Session 8.4, Activity 2; Workbook, Session 8.4; learners' topic words in Activity 1; A4 or A3 paper

   Description: Tell learners to look back at their topic words in Activity 1 and decide what they would like to include in their contents page.

Draw their attention to the Writing tips, which will support them in their writing.

You can use Workbook Session 8.4 in class, now, to help learners to practise organising ideas for a contents list.

You may wish learners to create their contents list on an A4 piece of paper or an A3 piece of paper folded in half. (See Activity 3 where they design their book cover for a display.)

Remind learners to use phonics where they can, to correctly spell the words. (See the Writing tip in Activity 1)

> **Differentiation ideas:** Support learners by working with them in a group to create a group contents page or ask them to work in pairs to create a contents page with fewer pages.

Challenge learners by asking them to think about the font they will use as well as their headings and layout.

Answers:
Learners' own responses

3 Design a book cover (10–15 minutes)

Learning intention: to design a book cover

Resources: Learner's Book, Session 8.4, Activity 3; a range of information books with exciting and varied cover designs; coloured pencils/crayons/paint

Description: Ask learners to design and draw a suitable cover for their topic and contents page.

If they have worked on an A4 or folded A3 sheet of paper for their contents page, they can now use the blank page they have left for their cover. If not, they can fix the cover to the contents page with glue or tape.

Where possible, create opportunities for learners to work in different media for their covers, including pencils, crayons, felt tips and paints.

Create a class display of the covers and contents pages. Ask learners to choose their favourite book cover and contents page.

> **Differentiation ideas:** Support learners by suggesting they create a draft sketch of the design

before they commit to their final piece of work. This will help with layout.

Challenge learners to experiment with fonts and sub-headings or star facts of additional information that can be found within the book, e.g. fun facts on each page!

Plenary idea

Play Animal Name Bingo (5–10 minutes)

Resources: empty bingo grids (3x3 boxes); paper or card; a bag

Description: Ask learners to work in pairs to write nine animal names on their bingo cards. Then ask them to write the same names in a list and cut up the list (so each piece of paper has the name of an animal).

Put the cut-up words from each pair in a bag and mix them up.

Then ask learners to swap their card with another pair.

Pick out words from the bag and call them out. Learners should cross out any matching words on their card.

The winners are the first pair to cross out all their words.

CROSS-CURRICULAR LINKS

Science: Explore creating contents pages for other science topics, e.g. materials, or Planet Earth.

Art: Explore the creation of contents pages in other subject areas. Can learners create a contents page for a history or geography book?

Homework ideas

Learners complete the Workbook Session 8.4 activities if not completed in class.

They practise writing numbers 1–25 neatly.

Answers for Workbook

1 Learners' own ideas and drawings

2 Learners' own responses (but not gardening and probably not food or weather)

3 and 4 Learners' own ideas and drawings

8.5 Exploring pictures and captions

LEARNING PLAN

Learning objectives		Learning intentions	Success criteria
Main focus	**Also covered**	• To explore pictures and photos.	• Learners can explore pictures and photos.
1Rv.01, 1Rs.04, 1Ri.08, 1Wc.04, 1Wp.05	1Rv.02, 1Rv.03, 1Rg.02, 1Rs.02, 1Ri.01, 1Ri.03, 1Ri.04, 1Ra.03, 1Wv.01, 1Wv.03, 1Wg.01, 1Wg.04, 1Wg.06, 1SLm.03, 1SLs.02, 1SLg.02, 1SLg.03, 1SLg.04, 1SLp.01	• To listen to captions and match to photos. • To read and write captions.	• Learners can listen to captions and match to photos. • Learners can read and write captions.

LANGUAGE SUPPORT

Check vocabulary and knowledge of pictures – black and white, coloured, photos, illustrations, cartoon, clip art, etc. – and pre-teach if necessary.

Ensure that there are captions in the classroom so that learners can see their use in an authentic context.

Practise writing sentences with capital letters and full stops.

Common misconception

Misconception	How to identify	How to overcome
–tions is pronounced: *–tie-ons*. *–ture* is pronounced: *–tyor*.	Ask learners to read the word *caption*. Do they say: *cap-tie-on*? Or *cap-shun*? [correct] Repeat with *picture*. Do they say: *pic-tyor*? Or *pic-chur*? [correct] Do they know other words ending in these letters? (*information, adventure*)	Make a class list / working wall of other words learners may know or find that end in *–tion* or *–ure*. They may find these a useful reminder when reading or spelling.

Starter idea

Drawings and photos (20–30 minutes)

Resources: Learner's Book, Session 8.5: Getting started; a variety of information books; a range of illustration styles to share (either in print or online)

Description: Provide groups with up to three non-fiction information books. Ask them to talk about the pictures.

After 5 minutes, ask groups of learners to say what they noticed about the pictures and what they preferred.

See how many learners are able to use precise language relating to pictures, e.g. *illustrations*, *photographs*, *colour* or *black and white*.

Draw learners' attention to the examples in Getting started. Discuss these in a similar way, modelling the correct language.

Ask learners to tell you how each picture might be used in a book (its function). Talk about how the way an illustration is used affects the type of illustration it is (e.g. cartoony, life-like, etc.).

Ask learners to reflect on whether they prefer to look at a photo or a drawing and to say why.

Main teaching ideas

 1 Listen and point (10–15 minutes)

Learning intention: to listen to captions and point to the matching photos

Resources: *Captions about crabs* (Learner's Book, Session 8.5, Activity 1); Track 52

Description: Ask learners what they know already about crabs. Try to elicit some of their previous knowledge and rehearse some of the vocabulary.

Tell learners to listen carefully to an information text about crabs.

Show them the photos in Activity 1 and ask them to listen and point to the matching picture.

You may wish to repeat and model correct pointing as you do so.

> **Differentiation ideas:** Support learners by working with them in a group and modelling pointing and/ or pause the audio to give them time to work out the answer.

Challenge learners by asking them to say their own captions for each picture.

> **Audioscript: *Captions about crabs***
>
> Listen to these captions. Point to the correct picture or photo.
>
> Some crabs are big and some crabs are very small.
>
> The claws are bigger than the other legs.
>
> This crab is eating a jellyfish.
>
> This crab lives on land.

Answers:

The photos in the Learner's Book match the following captions, but note that other answers are possible. Encourage learners to explain their answers.

a   The claws are bigger than the other legs.

b   This crab is eating a jellyfish.

c   Some crabs are big and some crabs are very small.

d   This crab lives on land.

2   Read captions (15–20 minutes)

Learning intention: to read captions and draw matching pictures

Resources: Learner's Book, Session 8.5, Activity 2; Phonics Workbook B; pictures of a giraffe, butterfly, shark and jellyfish

Description: Show learners pictures of a giraffe, butterfly, shark and jelly fish to check vocabulary.

Phonics (Phonics Workbook B, pages 12–13, 40–41, 50–51, 52–53): these deal with some of the grapheme-phoneme correspondences raised in the Learner's Book:

- g in *giraffe* is /j/ not hard /g/.

- *flower* can be split as /f/ /l/ /ow/ /er/ (unstressed *er*)

- *shark* can be split as /sh/ /ar/ /k/.

- *sea* and *deep* both have the /ee/ sound but are spelt differently.

Note the difference between:

- *butterfly* – two words to make one (compound)
- *jelly fish* – two words with a space.

Ask learners to write the captions and draw matching pictures.

⟩ **Differentiation ideas:** Support learners by asking them to choose one picture and write one caption each within a group.

Challenge learners to write another sentence for each picture.

Answers:
Learners' own drawings to represent the captions they have read and copied

3 Write captions (20–30 minutes)

Learning intention: to write captions

Resources: Learner's Book, Session 8.5, Activity 3; Workbook, Session 8.5; Phonics Workbook B; funny animal pictures to share

Description: Show learners the pictures in Activity 3 of a panda, monkeys, penguins and a bear to check vocabulary.

Together, look at a funny animal picture. Model how to write a caption for the picture, drawing learners' attention to the capital letter and full stop.

You can use the Workbook Session 8.5 in class now, to explore using captions further.

- *Panda* finishes in an /ugh/ sound (unstressed vowel) and not /a/.
- *Monkey* has an /o/ that we need to say as /u/ – we say *munkee*.
- The *ui* in *penguins* is tricky to read – we say *pengwins*.
- The *ear* in *bear* sounds like /air/.

For further practice of these trickier grapheme-phoneme correspondences, see Phonic Workbook B, pages 34–35, 52–53, but teach ui as /w/ and ear as /air/ as exceptions.

Ask learners to write their own captions for each photo.

As you circulate, support them with spelling as well as checking sentence punctuation and handwriting.

⟩ **Differentiation ideas:** Support learners by building a word bank with them first so they may use it to write their captions.

Challenge learners to check each other's handwriting and punctuation, too.

Answers:
Learners' own captions, matching the photos

Plenary idea

Caption it! (5–10 minutes)

Resources: a selection of pictures of animals

Description: Give each pair of learners a picture or photo.

Ask them to say a caption for their photo before they leave the classroom.

CROSS-CURRICULAR LINKS

Art: Explore how photos and illustrations are used in other subject areas. Ask: *Are photos used when we learn about events in history?*

Homework ideas

Learners complete the Workbook Session 8.5 activities if not completed in class.

They ask a family member to help them look online or in a book or magazine to find some unusual or dramatic animal photos (e.g. *National Geographic Kids*).

Answers for Workbook

1 Pictures joined to matching captions
2 Learners' own captions
3 Learners' own responses

8.6 Exploring topic words

LEARNING PLAN

Learning objectives		Learning intentions	Success criteria
Main focus	**Also covered**	• To explore topic words.	• Learners can explore topic words.
1Rv.01, 1Rv.02, 1Rv.03, 1Ri.05, 1Ri.13, 1Wv.01	1Rw.06, 1Rg. 03, 1Ri.08, 1Ri.09, 1Ri.11, 1Ww.06, 1Ww.07, 1Wv.03, 1Wp.04, 1Wp.05, 1SLm.02, 1SLm.03, 1SLs.02, 1SLg.03	• To listen to, read and answer questions about information that includes topic words. • To explore the use of pictures as icons.	• Learners can listen to, read and answer questions about information that includes topic words. • Learners can explore the use of pictures as icons.

LANGUAGE SUPPORT

Check knowledge and vocabulary of plants, fish, meat and the habitats of the rainforest, mountains, seas, ice lands and deserts, or pre-teach these if necessary.

Encourage learners to make their own topic charts (words and/or pictures) to help them remember topic words they may need later for writing.

Common misconception

Misconception	How to identify	How to overcome
Words with two syllables are always compound words.	Ask learners to talk about the words: • *rainforest* • *mountains*. Ask learners which words have two syllables and which are compound words (made up of two words).	Show learners that: • *rain* and *forest* are both words on their own • *mount* is a word on its own, but *–ain* is not. As they read and write, remind learners that splitting words in this way may help with decoding and spelling.

Starter idea

Talking about diet (10–20 minutes)

Resources: Learner's Book, Session 8.6: Getting started; Workbook, Session 8.6

Description: Ask if learners know what *diet* means. If necessary, clarify that it is the food we eat. Talk with learners about their diet. Ask: *What do you eat and what do you avoid?*

Use learners' knowledge and experience to reinforce what makes a healthy diet.

Draw simple picture icons on the board to represent plants, fish and meat. Ask learners what they mean.

Ask learners to match the pictures in Getting started to the correct labels.

Explain that for any topic there are special words, and that we call these 'topic words'. Give the example of *diet* as a topic word we would use in an animal topic. (We would talk about what animals eat.)

You can use the Workbook Session 8.6 activities in class now.

Main teaching ideas

1 Learn about the diet of baby animals (15–20 minutes)

Learning intention: to listen to and read information sentences

Resources: Baby animals (Learner's Book, Session 8.6, Activity 1); Track 53

Description: Tell learners they are going to listen to a short text. It gives information about the diets of baby animals (what they eat).

Play the audio or read the sentences aloud.

As they listen, ask learners to point to each word to follow the text.

Point out the change from singular *baby* to plural *babies*. Can learners remember other words that change in the same way? (*story* → *stories*)

Ask for volunteers to read the sentences aloud, paying attention to capital letters and full stops.

Ask learners to identify the animal diet topic words. See words underlined in the sentences that follow.

> What are <u>baby animal diets</u> like?
>
> Some <u>baby animals</u> only eat <u>meat</u> or <u>fish.</u>
>
> Other <u>animal babies</u> only eat <u>plants</u>.
>
> Many <u>animal babies</u> like to eat <u>meat</u> and <u>plants</u>!

⟩ **Differentiation ideas:** Support learners by sitting with a group and modelling, pointing to the words as they listen.

Challenge learners to read aloud with expression.

2 Answer questions (20–30 minutes)

Learning intention: to answer questions to show understanding

Resources: Learner's Book, Session 8.6, Activity 2; text and pictures in Activity 1

Description: Together, read the questions in Activity 2.

Ask learners to write the answers to the questions in their notebooks. The text is short, but learners need to work with both text and picture information (in Activity 1) to answer the questions correctly.

Ask learners to write a sentence about a different animal and what it eats.

⟩ **Differentiation ideas:** Support learners by allowing them to write only the diet words, rather than full sentences.

Challenge learners to think what other animal photos they could show for each type of diet, e.g. polar bears and blue whales (meat), deer (plants), raccoons (both). Ask them to find out the definitions of *carnivore*, *herbivore* and *omnivore*.

Answers:

a   Baby tigers eat meat or fish.

b   Baby elephants eat only plants.

c   Baby bears eat meat and plants.

3 The topic word *habitat* (20–30 minutes)

Learning intention: to learn and use a topic word

Resources: Learner's Book, Session 8.6, Activity 3

Description: Use the Writing tip to discuss the idea of topic words.

Ask if anyone knows what the topic word *habitat* means (where animals live). Ask: *What animal habitats do you know?* Share ideas and experiences.

Ask learners if they live in or near these kinds of habitats. Ask: *Do you know any other habitats?*

Look at the pictures and labels in Activity 3. Together, match the habitat pictures to the labels.

Draw learners' attention to the Reading tip and model how to use their phonics to work out some or parts of these topic words:

• Phonics – /m/ /ou/ /n/ /t/ /ai/ /n/, *ce* in *ice* is pronounced /s/, *s* in *desert* is pronounced /z/.

• Point out that *rainforest* is a compound words (two words together make one word).

Ask learners to draw and write the habitats in their notebooks.

> **Differentiation ideas:** Support learners by reworking the phonic examples with them in a group.

Challenge learners to think of any other habitats, e.g. grasslands, towns/cities, lakes/ponds.

Answers:
Learners match picture icons to the correct labels.

Plenary idea

Play 10 Questions (5–10 minutes)

Description: Ask a learner to choose an animal.

Other learners must try to work out the chosen animal by asking yes/no questions only (encourage the use of topic words including *diet* and *habitat*).

They may have no more than three guesses based on the information.

Repeat with different learners.

Homework ideas

Learners complete the Workbook Session 8.6 activities if not completed in class.

They find out special names for collections of animals, e.g. *a pride of lions* and *a school of fish*.

Answers for Workbook

1   Learners' own drawings
2   Learners' correct labelling
3   Learners' own responses
4   Learners' own responses

8.7 Exploring a glossary

LEARNING PLAN

Learning objectives		Learning intentions	Success criteria
Main focus	**Also covered**	• To explore how a glossary helps us with word meanings.	• Learners can explore how a glossary helps us with word meanings.
1Rv.01, 1Rs.04, 1Ri.04, 1Ri.08, 1Wv.03, 1Ws.02, 1Wc.04	1Rw.05, 1Rw.07, 1Rv.03, 1Rg.03, 1Rg.06, 1Rs.02, 1Ri.03, 1Ww.02, 1SLs.01, 1SLg.01, 1SLg.04, 1SLp.04	• To create a picture glossary. • To listen to and read a report that includes a glossary.	• Learners can create a picture glossary. • Learners can listen to and read a report that includes a glossary.

LANGUAGE SUPPORT

Ensure learners understand that words have meanings (and sometimes more than one meaning; see Session 8.4 Common misconception).

Make a physical paper word chain (that can continue to grow throughout the unit).

Play games that require learners to match words to meanings.

Common misconception

Misconception	How to identify	How to overcome
When we see words in colour or in blackened print, it means we have to shout them.	Ask learners to look at a text that has words that are emboldened or highlighted in some way. Ask them what it means.	Show them how this styling can mean different things, but usually it is drawing your attention to a word for a reason. In this unit, it means there are glossary terms that help us to understand word meanings. Look out for other examples in texts when teaching, e.g. when used for emphasis, and return to this misconception to remind learners why, as necessary.

Starter idea

Word-chain (10–15 minutes)

Resources: Learner's Book, Session 8.7: Getting started

Description: Explain to learners that they are going to play a game to create topic word-chains.

Show learners the example in Getting Started.

Before you play, tell learners they will need to think quickly once a topic has been chosen.

Start by calling out a topic word about animals. As each learner joins the chain, they must say a different word connected to the last, but it should still be about animals!

Play several times and see how far you can get to really test learners' use of vocabulary.

Main teaching ideas

1 Read a picture glossary (20–30 minutes)

Learning intention: to explore a labelled picture/picture glossary

Resources: Learner's Book, Session 8.7, Activity 1; Workbook, Session 8.7; large crab picture and labels

Description: Remind learners of the text about crabs in Session 8.5 (Activity 1). Explain that they are now going to find out some special words about the crab.

Show learners the labelled photo in Activity 1. Discuss the fact that it is a photograph and that the parts are labelled.

Ask pairs of learners to talk about the labels and how the photo helps them to understand some of the words.

Ask learners to draw the crab or another creature with a shell. Alternatively, you can use the Workbook Session 8.7 activities now.

> **Differentiation ideas:** Support learners by providing labels and a crab picture, and asking them to label it as a group.

Challenge learners to list other animals with a shell.

2 Listen to and read a report (10–15 minutes)

Learning intention: to identify topic words in a report

Resources: *Barn owls* (Learner's Book, Session 8.7, Activity 2); Track 54

Description: Tell learners they are going to listen to a report about barn owls. Specifically, ask pairs to listen out for topic words they do not know or understand.

Play the audio or read the report aloud.

Ask learners to share any topic words they did not understand, e.g. *barn(s)*, *owlets*, *hatch*, *down*.

Give pairs a limited time to then read the report together so they can see that some words are emboldened. Ask them to talk about the words they do not know and to try to work out their meanings.

As you circulate, encourage learners to use their phonics knowledge to practise decoding words, drawing their attention to the Reading tip if necessary.

> **Differentiation ideas:** Support learners by pairing confident and less confident readers.

Challenge learners to ask each other questions about the text.

3 Use a simple glossary (20–30 minutes)

Learning intention: to understand how to use a glossary

Resources: Learner's Book, Session 8.7, Activity 3; word cards (optional)

Description: Tell learners they are going to learn about a glossary in this activity. Tell them what a glossary is and/or draw their attention to the key word box in Activity 3.

Play a quick game. Tell learners that you will try to explain some difficult words for them – just like a glossary does.

Say: *Ask me what a chameleon is,* to get them started, or create and hand out some word cards so you are prepared for the definitions required.

Provide a simple definition of each word you are given.

Now, ask learners to find the emboldened words in the report in Activity 2.

Then, together, find the words and their meanings in the glossary in Activity 3 to show how it works.

> **Differentiation ideas:** Support learners by talking with them in a group about the word meanings. Ask: *Can you use the words in a sentence?*

Challenge learners to first find a verb in the glossary and then to choose a word from the text and write a glossary definition for it.

Plenary idea

Find your partner (5–10 minutes)

Resources: words and definition cards cut into two (based on topic words); Worksheet 8.1

Description: Cut out (or ask learners to cut out) the cards from Worksheet 8.1 Find your pair.

Give out the cards. Ask learners to find their matching word or word meaning before they can leave the classroom.

Homework ideas

Learners complete the Workbook Session 8.7 activities if not completed in class.

They write lists of words that end in –*tch* (like *hatch*) or feature –*ow* (like *owl* and *down*) and a word that rhymes with *feather* (*weather*).

Answers for Workbook

1   Learners' correctly join matching animals to make a picture word chain.

2   Learners' correctly label: eyes, stalk, claw, leg and shell

3   Learners' own sentences to explain the meanings of eyes, stalk, claw, leg and shell

8.8 Exploring a dictionary

LEARNING PLAN

Learning objectives		Learning intentions	Success criteria
Main focus	**Also covered**		
1Rw.01, 1Rv.04, 1Rs.04,1Ri.04, 1Wc.04, 1Wp.05	1Rv.03, 1Rg.06, 1Rg.07, 1Ri.03, 1Ri.08, 1Ww.01, 1Ww.05, 1Ww.07, 1Wg.06, 1SLg.04, 1SLp.01	• To know there are 26 letters in the alphabet. • To explore how a dictionary helps us with word meanings. • To read and write a dictionary page.	• Learners know there are 26 letters in the alphabet. • Learners can explore how a dictionary helps us with word meanings. • Learners can read and write a dictionary page.

Show learners examples of 'first' dictionaries and model their use. Rehearse the alphabet (names and letter sounds) by singing songs and chanting.

Common misconception

Misconception	How to identify	How to overcome
If there are words with *zz* then you must be able to write words with *xx* and *yy*.	Ask learners to read the words *buzz, whizz, fizzy.* Ask them if they can think of any words that feature *xx* or *yy*. (There aren't any in English.)	Remind learners that many consonants can appear in words as double letters, but not *x* or *y* (and not *hh, jj, kk, qq* or *ww*). Consider making a class poster to summarise this learning message for reference during writing work.

Starter idea

The alphabet and numbers (10–15 minutes)

Resources: Learner's Book, Session 8.8: Getting started

Description: Ask learners to chant the alphabet. Invite solo or paired performances, too.

Remind learners that there are 26 letters in the alphabet, including five vowels.

Play a game asking questions about the 26 letters of the alphabet.

Main teaching ideas

1 A dictionary page (20–30 minutes)

Learning intention: to explore a dictionary page

Resources: Learner's Book, Session 8.8, Activity 1; Workbook, Session 8.8; Phonics Workbook A; a collection of simple dictionaries and/or access to an online dictionary

Description: Together, look at a collection of first dictionaries (usually illustrated) and agree what a dictionary is and does. Include online dictionaries if you can.

Model how to use a dictionary to look up a word.

Ask: *What is the difference between a glossary and a dictionary?* (A glossary is at the end of a text to help you understand words in a text, a dictionary is just a book of words and their meanings in A–Z order.) Draw learners' attention to the Key word text in Activity 1.

Together, read the dictionary page for X, Y and Z in Activity 1. Talk about the word entries with learners.

Draw learners' attention to the use of *a*, *an* and *the*. Can learners remember when they are each used? (*a*: for one of many; *an*: for one of many for words beginning with a vowel; *the*: for just one). Ask learners to find examples of these in the dictionary text.

You can use the Workbook Session 8.8 activities now, to practise using alphabetical order.

Phonics (Phonics Workbook A, pages 6–7, 28–31, 64)): you can link to phonics here by checking learners are using the correct letter names and sounds for *x*, *y* and *z* (*x* is /k/ /s/, y is /y/ and z is /z/).

> **Differentiation ideas:** Support learners by asking them to just look at one letter entry on the dictionary page.

Challenge learners to add a new word for each of the letters *x*, *y* and *z*.

2 Answer questions by using a dictionary page (20–30 minutes)

Learning intention: to use a dictionary page to identify features and find word meanings

Resources: Learner's Book, Session 8.8, Activity 2

Description: Together, read and answer the questions in Activity 2.

Model how to find the dictionary entries (using the initial letter and picture clues) and then, together, read each of the entries to answer the questions.

Encourage further questioning or group work using any age-appropriate class dictionaries you have found.

> **Differentiation ideas:** Support learners by working with them as a group to ask questions about the dictionary page.

Challenge learners to ask and answer questions about the page or to use other full picture dictionaries.

Answers:
a   A worm is a living creature with no legs that lives in the ground.

b   A yolk is the yellow part of an egg.

c   A zebra is an animal that looks like a horse with black and white stripes on its body.

d   It is an X-ray

3   **Write a dictionary page (20–30 minutes)**
Learning intention: to write a dictionary page using a model

Resources: Learner's Book, Session 8.8, Activity 3; Worksheet 8.2

Description: Tell learners they are going to write their own dictionary page.

Ask them to choose a letter. They should then use the layout and features shown in the example in Activity 1 (a large letter at the top, letter headings in bold or big letters, a description of each word and a picture for each word entry) to create their dictionary page.

> **Differentiation ideas:** Support learners to first create a letter *Z* dictionary page using Worksheet 8.2 Writing a dictionary page, and then add their own *Z* word if they can.

Challenge learners to create a second dictionary page choosing a different letter.

Answers:
Learners' own responses

Plenary idea

Find your partner (5–10 minutes)
Description: Say a letter.

Ask learners in pairs to think of a word beginning with that letter.

Ask learners to give a definition for that word.

Learners may leave the classroom.

Homework ideas

Learners complete the Workbook Session 8.8 activities if not completed in class.

They write three words in a list and look them up in a dictionary to find their meanings.

Answers for Workbook

1   Missing letters in the snake pattern: b, c, e, f, h, i, k, l, n, o, q, r, t, u, w, x, z

2   Words joined correctly to their first letters: b: bee, c: camel, e: elephant, f: fox, o: owl

3   bee, camel, elephant, fox, owl

8.9 Exploring a fact file

LEARNING PLAN

Learning objectives		Learning intentions	Success criteria
Main focus	**Also covered**	• To listen to, read and talk about a fact file.	• Learners can read and talk about a fact file.
1Rv.01, 1Rs.02, 1Ri.04, 1Ri.05, 1Wc.04, 1Wp.05	1Rw.01, 1Rw.04, 1Rw.06, 1Rw.07, 1Rv.02, 1Rv.03, 1Rg.03, 1Rg.05, 1Rg.06, 1Rs.04, 1Ri.08, 1Ra.01, 1Ww.02, 1Ww.07, 1Wv.01, 1Wv.03, 1Wg.02, 1Ws.02, 1SLs.02, 1SLg.03, 1SLg.04	• To identify true statements to show understanding. • To write a fact file.	• Learners can identify true statements to show understanding. • Learners can write a fact file.

LANGUAGE SUPPORT

Check that learners understand what a fact is and the idea of a fact file. Ask learners to give three facts about themselves, their school, etc.

Play phonics games to reinforce digraphs and different spellings for the same sounds.

Check vocabulary and pre-teach where necessary, e.g. *webbed feet, hooked beak, black and white fur/feathers.*

Common misconception

Misconception	How to identify	How to overcome
It is confusing when a word has more than one meaning.	Ask learners what the word *web* means to them. (They may say: *world wide web, spider web* or the *webbed foot of a duck.*) Ask learners if these multiple meanings are confusing. Ask: *If you were looking at a book about ducks, would you really think a webbed foot was something to do with a spider's web?*	Tell learners that, when they hear or read a word that has more than one meaning, they should stop to think about what meaning makes sense for the topic they are reading about.

Starter idea

Animal features (10–15 minutes)

Resources: Learner's Book, Session 8.9: Getting started; small model animals; picture of a penguin

Description: Use any class displays or picture collections to talk about the features of animals and special vocabulary. You may also use small model animals as in previous sessions.

Pre-teach vocabulary where necessary as in Language support and Common misconception.

Look at a picture of a penguin. Describe its features with learners.

Ask what animals have similar features. Share ideas and find out what learners already know.

Look at the photos and text labels in Getting started and discuss them.

Together establish what each animal has in common with the penguin (webbed feet, a curved beak, black and white colouring).

Draw learners' attention to the Reading tip which reminds learners to use phonics to help them to read eagle, duck and panda.

Main teaching ideas

1 Listen and read a fact file (15–30 minutes)

Learning intention: to listen to and read a fact file

Resources: *Emperor penguins* (Learner's Book, Session 8.9, Activity 1); Track 55; Workbook, Session 8.9; Language worksheets 8A and 8B

Description: Tell learners they are going to listen to some facts about Emperor penguins. Explain that we call this kind of information a fact file.

Tell learners to first listen and point to each labelled part of the penguin as they hear it. Play the audio or read the fact file aloud.

Ask what they learned. Invite learners to share what they heard and understood.

Then repeat, this time asking them to point to the headings and pictures in Activity 1 as they listen.

Discuss anything they notice before finally asking them to read the fact file together in pairs.

You can use the Workbook Session 8.9 activities now for phonics and sequencing practice.

You can use Language worksheets 8A and 8B now for practice of verb endings and listening for nouns.

> **Differentiation ideas:** Support learners by working with them as they listen and point so you can guide them, or by pairing readers with different strengths so they can help each other.

Challenge learners to read the text aloud to the class or share any other fun facts they know.

2 True or false (10–15 minutes)

Learning intention: to show understanding of a fact file

Resources: Learner's Book, Session 8.9, Activity 2

Description: Make a statement about penguins, e.g. *Penguins have black and white fur like a panda.* Ask: *Is that true or false?* (false because they have feathers not fur).

Say a few more true or false statements and then ask learners to read those in Activity 2 and write their response in their notebooks in two lists (one list for true and one list for false).

> **Differentiation ideas:** Support learners by modelling how to check back to the fact file before they answer.

Challenge learners to write their own true/false statements about the Emperor penguin.

Answers:
a True; **b** False; **c** False; **d** True; **e** True

3 Write a fact file (20–30 minutes)

Learning intention: to write a fact file

Resources: Learner's Book, Session 8.9, Activity 3; Worksheet 8.3

Description: Tell learners they are going to write their own fact file. Explain that they may choose an animal of their choice, but they must know some facts about it.

Encourage learners to plan by roughly drawing their chosen animal and listing or labelling what they already know about it, and also what they would need to find out about it. They may need support with online searching or using animal books to help them find out their missing knowledge.

Remind them that the Emperor penguins fact file included:

- a heading and opening statement
- information about habitat and diet
- seven labels
- four fun facts
- two words in the glossary.

You can provide Worksheet 8.3 Writing a fact file if a template is helpful.

> **Differentiation ideas:** Support learners by asking them to work in small groups or to use Worksheet 8.3 Writing a fact file.

Challenge learners to choose an animal that is very different from the penguin and so requires new facts – even some research.

Answers:
Learners' own responses

Plenary idea

Find reasons to pair (5–10 minutes)

Resources: animal picture cards

Description: Hand out the animal picture cards to all learners.

Ask them to find a partner with an animal who has a similar feature.

Encourage pairs to explain why they are similar, e.g. *Both our animals have long ears / webbed feet / are black and white.*

Other learners can decide if the reason given is good enough.

Continue until everyone has paired up or time runs out!

CROSS-CURRICULAR LINKS

Science: Explore how humans are similar and different to each other.

Homework ideas

Learners complete the Workbook Session 8.9 activities if not completed in class.

They make a model (2D or 3D) of an animal and label its features.

Answers for Workbook

1 **a** fox; **b** seal; **c** duck
2 **a** panda bear; **b** Emperor penguin; **c** golden eagle
3 Learners' own responses
4 **a** They cannot fly. **b** They have webbed feet for fast swimming. **c** They have strong claws for gripping the ice.

8.10 Exploring a report

LEARNING PLAN

Learning objectives		Learning intentions	Success criteria
Main focus	**Also covered**	• To listen to, read and talk about a report. • To answer questions to show understanding. • To identify report features.	• Learners can listen to, read and talk about a report. • Learners can answer questions to show understanding. • Learners can identify report features.
1Rg.03, 1Rs.02, 1Ri.04, 1Ri.05, 1Ri.08	1Rw.07, 1Rg.01, 1Rg.02, 1Rg.04, 1Rg.06, 1Rg.07, 1Rs.04, 1Ri.13, 1Ra.01, 1Ww.07, 1Wv.01, 1Wv.03, 1Wg.01, 1Ws.02, 1Wc.04, 1Wp.05, 1SLs.02, 1SLg.03, 1SLg.04		

LANGUAGE SUPPORT

Check learners' knowledge of ice land creatures and pre-teach if necessary.	Encourage learners where possible to play with ice (especially if this is not common where you live).

Common misconception

Misconception	How to identify	How to overcome
Saying each letter sound aloud always helps us to read words.	Ask learners to read the word *the*. Ask: *Did you use phonics or did you just recognise the word?* They may say that they recognised that *th* is /th/, but then they realised you do not have to say the sound for letter *e* in *the*.	Continue to model the way in which experienced readers try out different options to work out how to read a word, often drawing on their phonics knowledge for parts of the word.

Starter idea

Ice land animals (10–15 minutes)

Resources: Learner's Book, Session 8.10: Getting started

Description: Ask learners to say what they now know about the habitats we call 'ice lands'.

How many animals can they name that live in ice lands? (seal, polar bear, arctic fox, penguin …)

Look at the pictures in Getting started. Talk about them and name them together.

Why do learners think these animals look white? (They are camouflaged to keep them safe.)

Main teaching ideas

1 **Listen to and read a report (20–30 minutes)**

   Learning intention: to listen to and read a report

   Resources: Harp seal (Learner's Book, Session 8.10, Activity 1); Track 56; Workbook, Session 8.10

   Description: Show learners the picture of the baby seal in Getting started.

   Tell them to listen to a report about harp seals. Play the audio or read the report aloud.

   Ask learners to share some facts they heard.

   Now ask learners to listen again, following the text, before reading the report on their own or in pairs.

Draw their attention to the Language focus box. If necessary, explain or remind them that common words are words that we use often (*the, for, a, is, they, are, on, her, about, she, then, away, have, to, that, and, off*).

Draw learners' attention to the How are we doing? prompt about reading common words. Ask: *How easily can you read common words now? Which common words do you still find difficult?*

You can use the Workbook Session 8.10 activities now.

> **Differentiation ideas:** Support learners by modelling how to follow a listening text by pointing to the words.

Challenge learners to say how they think they could improve the report, e.g. a longer caption or more sub-headings.

2 **Answer questions (15–20 minutes)**

   Learning intention: to answer questions to show understanding

   Resources: Learner's Book, Session 8.10, Activity 2; Differentiated worksheets 8A–C; report from Activity 1

   Description: Together, read the report in Activity 1 again if necessary.

Together, read the questions in Activity 2 and answer them. Learners can then write the answers in their notebooks if you wish.

You can use Differentiated worksheets 8A–C now for further comprehension practice.

> **Differentiation ideas:** Support learners by working with them in a group, or asking them to work on just questions a–c.

Challenge learners to pose further questions about the report, and to find out what a male seal is called (a bull).

Answers:

a   A pup

b   For 12 days

c   Fish

d   Ice lands or on ice, snow or in seas

e   pup, cow (most likely)

3   Find features (10–15 minutes)

Learning intention: to identify report features

Resources: Learner's Book, Session 8.10, Activity 3

Description: Ask learners to work in pairs to look again at the report in Activity 1 and then find the features listed.

> **Differentiation ideas:** Support learners by asking them to find a few of the features rather than all of them.

Challenge learners to write the list of features they find first and then check against the features listed in Activity 3.

Answers:
headings, icons, photos, labels, captions, fact box and sentences that give facts

Plenary idea

Watch an online video (5–10 minutes)

Resources: a short Arctic/Antarctic documentary online

Description: Play a short online documentary about the Arctic and the Antarctic.

Encourage feedback and comments from learners.

Homework ideas

Learners complete the Workbook Session 8.10 activities if not completed in class.

They find an amazing animal fact and an amazing way to tell it.

Answers for Workbook

1   **a** of; **b** are; **c** her; **d** she

2   **a** to; **b** they; **c** away/off

3   have, are, they; called, Some, with; is, and, when

8.11 Planning and writing a report

LEARNING PLAN			
Learning objectives		**Learning intentions**	**Success criteria**
Main focus	**Also covered**	• To create a chart of report features.	• Learners can create a chart of report features.
1Wv.03, 1Ws.02, 1Wc.04	1Rs.02, 1Rs.04, 1Ri.04, 1Wv.02, 1Wg.01, 1Wp.05, 1SLm.01, 1SLm.02, 1SLs.01, 1SLg.04	• To plan a report.	• Learners can plan a report.
		• To write a report.	• Learners can write a report.

LANGUAGE SUPPORT

Provide opportunities for learners to read more reports about their favourite animals.

Revisit the language of information books and ensure there is no confusion with other non-fiction formats explored in previous units (recounts, instructions).

Encourage learners to continue to use posters or displays / working walls created during the unit to support them in their reading and writing.

Common misconception

Misconception	How to identify	How to overcome
What someone thinks is always a fact.	Tell learners that you think baby penguins love the sunshine. Ask them if what you have said is a fact. *Is it true? Or is it what you think?* Discuss the differences between something that is a fact (true) and something that is an opinion (someone's own view, which may not be true).	Encourage learners to question what they read in information books. Ask: *How do we know something is a fact?* Some books give lots of information to help us believe the facts. Tell learners to ask themselves: *How can we check?*

Starter idea

Features chart (10–15 minutes)

Resources: Learner's Book, Session 8.11: Getting started; Workbook, Session 8.11; learners' lists of features from Session 8.10 Activity 3

Description: Ask learners to remember all the things they noticed about the report in Learner's Book Session 8.10 Activity 1 – their lists of features from Session 8.10 Activity 3.

Show them the chart in Getting started. Talk about it together.

As you do this, ask learners to point to the chart together and to answer yes or no. Ask: *Do you want to add anything else to this chart of features?*

Explain that information reports:

- do not tell a story
- have clear headings
- give facts
- highlight and explain topic words in a glossary

- do not list things you need
- have pictures or photos with captions.

You can use the Workbook Session 8.11 activities now.

Main teaching ideas

1 **Write a features chart (20–30 minutes)**

Learning intention: to create a features chart and list the features of a report

Resources: Learner's Book, Session 8.11, Activity 1

Description: Tell learners they will now write their own features chart for a report. They will use this as a checklist later when they review their own report writing.

Ask learners to work in pairs to draw and write features to include in their chart. They can refer to the chart in Getting started, but encourage them to add their own ideas, too.

As you circulate, support and challenge learners.

Ask a few learners to share their ideas.

You can use the Workbook 8.11 activities now.

> Differentiation ideas: Support learners by re-using Worksheet 5.4 Features of a recipe and adapting it, if they would benefit from this structure.

Challenge learners to write a version like the chart in Getting started with some false statements and then ask them to share it with the class and see who can spot the mistakes.

Answers:
Learners charts, similar to the chart in Getting started, but with some of learners' own ideas, too.

2 Plan a report (15–20 minutes)

Learning intention: to plan a report

Resources: Learner's Book, Session 8.11, Activity 2; animal web pages and/or information books; sheets of paper (optional)

Description: Tell learners they are going to plan their own animal report.

Draw their attention to the planning questions in Activity 2 and discuss them together.

Talk about how learners can find more facts if they need them. Support them to use websites and/or to use information books.

Ask learners to write their ideas in their notebooks or on a sheet of paper.

> Differentiation ideas: Support learners by proving information about two or three animals for them to choose from.

Challenge learners to present their plans to the class to make their ideas clear. This will support other learners, too.

Answers:
Learners' own ideas

3 Write the report (20–30 minutes)

Learning intention: to write a report

Resources: Learner's Book, Session 8.11, Activity 3; Worksheet 8.4; learners' features charts from Activity 1 and plans from Activity 2; images of animals

Description: Tell learners they now need to write their report.

Remind them to use their features charts from Activity 1 and planning sheets from Activity 2.

Draw their attention to the headings in Activity 3 and encourage them to use these as a guide for their own report.

Give learners time to work on their reports and circulate to support these with spelling and presentation.

> Differentiation ideas: Support learners by providing Worksheet 8.4 Writing a report as a report template and working with them, modelling how to use their features list and planning sheet.

Challenge learners to write their report without the worksheet, by choosing their own layout and headings.

Answers:
Learners' own reports

Plenary idea

True or false? (5–10 minutes)

Resources: fact cards (some true and some obviously made up)

Description: Ask a learner to pick a card and read it aloud.

The learner should say if they think the statement is true or false.

The rest of the class decides if they agree.

Repeat with different cards and learners.

Homework ideas

Learners complete the Workbook Session 8.11 activities if not completed in class.

They ask a family member to explore a newspaper report with them. Can they find one about animals?

Answers for Workbook

1   Learners' correctly labeled report features.

2   Learners' own responses

3   Learners underline: **a** A report gives information; **b** A report can have photos; **c** A report is written in the present tense; **d** A report has a clear heading; **e** A report has facts.

8.12 Look back

LEARNING PLAN

Learning objectives		Learning intentions	Success criteria
Main focus	**Also covered**	• To check their writing and share reports.	• Learners can check their writing and share reports.
1Rs.02, 1Rs.04, 1Ra.04, 1SLp.01, 1SLp.05, 1SLr.01	1Ri.04, 1Ww.01, 1SLm.01, 1SLm.03, 1SLg.04	• To talk about reading for information in this unit. • To think about their learning from the unit.	• Learners can talk about reading for information in this unit. • Learners can think about their learning from the unit.

LANGUAGE SUPPORT

Encourage learners to use Unit 8 for recall, as well as any posters or displays in the classroom used throughout the unit.

Common misconception

Misconception	How to identify	How to overcome
A fact file gives facts, but a report does not.	Ask learners to tell you the difference between a fact file and a report.	Explain that both provide facts, but a fact file is more likely to have lists of facts and a report more likely to have sentences with facts in them. Try to incorporate fact files and reports into other areas of learning to consolidate experience.

Starter idea

Checking (5–10 minutes)

Resources: Learner's Book, Session 8.12: Getting started

Description: Ask learners to tell you how they check their writing, e.g. read it aloud, ask a partner to read it or check it for one skill at a time and so read it several times.

Ask them to talk about what they think it is important to check.

Share ideas and create a class checklist to ensure that everyone understands what to do when they are checking their writing.

Main teaching ideas

1   Check writing (10–15 minutes)

Learning intention: to check writing for layout and correct use of features

Resources: Learner's Book, Session 8.12, Activity 1; Workbook, Session 8.12; learners' charts and reports from Session 8.11, Activities 1 and 3

Description: Discuss the importance of layout and neat work.

Encourage learners to check their writing, using the features checklist they created in Learner's Book Session 8.11 Activity 1.

Invite learners to share their writing with the class. Select a few reports and use these for discussion.

Ask learners to swap reports with a partner and then talk about what they have learned from each other's reports.

Display the reports, if possible, or put them in a class book in the library for others to enjoy.

You can use the Workbook Session 8.12 activities now.

> Differentiation ideas: Support learners by working with them in a group when checking their report, or selecting one aspect of it for them to improve.

Challenge learners to check punctuation and handwriting.

2 Review ways of finding information (10–15 minutes)

Learning intention: to reflect on learning from the unit

Resources: Learner's Book, Session 8.12, Activity 2

Description: Ask learners if they can remember the different ways of finding out information that they have explored in this unit. Encourage them to use memory as well as class displays that you may have created.

List the different ways of finding out information, together. Ask learners to look at the images in the Learner's Book (Unit 8) if they cannot remember all of them.

Ask learners to talk about the most useful information they have learned. Ask: *What did you most enjoy finding out about? What information or skills will you not forget to use?*

> Differentiation ideas: Support learners by providing examples of information books and dictionaries, or classroom displays as reminders.

Challenge learners to look at an index and to say what information it provides. (It tells us if something is included in a book and if so, on which page.)

3 Skills review (10–15 minutes)

Learning intention: to think about learning in terms of language skills

Resources: Learner's Book, Session 8.12, Activity 3

Description: Remind learners of the language we use to describe language skills: reading, writing, spelling, listening and speaking.

Say each skill one by one, and ask learners to put their hand up when you say the skill they think they are best at.

Now ask learners to say or write one thing from this unit that has helped them with each of these skills.

These simple learner statements can be extremely useful for informing end-of-term reports.

> Differentiation ideas: Support learners to be positive in their skills review, providing models: *I liked the way you …*

Challenge learners to also think of one thing they still need to improve and how they think they can do it.

Plenary idea

Lucky Dip review (5–10 minutes)

Resources: Assessment for Learning (AfL) sentence starters; a soft ball or toy

Description: Put a selection of Assessment for Learning (AfL) sentence starters on the board:

- *One thing I must remember from this unit is …*
- *I still don't understand …*
- *I know how to … better now.*
- *I now understand …*
- *I know one fact about …*

Throw a soft ball or toy to a learner. They must choose a starter sentence and complete it. They then throw the ball or toy to another learner before leaving the class.

Keep throwing the ball or toy until you run out of learners or time.

Homework ideas

Learners complete the Workbook Session 8.12 activities if not completed in class.

They talk to a family member about something they still find difficult to do in English, or have only just learned.

Answers for Workbook

1   Learners' own responses
2   Learners' own responses
3   Learners' own responses

CHECK YOUR PROGRESS

1   A dictionary or a glossary.
2   A contents page tells us what is in a book and on what page.
3   Learners' own captions about monkeys
4   Learners can say the alphabet.
5   Habitat
6   A fact file lists facts, but a report puts facts in sentences. (or similar)

PROJECT GUIDANCE

These projects build on the reading, writing and understanding learners have developed throughout the unit. Since learners have just explored many different ways to find out more about words and topics, the project options here extend this focus and provide opportunities for the learners to choose to work in a group, as a pair or alone. You might prefer to allocate a project to the class.

Group project: Allocate a letter to each learner. Learners should choose an animal name that begins with that letter and then use their research skills to find out a fact about that animal. Once complete, the facts may be pegged on a washing line across the classroom for display. Simple pegs and string will be required.

Pair project: Learners will need to start by designing their hotel. (See online for images of bug hotels to support learners with this.)

Encourage them to then plan the resources they need to build the hotel (old pallets or planks of wood, cans, bricks, dead leaves and logs, etc.) including any adult help. Support learners to decide on a suitable (and available) location for the bug hotel.

Solo project: Learners choose an information book they find interesting. They then design a bookmark that shows what information can be found in the book. (This might be three key topic words, as suggested in the Learner's Book.) Learners can then leave the bookmark in the book for other readers to find. Some learners may need guidance or a template to help with this activity.

For more guidance on setting up and assessing projects, see Project guidance at the end of Unit 1.

>9 All kinds of weather

Unit plan

Session	Approximate number of learning hours	Outline of learning content	Resources
9.1 Whatever the weather	1.5	Identify weather as a theme and explore new vocabulary. Explore a collection of short rhymes. Write a short rhyme.	Learner's Book Session 9.1 Workbook Session 9.1 ⬇ Worksheet 9.1 ⬇ Worksheet 9.2 Phonics Workbook B
9.2 Words in shapes	2	Listen out for letter names to spell a word. Explore shape poems. Write a shape poem.	Learner's Book Session 9.2 Workbook Session 9.2
9.3 Describing weather	1.5	Talk about words for *snow* and *ice*. Read a poem that describes snow. Use the structure of an existing poem to write a new poem.	Learner's Book Session 9.3 Workbook Session 9.3 ⬇ Differentiated worksheets 9A–C
9.4 Weather is like a …	1.5	Talk about using imagination when comparing things. Read two short poems and listen to another. Write captions for pictures.	Learner's Book Session 9.4 Workbook Session 9.4 ⬇ Worksheet 9.3

Session	Approximate number of learning hours	Outline of learning content	Resources
9.5 Planning and writing an adventure poem	1.5	Talk about play on different weather days. Read a poem about an adventure on a wet day. Use own ideas to write a poem about play.	Learner's Book Session 9.5 Workbook Session 9.5 ⬇ Worksheet 9.4
9.6 Look back	1	Reflect on and edit writing. Look back at the content of the unit. Review learning.	Learner's Book Session 9.6 Workbook Session 9.6 ⬇ Unit 9 Language worksheets
Cross-unit resources			

Learner's Book Check your progress

Learner's Book Projects

BACKGROUND KNOWLEDGE

Before you begin to teach this unit, you may find it helpful to familiarise yourself with:

- the poetry and poets featured in this unit. Look online for film versions which often have music and are sometimes read by the poets themselves
- the language of poetry, including: rhythm; rhyme and non-rhyme; theme; structure; verse; shape; calligram; acrostic; description; comparison/simile
- examples of poems and picture books that are written around a theme to share with your class
- examples of poems and rhymes about the weather

- how to listen to, read and then recite poetry
- ways in which learners can borrow ideas or the structure of a poem to support their own writing
- the phonics and grammar elements in this unit, including:
  - phonics - the language of phonics, such as letter names and sounds; consonant and vowel digraphs and long vowel sounds
- the metalanguage used within the unit, such as: letters; sounds; phrases; sentences; nouns; verb endings; adjectives and adverbs.

TEACHING SKILLS FOCUS

Metacognition

Metacognition describes the processes involved when learners plan, monitor, evaluate and make changes to their own learning behaviours and become self-regulating learners. It is thought to be a high-impact, low-cost approach to improving learning for all.

Encourage learners to reflect on their overall thinking and learning skills rather than only their knowledge of or skills in a given topic. Challenge yourself to find different ways to encourage and support learners to reflect on their learning:

- Make sure you are confident about your own skills and professional understanding of English for any given lesson, so that you can think about the process of learning you are asking of learners.

- Wherever possible, create opportunities for learners to think, plan, do, talk and reflect alongside activities.

- Respect that sometimes learners need time and space to reflect on their learning and may need support, too.

- Explore and model innovative ways to display learners' thinking, e.g. charts, thought bubbles, audio recordings, short film captures (on phones), diaries, journals, pictures and performances. Ask yourself: *Do some ways support young learners better than others?*

- Do not forget the art of good questioning; delve deeper into a response with *Why* and *How* questions, but use *Tell me more about …* too, asking:

  - *What do you know already?*

  - *What made you think that?*

  - *What did you do to help you answer that question / think about that question?*

  - *What do you notice?*

  - *What did you have to pay careful attention to?*

  - *How will you remember that?*

  - *What does this remind you of in real life?*

At the end of this unit, consider which metacognition strategies you included in your teaching and which were most effective for learners:

- activating and using prior knowledge

- direct instruction to use a strategy

- modelling learned strategy

- memorising strategy

- guided practice

- independent practice

- structured reflection.

9.1 Whatever the weather

LEARNING PLAN

Learning objectives		Learning intentions	Success criteria
Main focus	**Also covered**	• To say what a theme is and talk about it. • To join in with words and actions in rhymes. • To change words to write a new rhyme.	• Learners can say what a theme is and talk about it. • Learners can join in with words and actions in rhymes. • Learners can change words to write a new rhyme.
1Rv.03, 1Rv.05, 1Ri.14, 1Ra.02, 1Wv.01, 1Wc.01	1Rw.02, 1Rw.06, 1Rv.01, 1Rv.02, 1Rv.03, 1Rg.04, 1Rs.02, 1Ri.01, 1Ra.01, 1Ra.03, 1Ra.04, 1Wv.03, 1Wg.05, 1Wp.06, 1SLm.01, 1SLm.03, 1SLg.04, 1SLp.01, 1SLp.02		

LANGUAGE SUPPORT

Prepare learners for this session by looking at weather vocabulary:

• Provide simple weather games, including board and card games.

• If making the weather chart, refer to it often to reinforce language and vocabulary.

Encourage learners to recite rhymes, stressing rhyme and rhythm with them.

Common misconception

Misconception	How to identify	How to overcome
In English, letters always represent the same sounds and are pronounced the same.	Ask learners which spelling is correct: *cloudy* or *clowdy* *rain* or *rane* *snow* or *snoe* Check they are making the correct phonic choices. Ask them to read: *Wind up the kite string.* *The wind is strong today.* Ask: *What is the difference in the word* wind? (The first has long vowel sound *i* while the second has short vowel sound *i*.)	Use Phonics Workbook B, pages 6–19, to reinforce the fact that different letters, or groups of letters, can represent the same sounds. Make a class phonics chart and add to it each time learners discover another spelling for a sound or words that may be pronounced differently with different meanings.

Starter idea

Look at weather pictures (20–30 minutes)

Resources: Learner's Book, Session 9.1: Getting started; Worksheet 9.1

Description: Ask learners what they already know about different kinds of weather where they live and elsewhere. Give them a few minutes to talk in pairs and then share their ideas. Make a class list.

Draw on their experiences and use the pictures in Getting started (which include representations of hot, cold, sunny, cloudy, stormy, windy and snowy weather) as prompts.

Use Worksheet 9.1 Weather Snap! cards to play Weather Snap!

Main teaching ideas

1 Short rhymes (10–30 minutes)

Learning intention: to join in with a simple action rhyme and identify a common theme

Resources: Four weather poems (Learner's Book, Session 9.1, Activity 1); Track 57

Description: Tell learners they will hear a collection of short rhymes.

Together, read or listen to the audio version of the rhymes and ask learners to say what the common theme is.

Encourage learners to repeat the rhymes using appropriate actions. Check that learners are pointing to the weather pictures as they sing.

Ask learners which of the short poems rhyme and which words rhyme. They all rhyme: **a** tree/me; **b** hat/flat; shine/time; **c** me/me; **d** too/through/you.

Link to phonics by encouraging learners to notice the spelling of weather words: *s-u-n; c-l-ou-d* and *s-t-or-m; r-ain-n; th-u-n-d-er; s-n-ow, w-i-n-d.*

See the Language focus box for infromation on the use of *and*. You can use the Workbook Session 9.1 activities now to practise writing sentences about the weather with *and*.

> **Differentiation ideas:** Support learners' listening skills. Ask them to listen for a weather word in the rhymes, e.g. *rain*. Each time they hear it, they must stand up and sit down, or clap. Repeat with each rhyme.

Challenge some learners to identify the rhyming words in the rhymes by listening only and making a list as they hear them. Check their spellings and link to phonics work as described in Description.

Answers:
They are each about a different kind of weather: rain, sun, wind, thunder.

2 Sing or say one of the weather poems (15–30 minutes)

Learning intention: to perform a group recital of a weather poem

Resources: Learner's Book, Session 9.1, Activity 2; poems from Activity 1; recording equipment, if necessary

Description: Ask learners to work in groups. Give each group one of the weather poems from Activity 1 to work on or let them choose.

Tell them they are going to work in groups to say or sing one weather poem.

Draw their attention to the Speaking tip in Activity 2 and/or to any class posters you have made during this unit about what makes a good speaker.

Ask learners to talk about how they will practise their recital and involve everybody in the group. Circulate as learners work to support their ideas.

Invite learners to speak well and to listen to others well, too.

Encourage peer feedback by asking learners to say two good things they noticed and one thing to improve.

Encourage reflection about how volume or speed can impact their performance.

> **Differentiation ideas:** Support learners by setting up groups comprising some learners who would like to be challenged and some learners who would benefit from additional support.

Challenge learners to experiment with intonation, volume and pace in their recitals.

3 Change words to write a new poem (15–20 minutes)

Learning intention: to extend vocabulary and write a new poem using a template

Resources: Learner's Book, Session 9.1, Activity 3; Worksheet 9.2; poems from Activity 1

Description: By now, learners should be confident reading the weather poems.

Ask a volunteer learner to read the poem about rain aloud.

Invite them to help you to change some of the words in the rhyme to create a new version.

Model how to rewrite the poem a few times using different vocabulary, before asking learners to write their own poems in their notebooks. Some learners may benefit from using Worksheet 9.2 *Rain* cloze as a writing guide.

Note which learners are confident to experiment with new vocabulary when writing their own version of the poem.

⟩ **Differentiation ideas:** Support learners by using Worksheet 9.2 *Rain* cloze.

Challenge learners to write their poems in a raindrop-shaped piece of paper for a class display.

Answers:
Possible variation:
Rain on the *brown earth / red flowers / school bus / elephants*
And rain on the *sea / mountain tops / blue flowers / old jeep / camels*
But not on me!
Rain on the *brown earth / red flowers /school bus / elephants*
And rain on you
Rain on the *mountain tops / blue flowers / old jeep / camels*
And on me too!

Plenary idea

Read aloud (10 minutes)

Description: Invite learners to share their new poems by reading aloud.

Ask them to clap after each performance and, as in Activity 2, to provide feedback for each other.

Note with learners which new versions rhyme and which do not.

CROSS-CURRICULAR LINKS

Science: Explore how the sun is a source of heat and light, and one of many stars.

Art: Create class versions of weather icons.

Homework ideas

Learners complete the Workbook Session 9.1 activities if not completed in class.

They find out more about weather around the world.

Answers for Workbook

1   **a** rain and snow; **b** sun and clouds; **c** wind and snow

2   **a** Tuesday is sunny and windy; **b** Friday is heavy rain and strong wind / very rainy and very windy; **c** Sunday is rainy and stormy / raining and thunder and lightning

3 and **4**   Learners' own responses

9.2 Words in shapes

LEARNING PLAN

Learning objectives		Learning intentions	Success criteria
Main focus	**Also covered**	• To explore shape poems.	• Learners can explore shape poems.
1Rs.02, 1Ri.12, 1Ww.01, 1Ww.05, 1Wc.01, 1Wp.05	1Rw.01, 1Rw.05, 1Rv.02, 1Rg.05, 1Rg.06, 1Rs.04, 1Ri.01, 1Ri.09, 1Ri.12, 1Ri.13, 1Ra.01, 1Wc.04, 1SLm.02, 1SLs.01, 1SLp.04	• To listen for letter names and write words. • To write words in shapes to make shape poems.	• Learners can listen for letter names and write words. • Learners can write words in shapes to make shape poems.

LANGUAGE SUPPORT

Provide letters on cards for learners to explore key weather-related topic words, e.g. *cloud*. Ask learners to sequence the cards to spell weather words, and then ask if they can arrange the letter cards in a way that matches the word's meaning, e.g. the letters *c-l-o-u-d* in a circle.

Support learners to create weather charts, which they can add to throughout the unit, to use as

a resource to support vocabulary and language structures, e.g. *The weather today is …*

Play rhyming SNAP! Search online for rhyming cards, e.g. picture to picture, picture to word or word to word, depending on the level of challenge required. This will support learners to hear rhyme and non-rhyme, e.g. *snow/low/toe, rain/train/same.*

Common misconception

Misconception	How to identify	How to overcome
We always read and write English left to right and top to bottom.	Ask learners how they read and write their first language. Ask: *Do you read and write to the right or across the left? Do you read and write top to bottom or bottom to top?* Ask them how we read and write English. (left to right, top to bottom) Ask them for examples of when we might see English written in different ways.	Make a class display of texts in English that are written in different directions, e.g. acrostic poems, calligrams, jokes, crossword puzzles, text on fun birthday cards, text in some advertisements, text in some picture books (e.g. you could research online the books of Dr. Seuss or Lauren Child).

Starter idea

 Listen to a poem (20–30 minutes)

Resources: *Sunshine* (Learner's Book, Session 9.2: Getting started); Track 58; Workbook, Session 9.2

> **Audioscript:** *Sunshine*
>
> S – Soft sun
>
> U – Ultra hazy
>
> N – Never dazzling
>
> S – Soft and lazy
>
> H – Hot and humid
>
> I – In the shade
>
> N – Never glaring
>
> E – Endless sunshine dreaming …
>
> *Gill Budgell*

Description: Ask learners to first listen to a poem. Tell them it is a kind of quiz. Say: *The first letter of each line of the poem spells a word. What is it?* (sunshine)

Encourage learners to work in pairs to write each letter of the alphabet as they hear it, to work out the word in the poem. You may give further support by providing the muddled letters of the word and asking learners to choose each letter as they hear it to build the word cumulatively.

Challenge learners to listen for the letters and work aurally to work out the word. Can they add a word beginning with each letter of the word *sunshine*?

Listen to the poem again and talk about the words in the poem learners are not sure about. These might include *ultra, hazy, humid, glaring*.

You can use the Workbook Session 9.2 activities in class now to further explore topic vocabulary and word class.

Main teaching ideas

 1 Look at *Rainbow* (15 minutes)

> **Learning intention:** to read a shape poem and understand direction of reading (See Common misconception)
>
> **Resources:** *Rainbow* (Learner's Book, Session 9.2, Activity 1); Track 59; other shape poems from the class library or a display, if possible

Description: Together, talk about actions that might be suitable to accompany types of weather, e.g. hands and fingers falling vertically to suggest a rainbow, or hands with open palms moving outwards to suggest sunshine.

Ask learners to look at the poem *Rainbow* in pairs. Ask them what they notice about the letters and words. They may notice:

- There are some lower-case and some capital letters.
- Words are repeated.
- Rain is written down the page with a capital R and then lower-case letters.
- SUN is written down the page in capital letters.
- Rainbow is written in a rainbow shape.

Ask: *Why do you think the words are written like this?*

Read the rhyme together. Then repeat and create actions to accompany it.

⟩ **Differentiation ideas:** Support learners by writing the poem on the board, and modelling the direction – tracing each word with a finger as you read.

Challenge learners to perform the word *rain* as it is written. They should look like raindrops falling as they say the word.

2 True or false (15 minutes)

Learning intention: to decide if statements about the features of a poem are true or false

Resources: Learner's Book, Session 9.2, Activity 2

Description: Ask learners to look at the sentences about the shape poem in Activity 1 and say either *true* or *false*.

You may ask learners to work in pairs or you may work as a class. Learners will be working orally, but may note down their answers.

If in pairs, share answers and check everyone agrees.

⟩ **Differentiation ideas:** Support learners by working with a group and physically sorting the questions into true and false piles.

Challenge learners to write another true or false statement for a partner.

Answers:
a True; b False (it's like a rainbow); c True;
d Could be true. Learners may have other ideas.

3 Write words in shapes (20 minutes)

Learning intention: to write words in a way to show their meaning

Resources: Learner's Book, Session 9.2, Activity 3; further examples of calligrams, if helpful; art materials or a variety of pens and pencils, if responding artistically

Description: Together, look at the two ways the word *sunshine* is presented in Activity 4.

*   Ask them to think about what is the same and what is different. (The letters are the same, the layout is different.)
*   Ask: *Which do you think works best for the word* sunshine? *Why?*

Talk about ideas to add to these examples.

Ask learners to work alone or in pairs to write the words *snow* and *breeze* (Activity 3) in their notebooks, or on larger pieces of paper, in a way that shows their meaning. You may decide to extend this into an art session if practical.

> **Differentiation ideas:** Support learners by getting them to write *snow* and *breeze* ten times and to cut the words out. Then ask them to arrange the words in a way that makes them look like snow or a breeze.

Challenge learners to add words to their shape to begin to make them look and sound more like a poem (rather than one word). Some learners may like to know this type of word play is called a 'calligram'.

Answers:
Learners' own responses

4 Write a shape poem (30–40 minutes)

Learning intention: to write a list of topic words; to write a shape poem in a template

Resources: Learner's Book, Session 9.2, Activity 4

Description: Tell learners they are going to write their own shape poem.

Together, on the board, model how to create a word list for each type of weather to get learners started.

Model how to use phonics to attempt to spell words using plausible grapheme combinations.

Ask learners to continue with their chosen weather shape.

Draw their attention to the Writing tip to think carefully about where they will place their words and letters within the outline.

> **Differentiation ideas:** Support learners by providing their chosen words so they can cut them out and physically arrange and stick them into place. They may then copy their poem into their notebook if necessary.

Challenge learners to create their own weather shape poem for a different kind of weather not included in Session 9.2. Challenge them to write the rules of writing shape poems.

Answers:
Learners' own poems

Plenary idea

Noughts and crosses (5 minutes)

Resources: a bank of questions, numbered 1–9, relating to Learner's Book Session 9.2

Description: Draw a noughts and crosses grid on the board and number each square 1–9.

Split the class into two groups so that Team 1 is *noughts* and Team 2 is *crosses*.

Ask Team 1 to choose a number from the grid.

Read the question or task that is numbered to match the grid numbers, e.g. *Does r-a-i-n spell rain? What does the first letter of each word spell: cotton, light, over, up, down?* (cloud)

If Team 1 answers correctly, they win a nought in the square. If wrong, Team 2 win a cross in the square.

Then it is Team 2's turn.

Continue until there are three noughts or crosses in any direction on the grid.

CROSS-CURRICULAR LINKS

Science: Explore how plants need light from the sun to survive.

Art: Make poems for a rainbow or sunshine in such a way that their shape supports their meaning and hang them in the classroom.

Music: Listen to and/or make music that suggests different kinds of weather.

Homework ideas

Learners complete the Workbook Session 9.2 activities if not completed in class.

They write an acrostic poem like *Sunshine* in Getting started about their favourite type of weather.

Answers for Workbook

1   Learners' own words, e.g. fall, splash, drip

2   sun, dazzling/glaring, shade, glaring/dazzling, dreaming

3   May include: settle, sing, stop; need, nest, note; open, order, offer; water, wish, wait

9.3 Describing weather

LEARNING PLAN			

Learning objectives		Learning intentions	Success criteria
Main focus	**Also covered**	• To explore words about snow and ice.	• Learners can explore words about snow and ice.
1Rv.01, 1Rv.03, 1Rv.05, 1Ri.09, 1Ri.13, 1Wc.01	1Rw.05, 1Rw.06, 1Rg.05, 1Rs.02, Ri.01, Ri.05, Ri.11, Ri.14, 1Ra.01, 1Ra.02, 1Ra.04, 1Ww.01, 1Ww.05, 1Ww.07, 1Wv.01, 1Wv.02, 1Wv.03, 1Wg.01, 1Wc.04, 1SLg.01, 1SLg.02, 1SLg.03, 1SLg.04	• To read and talk about a poem. • To write a description of weather.	• Learners can read and talk about a poem. • Learners can write a description of weather.

LANGUAGE SUPPORT

Learners may need support with descriptive vocabulary in this session, especially if they have not had first-hand experience of snow.

If possible, allow learners to make and play with ice to stimulate discussion. You could consider making fake snow for fun (see Cross-curricular links later) using baking soda, shaving cream or glitter.

Common misconception

Misconception	How to identify	How to overcome
We usually use colour and size to describe something.	Ask learners to describe the sun. They may say: *big, round, yellow, hot*, etc. Then ask if anyone can describe the sun, asking: *Can you say how hot it is? How round it is? How yellow it is?* Then explain that in asking these questions, you are already describing the sun!	Create a checklist for describing things: • Think about size, colour, position, shape. • Use your senses. • Ask questions: *How …? Isn't it funny how …* • Make statements: *I do not know how to tell you how …* Add to this list over the duration of the unit.

Starter idea

Snow and ice (10–15 minutes)

Resources: Learner's Book, Session 9.3: Getting started; resources for making fake snow or ice, if appropriate (see the Language support box); pictures of snow and ice

Description: Choose a snow picture and stick it on the board or wall. Cover it in sticky notes.

Tell learners that behind the sticky notes is a picture of the topic for this session.

Ask learners to take it in turns to choose a sticky note to remove. You may number the notes or just ask learners to come to the board to remove a note. As each sticky note is removed, learners can begin to identify the picture.

Keep going until learners correctly identify the topic: Snow and ice.

Ask learners to look at the pictures in Getting started. Talk together about which words they can use to describe each picture. What do learners already know and what would they like to know about snow?

Main teaching ideas

1 Read *How Do I Describe the Snow?* (15–30 minutes)

Learning intention: to listen to, read and talk about a poem that describes snow

Resources: *How Do I Describe the Snow?* (Learner's Book, Session 9.3, Activity 1); Track 60

Description: Tell learners they are going to hear a poem about snow. Share the title of the poem.

Say to them: *I do not know how to tell you how beautiful this poem is. Oh! I just did tell you how beautiful this poem is!*

Ask them to listen out for what the poem tells us about snow. Read the poem aloud.

Ask learners to share their ideas about the poet's technique after the first listening. Remind them of your initial statements: *I do not know how to tell you how beautiful this poem is. Oh! I just did tell you how beautiful this poem is!* and make sure they understand that, similarly, the poet tells us about snow without meaning to do so.

Then ask learners to listen again and/or read the poem in pairs or as a class together.

Ask learners to note any words they are unfamiliar with and share this list, e.g. *settles, crunches, swiftly*. Discuss how to use phonics to read these words and pronounce them, as well as how to use context for working out possible meanings.

Challenge learners to count the number of times the poet uses the word *how* (9, not counting *How* in the title) and to notice the phrases *how softly, how gently, how wet, how freshly, how quickly, how thickly, how easily, how swiftly*.

See the Phonics Workbooks for further practice of using phonics for reading and spelling.

You may draw learners' attention to the punctuation (or lack of it) – perhaps by reading the poem aloud and running your finger under the words to show how one line leads into another seamlessly, like falling or drifting snow.

> **Differentiation ideas:** Support learners by working with a group to read the poem again after listening.

Challenge learners to annotate the poem with small arrows to show where the reader has to go onto the next line to finish the sentence (even though each line begins with a capital letter).

2 Answer questions (15–30 minutes)

Learning intention: to share opinions and answer questions about a poem in a group

Resources: Learner's Book, Session 9.3, Activity 2; Workbook, Session 9.3

Description: Ask learners to listen to or read the poem again.

Ask them to work in groups to answer the three questions in Activity 2.

As you circulate, check learners are working well together: listening to each other; taking turns; trying to understand others; not interrupting; and expressing their own opinions.

Invite groups to tell the class their answers, thoughts and opinions.

You can use the Workbook Session 9.3 activities now to practise writing sentences about snow.

> **Differentiation ideas:** Provide a copy of the text to support learners who will benefit from physically marking up words they do not know, or a list of phrases of the word *how* with adverbs.

Challenge learners to read the last section of the poem and to answer: *What are they doing with the snow?* (Say what is implicit, i.e. snowballing) and *Where are they playing?* (Say what is explicit, i.e. they are in the school playground)

Answers:

May include: **a** Somewhere hot / Somewhere where it does not snow **b** Because snow is so many different things, she does not know where to begin **c** She makes snow sound exciting/fun/varied / impossible to describe as one thing

3 Borrow a structure to write a poem (30–40 minutes)

Learning intention: to write a poem using an existing structure

Resources: Learner's Book, Session 9.3, Activity 3; Differentiated worksheets 9A–C

Description: Tell learners they are going to write their own poem that describes the weather.

Together, talk about the weather options in Getting started. Choose one weather type to model how to write the poem using the structure provided by filling in the gaps.

You can use the Differentiated worksheets now to support learners in writing their poems.

Ask learners to discuss how their chosen weather type looks and feels, and then to create their own poem using the structure provided.

As you move around the classroom, check that learners are holding their pencils correctly and forming their letters correctly, too.

> **Differentiation ideas:** Support learners by providing an appropriate Differentiated worksheet (from 9A–C) and encouraging them to re-use word banks and lists created in Activities 1 and 2.

Challenge learners to create their own version of the poem going beyond the template in Activity 3 from Session 9.3 or using the most challenging Differentiated worksheet (9C).

Answers:
Learners' own responses

Plenary idea

I do not know how to tell you how … chain (5–10 minutes)

Resources: a light, inflatable ball

Description: Return to the language structure of the poem and the sentence starter: *I do not know how to tell you how …*

Give an example of a completed sentence by finishing the sentence starter. Then pass the ball to a learner and ask them to say and complete the sentence starter using their own ideas.

Continue until everyone has had a go at saying the sentence.

CROSS-CURRICULAR LINKS

Art: Make mini ice sculptures from ice cubes using manicure set tools, or make fake snow (see Language Support earlier).

Science: Describe what happens when snow melts and think about why it melts.

Homework ideas

Learners complete the Workbook Session 9.3 activities if not completed in class.

They find other poems that describe weather.

Answers for Workbook

1 Learners' own drawings and sentences. Answers may include: *I can touch it, pat it, build with it, throw it, catch it.*

2 Learners' own drawings and sentences. Answers may include: *Snow falls, flutters, sticks, melts, sparkles on my hair.*

3 Learners' own sentences using *–ly* words

9.4 Weather is like a …

LEARNING PLAN

Learning objectives		Learning intentions	Success criteria
Main focus	**Also covered**	• To explore words and ideas about what weather is like.	• Learners can explore words and ideas about what weather is like.
1Rg.07, 1Rs.02, 1Ra.03, 1Wg.01, 1SLp.01, 1SLp.03	1Rw.04, 1Rw.06, 1Rv.05, 1Rg.01, 1Rg.02, 1Ri.01, 1Ri.14, 1Ra.01, 1Ra.04, 1Ra.05, 1Ww.03, 1Wv.02, 1Wg.06, 1Wc.02, 1Wp.05, 1SLp.02	• To read poems aloud and notice punctuation. • To write sentences about what they imagine the weather to be.	• Learners can read poems aloud and notice punctuation. • Learners can write sentences about what they imagine the weather to be.

LANGUAGE SUPPORT

Learners may need support with descriptive vocabulary in this session, especially if they have not had first-hand experience of severe weather.

Simple matching games may help learners to consolidate vocabulary choices, e.g. matching the wind to a monster or the sun to a giant sunflower.

Common misconception

Misconception	How to identify	How to overcome
We only add –s or –es for plural nouns, e.g. *cloud – clouds, fox – foxes*.	Ask learners to look at sets of verbs and nouns on the board: Verbs Nouns *to kiss* *a kiss* *to dance* *a dance* *to flash* *a flash* Ask them to say the verbs in the third person (*he, she, it*) and the nouns as plurals. Ask: *What do you notice?*	Discuss with learners how they might remember to check their spellings when writing in the third person and when making nouns plural. You could create a class poster with them to use as they write.

Starter idea

Stormy weather (15–20 minutes)

Resources: Learner's Book, Session 9.4: Getting started; large pieces of paper and pens

Description: Ask learners to work in pairs or small groups. (Be sensitive to those who may have experienced trauma due to weather.)

What do they know about stormy or extreme weather?

What do they want to know?

How can they find out more?

Ask them to share their ideas.

Together, look at the pictures in Getting started and ask what each picture looks like or reminds them of. (Large wave looks like a sea monster; lightning looks like a snake; sun looks like a sunflower; tornado looks like a giant animal's foot.)

Main teaching ideas

1 Listen to and read two short poems (30–40 minutes)

Learning intention: to listen to and read two short poems that compare the weather to something else

Resources: *Thunder* and *Lightning* (Learner's Book, Session 9.4, Activity 1); Tracks 61 and 62; Workbook, Session 9.4

Description: Tell learners they are going to listen to two short poems.

Split the class into two groups. Ask Group 1 to listen to *Thunder* and specifically for what thunder is compared to. Ask Group 2 to listen to *Lightning* and specifically for what lightning is compared to.

Read the poems aloud or play the audio.

Establish what comparisons are being made: thunder is compared to an elephant's roar and lightning to a snake's kiss. Ask learners what they would compare these types of weather to.

Talk about learners' views on the poems. Ask: *What did you hear? What did you notice?* Share ideas. They may notice some or all of these things:

- Both poems are short.
- Both poems have a title that begins the poem.
- Both poems have the same structure for each line.
- Both poems have some rhyming words.

You may wish to draw learners' attention to the articles: *an elephant/a snake*. Ask them why these are different. (*Elephant* begins with a vowel.)

Ask learners to work in pairs to read the poems aloud. Ask them to take it in turns to read each line of each poem – alternating and maintaining fluency and meaning. Ask some pairs to read aloud to the class.

You can use the Workbook Session 9.4 activities in class now, for further practice of using punctuation to write sentences.

Ask learners to read both poems again and to draw an illustration for each poem in their notebooks.

> **Differentiation ideas:** Support learners by asking them to choose just one poem to illustrate.

Challenge learners to slightly change each poem but to keep the rhyme, e.g. *the roar of a tiger's snore*, *the bump of an elephant's trunk* (near rhyme), *the flashing screech of an eagle's speech*.

Answers:
Learners' own responses

2 **Listen and imagine (15–20 minutes)**

Learning intention: to listen to a poem and to use imagination

Resources: *Storm* (Learner's Book, Session 9.4, Activity 2); Track 63; online musical tracks of dramatic weather

Description: Ask learners to listen to another short poem that asks us to imagine something.

Play the audio of the poem. Ask learners to listen for what we are being asked to imagine (the storm as a giant). Ask:

- *What can we imagine a storm to be?* (a giant)

- *What is the giant's breath?* (the wind)

- *What cracks the clouds open?* (the noise)

Ask learners to listen again in pairs or groups and to then talk about what else we might imagine a storm to be.

If possible, play some online sound effects of storms and invite learners to say what they think a storm sounds like.

Ask them to draw what they imagine and write a sentence or two to explain what they imagine.

> **Differentiation ideas:** Support learners by asking them to work in pairs where one is a stronger writer than the other.

Challenge learners to include ambitious ideas and vocabulary in their imaginative responses.

Audioscript: *Storm*

Imagine the storm

a giant

When he shouts

his breath

is the wind

The noise cracks the

clouds

for the rain to fall.

Michael Buckman

Answers:
Learners' own responses

3 **Write captions for weather pictures (20–30 minutes)**

Learning intention: to write sentences that compare weather to other things

Resources: Learner's Book, Session 9.4, Activity 3; Worksheet 9.3

Description: If possible, begin the activity by quickly re-reading aloud the poem *Storm*. Copy out the poem to ensure learners can see the structure of the poem.

Play a Pick a card game. Ask learners to choose picture cards of different weather types and then to say *Imagine the ... a ...* to orally practise this structure from the poem *Storm* in Activity 2.

Draw learners' attention to the chart in Activity 3. If time, point out the verbs ending in –s or –es (see Common misconception earlier).

Tell learners to create a caption for each of the pictures in Getting started. Model how to use the chart to write captions.

You can use Worksheets 9.3 *Imagine ...* here as a template for caption writing.

Ask learners to use the chart and to write their captions in their notebooks with illustrations for each.

> **Differentiation ideas:** Support learners by working with a group and providing possible responses for the chart for learners to choose from. You could ask some learners to just write two captions rather than four.

Challenge learners to include ambitious ideas and vocabulary in their imaginative responses to each picture, and to extend their captions beyond one sentence. Some may be able to write their sentence as a poem, mirroring the structure of *Storm*.

Answers:
Learners' own captions

Plenary idea

Reflection (5–10 minutes)

Description: Ask learners to reflect on what helps them to be imaginative. Is it:

- *pictures*
- *music and sounds*
- *words in the poems*
- *something else?*

Share ideas around the classroom, encouraging learners to be open and responsive to ideas.

Is anything suggested that may have an impact on your classroom practice or provision, e.g. having more time to think quietly / to respond.

CROSS-CURRICULAR LINKS

Science: Describe the pushes and pulls created by storms as forces.

Technology: Search online sound banks for the sound of storms.

Art: Make paintings of extreme weather looking like monsters, giants and animals.

Homework ideas

Learners complete the Workbook Session 9.4 activities if not completed in class.

They find another poem about storms and share with the class.

Answers for Workbook

1   Thunder is nothing more than the roar of an elephant's snore.; Lightning is nothing more than the electric hiss of a snake's kiss.

2   Learners' own ideas for sentence endings

3   Imagine the storm a giant. When he shouts, his breath is the wind. The noise cracks the clouds for the rain to fall.

9.5 Planning and writing an adventure poem

LEARNING PLAN

Learning objectives		Learning intentions	Success criteria
Main focus	**Also covered**	• To talk about pretend adventures.	• Learners can talk about pretend adventures.
1Rv.05, 1Ri.09, 1Ra.06, 1Wc.01, 1Wc.02, 1SLp.04	1Rw.04, 1Rw.07, 1Rv.03, 1Rg.04, 1Rg.05, 1Rg.07, 1Rs.02, 1Ri.01, 1Ri.11, 1Ri.14, 1Ra.01, 1Ra.05, 1Ww.06, 1Wv.02, 1Ws.01, 1SLm.03, 1SLg.02, 1SLg.04	• To read and explore the meaning of a poem. • To plan and write a new adventure poem.	• Learners can read and explore the meaning of a poem. • Learners can plan and write a new adventure poem.

LANGUAGE SUPPORT

Learners may find a poster of sentence starters helpful in this session: *One sunny day ...*; *One snowy afternoon ...*; *One rainy morning ...*; *One windy night ...*

Sing songs about the types of weather explored in the poems and rhymes from this unit.

Worksheet 9.4 Writing chart provides a writing framework. This may be particularly useful as a structure for some learners.

Common misconception

Misconception	How to identify	How to overcome
We compare things to show how different they are.	Ask learners to compare Jackie and Zuleika. Notice if they only say how they are different or whether they mention things that are also the same.	Ask learners to compare other things, e.g. the weather yesterday and today. If you made a weather chart, use it to compare weather on different days. Emphasise how comparing things can show us both differences and similarities.

Starter idea

Outside adventures in all weathers (15–20 minutes)

Resources: Learner's Book, Session 9.5: Getting started

Description: Ask learners to say what they like to do in different weathers:

• *When do you like to play inside? Outside? Why? What do you do?*

• *What is the best weather to play outside in?*

Tell learners that this session is about having outside adventures and pretending.

Together, look at the pictures in Getting started and talk about what the children are doing (a boy is pretending to be a knight or soldier on a snowy day; a small child is pretending to be a firefighter on a rainy day; a girl is pretending to be a super hero on a sunny day).

What sort of pretending games do the learners like to play?

Ask learners to work in pairs to give each picture in Getting started a title and then to say a sentence for each picture that begins with one of the sentence starters provided.

Draw the class together and record the ideas shared. Remind learners that a title usually has capital letters.

Main teaching ideas

 1 Listen to and read *One Wet Day* (15–20 minutes)

Learning intention: to listen to and read a poem about a pretend adventure

Resources: *One Wet Day* (Learner's Book, Session 9.5, Activity 1); Track 64; picture-caption match

Description: Tell learners that this next rhyme is about two children who go on very different pretend adventures on a wet day.

Read the poem aloud or play the audio.

On the second listening, ask learners to point to the names of the children as they hear them and to listen out for what each child is pretending to be. (Jackie: a strawberry to go strawberry picking; Zuleika: a panther to go panther tracking.)

Talk about what is happening in the rhyme. Ask: *Can you go anywhere in your imagination? Is it like real life?*

Talk about the language features of the rhyme:

- There are two verses.

- A lot of the lines begin with *And*.

- Colour words are used.

- Some sentence structures are repeated, e.g. *And went out of the back door.*

Ask learners to read the rhyme aloud with you before asking them to read it in pairs or small groups.

> **Differentiation ideas:** Work with any learners to support them in their paired reading or ask some learners to read in groups.

Challenge learners to explain what the poet is comparing. Ask: *Why doesn't he say that Jackie is dressed like a strawberry and Zuleika is dressed like a panther?* (This should prompt discussion around implicit and explicit information).

Answers:
Learners' own responses

2 Compare adventures (20–30 minutes)

Learning intention: to explore the meaning of a poem and its language structures

Resources: Learner's Book, Session 9.5, Activity 2; Worksheet 9.4

Description: Split the class into two groups. Group 1 represents Jackie. Group 2 represents Zuleika.

Revisit the poem and ask each group questions about their character: *What did you put on? What did you do? Where did you go? Why did you go out?* Ask learners in each group to respond as if in a role play.

Ask learners how Jackie might dress to pick a coconut and how Zuleika might dress to track crocodiles.

Show learners the chart in Activity 2 and model how you could complete it to compare what Jackie and Zuleika are doing.

Tell learners to copy and complete the chart in their notebooks or to use the top of Worksheet 9.4 Writing chart to fill in the chart.

> **Differentiation ideas:** Work with learners to use Worksheet 9.4 Writing chart to support them in completing the chart.

Challenge learners to add another two rows in the chart to include the ideas of Jackie going to pick a coconut and Zuleika going out to track crocodiles.

Answers:

a

Name	Put on	Went	Where to?	Why?
Jackie	red shoes red coat red woolly hat	out of the back door	into the garden	to pick a straw-berry
Zuleika	one black and one orange shoe gold sash a feather	out of the back door	into the rainforest	to track panthers

b and **c** Learners' own responses

3 Plan and write a new adventure poem (30–40 minutes)

Learning intention: to plan a new poem based on the structure of *One Wet Day* …

Resources: Learner's Book, Session 9.5, Activity 3; Worksheet 9.4; Workbook, Session 9.5

Description: Tell learners they are now going to plan their own version of *One Wet Day* …, the poem in Activity 1. They will need to think of new ideas and words to use.

You can use the Workbook Session 9.5 activities in class now, for practice of planning and creating poems.

Show learners the chart in Activity 2 again and ask them to add a row to this for their own ideas. You can use the bottom half of Worksheet 9.4 Writing chart here.

Give them time to work on their ideas. Circulate among them, and support and challenge where necessary.

Ask learners to use their plans to write their own version of the poem.

As you walk around the class, talk to different learners about their ideas and their writing, adding support where necessary.

The room should be industrious, but encourage learners to help each other and to enjoy their writing.

› **Differentiation ideas:** Support learners to generate ideas by working with a group if necessary. Ask learners to complete just one verse – do they want to be like Jackie or Zuleika?

Challenge learners to write two verses for their poem, as in the original poem.

Answers:
Learners' own poems and drawings

Plenary idea

Where are you going? (5–10 minutes)

Description: One at a time, ask learners to leave the classroom by announcing where they are going and why, e.g., *On this* [cloudy] *day, I am going out of the classroom to* [the mountains] *to* [dig for gold].

Encourage imaginative adventures and good use of vocabulary.

> **CROSS-CURRICULAR LINKS**
>
> **Geography:** Talk about different terrains, e.g. mountains, deserts, jungle.

Homework ideas

Learners complete the Workbook Session 9.5 activities if not completed in class.

They find some story books and non-fiction books about adventures in all kinds of weather.

Answers for Workbook

1 put, on, her, And, out, into

2 Learners' own answers, but similar to: orange T-shirt; new green sunglasses; red hat; the farm.

3 Learners' own responses, but may include: wore/slipped on; put/pushed/fixed; ran/jumped/leapt; find/discover/see

9.6 Look back

Learning objectives		Learning intentions	Success criteria
Main focus	**Also covered**	• To check their spelling of common words.	• Learners can check their spelling of common words.
1Rw.07, 1Ra.04, 1Ra.05, 1Ww.06, 1WP.06, 1SLr.01	1Ww.07, 1Wv.03, 1Wp.02	• To read and check their own writing.	• Learners can read and check their own writing.
		• To think about their learning from the unit.	• Learners can think about their learning from the unit.

LANGUAGE SUPPORT

Use the images in the Learner's Book or any classroom displays or posters to support learners in the review process and to talk about self-assessment. Prompt learners to think about their enjoyment of the unit, how much or what they have learned and what they would like to improve.

Starter idea

Common words (10 minutes)

Resources: Learner's Book, Session 9.6: Getting started; Language Worksheet 9B; Bingo cards (3x3 grid)

Description: Ask learners to talk about common words, e.g. words we use a lot in our writing. Ask: *Which words do you know you find tricky to spell?* Reflect on how they try to remember these words.

Draw their attention to the list of words in Getting started. Are they all confident in spelling these words?

Ask learners to self-assess or peer assess by swapping books. They should choose one piece of writing from the unit and list any common words they see misspelled.

If time, play a game of Word Bingo as a fun way to revisit these words. Provide Bingo templates for learners (grids of 3x3 with a star in the middle square). Ask learners to fill in the grid with the words they find most difficult to spell correctly. Call out these words. Learners should tick off the words on their card as they hear them.

You can provide Language Worksheet 9B now for learners to practise writing and reading common words.

Main teaching ideas

1   Check your writing (15–20 minutes)

Learning intention: to think about and check own writing

Resources: Learner's Book, Session 9.6, Activity 1; Workbook, Session 9.6; Language Worksheet 9A

Description: Choose a learner to model how to check their writing for the class.

Ask them to show how to read quietly to check their work

Then ask them to read it out loud.

Ask learners what they found most helpful and why

Ask learners to repeat this process for their own poem.

When everyone has tried this, discuss again, asking:

• *What mistakes did you find in your work?*

• *Was it a useful thing to do?*

Take a class vote. Who prefers checking their own work quietly and who prefers reading it out loud?

You can use the Workbook Session 9.6 activities now for further practice of topic words.

You can use Language Worksheet 9A now for further practice of using full stops correctly.

> **Differentiation ideas:** Support some learners to check their own work, whether reading silently or out loud. Work with this group or ask each learner to target just two or three words from the list of words they use a lot in Getting started and/or the use of capital letters and full stops.

Challenge learners to correct their work and to think again about what sort of mistakes they are making, e.g. spelling, punctuation or grammar.

2 Look back at the poems in Unit 9 (10 minutes)

Learning intention: to enjoy re-reading and saying rhymes and poems

Resources: Learner's Book, Session 9.6, Activity 2

Description: Ask learners to identify all the poems they have read in the unit. Recite some of them. What was the common theme for these poems? (weather)

You could play all the Unit 9 audio tracks for a celebration of rhymes and poems.

Ask learners if they can remember the focus of each rhyme or poem. Ask: *What was it about? What did we learn?* Encourage learners to speak clearly.

Draw learners' attention to the chart in Activity 2. Ask them to copy and complete a chart like this in their notebooks.

Remind them to write neatly as they write the title of each poem. Check the use of capital letters. They should then draw a picture for each poem, too.

> **Differentiation ideas:** Support learners by working in a small group with them and finding the poems in the book or saying/reading them together.

Challenge learners to remember as many poems as possible without looking in the Learner's Book.

Answers:
Learners' completed charts

3 Read the chart and choose a favourite (10–15 minutes)

Learning intention: to use a chart of poems to express opinions and preferences

Resources: Learner's Book, Session 9.6, Activity 3

Description: Together, talk about which poems learners liked best and why.

Encourage learners to express their own likes and dislikes in relation to the poems in their chart from Activity 2, but ask for explanations.

Ask: *Did you like reading poems on a weather theme or would you have preferred a different theme? What would you choose?*

Encourage others to listen and respect opinions. Do they agree or disagree with each other?

Ask learners to draw and write which poems they liked best.

> **Differentiation ideas:** Support learners by working in a small group or asking them to work in pairs to talk about preferences. Alternatively, discuss preferences as a class and take some votes on which rhyme or poem they liked best and why.

Challenge learners to memorise one of their favourite poems or rhymes.

Answers:
Learners' own responses

Plenary idea

Play Topic Tennis (10 minutes)

Description: Ask two learners to stand at the front of the class.

Give them a topic word, e.g. *storms*.

Ask learners to take it in turns to say words that are linked to this topic word, e.g. *rain – wind – hurricane – stormy*.

Learners should keep going until one of them cannot think of a word. This learner is then out of the game.

Choose a new player to take on the winner of the previous round and start the game again with a new topic word, e.g. *snow*.

Homework ideas

Learners complete the Workbook Session 9.6 activities if not completed in class.

Answers for Workbook

1   Sun: warming, sizzling, glowing; Wind: gusty, wild, breezy

2   Learners' own responses, but may include: Rainbows: colourful, fading, glowing, looping; Storms: noisy, scary, rainy, flashing.

3   **a** ice; **b** snow; **c** a tornado/hurricane/a tropical storm (or similar); **d** a sandstorm

4   Learners' own ideas

CHECK YOUR PROGRESS

1   Learners' own responses, e.g. snow, rain, sun, thunder and lightning.

2   Learners' own responses, written in a sunshine way, e.g. gleaming, shining, hot, warm, bright, glow.

3   This weather is … [learners' own sentences]

4   A storm is like … [learners' own sentences]

PROJECT GUIDANCE

These projects build on the reading, writing and understanding learners have developed throughout the unit. Since they have just read several poems on the related theme of weather, the project options here extend the topic and provide opportunities for learners to choose to work in a group, as a pair or alone. It may be that you prefer to allocate a project to the class.

Group project: Learners create an imagination corner so that they can enjoy dramatic play. Make a suitable space in the classroom and provide cloth, decorations, writing tools, headphones, etc. to inspire learners.

Pair project: Learners choose a different theme and find three poems that match it. Provide poetry books at the appropriate level and/or a bank of suitable themes, e.g. nature, friends, transport.

Solo project: Ask learners to find a new weather poem and write it in a shape that matches. Provide some weather-shaped templates, if possible. Provide poetry books about the weather at the appropriate level so learners may read and select.

For more guidance on setting up and assessing projects, see Project guidance at the end of Unit 1.